LAN Times Guide
to Managing Remote Connectivity

Salvatore Salamone

Osborne **McGraw-Hill**

Berkeley   New York   St. Louis   San Francisco
Auckland   Bogotá   Hamburg   London   Madrid
Mexico City   Milan   Montreal   New Delhi   Panama City
Paris   São Paulo   Singapore   Sydney
Tokyo   Toronto

Osborne **McGraw-Hill**
2600 Tenth Street
Berkeley, California 94710
U.S.A.

For information on translations or book distributors outside the U.S.A., or to arrange bulk purchase discounts for sales promotions, premiums, or fundraisers, please contact Osborne/**McGraw-Hill** at the above address.

LAN Times Guide to Managing Remote Connectivity

1234567890 DOC 9987

ISBN 0-07-882267-X

Publisher
  Brandon A. Nordin

Editor-in-Chief
  Scott Rogers

Acquisitions Editor
  Wendy Rinaldi

Project Editor
  Mark Karmendy

Editorial Assistant
  Ann Sellers

Contributing Writers
  Terè Parnell
  Dennis Williams

Technical Editors
  Patricia Brown
  Terè Parnell

Copy Editor
  Jan Jue

Proofreader
  Stefany Otis

Indexer
  Rebecca Plunkett

Computer Designer
  Jani P. Beckwith

Illustrator
  Leslee Bassin

Contents at a Glance

Part III Connectivity Scenarios

Contents

PART III

Connectivity Scenarios

Introduction

*R**emote access.* It means a lot of different things to a lot of different users. Remote access can be the link that enables a telecommuter to work as effectively at home as if he or she were in the office. It can be the dial-up connection that lets a CEO keep up with urgent e-mails from anywhere in the world. Or it can be the dedicated wide-area telecommunications link that connects a small satellite office to headquarters, keeping those users "in the loop," despite their separation from the nerve center of the corporation.

But Does It Make Cents (and Dollars?)

Whatever remote access means to your organization, it represents huge new responsibilities for you, the network manager. The first of these responsibilities is determining whether remote access is cost-effective for your intended use. It's easy to think that providing remote access for your network users is a "slam dunk" budget decision: if you can keep people working productively even when they're not in the office, how can it *not* be good for the bottom line? However, as you'll find in Part 1 of this book, there are many hidden costs involved in building and maintaining a remote access system. It requires a great deal of thought, planning, and business acumen to budget these costs accurately and provide your management with a valid financial model for remote access. Chapter 1 will provide you with strategies and techniques for developing a solid budget for your remote access system. You'll also find that the resulting figures can be a very compelling argument for implementing remote access in your company.

And the Questions Don't Stop There

Even after you've determined that remote access is a good deal—from both a financial and production perspective—there are still many questions that you must answer before beginning to build your remote access capability. These questions begin with selecting the right remote access service.

Remote Access Service Questions

Selecting the right remote access service can be key to the successful use of the whole system. The service must be obtained from a telecommunications service provider, so you'll want to ask the prospective providers some detailed questions, including:

- Which wide-area service is best for your organization?
- Who should install and maintain the wide-area service?

Chapters 2 through 8 are devoted to describing the various service choices now available to you. Each type of service has its own advantages and disadvantages. Also, the services vary widely from region to region in both cost and availability. To make matters even more complex, service choices are expanding daily. After carefully reviewing the information in these chapters, you'll be well-advised to contact service providers in your area to conduct your own survey of service choices. And be sure not to lock yourself into a long-term service agreement until you have some experience with your remote access system. After using remote access for a while, you may find that your initial choice for remote access service isn't the best after all. Give yourself some room to experiment and adapt to new and changing usage of your remote access system.

Equipment Issues

There are also several issues surrounding the selection of the right equipment for your new remote access system. These are:

■ Which remote access equipment best fits your needs?

■ How do you select equipment?

■ How do you install and maintain this equipment?

■ Who should install and maintain the equipment?

Chapters 9 through 13 deal with the various ways in which you might want to provide remote access to your users. Remember, "remote access" is a blanket term that covers many different connectivity scenarios. The type—or types—of connectivity you plan to provide will determine to a large degree what type of equipment you will need to build your remote access system. For example, providing remote connectivity to half a dozen telecommuters might require installing a single desktop PC with a modem, remote access software, and network adapter. On the other hand, linking several remote offices would require one or more remote access routers with appropriate local area network interfaces.

This leads to another issue. The type of remote access connectivity you are planning to provide will also determine what protocols your remote access system must support, as well as the type of management you will need to employ to monitor the remote access system to make sure that all is running smoothly. This means that if you are linking a remote Token Ring LAN to the Ethernet LAN at headquarters, you are going to have to supply both the appropriate LAN interfaces on the routers, as well as the necessary protocol translation bridges so that both LANs can interpret packets sent from the other.

Another issue covered in these chapters is the *amount* of equipment you will need. Providing remote access to a handful of telecommuters requires far less equipment than providing remote backbone connectivity to a hundred small remote offices. This will also affect the number of wide-area service connections you need, so be sure to study these chapters carefully before you order any services!

Remote Access Software Considerations

A remote access system involves not only hardware, but software as well. The software you select falls into two categories: server software, which resides in the remote access server, and client software, which is installed on the users' personal computers. This leads to some obvious—and important—questions:

■ Which remote access software is best—both for the users and the remote access server?

■ How do you install and maintain the remote access software?

Your choice of remote access software is determined by both your needs and the type of remote access connectivity you want to provide. However, you should also take into consideration your users' needs and the support requirements they will have. The more users you have on your remote access system, the more you will want to consider standardizing on a single vendor's remote access client software to minimize training and support time. You'll also want to consider which types of remote access software can be managed with your existing network management tools, and which provides the easiest upgrade routes. After all, when it comes time to upgrade the client software for all your remote users, you probably won't be able to have them bring their PCs into your office for your staff to upgrade. Therefore, a software package that is easy enough for even an inexperienced remote user to upgrade and maintain will often be your best bet.

Remote Access Management Concerns

This book is entitled *LAN Times Guide to **Managing** Remote Connectivity*. And management is the biggest challenge for remote access. With your users spread far and wide—and with support resources limited—you must give careful consideration to how you are going to provide for their needs. This is especially important when you consider that the remote access system will soon become the lifeblood of your remote users. It is what connects them to the home office and keeps them working productively while in the field.

Therefore, some of the questions you must answer before implementing your remote access system are:

■ Should you outsource the maintenance of your remote access system?

■ How do you prepare your users to get the most benefit from your remote access system?

■ Who will design and conduct user training?

■ How will you support remote users?

- How will you handle software upgrades and routine maintenance for remote users?

- How will you keep track of all the software and hardware traveling around with your remote users?

- How will you establish and enforce a corporate remote access policy?

Chapters 14, 15, 17, 18, and 19 are devoted to helping you identify all the issues surrounding these questions and crafting effective answers to them. Remember, however, that the management issues involved in your remote access system are as fluid and changing as the system itself. The key to successful management is periodic review and updating of corporate remote access policies.

Security: The Final Frontier

How will you handle the increased security challenges that a remote access system introduces? After all, the point of a remote access system is to make your corporate network accessible from virtually anywhere at nearly any time. Therefore, how do you prevent unauthorized access in such an "open" environment?

Chapter 16 provides a thorough checklist of security measures and precautions, as well as valuable information on security systems you will want to investigate. It is absolutely essential that your security program be firmly in place well before your remote access system is implemented. It's much easier—and far less costly—to fix security problems before they occur!

A Lot to Ponder

As you can see, there is a lot to consider before, during, and after implementing a remote access system. While it can increase corporate productivity and make life easier for the "road warriors" of your organization, without careful planning, a remote access system can become one frustration after another. In fact, a poorly-implemented remote access system can be a major headache and embarrassment for a network administrator. However, this book is here to guide you through the maze and help you avoid the pitfalls. By following the advice provided and using the techniques described here, building a remote access system won't be disastrous, but rather one of the crowning achievements of your network management career.

PART ONE

The Hidden Costs of Remote Connectivity

If you are like most managers, you are increasingly under pressure to provide connectivity for more and more remote and mobile users. This pressure includes keeping the costs of such connectivity down. The trouble is, costs are hard to figure. While you likely have in mind ballpark prices for remote connectivity equipment like modems and dial-up routers, it is also likely that you would be hard pressed to peg the costs of the two largest portions of a remote connectivity solution: the recurring telecommunications charges to keep users connected and what are often called the hidden costs of remote connectivity—the management costs and the time spent by the users in diagnosing and fixing problems.

This section of the book will give you a framework to help you price remote connectivity solutions. This framework will then be used throughout the book to help you cost justify your remote connectivity choices.

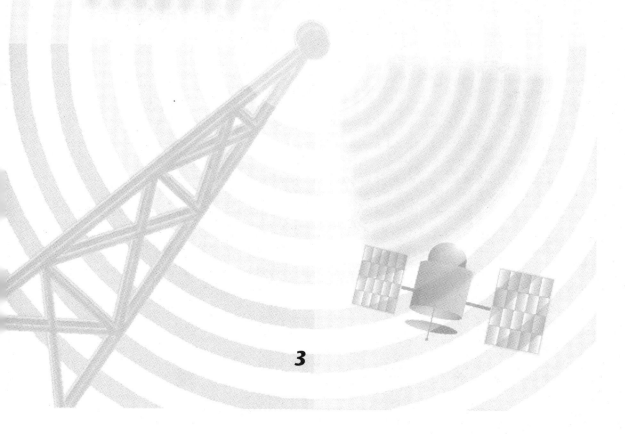

Chapter One

Pricing Out Remote Connectivity

3

These days when you buy a car, you get to see the fuel economy printed right on the sticker. Same thing goes for any large electrical appliance. If you buy a refrigerator, microwave oven, or an air conditioner, there's a tag on the product telling you how much electrical power the thing will consume per hour.

A savvy shopper takes the fuel economy and rating of power efficiency into account before buying the product. If two products are comparable in features and close in price, but one is much more energy efficient, it's a simple matter to pick the one that would use less gas or electricity over the course of its lifetime.

The even more savvy shopper goes further, looking into the service history of a particular car model or the repair history for an electrical appliance. After all, you want something that won't cost you a lot of money for repairs down the road.

What does any of this have to do with remote connectivity? You should be looking at your remote connectivity choices in the same way you look at buying a car or appliance. You should be considering the costs associated with owning the equipment and using a product. Basically, you should be trying to determine the total cost of ownership for your connectivity solutions.

Unfortunately, there is no cost-of-ownership guide to remote connectivity services and equipment. But that shouldn't stop you from using the same type of reasoning when selecting a remote connectivity solution for your company. You simply have to do more work on your own to understand the long-term cost implications of one remote connectivity solution versus another.

And you had better believe there are major long-term cost differences between the various solutions. To start, there is the choice of which service to use to connect remote and mobile users. The type of analysis you will need to make before selecting a service is comparable to looking at the miles per gallon rating on a new car's sticker or the kilowatt-hour rating on an electrical appliance. Basically, you will need to determine which service is the most cost-effective for the types of traffic your remote users will generate.

The Challenge of Remote Connectivity

In today's competitive corporate world, access to information is essential. And increasingly, companies are finding they must make information available to more and more remote and mobile users. This presents one of the greatest challenges you, a manager responsible for connecting these folks, will face.

Connecting remote users presents a very different set of requirements to you and your staff than connecting users to a network within the company. The main differences are that you have to pay for bandwidth; the bandwidth typically will not be as great as that offered LAN-attached users, and it is harder to support users who are beyond the walls of your corporation.

Dealing with these differences represents both a technical and financial challenge that requires constant evaluation and trade-offs. The remaining chapters in this book give you the information you will need to properly evaluate the different connectivity services, equipment, and scenarios so that you can choose the most appropriate for your users. Throughout the book you will see that there are many connectivity solutions that will give your users the basic level of connectivity they need. You may find, for example, that there are several connectivity service offerings that provide your users with enough bandwidth for them to get their jobs done. However, as with most decisions concerning the implementation of networking technology, you must choose a solution that not only satisfies the technical requirements of your users' needs, but one that also makes business sense. In other words, you have to find the most cost-effective connectivity solution.

And here is where remote connectivity differs greatly from other network situations. Basically, it can cost a lot more to connect remote users. The best way to look at the cost to support remote users is to consider what is commonly called the *total cost of ownership* (TCO), which, as the name implies, is the total cost to get remote users up and running and to keep them up and running. The special box "Components of the Total Cost of Ownership for Remote Users" lists the cost components in the TCO for a remote user. As you can see in the box, the cost includes much more than the purchase price of the equipment a remote user needs. So, when you are trying to estimate the cost of one remote connectivity option over another (or simply what it would cost to let a user work at home or in a remote office), you must budget money for the normal things like a desktop computer, a modem, and telecommunications services. But you must also allocate money for the time your staff will need to spend supporting the remote users.

Components of the Total Cost of Ownership for Remote Users

Equipment-Related Costs

- Hardware and software purchase price
- Labor charges for installation, setup, and configuration of equipment and software
- End-user training
- Network staff's time to handle administrative tasks associated with remote users, equipment, and services
- Network staff's time to manage remote equipment
- Network staff's time to service and maintain remote equipment

Telecom-Related Costs

- Charge to start service
- Installation fee for access lines
- Cost of any special equipment needed to connect to the service
- Monthly charge for the service
- Usage fee for the service (in some cases)

How much should you allocate for these things? That is the main question facing network managers when they develop remote connectivity solutions for their companies. It is very hard to estimate the costs to connect and support your users. There is no simple answer—except to say remote connectivity can cost a lot more than it first appears. One way to get an estimate of the expected costs is to look at some of the research on this market done by industry consultants.

Probably the most pertinent study about the costs of remote connectivity was done by Infonetics Research Inc. (San Jose, California). In 1995, Infonetics Research surveyed 161 organizations that used remote access networks to connect remote sites, telecommuters, and mobile workers. At that time, the companies in the survey were spending on average $4.79 million per year in total remote access costs. Of these costs, only $726,000 per year, or 15 percent, went toward purchasing equipment and software.

Figure 1-1 shows that the largest portion, about 50 percent ($2.4 million annually), of the cost to connect remote users is for recurring operations costs of which telecommunications charges are the bulk. Companies spend about another 35 percent ($1.6 million annually) on hidden user costs, which include the lost time users spend installing, configuring, and solving equipment and software problems, according to Infonetics Research. Other market research studies by Stamford, Connecticut-based Gartner Group and Cambridge, Massachusetts-based Forrester Research point to the same high TCO for remote connectivity, where the purchase price for equipment and software is roughly one-fifth the total TCO.

What does all of this mean? It means you have to be aware of the recurring operational costs and potential hidden costs. Many times, products are purchased strictly on price alone, but as you can see, the real key to keeping costs down is to reduce the recurring charges and to identify and reduce the

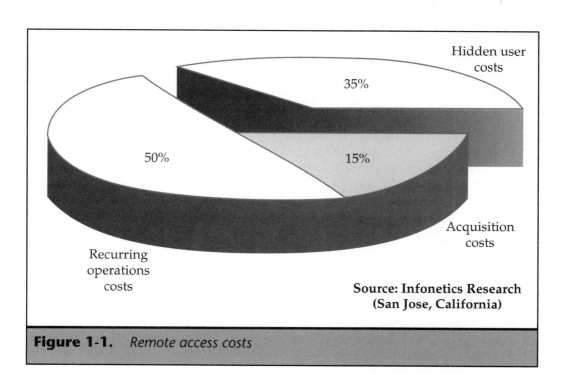

Figure 1-1.   *Remote access costs*

hidden costs. Throughout this book, I will give you examples of how to calculate the TCO of the different remote connectivity solutions. In the examples, I include the cost to buy equipment and establish the appropriate telecommunications service, and the recurring telecommunications charges for the service. I also will give you tips on how to save money on recurring costs. For example, in Chapter 2 on analog services, I point out that a higher-end modem, while costing more up front, might save you money in the long run if your users take advantage of the 4:1 compression that comes with it. Throughout the book I also try to point out potential hidden costs and in some cases suggest ways to reduce these costs.

Not All Users Are Created Equal

When trying to address the hidden costs of remote connectivity, you must realize that not all users need the same level of support. As Table 1-1 shows, there are basically four distinct types of remote users—users in small offices with no onsite technical staff, full-time telecommuters, part-time telecommuters, and mobile workers. Each type of remote user requires very different kinds of support. You will have to take this into account when trying to determine how much it will cost you in staff hours of labor to keep these users up and running.

Users in Small, Remote Offices

The first group is made up of users in small remote offices where there is no onsite technical support. This includes a wide variety of situations, all of which have different support needs. For example, this might include a company with a half dozen small regional offices. Or, it might be a bank with dozens of branch offices where workers in each office are on a small LAN. It could also be a retail store chain where each store has a single point-of-sales terminal that is a computer linked to the chain's central site.

With such small offices it is likely you will dispatch a network staffer to the site to install or upgrade networking hardware and software. For example, your staff would typically perform such tasks as adding a new server or wiring hub, or the installation of a new version of the network operating system running on that site's servers. You may opt to outsource these tasks to a systems integrator or buy the equipment from a local VAR (value-added reseller) who would handle the installation.

When it comes to the client software, you might try to save your staff's time. You could opt to invest in an electronic software distribution system that

Type of User	How Equipment and Software Installation and Upgrades Are Handled	How Support Is Handled
Users in remote offices with little or no technical staff	Networking equipment and software typically installed by a visiting networking staffer; client software typically installed by users.	Either network staff handles support or it is outsourced.
Full-time telecommuters	Client software and equipment often installed by the user.	Support typically handled by network staff remotely (sometimes requires a visit to the user's home).
Part-time telecommuters	Installations can be done by networking staff in the office.	Users can often wait until they get into the office and have the problem solved by network staff.
Mobile workers	Installations and upgrades can be handled by networking staff.	Problems require immediate attention of the network staff.

Table 1-1. *The Types of Remote Users*

lets you centrally administer the automatic installation of new software or the upgrading of existing programs. (I discuss software distribution in Chapter 17, "Software Distribution and Asset Control.") But most likely, you will choose the traditional method of using floppy disks and leaving client software installation up to the end users. For example, in 1996, The McGraw-Hill Companies (LAN Times' parent company) purchased an enterprise license for a McAfee antivirus product that scanned for and removed a particularly nasty virus that upon execution would overwrite your hard disk destroying all the data on it. The McGraw-Hill Companies is like many organizations—a collection of semiautonomous business units with many regional offices, all of which may or may not have users connected to a network. Electronic software distribution was not an option. And it would have taken too long for the corporate systems staff to get to everyone's machine. The best solution was to send all the people in remote LAN Times offices an overnight package with a floppy and have them install the antivirus software.

Having users in remote offices load their own client software is an effective way to save your staff's time. It works for many retail store chains. Some chains do use electronic software distribution, but many still ship to their stores floppies with upgrades to customized software packages. This is particularly true in mom-and-pop retail industries like florist shops.

If a remote office is large enough, you might want to hire a support firm to install the software for you. That would be a good solution if the installation is complicated. For example, if you are installing a new communications package or piece of hardware that requires the user to select the proper comm port or IRQ for the device, you might decide it would cost less (by virtue of fewer calls for help to resolve problems) to have someone handle this. Of course, one point that will be raised later in the book is that you might want to consider migrating users to an operating system like Windows 95, which touts plug-and-play capabilities, and select only plug-and-play components, such as modems and network adapter cards, to make installations easier (in theory) for your users to handle.

When there are problems with networking hardware and software in remote offices, you might send one of your network staff to the site or have it handled by a firm you have hired. Either approach costs money. If you have geographically dispersed sites, sending a person requires paying for air fare, hotel, food, car rental, and other travel-related expenses. You are also losing that person's time in your main site. On top of that, you have to make sure you send the right person. It is likely that the people in the remote site will not be able to offer much useful information over the phone. If the problem is fairly complicated, it might require a network staffer with a specific set of skills to diagnose and fix the problem. If you send the wrong person, you have wasted the travel money, that person's time, and the time of the users in the remote office who have sat idle for a few extra days while you fix the problem.

If you are lucky, you might have a person onsite who can help you handle some simple tasks and help diagnose a problem. It is a good idea to actively groom a person or two in your remote sites to act as a liaison (see "Training Remote Site Liaisons") who can help the people onsite with simple problems, and who can also provide accurate and useful information about a problem.

Training Remote Site Liaisons

The idea of grooming people in the remote sites to help your staff is a way to extend your support structure beyond your network staff. You should choose a person who is interested—you can usually find one or two people in each site who are interested in computers and who seem to know more than the basics. Train these people on a regular basis so that they can help your staff. You do not have to turn these people into CNEs (Certified NetWare Engineers), but each month teach them something about some aspect of remote access and network administration.

You can do something as simple as educating them about the "corporate" view on virus protection. If your company, for example, relies on users to scan floppies and mail attachments for viruses, your liaison may want to remind users at his or her site to do so. This reminder by the onsite person might prevent a virus infection and thus save you and your staff the time it would take to correct any problems an infection might bring with it.

You might also consider developing some simple troubleshooting checklists for the liaison. Such checklists help the liaison diagnose problems so that he or she can pass this information along to your staff. Creating troubleshooting checklists is fairly easy. You start with the most generic and frequently occurring problems that happen at your remote sites. For instance, many calls to network support from remote sites are for PCs or modems not being turned on or plugged in. This holds for even more sophisticated remote access equipment like a remote access server or a DSU/CSU (data service unit/channel service unit). So checklist item 1 is "Is there power?" Then offer a solution. "If not, check the cords and make sure the unit is plugged in and turned on." That is a simple example, but it is also a very common problem.

The troubleshooting checklist should get into more detail. Remember, the purpose of the list is to help the onsite liaison isolate a problem. If the liaison can, for example, determine that a device, such as a branch office router, is up and running, and there is still a problem with users connecting to the main office, it might help your staff determine that the telecommunications service is out, saving a trip to the site.

The onsite liaisons can also help fix some minor, common problems like printer jams. However, make sure your use of a liaison stays within any company boundaries. After all, this person is not a network staffer. He or she has a job to do. You are essentially using this person to reduce your operational costs. Unfortunately, the liaison's time to help you is still a cost to your company.

Full-time Telecommuter

Full-time telecommuters are just that—people who work at home full time. While full-time telecommuters are not a large part of most corporations' user base, they are growing in number. The typical full-time telecommuter is usually either an independent worker, such as a writer, or a service-oriented person, such as a travel-reservation agent. The common thread among all full-time telecommuters is that they need their computer, phone line, and a link to corporate e-mail and data.

The level of connectivity can be the simple need to check e-mail every once in a while. Or, it can be much more complicated, requiring a centrally located automatic call distributor to direct an incoming call to the next available agent's home, and a high-speed or dedicated link connecting the agent to the numerous databases required to arrange a caller's trip, including booking a flight, a rental car, and a hotel room.

It should be clear that these examples represent two very different types of connectivity scenarios—each requiring very different types of support. For example, you might simply ship a new home-based writer a laptop or desktop computer with a preconfigured modem and communications software package. You might also bundle the necessary productivity software, such as word processing, spreadsheet, and presentation graphics packages, with the computer before you ship it. And you might rely on such full-time telecommuters to load any new software or upgrades by themselves. For instance, if you are migrating users from Windows 3.x to Windows 95, you might send them more memory and Windows 95 software and ask them to install the memory in their system and load the new version of Windows.

You can probably do many of the same things with a travel-agent type of full-time telecommuter. You could ship out a preconfigured computer with all the appropriate software installed. However, if the user requires something more sophisticated than a modem connection—an ISDN line, for example—you might need to send a person to the home site for the installation. Similarly, for software upgrades and hardware changes, you may be able to simply offload this task to the home user. There are potential hidden costs in this approach, as the user may have trouble and will spend his or her time trying to diagnose the problem.

When it comes to supporting full-time telecommuters, again, your options will depend on the type of user. For example, a home-based writer working on the text for a corporate brochure or an article for a publication might have trouble dialing into a mail server to get e-mail. While this can be very annoying to the user, it might not be disastrous if the problem is not resolved instantly. You may be able to talk the users through the problem, or simply ask them to send their laptop by overnight delivery to you to fix. (The assumption is that they can get by without the system for a day or two. Or, more likely, you will need to ship them a loaner unit for their use while you repair their system.)

On the other hand, any problem the reservation-agent type of telecommuter has, needs immediate attention. Down time for such a person means that person cannot take orders, and that means there is a potential loss of revenue to the company. If the problem cannot be resolved over the phone, you might have to dispatch a staffer to the user's home to fix the problem.

Part-time Telecommuter

Part-time telecommuters are people who either work at home a few days a week or are what the Cambridge, Massachusetts, consultancy Forrester Research calls "white-collar workhorses," people who work a full day in the office and put in a few more hours working at home at night or on weekends.

Typically, part-time telecommuters need access to e-mail, the Internet, or other network resources. For instance, a department manager might need budget information stored in spreadsheets on a departmental server. Or, a sales manager might need to get quarterly performance numbers on his or her staff from a mainframe database. The way the user connects will likely be by using an analog phone line and a modem, or in some cases, an ISDN line and an ISDN terminal adapter.

There are several ways to handle part-time telecommuting situations that will help you reduce your recurring management and hidden costs. If your company allows, you might suggest or mandate that all part-time telecommuters use a specified list of equipment and software, and install it themselves.

Limiting the number of parameters, like which communications packages a part-time telecommuter can use, simplifies support. You might, for example, require that all users run the same operating system and communications software. If the user is simply taking home a company laptop, you may be able to control what is installed on it. You will be able to install software and new hardware (for example, a new PC Card modem or memory for a system upgrade). Your staff will be able to take some control over the configuration of the system. That might help reduce the number of problems from equipment or software conflicts.

But you may find that many part-time telecommuters are using the family PC to do some extra work. So your efforts to limit the person's choices may not be successful.

One thing in your favor with part-time telecommuters is that their problems can often wait to be fixed until the user is in the office. If part-time telecommuters are simply getting some extra work done at night on a presentation and they cannot connect to get e-mail, they can probably wait until morning. (However, if these users must be supported, you might need to have staff available 24 hours a day, since the problems that interfere with these types of workers occur during off hours.)

On the other hand, if the part-time telecommuter is the head of marketing or production working at home for two days to nail down the year-end projections for a project and this person needs access to the network, his or her problems will need to be handled immediately.

When problems occur with either type of part-time telecommuter, you or a member of your staff might need to diagnose the problem with help from the user. If this is just a person working a few extra hours on his or her own, how much of your staff's time do you really want to allocate to this type of support? You can probably imagine cases where it might be difficult to resolve a problem over the phone. You have much less control over this situation, since the user can be running anything from an old IBM PC XT to a high-end, self-built multimedia PC (where the user has added lots of hardware and software without regard for conflicts). If users own their computer, they can load anything they want on it and add any hardware their heart desires. Just try troubleshooting a problem over the phone in that situation. I've seen many problems with remote access that are just impossible to diagnose without the pertinent information—information that the person at the other end of the line might not be able to supply. (See "Remote Frustration.")

Mobile Users

The last type of remote user is the mobile user. This person typically is a traveling professional who needs information to do his or her job from the road.

On the plus side, mobile users usually start their trips from an office with a networking staff. So you can at least have control over the type of equipment (laptop and modem, for example) the user takes on the road and the software that is installed on the laptop. And since the user is mobile, the choices of service are limited. Most often the person will use analog phone lines and a

Remote Frustration

When you're trying to help a remote user with a problem, it is very hard to get even simple information over the phone from a person who doesn't know computers. For example, at a previous job, one fellow worker called me at home because he was having trouble with e-mail. Within the office we used MCI Mail communications software to dial out. But at home, we all had our own favorite package installed. My friend was having trouble uploading a file as a binary attachment to his message. At that time, MCI Mail was a strictly command-line system, and it required that you change your standard parameters to specify the transmission protocol you would be using (XMODEM, ZMODEM, and so on) if it wasn't the default setting. Once you correctly specified the file transfer protocol, you had to specify, within the text of the message, that you were adding a binary attachment and which protocol you were using (the command was \upload binary xmodem). Then you had to upload the file from your PC's hard disk to the MCI Mail system.

Considering that every communications package uses a different set of hot keys or menu items to define the transmission protocols and to upload a file, I ran through the most common ones I could think of for my friend. We eventually came across the right combination. The entire process took about an hour. And that was for something most would consider a minor task.

modem. Some may use or need a wireless connectivity solution. But for the most part, we are talking about laptops and PC Card modems.

There are many types of mobile users, and each type requires a different kind of support. You may have a group of traveling professionals who simply need to check e-mail at night from a hotel. These folks may also need access to the corporate network from their hotel room, too. For instance, they may need to access a group scheduling program to check on meetings later in the week, or they may need to run a query in a database application for a customer who left a voice message during the day.

The other type of mobile user requires connectivity as part of his or her job on the road. Such users include service and support people who, while at a customer's site, need to dial in to your company's bulletin board service or web site to download a software patch or remedy to a problem. This type of mobile user also includes salespeople who need to check price lists and availability of stock while at a customer's site to give customers a quote or confirm their order.

With the first type of mobile user, the ones accessing mail at night from their hotel rooms, problems often occur after hours. Depending on the number of mobile users in your company and the extent of their travels, you might need to have network staffers on duty 24 hours a day to help these people when problems occur. If there are only a handful of such travelers, you might be able to get by with having one staffer be on call each night and simply have the mobile user page this person. Or, you might simply decide these people are on their own during off hours and make them wait until your staff is on duty to help them.

With the other type of mobile user, problems require immediate attention. However, the problems normally occur during business hours, so your staff will be around to help them out. This means of supporting such users breaks down if you have many people who travel great distances. If your office is on the West Coast and you have a strong push in Eastern Europe or the Far East, we are talking about a 10- to 12-hour time difference. So you may still need some way to cover these folks when they have problems. Having a person on call with a pager is usually the most cost-effective method of supporting such users.

What Does It Cost?

In discussing the types of remote users, I have touched on the basic levels of support you must provide for these users. The cost of this support comes out of your network operations budget. If you need people to work overtime or be on call at night to support remote users, you pay for this out of your budget.

Most companies have not allocated staff to mobile and remote users, according to Infonetics Research. That is in contrast to network-attached users, who can expect a network staffer to come by and fix a problem. Infonetics Research believes that 95 percent of the time remote users have to fix their problems by themselves, estimating that mobile users spend six hours per month, telecommuters spend five hours per month, and users in remote offices with no technical staff spend three hours per month trying to resolve problems.

I would consider these estimates to be on the conservative side. I have worked in a remote office for four years and consider myself more knowledgeable about software installation, configuration, and troubleshooting than your typical office worker. But it still takes a lot of time to resolve problems, even when you know what to look for. I spend much more than three hours per month trying to get new equipment to work with existing computer systems. Particularly challenging tasks have been trying to install an external CD-ROM that uses the parallel port (the systems manager shipped a floppy disk with the drivers, but the disk was blank), and installing a tape backup system (again, one that used the parallel port) that seemed to only work with one of our four computers.

The main point to consider is that if your company is going to approach remote connectivity from an enterprisewide, systematic perspective, these hidden costs must be considered before any solution is tried. The reason is that the payback for remote access equipment comes not from lower initial purchase costs, but from lowering the recurring operational and hidden costs.

If you are like most managers, the technical aspects of connecting remote users, while challenging, are either well understood or something that, with research, you feel comfortable with. The areas that most managers seem to be less comfortable with are preparing the cost justification of a remote connectivity solution, demonstrating the cost-effectiveness of that solution, and ensuring that the hidden costs to manage a large remote connectivity solution are kept to a minimum. Your success in these three areas will determine the success (or failure) of your remote connectivity ventures.

This book will look at both the technical and business aspects of planning, deploying, and managing remote connectivity solutions for your company. Most chapters in this book will reacquaint you with familiar technologies, such as dial-in connectivity using analog phone lines and modems, and will introduce you to some of the new services, such as those based on Digital Subscriber Line technologies, that might be useful when linking remote users.

Throughout the book, I will try to give you information about the technology and the cost of using the technology. Specifically, I will guide you through the cost justification process, giving you examples on how to prove your solution is cost-effective. Additionally, I'll point out issues you should be aware of and will need to address to ensure that the hidden costs to manage your remote connectivity solution are not out of line.

The book especially focuses on how to select the right connectivity solution to reduce the total cost of ownership (TCO) of remote connectivity. As noted, studies by several market research firms find that the costs for telecom services and labor are four times the initial purchase price of connectivity hardware and software.

Why This Matters

The reason you will need to pay close attention to the cost of remote connectivity is because within most companies there is explosive growth in the need to connect remote users. And the remote connectivity trend is accelerating rapidly. In 1995, Forrester Research surveyed Fortune 1000 companies and found that 62 percent reported that they had at least 50 work-at-home employees. Of these workers, 11 percent were full-time telecommuters who did not come into an office at all. The other 89 percent worked from home at night or a few days a week (the white-collar workhorses).

The telecommuting trend is not limited to Fortune 1000 companies. A survey by the Boston, Massachusetts-based Yankee Group found that more than 41 percent of all U.S. households engaged in some form of at-home work. And the Gartner Group finds similar numbers of remote workers in its surveys. For example, Gartner estimates that by the year 2000 there will be 55 million users who are regular telecommuters working out of a small office or home office.

That's a lot of remote users, and it doesn't even count the mobile professionals such as sales reps and tech support staffers who need access to e-mail and corporate data from customer sites, hotel rooms, and pay phones.

Additionally, companies are spending more to connect remote users. The International Data Corp., a market research firm in Framingham, Massachusetts, estimates that revenues for the remote access server market will grow from $1 billion in 1995 to $4.9 billion in the year 2000. Remote access servers are essentially the corporate entry points into which telecommuters and mobile workers access corporate networks.

All of this growth reflects four major trends: decentralization of corporations, increased levels of telecommuting (be it full-time or after-hours work-at-home users), a growing need for mobile professionals to have access to data and e-mail, and an increased need to connect to the Internet from home or on the road.

When it comes to decentralization of the workforce, many companies no longer have a single corporate headquarters where just about the entire workforce is located. Instead there are many smaller offices with workers who need to share e-mail, documents, and spreadsheet files, and who need access to corporate databases. One factor driving this decentralization is the large number of corporate acquisitions, which lead to many regional offices.

When it comes to telecommuting, there are many reasons this type of remote connectivity is increasingly becoming important. The reasons have to do with economics and environmental issues. On the economic side, some companies have come to the conclusion that office space in corporate headquarters is just too costly to use for people who can easily do their job at home. And some workers believe quality of life is more important. They would rather work at home and be with their children, pets, or loved ones, rather than placing kids in day care or leaving animals home alone all day. And some people simply do not want to commute.

Increasingly, companies are being forced to adopt telecommuting to meet local and federal laws. The Clean Air Act requires significant reductions in the number of cars traveling into some cities. To force compliance, some states have passed legislation that mandates telecommuting.

Also increasing the demand for remote connectivity is the desire to connect to the Internet. The Internet gives mobile users access to information from the road and lets telecommuters perform research from home. And as I discuss in Chapter 8, "The Internet as a Backbone," some companies are leveraging the Internet to enhance connectivity to remote users and to reduce recurring telecommunications charges.

Regardless of the reason for the increase in the demand for remote connectivity, the demand is there. And the cost to support your remote users will be yours to determine. You, as the manager responsible for the solution, will likely be called upon to discuss, document, and justify the costs associated with any remote connectivity solution planned by your company. The most important thing to keep in mind is that you must look at the total cost of ownership for any solution, not just the up front costs to get a user connected.

PART TWO

LANTIMES

Connectivity Choices: Services and Equipment

In the past, your options for connecting your remote users were fairly limited. Today, that's hardly the case. This section looks at the choices you have when it comes to connecting your remote users. I start with the most common methods—analog and ISDN lines. And then move on to some of the emerging options including wireless, Digital Subscriber Line services, cable access, and using the Internet as an extension of your corporate backbone. In each chapter, I discuss the specifics about one of the service offerings and the type of equipment needed by a user to connect to that service.

Since a successful remote connectivity implementation requires a combination of good technology and a good business model, I also discuss the pricing of the services and equipment. Throughout the chapters in this section, I point out ways to cost-justify a service, as well as ways to get the most out of a particular service. I also give examples of how to choose a service so it is a good match for the applications you are running.

Chapter Two

Analog

A nalog phone lines have always been, and will remain for many years, the primary way to connect remote users and telecommuters. So how do you, a manager responsible for the future connectivity needs of your company, get the most out of these analog line connections?

Before considering this question, you may want to ask another: Why stick with analog in the first place? There are other access technologies, established and emerging, such as ISDN and those based on cable modems, that offer higher bandwidth. And there are a number of wireless technologies that offer users freer range when trying to connect. (Subsequent chapters in this book will discuss these connectivity services and equipment.) Why not use these services?

You may decide some of these other services are right for some of your connectivity needs. But the bottom line is that using analog lines to connect telecommuters and remote users has many advantages—advantages that will keep analog the most common remote connectivity method used by companies. These advantages include relatively low cost for the service and an ubiquity guaranteeing that a user can find a line to connect to from anywhere on the road. In addition, using analog lines as the primary connectivity means that you will buy connectivity products from a well-established, highly competitive (read that: cutthroat pricing by vendors) modem industry that has based its products on international standards, which guarantees interoperability. That is not necessarily the case with other access technologies—many of which use proprietary techniques. Or, as is the case with some ISDN and ATM equipment, the standards are either broad enough for vendors to offer different implementations, or the vendors use proprietary extensions to the standards. Because modems are standards-based, you can select the best product on the market today that meets the immediate needs of your users, knowing you are not locking yourself into any one vendor's product line when it comes to your future purchases.

Making the Connection

In the basic analog line connectivity scenario your users typically have two ways of connecting to the corporate network. Users can access the network as if they were a node operating remotely, or they can control an application running on a server within the company from a remote location. These approaches to remote connectivity are called *remote node* and *remote control*, respectively.

Remote node and remote control access to a network are quite different. With remote node, the remote user's computer acts as a client on the corporate network. With remote control, the user, as the name implies, controls an application running on a server or workstation located on the network. (Chapter 12, "Single User-to-LAN," provides more detail about the differences between the two types of connectivity and when to use one over the other.)

In either mode of operation, the user dials into the network, typically by calling into a modem pool, which is connected to a communications server as shown in Figure 2-1. With remote control, sometimes a user dials directly into an application server that may or may not be attached to a corporate network.

Cutting Phone Costs

Each time a user dials into your network, he or she is racking up phone charges—something you obviously want to keep to a minimum. There are a couple of ways to do this.

One way that is getting a lot of attention is to use the Internet as an extension of your corporate backbone to save telecommunications charges. The basic idea is to have users in remote offices dial into an Internet service provider (ISP) with a local point of presence and let the traffic pass over the Internet to the corporate network as shown in Figure 2-2. By using this method telecommunications charges can be greatly reduced. For example, the user in the remote office typically only pays a local phone charge to connect to the ISP. The user might be billed per minute by the phone company for this

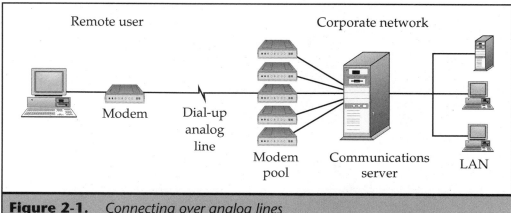

Figure 2-1. *Connecting over analog lines*

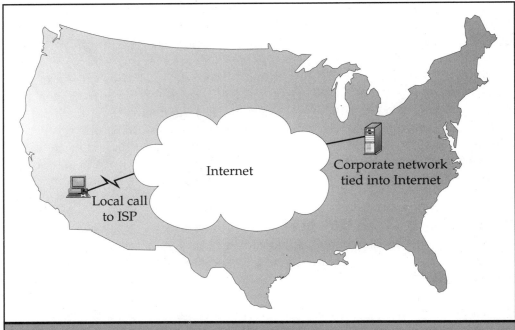

Figure 2-2.   *The Internet as an extension of the corporate backbone*

connection, but it is a local call, so the charge is much less than for placing a long-distance call. A user in New York, for the cost of a local call, might connect with a network in San Francisco. Sometimes there is no extra charge for the local call—for example, some phone companies offer a fixed rate per month for unlimited local calls.

This Internet-as-backbone approach has lots of appeal because of the potential cost savings that you could get if most of your remote traffic were carried for the price of a local phone call. There are, however, many obstacles to this approach, including security considerations and the issue of how you get existing client/server applications to work over the Internet. Chapter 8, "The Internet as a Backbone," looks at these issues in great detail.

Another way to reduce telecommunications charges is to cut the length of each call to connect to the network. The general approach to trying to reduce line-usage charges for telecommuters and remote users is to reduce the time it takes for each call. For example, many companies find they can reduce the connect time of some of their users by teaching them how to compress large files, such as image files or files created with presentation graphics software like Microsoft's PowerPoint or IBM's Lotus Freelance. File compression seems simple, but it is not as widely practiced as you might think (you'll see why a little later in the chapter). That's too bad, because the investment is minimal and the cost savings can be significant. For example, shareware and commercial compression programs, such as PKZip, Double Space, Stacker, and WinZip, some of which are easy to download from CompuServe or other online services, have site licensing agreements that go as low as $10 per PC. Depending on your users' file-transfer requirements, that dollar amount can easily be made back in a short time (see the special section, "Cost Savings Using Compression Software," provided next).

Cost Savings Using Compression Software

A site license for shareware compression software, such as PKZip, can be obtained for about $10 per PC—an amount that will be returned many times over by cutting the length of time it takes users to send files over an analog phone line.

Example of cost savings from compression:

Calling from New York to Miami, it takes me three minutes to send a fairly small 350K PowerPoint file using a 14.4-Kbps modem. The call costs $2.10 using my NyNex calling card (and AT&T service). Using PKZip, I can compress the file to about 90K, and the call takes 1 minute at a cost of $1.40. I save $0.70.

If your users are typical, the flow of information is two way—for example, a salesperson sends the document or presentation file to an assistant for modification, and that person later sends it back. If I needed to pull down the reworked version of my file at the end of the day, I'd save another $0.70 if the user on the other end used compression. Now I'm up to a $1.40 savings for just one file.

Most business trips last at least one night, and I probably would need to do the same thing the next day. That means I've saved $2.80 by using compression (again, on just one file).

You can see that the savings add up. If I travel once a month and have to do the same type of file exchange, I save $33.60 for the year. That more than covers the $20 it costs for my copy and my coworker's copy of compression software.

Your remote users most likely will be on the road more often than one night a month. If they send many large files, you can see that a small investment in software can easily pay for itself in reduced phone charges in a few months with moderate usage.

Many companies do not make file compression a high priority. One reason is that nontechnical users often find it hard to compress and decompress files. This is particularly true if there is no corporate standard for compression. A user may get a ZIPed file from one person and an ARCed file from another. Technical and nontechnical folks alike will not be enthused about compression if they need to use two or three programs to compress and decompress files.

In companies where there is no corporate standard for compression, there can be other problems that limit the use of the technology—for instance, if different departments use different compression software. A user who cannot remember which compression software the marketing department uses will likely send files in uncompressed form just to be on the safe side. Even when only one program is used, there can be issues that limit the use of compression software. For instance, suppose you have a mix of IBM clones and Macintosh computers. If you use PKZip and create self-extracting, executable files, the folks using Macs will not be able to easily extract the compressed file (unless, of course, they are running some type of PC emulation software on their Mac).

The point is that if you do not make compression easy for people to use, users will not take advantage of the software. If you want to reap the cost-saving benefits of file compression, you must develop a corporate policy on compression, educate users on the importance of compression, and train users how to run the software.

An alternative to file compression is to use compression algorithms that come with higher-end modems. Typically, when shopping for a modem, you will find that it costs more for one that includes compression than for a comparable model without compression operating at the same speed. You can cost-justify the purchase of the higher-end model by looking at the total cost of ownership—the more expensive model will save you phone charges every time it is used.

The two most common modem compression protocols are V.42bis and MNP5. Typically, it costs about $50 to $100 more for a modem with either of these protocols. Using modem-based compression requires that the modems at both ends of a connection support the same compression protocol. In some ways, that's why modem-based compression is not used as often as it could be.

Modem-based compression works in this way: the data sent to a modem through a computer's serial port is compressed by use of the V.42bis or MNP5 algorithm. The modem at the other end uses the same algorithm to decompress the data. MNP5 compression typically cuts in half the time to transmit a large file. V.42bis typically cuts the time to about one-third to one-fifth of the time if no compression is used.

Moving to Higher Speeds

Compression is not the only way to cut phone costs when using analog lines to connect remote users. The other common approach is to use higher-speed modems. If your company is typical, many of your users still have 14.4-Kbps modems. A simple move to 28.8-Kbps modems obviously provides a much faster connection—in theory, cutting the connect time in half.

You do not usually get a 50 percent reduction in connect time when you move from a 14.4-Kbps to a 28.8-Kbps modem, because there are many factors that determine the length of time to connect. For instance, the time it takes for the modems to perform all of the handshaking required to establish a connection is about the same for a 14.4 and 28.8 modem. And the time it takes for a connection session depends on the type of session, the communications software, and the transfer protocol being used. For example, if I am connecting to a database application server, the bulk of my connect time may be spent waiting for a query to be processed. Or, similarly, I may connect to a Web site and find I am waiting minutes for a response from the Web site's server. In either case, a higher-performance modem does not speed up these parts of my connection session.

Still, higher-speed modems do speed up the delivery of data over analog lines and cut the length of each call. By the time this book appears in print, 33.6-Kbps modems should be the norm with any new computer purchase (see the special section, "33.6-Kbps Modems Debut," provided next). In the summer of 1996, 33.6-Kbps modems started to appear preinstalled in many home computer bundles from the mail-order PC firms. At that time, many modem vendors had announced they would have 33.6-Kbps products available in the fall. There were few 33.6-Kbps modems discounted in the back pages of computer magazines when this book was written. But there were only a few. The price difference between a 33.6 and a 28.8 at that time was minimal (about $30 for an internal OEM version of the modem sold through a mail-order house). When this book appears, there will be no difference in price, according to many modem vendors.

33.6-Kbps Modems Debut

The 33.6-Kbps modems are essentially a better V.34 modem. Many higher-end 28.8-Kbps modems use V.34, which is a communications standard developed by the International Telecommunications Union (ITU). By the fall of 1996, the ITU was expected to ratify a new version of V.34 that improved modem interoperability and that supported higher transmission rates—namely 31.2 and 33.6 Kbps.

If there is virtually no difference in price between a 28.8- and a 33.6-Kbps modem, you obviously will buy the higher-speed modem if you need a new modem. But what if you don't need a new modem? Does it make any sense to junk a perfectly good 28.8-Kbps modem just to have the latest and greatest technology?

You might be able to cost-justify tossing the 28.8 and buying a new 33.6-Kbps modem based on line-charge savings. But you have to be careful here. When the decision was 14.4 versus 28.8, it made sense—you doubled your transmission speed, theoretically cutting your connect time in half. Going from 28.8 to 33.6 is not that much of an incremental gain.

And what if your boss rightly points out that the majority of installed modems would be, at least for a year or two, 14.4 or 28.8 Kbps? He or she might question whether you would make enough connections at the higher 33.6 rate to get the benefit of shorter calls. The way to convince your boss that you need to supply your remote users with 33.6-Kbps modems to save the company money is based on reduced connect time, not the traditional argument.

The way to cost-justify 33.6-Kbps modems is based on the better quality connection your users will get. Because of the improved nature of the 1996 version of V.34, your users will be able to reliably connect at higher rates more often. As anyone who works remotely knows, connection quality varies greatly from modem to modem. For example, Xircom claims that the 1996 version of V.34 yields average connects that are 30 percent higher. So you get more reliable high-speed connections using a 33.6-Kbps modem than when using a 28.8-Kbps modem. For example, some research studies have found that a 33.6-Kbps modem will operate at 28.8-Kbps connection speed about 80 percent of the time, while a 28.8-Kbps modem will only connect at that speed about 35 percent of the time. Typically, the 28.8-Kbps modem operates at a slightly lower connect speed of either 26.4, 24, or 21.6 Kbps.

So you might want to use this logic when lobbying to replace your company's existing 28.8-Kbps modems. You may, for example, argue that you will have a higher throughput more often with the better V.34 technology that is incorporated into 33.6-Kbps modems.

Sharing the Line: Combining Other Traffic with Data

If your remote users only need to access LAN-based applications on your corporate networks or to exchange e-mail and files, analog lines and modems can often be used to provide connectivity. But what happens when you want to send other forms of traffic on the same line?

For example, many companies are starting to deploy applications, such as collaborative work applications, that let workers display a shared document while allowing users at both ends of a connection to jointly edit the work. Such collaborative work programs, which are touted as productivity boosters, work best if the two users are also talking to each other. Quite often, companies equip their telecommuters with two telephone lines for just such situations. That solution doesn't work for the mobile user. Fortunately, there are a couple of techniques that provide users with a way to share voice and data over a single phone line.

DSVD Takes Off

Until recently, there were few practical ways to share voice and data over an analog line. Fortunately, a new line-sharing technique called Digital Simultaneous Voice and Data (DSVD) that works over existing copper wire phone lines is emerging. DSVD promises to give the small office or home office user a level of voice/data integration that has not been available before.

DSVD operates over unshielded twisted pair cabling—the common wiring that runs to every home and office. Because it uses existing lines, this eliminates one problem linked with the installation of Integrated Services Digital Networks (ISDNs). Many users have found that to get ISDN service, they have had to install new lines to their home—not a trivial task. In some cases, users have had to dig a trench from the curb to their house for the ISDN line to be installed by the regional telephone company. Users of DSVD-based modems do not need the phone company to make any changes in their central offices or on their switches as is the case with ISDN. That means you do not need to wait for service to be installed.

DSVD is an international standard modem technology that lets a user run voice and data over a single telephone line. All that's required is that users at each end of a connection have a modem that supports DSVD. DSVD is a protocol added on top of a V.34 modem. Products that support DSVD convert voice traffic into a digital format and compress this signal to about one-eighth the size of the analog voice signal. The stream of digital voice is then mixed with data from any communications application running on a PC or Macintosh computer (see Figure 2-3). The combined signal is carried over the public telephone network, as is the case with any dial-up modem. At the receiving end of a link, the digitized voice traffic is separated from the data, then it is decompressed and converted back to an analog voice signal.

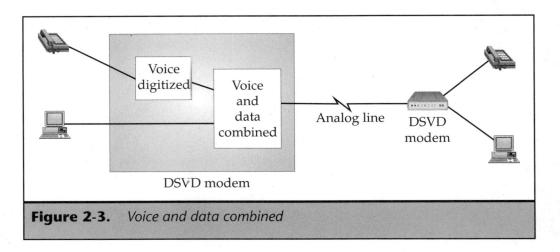

Figure 2-3. *Voice and data combined*

Using DSVD, a modem, which operates at 28.8 Kbps for data only, will typically transmit data at a rate of 19.2 Kbps when voice traffic is being carried over a line. Once the connection is made, users at each end of the link will have a channel that supports voice and data sharing. A person on one end of the call can pick up a telephone connected to the modem and talk with a person on the other end of the link—all while transferring files and data over the same link. This would be the way the technology would be used for a collaborative work application.

Alternatively, a user might place a telephone call by dialing through a DSVD-enabled modem to another DSVD-enabled modem. While the users are talking, they may decide to transfer some data. A good example of how this technology would be used is to provide technical support to remote users. Suppose a user in a remote office is having a problem printing a document. The user calls a helpdesk or tech support person in corporate headquarters and explains his or her printer problem. While the conversation is going, the tech support person can start diagnosing the problem by checking the user's systems files and looking at the version numbers of the user's printer drivers. During this process, the support person might see that the user needs a new print driver, install it remotely, and tell the user the problem has been fixed.

DSVD is also useful when doing collaborative work. Existing whiteboard applications can run over the modem, allowing users to annotate a shared document. Such applications give each user the equivalent of the common white drawing board found in many conference rooms. The *whiteboard* in a whiteboard application is essentially displayed in an open window on each user's computer screen. A remote user can make an annotation on his or her whiteboard using a mouse and the annotation shows up on the other user's screen. In this way, two users may share a graphic, spread sheet, or document, and jointly annotate it from two locations. The twist with using DSVD is that now the two users can also talk about the annotations by using the single phone line. Without DSVD, the same collaboration can be accomplished by use of two phone lines (one for the whiteboard application and one for voice). However, there are many situations where a second phone line is not available—in a hotel room or a busy airport terminal, for example.

DSVD modems typically cost about $100 to $200 more than comparable V.34 modems. You could argue that this cost difference could quickly be made up when you consider the alternative: installing a second phone line to a user's home or office. If you do the math, you can easily make a case for DSVD. A second phone line typically costs about $50 to have installed and about $10 to $15 per month for basic phone service. So in two years, you pay between $290 to $410 for that extra line. (There are also monthly line charges adding to this cost.)

However, while you can make a compelling case for DSVD based on cost, this is the wrong reason to buy a DSVD modem. Most often a person in a remote office will still want two phone lines (one to connect to an online service and another for phone conversations). The right reason to buy a DSVD modem is to exploit the technology to improve the productivity within an organization. (Some network managers would argue that the real reason to do anything in their organizations is to save money.) Currently, the most common uses of DSVD technology are for providing better technician support to users in the field and for conducting collaborative work.

In the first case, users having difficulties can have a helpdesk technician dial into their PC. Both parties can maintain a phone conversation to discuss the problem. At the same time, the helpdesk technician can transfer system files, examine them, edit them, and download updated versions to the remote user's machine. Since DSVD is a transport technology and independent of the application running over it, a helpdesk staffer can use any program he or she has used in the past without modification. That means, for example, the technician can run any existing remote control or file-transfer utility program.

Cost-justifying a higher-priced DSVD-enabled modem for such usage is quite easy. The argument should be based on reducing the cost to support remote users. The Gartner Group (Stamford, Connecticut) estimates that over a five-year period, it costs about 50 percent more to support remote users than it does to support LAN-based users. One of the reasons it is so much more expensive providing support to remote users is that the manager needs to get very detailed technical information from nontechnical users. If you have ever had to support remote users, you probably have lots of great stories of head-banging experiences trying to get the simplest information from a person. A DSVD modem gives the tech support person the best of both worlds—voice contact with the person having the problem and the ability to "look" into the user's computer and install patches and fixes as needed.

You can easily make up the $100 to $200 more it costs for a DSVD modem if, just once, you can fix a problem that would have required you to send a staffer to a remote site. Some companies do not send technicians to remote sites, but rather have the user pack up his or her system and send it via express delivery to the support staff when there is a problem that cannot be fixed by talking with the user. If a DSVD modem can be used to solve problems and reduce the number of times this process has to be carried out, the payback can easily happen in months. You can also cost-justify the price difference if you can more quickly solve a problem by gathering information about the caller's system. For example, you might be able to show your boss that it takes ten fewer minutes to resolve calls into your helpdesk when a staffer can gather basic information over the data channel. This means the same number of helpdesk staffers will be able handle more calls, or fewer staffers can handle the same number of calls.

A Software-based Approach

For those who want the ability to share voice and data for tech support, but think DSVD is overkill for their company, there is another alternative—one based on software. About two years ago, Raddish Communications developed a software product called VoiceView that lets voice and data traffic share a single analog line. The product is now bundled with many modems and preinstalled on many modem-equipped PCs.

The difference between VoiceView and DSVD is that with VoiceView only one type of traffic can pass between the modems at any one time. So you can either have voice or data being exchanged, instead of both simultaneously. When a user talks into a phone attached to a modem running VoiceView, data stops flowing between the two modems. Once the voice message has ended, the exchange of data traffic resumes.

VoiceView-equipped modems cost less than DSVD, since they use software to perform the switching rather than hardware to mix the signals. Many PC vendors are bundling VoiceView with their modem-equipped units so that they can reduce their cost to support customers. If you have VoiceView installed for that reason, you can take advantage of it to cut your support costs.

Another difference between VoiceView and DSVD modems is that VoiceView can work with lower-speed modems. For instance, last year Boca Research offered VoiceView with its 14.4-Kbps modems.

Videoconferencing over Analog

Combining voice and data over an analog line for collaborative work or tech support is just a first step. Some companies would like to add video to the mix. There are concerns about bandwidth when providing such connectivity into a network. Many interesting applications, such as videoconferencing and collaborative work programs, crawl when using analog lines.

Most companies would like to use ISDN for these applications, but find that they can no longer wait for ISDN service to reach every one of their sites. Eventually, companies decide to look for technology that will help. After all, for many companies, collaborative work projects, high-speed access to the Internet, videoconferencing, and delivery of multimedia applications are being held up for the lack of a telecommunications service.

Intel has proposed an interesting approach to the analog line bandwidth problem—one that, not surprisingly, relies on Intel chip technology. In 1996, Intel rolled out an analog phone line version of its ProShare videoconferencing software. ProShare was originally designed to run over ISDN links, so a version aimed at the analog phone line market was a very great departure.

Why didn't Intel bring this product out first? Or at least earlier? Intel, like many in the industry, thought the time was ripe for ISDN when it introduced ProShare several years ago. But the company has not been satisfied with the deployment of ISDN. Andy Grove, Intel's president and chief executive officer, has noted the lack of a mass market, pointing out that making a half million ISDN lines available in 15 years (as the telephone companies have done) was not very good progress. He said that for videoconferencing to reach a mass market, vendors had to leverage a processor's power to compensate for the lack of bandwidth when using analog phone lines. Some at Intel expressed frustration at this lack of bandwidth and the inability of the telephone companies to deliver high-speed services. In a comical yet telling way, Craig Barrett, an executive vice president at Intel, displayed a slide showing Intel Chairman Gordon Moore's postulation that is frequently referred to as Moore's law: the number of transistors per chip will double every 18 months. Barrett said that the telecom industry version of this law was that bandwidth will double every century.

Intel wants mass-market opportunities. Bandwidth was the issue. When ProShare was first introduced, Intel engineers deemed the bandwidth of your typical analog line inadequate to run a videoconferencing session.

So what changed? The analog version of ProShare requires a minimum of a 133 MHz Pentium. The CPU in such a system is fully taxed because it has to handle the communications and display needs of a videoconferencing session. Intel realized that if analog was the way to go for applications such as video-conferencing and collaborative work, it would not be enough to simply leverage raw processing power to improve the quality of these programs. Intel decided a new architecture would be needed to make these applications run more efficiently. In 1996, Intel announced its MMX technology was geared to the needs of videoconferencing, communications, and multimedia applications (see the special section, "How MMX Technology Works," provided next).

MMX technology consists of general-purpose instructions that enhance the performance of a large body of multimedia and communications software, all while maintaining compatibility with the Intel architecture. MMX technology is fully compatible with existing operating systems and application software. Programmers need only modify a small portion of code to get the performance benefits of MMX—developers simply call MMX technology-enabled drivers and library routines through existing application programming interfaces (APIs).

PCs that use MMX technology will be able to compensate for the low bandwidth of an analog line so users can run videoconferencing, Internet multimedia, and collaborative work programs. While you can do these things today with varying degrees of success, MMX technology will enable this kind of usage on standard PC platforms. What MMX technology does is handle some of the most time-consuming tasks a processor must perform in these applications. This frees the processor to do other tasks. For example, if the same 133 MHz PC that was fully taxed were to use MMX technology, about 40 percent of the CPU load would be freed up.

How MMX Technology Works

Intel believes you can leverage a computer's processing power to get applications such as videoconferencing, Internet-based multimedia, and collaborative work programs to run over analog lines. In the past, the way to do this was to boost clock frequencies of the processor and to use micro-architecture techniques such as branch prediction, superscalar execution, and superpipelining. With MMX, in addition to these traditional means, Intel has added 57 new instructions to its architecture to speed up certain compute-intensive loops in multimedia and communications applications. These loops typically account for 10 percent or less of the overall application code; however, they can account for up to 90 percent of the execution time.

In addition, to further boost performance with videoconferencing and collaborative work applications, MMX instructions process multiple data elements in parallel using a technique called Single Instruction Multiple Data (SIMD).

Analog Forever?

As you can see, there are many ways to get around the bandwidth limitations of analog phone lines. However, even with the strong points in its favor, you may still be concerned that analog lines will not meet your remote user's bandwidth needs. Most people who use dedicated, high-speed links into the Internet in their office, loath accessing Web sites from the road. There's no comparison. Many companies have at least a 56-Kbps dedicated link into the Internet and many have T1 links that pump data down at 1.544 Mbps. Even with the newest modems, a user can get at best 33.6 Kbps.

Add to that the fact that most client/server applications do not work that well over analog links. There are, of course, ways to partition a client/server application so that it runs more efficiently over a remote connection. Such techniques are discussed in Chapter 14, "Server Tools." For those of you who simply need more bandwidth than analog affords, the next six chapters will discuss existing and emerging higher-bandwidth services and the equipment you'll need to use these services.

Quick Summary: Ways to Save Using Analog

- Use the Internet as an extension of corporate backbone to cut long-distance phone charges.
- Use file compression software to reduce length of time it takes to transmit files.
- Use modem compression technology to cut phone charges.
- Use technology that combines voice and data to cut support costs.

Chapter Three

ISDN

ompanies trying to meet the connectivity needs of their remote users often find that analog phone lines do not deliver the required bandwidth. Many client/server applications that work quite well when running over a LAN suffer performance problems when running over an analog connection. And multimedia, collaborative work, and videoconferencing applications, which support voice, images, and video, need higher speeds than those offered through a modem and an analog phone line. Additionally, a dial-up user's patience can be strained if he or she needs to connect to the World Wide Web—the rich graphical content of the Web means lots of waiting while images are downloaded.

For many companies, ISDN service is an economical way to solve most of their remote users' bandwidth cravings. ISDN (Integrated Services Digital Network) is a digital telecommunications technology that allows the transmission of voice, data, images, and video in digital format over the public switched-telephone network. ISDN is based on international standards and is well-suited to the higher bandwidth needs of today's telecommuters. ISDN also does a good job supporting the delivery of time-sensitive data types such as voice and video.

One point of interest before proceeding. ISDN has led a crazed life. At first, proponents hailed ISDN as the universal unifier for voice and data services. Then, about five years ago, after years of slow deployment, many users got frustrated and pretty much wrote off ISDN, choosing instead to look to the newer data services such as frame relay and even ATM (asynchronous transfer mode). Within the last year or two, ISDN's status has risen in the eyes of many network managers because of the growing demand for high-speed access to the World Wide Web by users working in small offices and telecommuters working at home.

What Is ISDN and How Is It Used?

ISDN service comes in two forms: Basic Rate Interface (BRI) and Primary Rate Interface (PRI). A BRI link consists of three channels—two 64-Kbps B (bearer) channels and one 16-Kbps D (data) channel—commonly referred to as 2B+D. PRI has 23 B channels and one 64-Kbps D channel (commonly referred to as 23B+D). Typically, remote users and telecommuters would use BRI service, and a central site would use either BRI, PRI, or a mix of the two types of service. (Chapter 11, "LAN-to-LAN Connectivity," discusses the economical and support issues that you should consider to help determine when to use PRI service versus BRI service in a central site.)

The primary function of the D channel is to handle the communications between the ISDN termination equipment located on the user's premises, called the *customer premises equipment* (CPE), and the switch in the telephone company's central office. The signaling between the central office switch and the CPE helps handle such things as managing a call. For example, when a user tries to establish an ISDN link, signaling information is sent to the central office switch. The switch then knows, in effect, to turn on the dial tone in the equipment.

The D channel of an ISDN BRI connection does not need the full 16 Kbps bandwidth to perform the signaling. That means a user could take advantage of the "spare" bandwidth and run additional data over the channel—it is as if that remote user had a third data channel (that is, in addition to the two B channels). Used in this way, the D channel supports asynchronous communications—like the traffic running from a PC's serial port— at a 9.6 Kbps rate.

The primary function of the B channel is to carry information. Each B channel can carry voice, video, or data traffic independently of other B channels. Thus, a remote user can use one B channel for, say, surfing the Web at a higher data rate than when using an analog phone line and modem, while simultaneously using the other line for a phone conversation. Or, the two channels can be combined to yield a 128 Kbps bandwidth connection. Combining bandwidth, however, is not as straightforward a process as it might sound. There are two main approaches that are discussed in the special section, "Aggregating Bandwidth."

In general, you are not limited to combining just the two B channels of an ISDN link. You may, in fact, want to allocate even more bandwidth. ISDN allows for this through what is called *dynamic bandwidth allocation,* where the effective transmission rate between two sites is increased in increments of 64 Kbps. This process, which is known by several names including bandwidth-on-demand, inverse multiplexing, and channel aggregation, is sometimes referred to as Nx64 Kbps, where N is the number of B channels merged together.

Aggregating Bandwidth

One of the appeals of ISDN is the potential to combine the two B channels of an ISDN BRI link into one 128-Kbps link. Currently, there are two ways to accomplish this feat.

First, there is bandwidth-on-demand interoperability (BONDing), which is commonly used to provide more bandwidth for videoconferencing sessions. BONDing is implemented in hardware (making it fairly efficient), and the actual combining of the B channels (two or more) is carried out when the call is set up. The downside to BONDing is that it is fairly inflexible. Once the bandwidth is negotiated at the start of a call, you cannot allocate additional bandwidth or drop a channel to free it up for another application.

The second approach is Multilink PPP (ML-PPP), which is commonly used to support the exchange of LAN traffic between two sites. ML-PPP is an Internet Engineering Task Force (IETF) standard specified by Request For Comment (RFC) 1717. ML-PPP, which is carried out in software, lets you open multiple channels between two systems, creating a single logical connection. This process is dynamic, meaning that even after an ISDN link between two sites is established, you can add or drop channels to match the bandwidth needs of that connection. The standard is written for PPP, the Point-to-Point Protocol, which is the commonly used TCP/IP link-layer standard for Internet and remote LAN access.

Today, it is quite common for a line termination device, be it a terminal adapter, ISDN bridge, or ISDN-enabled router, to support one or both of these bandwidth-aggregation methods.

ISDN Line Termination Equipment

Connecting to an ISDN line requires equipment that links the device, be it a PC, router, or telephone, to the service. In the analog world you would use a modem. With ISDN, there are two devices that must be located in the remote user's office or telecommuter's home.

First, you need a *network terminator,* which is commonly referred to as an NT1. The function of the NT1 is to take the two-wire connection that terminates the line running from the central office telephone switch and convert it to an S/T interface. Comparable to the RJ-11 jack for an analog line and modem, the S/T interface is commonly incorporated into ISDN devices and used for connecting equipment to an ISDN line.

The other piece of equipment needed is a *terminal adapter* that connects, for example, a PC's communications port or a router's wide-area networking port to a B channel of an ISDN line. A terminal adapter, which like a modem can be in the form of a stand-alone unit or a plug-in card for a PC or a router, plugs into the NT1. Figure 3-1 shows a typical configuration that would be required in a telecommuter's home. Basically, the user would have a wall jack with the ISDN two-wire U interface, an NT1, an ISDN terminal adapter, and the user's computer. Some ISDN devices come with an integrated NT1 and plug directly into an ISDN wall jack. You can buy ISDN terminal adapters from ADTRAN (Huntsville, Alabama), Digi International (formerly Digiboard of Minneapolis, Minnesota), Motorola (Mansfield, Massachusetts), MultiTech Systems (Mounds View, Minnesota), and from most modem vendors.

Besides acting as a physical conduit to an ISDN circuit, terminal adapters perform another function. Many devices are not designed to operate at the 64 Kbps rate of an ISDN B channel—a PC's serial port, for example. ISDN terminal adapters handle the difference in speed by performing what is called *rate adaption* through a process called *bit stuffing*. Essentially, the terminal adapter slows a B channel's effective data transmission rate by inserting extra bits (hence, the name "bit stuffing") in the data stream sent from or received by a slower-speed device. The terminal adapter at the other end of a connection must use the same bit-stuffing method to extract the real data. There are a few proprietary rate-adaption protocols, which are not commonly used. There are also two standard rate-adaption protocols—V.110 and V.120—that are widely used. Most terminal adapters on the market today support at least one of these two protocols.

In addition to handling this difference between the rate a device can operate at and the speed of an ISDN link, terminal adapters can also be configured to

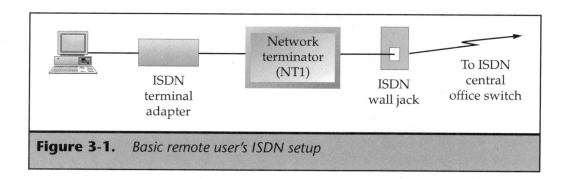

Figure 3-1.   *Basic remote user's ISDN setup*

handle different forms of communications including synchronous/asynchronous, automatic dialing to a preprogrammed number, or terminal-controlled dialing by use of either the AT-command set or V.25bis synchronous dialing method. These features can be quite handy. For instance, a remote office worker who uses several communications programs might want to keep using the AT-command set he or she is already familiar with from working with modems.

For some users, a simple terminal adapter with an NT1 is all that is needed. However, some users need an ISDN access router. For example, you might have a user who needs to enter a network as if he or she is a full-blown node on that network complete with an IP or IPX address. Typically, a person who simply needs high-speed access to the Internet from home and occasional connectivity to the office (to check e-mail, for example) would only need an ISDN terminal adapter. On the other hand, a person who requires full access to applications running on network-attached servers and other computer systems would probably need to use an ISDN-enabled access router.

You are also likely to use an ISDN router to connect a LAN in one office to a LAN in another office. Many router vendors offer what are often called ISDN-enabled access routers that let users in one site connect to users and applications running on networks in another site on demand—bringing up an ISDN connection between the sites only when a user needs access to resources in the other site. This is a different approach to connectivity than you would see when using higher-end routers and backbone network routers, which support dedicated and higher-speed links between sites. Chapters 10 and 11 discuss how to determine which service and type of router to use. Since this chapter is about ISDN service and how to use it, I will discuss the specifics of ISDN routers here. In the later chapters I talk more about how you would decide when to use a dedicated, leased line to link one site with another versus when it is appropriate to use a dial-up ISDN connection that uses the public switched-telephone network.

ISDN-enabled access routers usually have one LAN port and one wide-area networking port. Typically, they support one ISDN BRI connection, although there are some that support more. Figure 3-2 shows a typical setup where an ISDN-enabled access router has been added to the LANs in two locations.

Because these routers are usually installed in small sites with little, if any, technical staff to support them, access routers are designed to be fairly simple to configure and manage. The configuration and management tools could be a key differentiator between two vendors' offerings. Look for good tools and any features that help set up or manage a router. These characteristics are important because routers are fairly complex internetworking devices, and they take time to set up and manage. And since they are being put in small

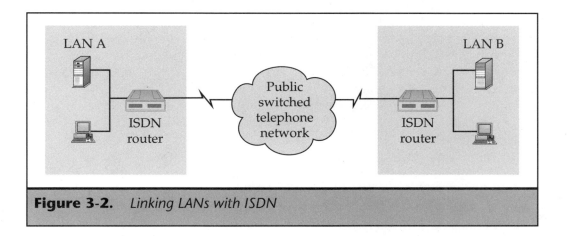

Figure 3-2. *Linking LANs with ISDN*

offices, you may not have anyone on site to diagnose a problem when one occurs, or even to answer a simple question about the router's configuration to help you troubleshoot remotely. For instance, a typical access router will accommodate two or three types of Ethernet cabling including twisted pair and coaxial cable. So a router might have a BNC and a 10Base-T connector. If that is the case, one thing you might want to look for in an access router is what is called a self-sensing or autodetecting LAN port. Without this feature, a user would have to configure the LAN port for the appropriate cabling as part of the router's setup process. That is not a major task, but it still requires that the user know the difference between, for example, 10Base-5 coaxial cabling and 10Base-2 coaxial cabling. A router that self-senses or autodetects knows which type of connection you are using once you attach a cable to the router. Such a router would then configure that LAN port automatically to work with that type of cabling connection.

You should also compare the configuration and management tools that come with ISDN-enabled routers. These tools are typically either Windows based or menu driven, where you enter information about the LAN (such as the Ethernet frame type and addressing information about the router and devices on the LAN) and information about the ISDN connection. With Windows-based and menu-driven configuration programs you are led through the configuration process by answering questions about the LAN, ISDN connections, and the way ISDN calls are to be handled.

NOTE: *Some access routers still require the use of cryptic command-line entries to configure the router or to troubleshoot a problem.*

Specifically, you will need to set the parameters that manage and control calls made and received by the router. For example, you may only use the ISDN link through the router to give LAN-based users high-speed access to the Internet. If that is the only use of the router, you may not want the router to receive incoming calls for security reasons.

Another use for dial-up connectivity is to give a user in one office access to network resources in another office. For example, you could use ISDN to access an application that runs on a server in another site, attaching to that remote server as if it were local. This process needs to be transparent to the user. Figure 3-3 shows how this process would work. In the figure, a request to connect to a device not on the local LAN comes into the router. The router has a table that associates, for example, the name of the remote server or network drive, with a phone number.

A manager can build a set of associations so that a user can, for example, access a database server in one office, a mail server in another office, and make an ISDN connection into the Internet. Again, the important point is that for the user, all of this is transparent. The user simply clicks on application icons, launches an application, or accesses a network drive as he or she would if the application or drive were on the same LAN. The router handles the connection with no assistance from the user.

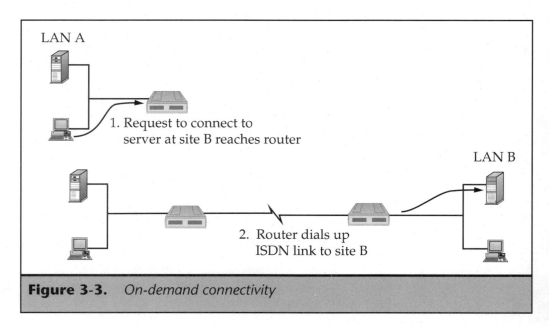

Figure 3-3.   *On-demand connectivity*

The Financial Case for ISDN

Obviously, you can make a case for using ISDN based on its technical merits. ISDN certainly provides more bandwidth than an analog line. Often you will be able to convince upper management that ISDN is essential for remote users based purely on such technical arguments. For instance, your company may rely on an ISDN-based videoconferencing system to cut travel costs and give members of geographically dispersed product teams a way to "meet" each week.

Such an argument might work some of the time. But most often you will need to convince upper management that there really is a cost justification for using ISDN. And that may be a tough task. ISDN tariffs vary widely, making it important to ask the telecom carrier questions before ordering the service. ISDN is most frequently billed like your analog service. There is a fee to establish the service, a fixed monthly fee for the service, and a usage fee where you are billed for connect time. Table 3-1 gives an example of the monthly fee you can expect to pay for an ISDN link based on different levels of usage. Keep in mind that there are significant differences in pricing between the various regional Bell operating companies (RBOCs) and the long-distance carriers, such as AT&T, MCI International, and Sprint. So use your own billing rates and insert them into this table to calculate your total costs.

	$0.05/ minute	$0.10/ minute	$0.20/ minute	$0.40/ minute
2 hours/day	$165	$285	$525	$1,005
4 hours/day	$285	$525	$1,005	$1,965
6 hours/day	$405	$765	$1,485	$2,925
8 hours/day	$525	$1,005	$1,965	$3,885

Table 3-1. *The Cost of One Month of ISDN Service Based on Connectivity Needs of Your Users**

*Assumes a monthly service charge of $45 and 20 business days per month.

Another way to look at the cost of using ISDN is to compare it to the cost of analog service. You might want to, for example, compare the likely costs for the first year of using each technology. Figure 3-4 shows the total first-year costs to get a user up and running for three situations: an analog phone line using a modem, an ISDN BRI line using a terminal adapter, and an ISDN BRI line using a router capable of combining the two BRI B channels into one 128-Kbps link. The cost calculations include the cost of the equipment needed to connect to the service, the startup fee for the service, the monthly charge for the service times 12, and the total charge for three hours of connectivity per day, 20 days per month. I have based the numbers on the typical costs in the NyNex region. Your fees may be different.

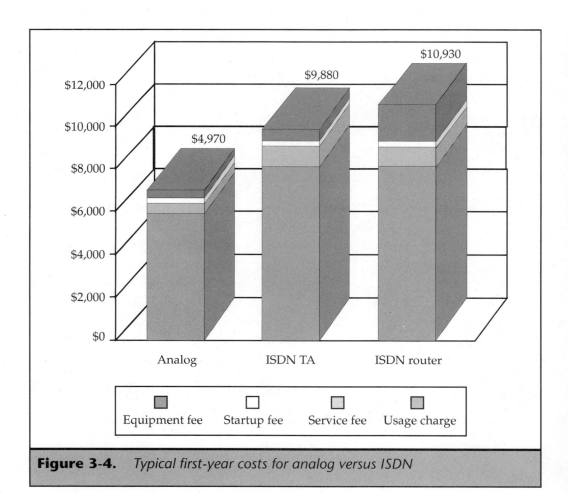

Figure 3-4.   *Typical first-year costs for analog versus ISDN*

For example, I've estimated that it would cost $100 to get the analog service started—this might be on the low side if you need to have a line installed. And I have used a $250 startup fee for the ISDN service. I assumed it would cost $250 for a decent analog modem, $450 for an ISDN terminal adapter, and $1,500 for an ISDN access router capable of combining the two BRI B channels into one 128-Kbps link. For my calculation, I used a monthly rate of $25 for analog and $45 for ISDN service. The usage charges are $0.10 per minute for analog and $0.20 per minute for ISDN. Again, these numbers may vary; you should use my figures as an example and plug in your own numbers.

Calculating First-Year Costs

To calculate the first-year fee for ISDN service and equipment use the calculation below as a guide. Insert your own numbers to determine your costs.

Equipment fee: ISDN terminal adapter	$450
Startup fee for service	$250
Monthly charge for service times 12 months[1]	$540
Usage charge for the year[2]	$8,640
Total for year	$9,880

[1] based on a monthly fee of $45 per month
[2] based on three hours of connectivity per day, 20 days per month, and a usage charge of $0.20/minute

Some RBOCs and carriers offer lower rates for residential ISDN service versus what they charge for the same line used as a business line. For example, residential users in the Pacific Bell region do not have to pay usage charges for local ISDN calls made during evening hours and on weekends, while business customers do have to pay. (This may have changed by the time this book appears. Most of the RBOCs had petitioned their respective public utility commissions for higher ISDN rates.)

Will your local carrier give your users the residential rate? To get the better rate, you could just tell your users to sign up for the service claiming the line is not for business but for personal use. However, be warned that such an approach may open up your company to many problems. For example, your company may not be able to write off the phone charges by deducting them as business expenses. Typically, if the line is billed as a residential service, the basic monthly fees cannot be written off, but the usage charges can. If the line is billed as a business line, both the monthly service fee and the usage fee can be deducted.

NOTE: *Consult your corporate tax experts on this issue.*

In a way, the telecom carriers have tried to structure ISDN pricing so that it is similar to your traditional analog phone service pricing—that is, offering free local calls ("free" meaning no usage charge). In many areas, however, only residences qualify for unmeasured service.

With some telcos, each call within a local area costs the same regardless of the duration of the call. In other areas, data calls cost more than voice. If this is true in your area, order two voice channels and program the ISDN terminal adapter to tag the calls as voice.

ISDN pricing has been fairly tough to nail down. Each of the regional Bells has charged tariffs on their services in different ways. At this writing, the rates were in a state of flux. The main thrust of the pricing changes proposed in summer 1996 was to move away from a flat-rate pricing structure that was offered by some of the RBOCs to one where you would be billed per minute of usage. Still, some of the RBOCs were proposing flat-rate pricing, but often it was at a much higher monthly rate than previous rates, and it had a cap on the number of hours a user could connect within a month before being charged extra.

For instance, prior to the rate increases proposed in late summer 1996, Pacific Bell offered its residential ISDN customers unlimited free access on evenings and weekends; in the GTE region, some users could order ISDN service for a flat rate of $70 to $75 per month. Such pricing is an incredibly good deal if your remote people spend lots of time surfing the Web. The RBOCs felt that many people were taking advantage of the flat-rate pricing to use ISDN almost like a dedicated link, keeping the connection between sites up most of the time.

For that reason, the RBOCs tried moving away from the flat-rate pricing to one based on usage. For example, US West proposed a monthly charge of $63 to $84 for 200 hours of usage per month or $184 per month for unlimited access.

Bell Atlantic proposed a $249 flat rate per month for residential service. The Delaware utility commission counterproposed a $28.02 flat monthly rate.

That led Bell Atlantic to withdraw its proposed tariff change and file suit in the Delaware Superior Court. Other regions of the country are experiencing similar differences of opinion between the proposed rate from the carrier and the rate the utility commission deems appropriate. If the telcos are granted the higher rate, this may lead users to other emerging connectivity services such as those offered by cable television companies and new high-speed services, such as Asymmetric Digital Subscriber Line (ADSL), which are starting to be offered by the telcos themselves. Chapters 6 and 7 look at these services and discuss the financial aspects of using them.

One last thing about straight ISDN pricing. If you want to use ISDN for high-speed access into the Internet, check with your Internet service provider. Many providers now offer such service, but most offer it at a premium. Make sure you take that into account when calculating the cost of an ISDN connection.

Price/Performance Counts

Sometimes ISDN does not compare very well economically with analog on a minute-by-minute billing plan. And if the proposed rate hikes come to fruition, a straight economical argument of ISDN versus analog will not work. Often you will have to make a price/performance argument to convince management that ISDN is needed over analog lines and is a cost-effective alternative.

To select the most appropriate connection service, determine the minimum performance requirements for remote users, the expected amount of usage, and the pricing policies of the telephone companies involved.

You want to be able to fairly compare costs on a price/performance basis. To do this, make a realistic prediction of the number of hours of connect time a user will need per month, and calculate the total costs for a year of service. To be fair, you should factor in the installation costs the phone company will charge to establish the service and the cost of termination equipment—a modem for analog lines, an ISDN terminal adapter for dial-up ISDN links. Once you have established that figure for both analog and ISDN links, divide the cost for a year of service by the data rate of the service. For the ISDN link, divide by the 64 Kbps data rate of one ISDN B channel (representing the most common type of connectivity). For the modem, divide by 14.4, 28.8, or 33.6 Kbps, depending on the modem your users have installed at home or in their laptops. This will give you a dollar per Kbps measure of the cost of the two services for a year.

There are some things you should take into account with this type of analysis. First, your ISDN users will have two B channels compared with one analog line. You might want to calculate ISDN's price/Kbps by dividing by 128 Kbps. Do that only if your users will be aggregating the bandwidth of the two B channels on a regular basis. Second, you might want to factor in how much less time a user will need to connect when using an ISDN link versus an analog connection. You can get a crude idea of the time savings by dividing the ISDN data rate of 64 Kbps by the modem rate. However, keep in mind that the connect time might be controlled by the application a user is accessing. For instance, the fastest connection in the world will not speed up a database query on a busy server.

Beyond a straight cost-per-Kbps analysis, you need to consider the nature of the traffic that will run over the ISDN links. For example, you must consider how the volume of traffic is distributed over the course of a typical day. For instance, in many retail store environments, LAN-attached point-of-sale cash registers update an on-site inventory database as sales are made during business hours. Once the store is closed for the day, all of the inventory data pertinent to that day's sales is uploaded to a centralized host computer. In other words, the connectivity needs are not terribly time critical—once a day, a bulk file is transferred from every store in a chain. If that's the case, an analog modem solution, while costing more per Kbps, might be a good solution, since there is no installation charge to pay for each site.

On the other hand, consider a bank branch office user who runs LAN-based word processing and spreadsheet programs in the branch office and who requires frequent queries of a centralized database. This is quite common in banking environments. For instance, the bank may have an Excel spreadsheet that calculates what size home owner's loan a customer is eligible for based on his or her salary. The application may require the branch employee to enter some basic information into spreadsheet cells, and some of the information—such as the current loan rate the bank is offering and the amount of equity the customers have in their existing home—might need to be gathered from mainframe databases residing at the bank's headquarters. In such a situation, a dedicated line to headquarters might not be necessary, and an analog modem link might be too slow. However, a dial-up ISDN connection could meet the need to transfer customer data files.

To determine whether ISDN is economically feasible, you must also consider where the calls are being placed. While local calls are always less expensive than long-distance calls, shorter distances are not always less expensive than longer distances. In fact, the most expensive long-distance calls are typically those in the 20- to 50-mile range.

Another important aspect of minimizing the cost of dial-up access is minimizing the amount of connect time. Call setup time is faster with ISDN compared with analog. Both ISDN and analog take about the same amount of time to establish a call—about three to five seconds. However, ISDN devices take very little time to get into synch and work together. With modems, it typically takes about 15 seconds for the negotiation process to take place—during that time, no data is exchanged. With an ISDN connection the time is closer to one second.

Reducing the number of times a connection is made can substantially lower costs by reducing the amount of overhead required to establish the link. Also, shortening connect times will lower costs. One way to achieve these goals is to select software and hardware products that use the dial-up connection intelligently. For example, some e-mail programs can store messages for forwarding at a later time, allowing several messages to be sent at once, rather than bringing up the link between sites every time a message destined for another site is created.

Another way to reduce the line charges is to adopt a client/server-style application that allows users to work locally. Once the work is completed, it sends the updated information to the remote server. Client/server applications do not require the connection to be kept up for the entire time information is being processed; this minimizes connect time.

An additional way to save line charges is to use bandwidth-saving features such as data compression, which will reduce connect times. Many ISDN products offer 4:1 data compression, thus turning a single B channel into a 256-Kbps link. Also look for internetworking products that perform spoofing and link optimization techniques that can keep nonessential traffic off the lines. These techniques are essential in NetWare environments in which the remote ends constantly poll each other for status information. Without some kind of limitation, this constant polling can significantly increase line charges. (There will be more on this topic later in this chapter.)

Improved Productivity

Another way to cost-justify an ISDN line is to argue that remote users will be more productive. For the remote user, BRI service offers more bandwidth than analog phone lines. A single channel provides 64 Kbps, and the two B channels combined offer 128 Kbps. To put this into perspective, a remote user can send a 2MB file in about four and a half minutes using a single B channel, while it would take about nine minutes using a 28.8 connection.

If your remote users exchange many large files, or if they download many big files from the Internet, you might be able cost-justify the ISDN links based on a pure productivity argument. Telecommuters and remote users with an

ISDN connection will spend about half the time waiting while files are transferred than analog line/modem-linked users will.

The cost justification is quite simple to make. Assume the average user sends or downloads at least one large file (for example, 2MB or larger) a week. That is a pretty modest assumption, according to a survey of business users (see the special section, "How Much Is Being Downloaded from the Web?").

How Much Is Being Downloaded from the Web?

A study conducted by Fleishman-Hillard Research (St. Louis, Missouri), a market research firm, in summer 1995, just as the World Wide Web portion was taking off, found that 68 percent of all business users downloaded files from the Internet weekly. Twenty-two percent of the survey respondents said they downloaded information daily. Thirty percent of the users said they downloaded files of between 1MB and 5MB. And 65 percent of the survey respondents expected the size of files they downloaded to increase within the next year (22 percent expected the size to increase substantially).

If your remote users are typical and use the Internet as a research tool and for an occasional look at some nonbusiness-related sites, they are downloading programs, movie animation clips (just about every new movie has a URL and short clips available for downloading), and other forms of information.

If a remote worker spends two hours per session online with a 28.8-Kbps analog modem, the user might cut his or her connect time by about 30 to 40 minutes by using an ISDN connection. (Note: the ISDN link cannot speed up responses from busy servers or a congested Internet segment.) If the worker does this twice a week, he or she is saving between one hour and one hour 20 minutes per week. That works out to about 50 to 67 hours per year (based on two weeks of vacation). If you have 20 remote users who work the same way, ISDN links will save the company 1,000 to 1,340 hours per year—or about the equivalent of half of one person's total labor for a year.

ISDN's Downside

ISDN makes sense in many ways. It is often comparable in price to analog service. It offers better performance than analog. It boosts productivity by reducing the amount of time workers need to stay on the line during a connection.

So, if ISDN is that good, why doesn't everyone use it? There are several reasons, including availability, difficulty in ordering the service, difficulty with configuring ISDN devices, and a wide-area networking device's trouble handling ISDN's dynamic links. The rest of this chapter will discuss these problems and give you an idea of where things stand with each.

Lack of Availability

The telcos did a lousy job deploying ISDN. Even today, there are still areas of the country that cannot get ISDN service. In some parts of the United States, the service is available, but you need to dig a trench in your front lawn in order for the carrier to bring the wires from the curb to your house. In other parts of the country, the telcos have not upgraded their central office switches to support ISDN service. And even in areas where the switch supports the service, you might live too far away from the switch—ISDN has an 18,000-foot (about three-mile) limitation between a switch and a remote user's home.

 NOTE: Three miles is the length of wire run from the switch to the home; not the distance from the telco's central office to the home. That means you may actually live geographically close enough to a switch that is capable of supporting ISDN and still not be close enough to get service.

The telcos are trying to handle the availability problems in several ways. First, they have been upgrading switches so that most central offices in the United States have at least one switch that supports ISDN. Some telcos have also tried deploying what are called *midspan repeaters,* which take a signal that has passed the 18-kilofeet distance and boosts it so that it can travel another 18 kilofeet. Figure 3-5 shows how this can double the possible distance between an ISDN switch and a user's home.

Another approach the telcos are taking to make ISDN available to more users is to offer what is called "ISDN-anywhere" programs. Basically, the regional carrier promises you ISDN even if the closest switch to your remote user's home does not support ISDN. For example, NyNex offers what it calls Virtual ISDN service, where they bring ISDN to your location from the nearest switch capable of supporting ISDN. Typically, the carriers offering such ISDN-anywhere services use idle Switched 56 K lines to connect you to the nearest switch.

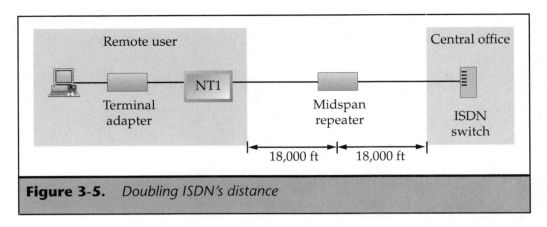

Figure 3-5.   *Doubling ISDN's distance*

Other Issues to Consider

There are a couple of other issues to consider when you look at ISDN for your remote users. First, even if ISDN is available in your area, you may have a hard time ordering the service. Many network administrators say it is still harder to order ISDN service from a telco than to establish analog service. In many cases, managers say that they get people on the phone who do not know what ISDN is or that their company offers it. This problem is being addressed. Most of the RBOCs have special phone numbers you can call to order ISDN service. Typically, these numbers connect you to a person who specializes in helping you with ISDN. They know what services are available and can tell you specifically what type of equipment you will need to connect to the service.

Many of the RBOCs also have fax-on-demand services set up for their ISDN offerings so you can get details about availability, pricing, equipment needs, and even examples of how to use ISDN. Most RBOCs and long-distance carriers, such as AT&T, MCI International, and Sprint, have Web sites with similar information.

There is an industry initiative under way to make it easier to order ISDN service and equipment. The North American ISDN Users Forum has developed a set of specifications called the EZ-ISDN ordering codes specifications that should make it easier for you to deploy ISDN. When this book was being written in fall 1996, Motorola and Bay Networks had announced the first ISDN products to support EZ-ISDN. The idea behind EZ-ISDN is that when you order ISDN service, establishing voice and data services, such as adding call waiting, would be simplified.

Second, if you plan to use ISDN to give remote users high-speed access to the World Wide Web, there are a couple of issues you might want to take into account. Some Internet service providers (ISPs) do not support ISDN connections at all. Some only support ISDN links in major cities—making it less economical if your users must dial long-distance to connect to the ISP's closest point of presence. And all ISPs will charge you a higher monthly fee (and possibly a higher hourly usage fee) for an ISDN account than they do for an account that uses a modem and analog line.

Additionally, some ISPs only support one vendor's access router to make the link into their account. Others might bundle a preconfigured (down to the ISP's local access number) ISDN access router to use to connect to their service. There are mixed feelings about such routers. Some network managers see them as filling a need in an economical manner. That is because some ISPs bundle the router with the service, so you pay a monthly fee for the service and not the router. In this way, you do not actually feel like you are paying for a router. The downside to this approach is that the routers typically cannot be used for anything else but connecting to that ISP's service. Because of this, some small offices actually have two ISDN access routers—one for their Internet connectivity needs and one for all of their other dial-up connectivity needs.

Still, the ISP approach to giving you a preconfigured ISDN access router has a lot of appeal to some managers. That is because ISDN devices—routers and terminal adapters alike—are hard to configure. Unlike the process of installing a modem, an ISDN device requires some knowledge of ISDN terminology and the equipment used by the telephone companies. At a minimum, a user must enter a Service Profile Identifier (SPID) and information about the ISDN switch in the telco's central office from which the user is getting his or her service. There are still many network administrators who say they have difficulty getting this information from the ISDN provider. Often, it is a matter of finding a person within the telco's support department who knows ISDN. Some managers say this is still a frustrating process that requires multiple calls to find such a person. The RBOCs and other carriers have made strides in this area, and most have special support numbers for ISDN users.

Call Management

If you are using an ISDN router, another thing that must be configured is how and when the router should tear down the connection. Routers were originally designed to connect sites using dedicated leased lines that did not incur any usage charges—a company paid a fixed amount per month for the line. So the connections were always up, and there was no need to build into a router any process that would disconnect a line simply because no traffic ran over the line.

Many early users of analog and ISDN dial-up routers did not even think about tearing down a connection when they first installed their routers. This led to numerous cases of managers getting a shock when a phone bill came in after one month of ISDN router use. What would often happen was that a dial-up connection would be made late in the day, and the connection would stay up all night. If no one noticed, the usage charges would simply keep adding up until the line was dropped. If this happened just once over a weekend, a manager could get a bill for twice the amount he or she had expected to pay for the entire month (see the special section, "A Costly Mistake").

A Costly Mistake

To give you an idea of the costs that you can incur if you do not take line-disconnection seriously, consider the following example.

Suppose an ISDN line is left up all weekend and no one uses it. That means from 6 P.M. Friday to 9 A.M. Monday morning, a total of 63 hours, you have no traffic running over an ISDN link. If you pay $0.05 to $0.20 per minute for an ISDN usage charge, that means you will pay between $189 and $756 for nothing.

To put that cost into perspective, consider that many remote sites that use ISDN lines for dial-up networking only require about two to three hours of connectivity a day. That translates into 40 to 60 hours per month—less time than the one-weekend mistake.

ISDN-enabled access routers must, therefore, be configured to automatically disconnect when a link sits idle and carries no traffic for a manager-selected period of time. For example, you may decide that if a link is idle for five minutes, it is likely that there is no need to maintain the connection, and the router should drop the link. If a user needs to access an application running on a remote server after the link is torn down, that user's launching of the application will bring the connection back up.

You might ask what happens if a user is waiting for some response when the link drops. The way this might happen is if a user submits a query to a database running on a server at another site and it takes the server more time (say ten minutes) to perform the manipulations and return an answer than you have allocated for the link to remain open. If that is the case, when the database calculation is done and the query's answer is headed back to the user, the router at the other site will initiate a call and bring the connection back up. In this scenario, where you have configured the ISDN-enabled router to disconnect after five minutes of no traffic, you have saved five minutes of connect time.

Shutting down inactive links is not straightforward. WANs have peculiarities that are not found in LANs. For example, to reduce charges, it is preferable not to keep a connection in place when the user is not accessing the network. Therefore, network devices are customarily programmed to drop calls when there is no user data to send across a WAN link. However, network traffic, such as routing updates and *keep-alives*, which are packets sent out by network devices and servers to let other devices know the device is up, running, and attached to the network, must still pass over the WAN even when no user data is present.

A major problem comes from a characteristic of LAN networking and routing protocols. Router-to-router protocols such as the routing information protocol (RIP) and Open Shortest Path First (OSPF) frequently pass information between routers so that the routers can calculate routing paths. Both protocols use periodic updates to ensure that information about changes to the state of the network are shared among all routers. For instance, routers running RIP send out updates every 30 seconds. Additionally, devices on a NetWare LAN generate traffic broadcasting their presence using NetWare's Service Advertising Protocol (SAP).

WAN equipment vendors attempting to deal with this dilemma have met with only limited success. One approach is called *spoofing,* which is a technique used by network devices to trick a NOS (network operating system) into thinking that a connection is in place when it really is not. Spoofing is far from the ultimate WAN solution because it is a proprietary solution. The place to deal with WAN-related issues is not in network devices, such as bridges or routers, but in the OS or NOS itself. If the NOS/OS is smart enough to realize that it is dealing with WAN connections, it can control the calling patterns and adjust keep-alives and updates accordingly.

With better WAN support in mind, vendors such as Microsoft and Novell have begun incorporating ISDN into their operating system and network operating system. Your users should benefit from both vendors' efforts. Specifically, the remote user dialing into a network or the Internet over an ISDN link should be able to more easily set up the connection. And, managers connecting LAN-based users in remote offices to corporate backbones will not have to worry about interoperability problems arising from incompatible, proprietary spoofing implementations.

A tighter integration between the network operating system and ISDN could help simplify the situation. For example, Novell is relying on the NetWare Link Services Protocol (NLSP) and APIs to make a tighter integration between NetWare and ISDN.

NLSP was designed to reduce the bandwidth consumption of IPX routing information protocol (RIP) and Service Advertising Protocol (SAP) broadcasts over a network. Instead of the traditional updates every 30 seconds, as is common with RIP, and the constant SAP broadcasts, NLSP sends out a "hello" packet once every ten minutes. When changes in a network do occur, routers running NLSP only pass along the changes, instead of sending all of the information about the state of a network.

The combination of fewer updates and the passing of less information in each update saves bandwidth over any link, be it a backbone Ethernet network, an internetwork with sites connected by dedicated lines, or a network where sites are connected by dial-up ISDN links. While NLSP is a significant improvement over traditional RIP and SAP, you still do not want to pay phone charges just to pass along hello packets when nothing has changed. Bringing up a link every ten minutes translates into 144 calls every day. For that reason, Novell still relies on third-party vendors for spoofing to summarize the topology behind a link and to propagate the changes once a connection is made by a user's initiative.

Another area where Novell helps integrate ISDN with the NOS is through its Open Data-Link Interface for Wide-Area Networks (ODI WAN) specification. The specification gives WAN adapter developers a way to tap Novell's configuration and connection management software.

ODI WAN plays a role similar to that of a traditional network adapter card driver, except it works for WAN connections. Basically, ODI WAN is an interface layer between a WAN adapter, the LAN communications protocols (IPX/SPX), and the WAN protocols. To integrate with the NetWare environment using ODI WAN, a developer need only write a driver and a configuration database module for its WAN adapter.

Microsoft wants to make ISDN as easy to use as installing a modem by making ISDN an integral part of the operating system. Microsoft developed an NDIS packet driver WAN Miniport ISDN architecture for its Windows NT product line, and the company ported this to Windows 95.

Windows 95 supports the Internet Engineering Task Force's (IETF) Point-to-Point Protocol (PPP). PPP allows network protocols, such as TCP/IP (Transmission Control Protocol/Internet Protocol), IPX/SPX (Internetwork Packet Exchange/Sequenced Packet Exchange—Novell's network protocols), and NetBEUI (NetBIOS Extended User Interface) to operate over ISDN WAN links. Microsoft has developed PPPMAC, an NDIS 3 PPP driver that installs in the network control panel. To network protocols, PPPMAC looks like a network (LAN) driver. You can see this architecture in Figure 3-6, which illustrates the ISDN WAN driver architecture.

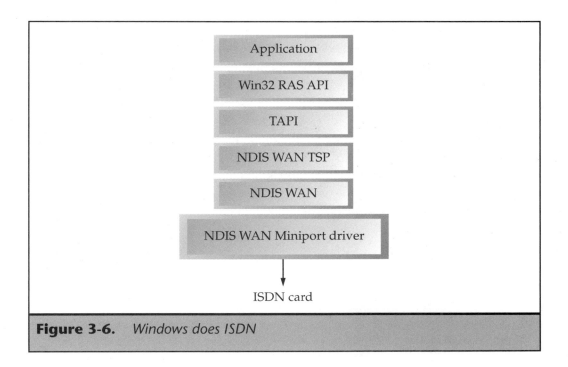

Figure 3-6. *Windows does ISDN*

Windows 95's ISDN support is relatively transparent. From an application or user point of view, when compared with an analog connection, nothing changes except the connection speed. Applications continue to create connections, by use of remote access services (RAS), APIs (application programming interfaces), or a Winsock connection. For example, when a user creates a new connection in the Dial-Up Networking folder, he or she simply chooses the ISDN adapter instead of a modem in the dialog box.

Third-party product integration is relatively straightforward. Using the built-in ISDN protocol stack, the vendor's driver talks directly to WAN Miniport architecture. This eliminates the need to use third-party IP protocol stacks.

Native ISDN support also means that vendors will be able to release products with shorter development cycles. This will result in ISDN products being brought to the market faster with lower cost than was possible when the vendor had to write its own device driver. The reason: an independent hardware vendor only needs to create an ISDN WAN Miniport driver for its product. The driver uses the Windows API to send information to the RAS. The RAS makes use of telephony API (TAPI) calls to create the connection. A TAPI service provider, called the NDIS WAN, then passes the TAPI calls to an NDIS WAN Miniport via the NDIS Wrapper. Once the connection is made, PPPMAC sends and receives data to the NDIS WAN Miniport. Therefore, the RAS becomes the interface for all ISDN remote LAN access.

Basically, the Novell and Microsoft efforts in this area will make it easier to use ISDN. Ideally, you would like it so that users will not need to bother themselves with the distinction between an ISDN connection and an analog connection. We are not at that point yet, but Novell, Microsoft, and many ISDN-equipment vendors are at least trying to address the configuration and call-management issues that today are still different for an ISDN and an analog link.

Chapter Four

Mixed Analog/ISDN Environments

The two previous chapters discussed how to link your remote and mobile workers by use of analog and ISDN connections as if the two approaches were mutually exclusive. The approach in these chapters was to focus on each type of connection and discuss the technical merits, costs, and trade-offs of using either one or the other. If your company is like most, you will not be able to treat your analog and ISDN connectivity needs as distinct offerings. Most likely, you will need to support your users by dealing with mixed environments, where a combination of analog and ISDN connections is the norm.

Such mixed environments take many forms. Supporting users in a mixed analog/ISDN environment might require something as simple as providing one group of users with modems to dial into your network from the road over analog phone lines, and establishing ISDN service and installing a line and equipment in the homes of telecommuters or small branch offices. However, supporting users in a mixed environment might also mean finding a way to use existing analog equipment, such as telephones, fax machines, and modems, so that this equipment runs over digital lines. Or, it might mean giving a telecommuter a way to dial into your corporate network over an ISDN connection, while still providing a way for that user to dial into an Internet service provider or a commercial online service, such as America Online, CompuServe, or The Microsoft Network, using an analog connection.

Of course, the heart of the matter is to do any and all of this in the most economical way. In many cases, it makes no sense to pay for both an analog and an ISDN connection when one will do. Yet it does make sense to let your remote workers use the existing analog equipment (telephones and faxes, for example) with an ISDN connection.

Simplifying the Central Site

The first place to start planning to support users in a mixed analog/ISDN environment is your central site. You will need a way to economically bring in mixed analog and ISDN traffic and a way for your users to dial into your network.

For most companies, such systems are not necessarily planned, rather they evolve (that's a polite way to say they just happen). For example, you might start by giving some traveling users dial-up access over analog lines. This capability might expand so workers can dial into the network from home.

Then, some of these home workers might need higher-speed access, and ISDN would seem like the best choice. At about the same time, users in small remote sites, which have been isolated from the network, might be given access to network resources in a central site. Typically, users in these remote sites have exchanged, at most, e-mail with their fellow workers in the central location by dialing in over an analog line and have relied on overnight delivery packages to ship off floppy disks with large document and graphics files.

If users in a remote site need more access—the ability to transfer large files or access to database applications, for example—it might make sense to install a dial-up ISDN router. This would give LAN-attached users in smaller sites a transparent and somewhat high-speed link to network resources in a central site.

Basically, you are adding connectivity as remote users need it. The result of such an "add-connectivity-as-you-go" approach is a central site with many access lines. Figure 4-1 shows what a typical configuration might look like. In the figure, you can see that the telecommuters dialing in over analog lines reach a modem pool that connects them to some form of remote access server, which gives them access to the network. You can also see in the figure that you might provide a set of analog phone lines and a modem pool so your traveling users with PC Card modem-equipped laptops can gain access into the corporate network. Similarly, those telecommuters requiring more bandwidth than that available over an analog line will dial in over ISDN BRI links. Using such links, telecommuters access the network through a pool of ISDN terminal adapters. Additionally, you might have to support additional ISDN lines so that users in small remote sites with ISDN-enabled access routers can connect to your backbone.

For purposes of discussion, this scenario will be referred to as a *multiline approach*. For most companies, there will be little incentive to change from this multiline approach. But that might not be the best bet—there are many costs associated with such a mixed networking environment. You might be able to reduce these costs by selecting a more appropriate service for the central site.

What you will have to do is determine the costs for two different scenarios. The first scenario is the multiline approach illustrated in Figure 4-1. The other is to consolidate all of the incoming traffic onto one (or more) higher-speed links, such as an ISDN PRI or T1 connection coming into the central site. Figure 4-2 shows architecturally what this scenario would look like. This scenario will be referred to as the *consolidated approach*.

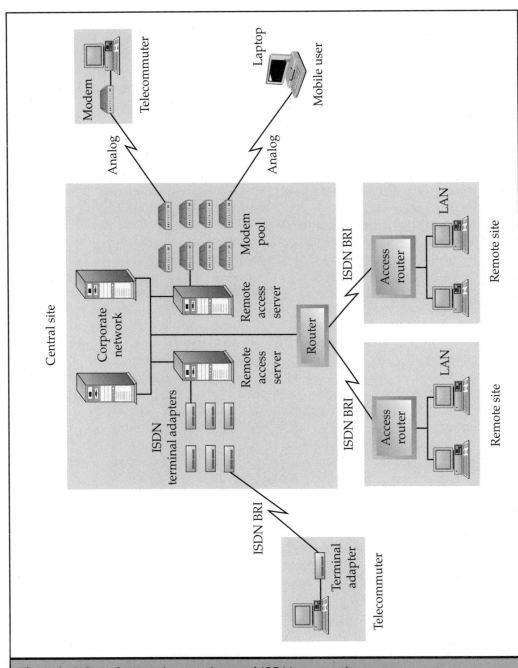

Figure 4-1. *Supporting analog and ISDN connections*

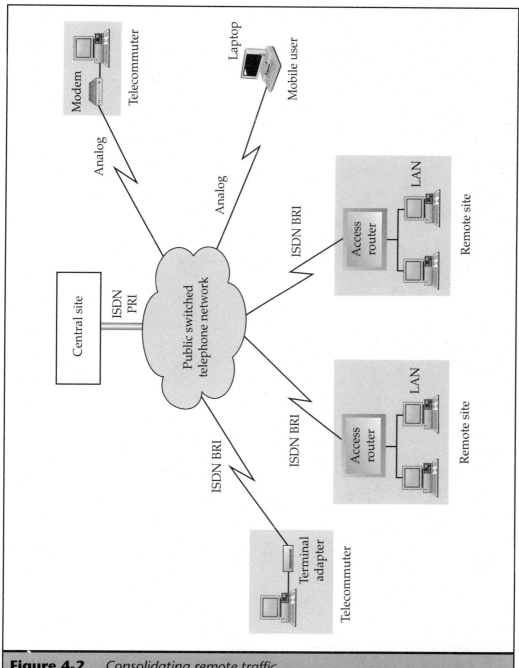

Figure 4-2.   *Consolidating remote traffic*

Calculating the Cost of Connectivity

The way to determine which of the two approaches—multiline versus consolidated—is most cost-effective requires a fairly straightforward calculation. We will determine the price of equipment for each scenario and the telecommunications charges for the services. Since everyone's networking situation is different, the calculations should be used as an example to guide you when deciding between the two scenarios.

Note, however, that even with the cost comparison we will go through, there is one caveat: It is very hard to come up with an exact formula to tell you when one scenario is more cost-effective than another. It is hard because there are many hidden costs involved in supporting users in both environments. For example, in the multiline approach you will have to maintain all of the modems in the modem pool. What does it cost to do that for a year? Is this support something you can delegate to a less-experienced technical staffer? You will also need someone to manage all of the terminal adapters and the access routers. Again, what does it cost to support these devices? Such support costs are hard to quantify since they are typically buried in operations budgets and are considered the cost of doing business. Yet studies by market research firms such as the Meta Group, Forrester Research, and the Gartner Group, say that these costs are substantial—often the annual support costs to manage and maintain such remote connectivity equipment is several times the purchase price of the equipment. As we go through the calculation of equipment and service costs, I'll point out some trade-offs in these soft costs to give you at least an idea of where to look for hidden support costs.

We'll now calculate the costs for the two scenarios and see whether a multiline or consolidated approach is more cost-effective.

Calculating the Cost of Remote Connectivity

To calculate the cost for the two scenarios, we will need to make some assumptions about the level of usage a company will need. Suppose we have a company with a sales staff of 100 people who need occasional dial-up access to inventory and pricing information from the road. Suppose also that there are five engineers who use ISDN BRI service for high-speed access into the corporate network when they work at home. These engineers also need high-speed access to the Internet from the office. In addition, assume the company has three small remote offices, each with a LAN that supports about ten people in each site. The users in the remote sites use ISDN-enabled access routers to send and receive e-mail with users in the central site, transfer files between sites, and access applications running on servers, minicomputers, and mainframes in the central site.

ANALOG COSTS   Assume the sales staff only needs access to the data after they have completed a customer call. They enter the orders while in their cars or hotel rooms after making the sale, and it only takes a few minutes of access time to send or retrieve the information they need. If the typical salesperson dials into the network and gets a busy signal, he or she can dial back later. That means you can get by with something in the range of ten modems to handle the calls of 100 salespeople. This ratio of modems to remote users can vary depending on the requirements of the dial-up users and the length of time each user stays on the phone. Some companies get by with proportionately far fewer modems. I've seen one company use two access lines and modems in its central site for 50 remote users who only needed to check e-mail throughout the day.

The number of modems required to support remote users also depends on the geographical distribution of the users. If all remote users are in the same time zone, you may need more modems since it is likely they all will be dialing in at the same time each day—in the morning before heading out on sales calls, or at the end of the day to get e-mail, for example. You will have to decide how many users per modem works best for your users from experience and from the feedback you get from the remote users.

For the purposes of this discussion, we'll assume ten modems will be sufficient in the central office. That means you will need ten analog lines into your central site and ten modems. Figure each modem costs about $250, and it costs $100 per line to establish the service. That means it costs $3,500 to set up the analog portion of the central site. The monthly fee for analog service varies greatly with the carrier or service provider (with the deregulation of the telecommunications market brought about by the passage of the Telecommunications Reform Act of 1996, you may be able to get lower rates from long-distance carriers entering the local service market). For this example, let's take a conservative amount of $25 per month per line. The total monthly fixed fee for the analog service for the ten lines comes to $250 per month or $3,000 per year.

The usage fee for the phone service in this scenario can vary greatly depending on the communications requirements of your remote users. For the situation I've described with remote users dialing into the network from the road to retrieve e-mail, to query an inventory and price database, and to enter orders in a database, most of the calls will originate from another location, and the costs to the central site will be minimal. Obviously, someone will have to pay for these calls, but for the purposes of this example, which compares central site costs for different scenarios, we will not take the cost of calls that originate from another location into account.

Still there will be usage charges. For instance, you might use one line to dial out to a network device, such as a router or server, located at another site and obtain out-of-band information about that device's status. Or, you may allocate one of the modems as a dial-out modem for onsite LAN staffers to dial up vendor bulletin board systems for software updates and patches. Still again, you may let onsite employees use one or two modems to dial out to a commercial online service.

In any event, the outward-bound calls from the modem pool in this scenario will be limited. Assume the usage fee is $.10 per minute, and you use two of the modems for one hour each per day. That's $12 per day or $240 per month based on 20 business days per month. That works out to $2,880 per year for the usage fee for the central site's analog lines. Remember, these amounts are based on fairly conservative estimates of the service fees and limited usage of the phone lines. Still, the first-year grand total for the ten modems, analog lines, and usage of the lines in this scenario adds up to $9,380.

SINGLE-USER ISDN COSTS   We'll now calculate the cost for the ISDN portion of the network. Again, we'll have to make assumptions about the usage levels. Assume that the five engineers, who need high-speed access into the network from home and high-speed Internet access from the office, can easily share two connections. That means the central site will need two terminal adapters and two ISDN BRI lines. The cost of an ISDN BRI terminal adapter varies, but we'll pick a conservative $450 for a low-end unit without many bells and whistles. Also assume the startup fee to establish ISDN service is $250 per line. That means the cost to get these two connections off the ground comes to $900 for the equipment and $500 for the ISDN BRI service, or $1,400 before you send or receive a single bit.

You will have to pay a fixed monthly fee for the ISDN service and a usage fee based on connect time. The monthly fee for ISDN BRI service varies with the region and telecom carrier. For this example I'll use a fairly common yet conservative $45 per month per line. That means it will cost you $1,080 per year for the basic service. The usage fee for an ISDN BRI link also varies, but for purposes of this calculation I'll assume that the usage rate is $.20 per minute, and connect time for each line is three hours per day, or six hours total per day for the two lines. That comes out to $72 per day in usage fees, $1,440 per month based on 20 business days per month, or $17,280 for the year.

That brings the first-year total for the central site termination equipment and two ISDN lines for the five engineers to $19,760. Again, these numbers are based on my specific example and should only be used to give you an idea of how to calculate the costs. Your numbers will likely be different; just make allowances in your calculations.

COST TO LINK REMOTE LANS My hypothetical company also has three remote sites that need dial-up connectivity into the backbone network located in the central site. That means you will need three more ISDN BRI lines into the central site.

The pricing for the service will be similar to that calculated in the previous section. Namely, it will be $250 per line to establish the service and $45 per month for the service. That means you will be spending $750 to establish service for all three lines and $135 per month or $1,620 per year for the basic fee for the lines. The usage fee for the service will vary with connect time. But, as I have done in the past, I'll assume each site needs three hours of connectivity a day and the ISDN usage fee is $.20 per minute. That means it will cost $2,160 per month for the three sites to connect to the central site (that's based on 20 business days per month). That means you will spend $25,920 a year in usage charges for all three sites to connect an average of three hours per day by use of ISDN BRI service. Let's assume that half the time the ISDN link is brought up by the remote site and half the time the connection is established by the central site. That means the central site telecom allocation will be half this amount, or $12,960 for the year. Again, this amount is based on my specific example. Your numbers will vary with your network situation. For example, you may find that a higher percentage of the calls originate from the remote sites. Take that into account when you calculate your own expenses.

The termination device needed to support connectivity between remote offices and the central site will be slightly more expensive than that required for single users to connect. You will need an ISDN-enabled router instead of just a terminal adapter. You might choose to use one access router for each line entering the central site. Access routers can vary in price from about $700 for a no-frills low-end model to about $2,500 for a higher-end version with more features, such as more built-in management, built-in SDLC conversion (which converts SNA session traffic between a mainframe and terminal so that it can be carried over a network), and support for multiple protocols. Let's assume we want an access router with some management features and support for IP and IPX. The router will also need one LAN port and one ISDN WAN port. Such a router will cost about $1,500 (again, prices do vary greatly, so when you calculate your costs, substitute your price for this value). That means you will need to spend $4,500 for the three routers. You will also have to manage three separate devices—that's one of the hidden costs of remote connectivity. For about the same amount of money, you can get a higher-end router with three or more ISDN WAN ports.

Table 4-1 summarizes the first-year costs to connect 100 salespeople to the central site using ten analog lines and a modem pool, five engineers using ISDN service to dial in and out of the network, and connecting three remote sites in the manner I just described.

Combined Approach Costs

As you can see, the costs for equipment and telecommunications services in my example are fairly steep. The connectivity alternative for the hypothetical company I've created is to consolidate all of the incoming traffic onto a single ISDN PRI line to handle all of the traffic from the sales force, the engineers, and the remote sites. For both the multiline and consolidated scenarios, the cost of the equipment in the home or remote office will not change, and the services to those locations will not change. What changes is the equipment in, and the services to, the central site. For that reason, I am keeping the costs of the equipment and telecom services for remote users and remote sites out of this calculation.

For the consolidated scenario, you only need a single device in the central site—one that is capable of taking the mixed analog/ISDN traffic combined by the telephone company and separating it into its distinct components. All of the major router vendors, including Cisco Systems, Bay Networks, and 3Com

	Ten Analog Connections	Five Single-User ISDN Connections	Three Remote-Site ISDN Connections
Termination equipment	$2,500	$900	$4,500
Fee to establish service	$1,000	$500	$750
Monthly fee for service for one year	$3,000	$1,080	$1,620
Usage fee for service for one year	$2,880	$17,280	$12,960
Total first-year costs	$9,380	$19,760	$19,830
Grand total for all connectivity: $48,970			

Table 4-1.   *First-Year Costs for Multiline Approach*

Corp., offer such units. You'll also find similar products from Ascend Communications, a company with lots of inverse multiplexing expertise. There are other vendors that offer such high-end routers, and there are more joining the market every month. The ISDN router market is rapidly changing and rather than give you specific models, which will be outdated by newer models in a month or two, I'll simply tell you that you will need a router with enough processing power to handle the traffic load. For the levels of connectivity I have described, we're talking about a mid-level router and not a high-end backbone model. So the price for such a router with an ISDN PRI interface will be somewhere in the range of $12,000 to $25,000. Essentially, you can expect to spend a little more than it costs for the router in the previous example that could accommodate multiple ISDN BRI connections. For the purposes of this calculation, we will use $20,000 for the price of the router. That is all the termination equipment you will need.

Next, you will have to calculate the price of the PRI service for the year. This can be tricky. The price varies greatly. You must pay a price to establish the service, a monthly fee for the service, and a usage fee. Many of the regional Bells and other ISDN service providers have not priced ISDN PRI service inexpensively enough to make it worthwhile in many situations. A PRI link delivers 11.5 times the bandwidth of a BRI link. If the price for PRI service were about eight times that of BRI, you would have a great deal. But at this writing, many of the carriers were charging users a monthly fee of about ten times the cost of a BRI link for a PRI link. The monthly fee can vary from about $450 per month to $1,500 per month.

Because of this pricing policy on PRI links, many companies choose to use a T1 line instead of a PRI link. The bandwidth is comparable and the monthly fees for both services are about the same in many regions of the country, yet

A Better Buy in Europe
Within the United States, the pricing of ISDN PRI service varies greatly, but in most cases, it is based on T1 tariffs. Such tariffs make it more expensive than the price of an equivalent number of BRI lines. In Europe, the pricing also varies greatly, but in some cases a single PRI line costs about the same per month as about a half dozen BRI lines. That makes PRI very economical when you're trying to aggregate traffic coming into a central site in Europe.

there are no usage charges associated with using a T1. A router with a T1 interface is comparably priced when compared with a similarly performing router with an ISDN PRI interface.

Let's assume then that we will use a T1 line into the central site and that it carries a fixed monthly fee of $1,500, or $18,000 per year. Also assume that the one-time cost to establish the service is $2,000. Table 4-2 summarizes first-year costs to establish service, pay for the equipment, and pay the monthly fee for the service. As you can see, it is $40,000, which is significantly lower than the $48,970 first-year costs for the multiline approach. If you have about eight or more ISDN BRI lines coming into a central site, it is more cost-effective to replace the individual lines with a T1 or PRI connection.

One of the trade-offs that you must factor in when choosing between a consolidated versus multiline approach is the cost to manage the termination equipment. Typically, you will need a more experienced (read that more highly paid) person to manage the type of router that can handle the mixed, multiline traffic in the consolidated traffic approach. With the multiline approach, you may be able to get away with using a less skilled person to manage the termination equipment; however, that person will need to spend more time, since he or she is dealing with many more pieces of equipment.

	Using a Single T1 Link and One Mid-Range Router
Termination equipment	$20,000
Fee to establish service	$2,000
Monthly fee for service for one year	$18,000
Usage fee for service for one year	$0
Total first-year costs	$40,000

Table 4-2.   *First-Year Costs for Consolidated Approach*

Single-Line Considerations

Now we will shift attention from the central site to the users in the remote sites. The issue you must consider when trying to support a mix of ISDN and analog equipment in remote sites is the retention of existing office equipment.

Suppose you install ISDN to a telecommuter's home or to a small remote office. Do you want to maintain two lines—one ISDN and one analog? Probably not in most cases. After all, an ISDN BRI link has two B channels, so a telecommuter can use one channel to connect to the corporate network or the Internet and the other to place phone calls and send and receive faxes. Given that type of connectivity, you may elect to drop existing analog service in favor of the ISDN link.

However, you will either need to buy new telephones and other equipment that connect to an ISDN terminal adapter or, more sensibly, pick an ISDN terminal adapter that allows you to use existing analog equipment. That's the most practical approach in a small remote office or for a telecommuter. Terminal adapters that support analog equipment are only slightly more expensive than terminal adapters that do not support analog devices. The price difference is usually less than $100—much lower than the cost of replacing a couple of phones and possibly a fax machine.

When someone calls a user in a remote site using one of these terminal adapters, there is no perceivable difference to the outside caller. Most ISDN terminal adapters can route an incoming call according to the type of caller. If a user in a remote site receives a call from another ISDN device (an access router, for example), most terminal adapters will be able to recognize that the incoming call is digital, and the terminal adapter will answer the call as a digital data call. Conversely, if a person calls into a remote office or telecommuter's home using a regular analog phone line, the terminal adapter recognizes this and routes the call to an external analog phone plugged into the terminal adapter. To make matters even easier, some ISDN service providers let you have different phone numbers for analog and digital calls.

Hybrid Modems: ISDN and Analog Access Combined

Another area to consider when providing remote users with ISDN access is that the rest of the world is still mostly analog. Your central site may be equipped to handle incoming ISDN calls, but your remote user's Internet service provider may not. Or, your remote users may need to occasionally dial into a vendor's bulletin board or an analog-only online service. That means a remote user will need both ISDN connectivity and the functions of a regular modem.

One way to give users this level of connectivity is to, as the previous section said, buy terminal adapters that accept analog devices. In that way, a user with a modem can plug that modem directly into the terminal adapter. An alternative approach is to use a new class of product called a *hybrid* modem.

For users who do need both types of access, a hybrid device that connects to an ISDN line and that also supports analog modem communications might be the best bet. Such products are essentially enhanced ISDN terminal adapters, but a more apt name for them would be an ISDN modem.

NOTE: *These are not ISDN terminal adapters that can handle analog devices. The hybrid devices have both ISDN terminal adapters and analog modems bundled together. Some vendors blur the distinction between these vastly different offerings, so be forewarned—there is a distinction. The way to make sure you have an integrated device is to see if it supports the common International Telecommunications Union (ITU) standards. For a modem, those standards are V.34, V.32bis, V.32, V.22bis, V.22, and V.21. For fax modems, the device should also support V.17, V.21, V.27ter, or V.29.*

Hybrid ISDN/analog modems typically cost more than modems that incorporate V.35 technology. They are usually a little more pricey than a standard ISDN terminal adapter. You can buy a low-end hybrid product for about $500. That means they cost less than the combination of an ISDN terminal adapter and a high-performance modem. So if you are outfitting a new telecommuting office, it would cost less to buy a hybrid device than to buy an ISDN terminal adapter and a modem.

Hybrid modems let a user take advantage of an ISDN link's higher bandwidth when ISDN is available at the other end of the line. For example, a user may connect to an Internet service that offers ISDN connections. And if the endpoint on the connection does not support ISDN, the device can support a link to a traditional modem.

Such hybrid products, which give the user access to both ISDN and analog connections, can be considered a modem replacement. They should not be confused with higher-end products like access routers that also combine ISDN and analog access into one device through separate ports. The hybrid modem-like products are just that, modem-like. For example, for analog access they use the same communications software programs as a regular analog modem. And many use standard AT commands (with slight modification) for ISDN connections.

The biggest difference between these hybrid devices and a regular modem is that they are more difficult to configure. (So you might need to train members of your staff on how to configure these devices.) This has to do with the complexity of making an ISDN connection. If you do not have the equipment configured correctly for the local exchange carrier's central office equipment, an ISDN hybrid modem will not work.

That is in contrast to the case of two modems trying to set up a connection. If the two modems are configured differently, say to operate at different rates, they negotiate at the start of the call and settle on a default transmission rate that both can handle. With an ISDN modem, a person must usually enter information about the type of switch that is used in the central office, the Service Profile Identifiers (SPIDs) associated with the channels over which the connection is being made, and the telephone numbers of the SPIDs. All of this information varies with the local exchange carrier whose equipment you're connecting with. All of the products support connections with the major ISDN switches that you're likely to find in a local exchange carrier's central office. Those switches include AT&T's 5ESS, Northern Telecom's DMS-100, and switches that are compatible with the National ISDN-1 specifications.

There are other parameters that sometimes require setting. However, the switch type, SPIDs, and numbers are the basic ones required to get an ISDN modem up and running. To help the user, the manufacturers of these hybrid devices include configuration tools to make setup easier. For example, U.S. Robotics offers an easy-to-use configuration menu and includes a test routine that checks to see if you can establish a connection with its hybrid product. Motorola includes a Windows-based configurations manager with its product.

The ISDN/modem combination products can have many uses, but one place they are likely to be installed is in a home that has ISDN service. For instance, a telecommuter might use one to dial into the corporate network at high speeds or to access the Internet over an ISDN link. The same person using the same "two-in-one" device may also connect into an online service or another corporate site, where analog modems are used to accept incoming calls.

I'm Analog, You're Digital

Most of the discussion so far in this chapter has centered on how to support your existing analog products or give users access to analog services in a mixed ISDN/analog environment. A subset of this discussion is how to give an analog user dial-up access in a purely digital environment.

One example of this is a hotel room where the phone system is purely digital and the telephone has no data port. Or you might have mobile workers—salespeople or technical support folks—who need dial-out access from a customer's site, but the customer's location is all digital.

In either case, there are two points to consider. First, you must figure out a way to protect analog modems from accidentally being destroyed when a user unknowingly connects his or her laptop PC Card modem into a digital line. And second, you must give users a way to dial out if all that is available is a digital line.

With most of the major hotels installing digital Private Branch Exchanges (PBXes), many a traveler has fried a PC Card modem by accidentally plugging it into a digital line in a hotel room. One way to avoid this problem is to give each traveling user a line-sensing device that detects whether a line is digital or analog. The device looks like a pen and costs about $25. One end of the device is shaped like a telephone jack and plugs into a wall jack. If the outlet is a digital line, a red light or LED (light-emitting diode) lights up to warn the user. These pen-like digital-line detection devices are commonly available from mail-order catalogs that specialize in mobile equipment.

The digital-line detection devices are worth the $25 cost. If your company has 100 salespeople on the road, it would cost you $2,500 to equip all of them with a unit. If you save five $250 modem cards per year using the detection devices, you will earn back the initial purchase price in two years. And every modem you save after that is money in the bank (at least it is money you don't have to spend).

One problem with the digital-line detection devices is that people have to use them. A person can simply forget to use it every time, or forget to bring the unit. In either case, without the device, the mobile users cannot test the line before plugging in their modem. If you think your users will not be vigilant in their use of these devices, you might want to look for modems that offer built-in protection against digital-line burnout. For example, Xircom offers this feature in its line of PC Card modems, where the card is protected from damage if the user plugs it into a digital line.

Let's assume the protection of the PC Card modems is taken care of. You still need to give your users a way to communicate using their analog modems over the digital line. You have two choices here: a line converter or something that is the equivalent of an acoustic coupler.

I have tried to avoid the discussion of specific products in this book for a number of reasons. First, the thrust of this book is to get you thinking about deployment and support strategies. I've done this by discussing classes of products and explaining what issues you should consider to select among the different offerings within the class of products. Second, I do not want to appear to be endorsing any one vendor's product. And third, and perhaps most importantly, I do not want to steer you into a dead-end direction. The industry is rapidly changing. Technological changes are giving us higher-speed products (such as the 33.6-Kbps modems), the telcos are poised to offer new connectivity services, the pricing of the telecommunications services and products changes frequently, and there is consolidation within the connectivity and internetworking industries, so that service providers and equipment manufacturers might be here today and gobbled up tomorrow. Having said all of that, I do want to mention one product that I find indispensable for the road.

The Konexx Mobile Konnector from Unlimited Systems costs about $150, and it gives a user with a modem a way to connect to a digital phone to dial out as normal. The connector takes advantage of a little-known fact with digital phones—the headset with the mouthpiece and receiver is analog. The way you use the Konexx connector is to disconnect the headset and plug the connector into the jack previously occupied by the headset. The Konexx Mobile Konnector gives you an RJ-11 jack that you then plug your modem into, allowing you to dial out using your analog modem. (I know "analog modem" is a redundant phrase, but you might have to state it this way to emphasize to your users that they are really tapping into a digital network.)

The other type of device you might look for is a *coupler,* similar to the old-time acoustic couplers used years ago to connect to telephones. There are several couplers on the market today that work by bolting onto a digital phone's handset. The device has two cups—one fits over the mouthpiece and the other over the earpiece. A user then plugs his or her analog modem into this coupler and dials out.

Such conversion devices are useful in several situations. Obviously, a traveling user who stays in a hotel room that only has a digital phone system and no analog port to connect his or her modem would find such devices handy. Sales staffs or consultants might find these devices useful, too. For instance, many service professionals need connectivity from a client's office. You might have a systems engineer at a customer's site to troubleshoot a problem with some equipment. The systems engineer might need a patch to get the equipment running and might need to dial into your company's network, bulletin board system, or web site. If the client's office is fairly new, it might have an all-digital phone system and provide users with limited dial-out capabilities (for example, the user can only dial another company site or the Internet) through a LAN-based modem or router. If that is the case, the systems engineer might have to return to your company just to pick up a floppy disk with the patch. With a connector or coupler that plugs into a digital phone, the systems engineer can make the call from anyone's desk and pull down the software he or she needs.

Your sales agents might find themselves in a similar situation. They may need to dial into an inventory database to check on availability or pricing of your company's products or services. Without a link, they might have to call the client back later with the information—something that might delay or kill a sale.

Wrapping It Up

This chapter has discussed several scenarios where you must support users in a mixed ISDN/analog environment. The bottom line is that ISDN and analog connectivity will both be around for a long time, and neither will fully replace the other. Given that, you should look for ways to most economically leverage the strengths of each service to give your remote users the connectivity they need to perform their jobs.

Chapter Five

Wireless

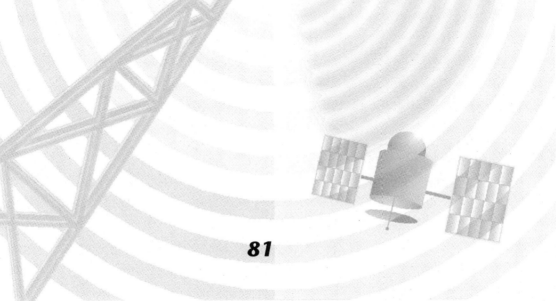

The previous three chapters discussed what are likely to be the most common ways you will connect the majority of your remote users (be they telecommuters or travelers) who need access to e-mail, the corporate network, or the Internet. This chapter will look at wireless communications technology, which, while holding much promise for meeting remote connectivity needs, is still relegated to connecting only a small percent of remote users. This is because of the limited availability of wireless services, lack of interoperability between wireless systems, or other reasons, all of which we will examine in this chapter.

For many of us, wireless communications is fascinating. The idea of being in contact whenever and wherever you choose is very appealing. Unfortunately, such connectivity is not realistic today. And that's too bad. I don't know how you feel, but I expected wireless communications to be much more advanced than they are. Maybe I put too much credence in the old Dick Tracy comic strips, where the detective's two-way wrist-radio played such a vital role in many of his cases.

That's not to say that today's wireless communications methods are worthless. It's just that the ubiquitous nature of Dick Tracy's wrist-radio communications system and the miniaturization of the device set my expectations for wireless communications at a fairly high, most would say unreasonable, level.

Today's wireless communications offerings—including the services and the equipment to connect to those services—are not practical for most applications. Still, there are some situations where wireless connectivity might be your best (or only) choice. In this chapter, I'll discuss the basic shortcomings of wireless communications as a generic form of connectivity technology. Then I will look at the available wireless service offerings. When discussing the differences in the various wireless services, I will show you how to match a service's technical and economical strengths to your applications. And then I will look at some of the wireless services that are either just starting to be deployed or that have the potential to be deployed in the near future.

Generic Issues to Consider

As I have discussed in the previous three chapters, connecting to the office from the road has certainly gotten easier over the last few years—many hotels have added data ports to phones, and most airport terminals have pay phones that accept modular jacks. But there are still many cases where a hard-wired modem connection is tough to make or impractical—when you're sitting in a car, for example, or while you're in a client's office where there are only digital lines.

For these reasons, and perhaps because of the freeing effect cellular phones have had on business travelers, many companies are interested in wireless connections for their mobile employees.

There are for practical purposes three wireless service alternatives available today. Currently, your generic choices when looking for established wireless services are *circuit-switched cellular, packet radio,* and *Cellular Digital Packet Data* (CDPD) service. Circuit-switched cellular is the common cellular service used for cellular telephones, and it is offered to you by your traditional long-distance telephone carriers, regional Bell operating companies, and other cellular providers throughout the country. Packet radio is, as the name implies, a packet-switched service that is offered predominately by two companies: RAM Mobile Data and Ardis. Both companies operate networks throughout the United States and internationally and offer a way to send information over a packet-based radio network. The other alternative is CDPD, which is typically offered by your cellular carriers.

The most common wireless communication between a mobile worker and the office, or between two mobile workers, is an exchange of e-mail. And that's where the first wireless service providers aimed when offering services. For example, for several years, RadioMail Corp. (San Mateo, California) has offered wireless e-mail services that rode over the Ardis and RAM Mobile Data commercial wireless networks. Figure 5-1 shows the typical RadioMail user's setup. Usually, the early users of RadioMail's wireless service used a Hewlett-Packard palmtop computer and an integrated (or at least strapped on the back of the palmtop) wireless modem that allowed the person to send and receive e-mail. Today, it is more likely that the wireless modem is a PC Card with an antenna (more on this later). RadioMail also offered (and still does offer) other services that proved useful to the traveling users. For instance, one service let a user check airline schedules.

Within the last two years, the advent of fairly powerful *personal digital assistants* (PDAs), offered by a number of vendors including Apple, Psion, Hewlett-Packard, and Sony, has opened up the wireless e-mail market. Today, RadioMail and Wynd Communications are aggressively going after this market, giving network managers more choices for linking remote users.

While e-mail is the most common form of wireless communications, many companies would also like to use wireless connections to link users to corporate data, which resides on servers, minicomputers, and mainframes in the office, or to the Internet. To accomplish this level of connectivity requires more components. As Figure 5-2 illustrates, you will need a wireless modem,

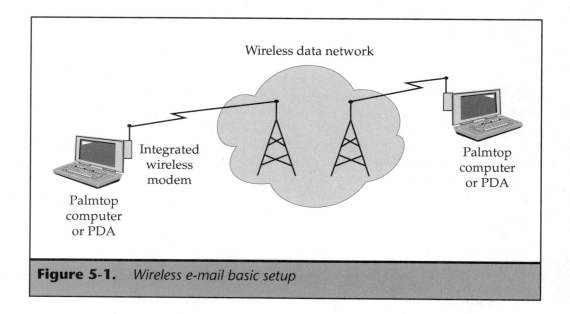

Figure 5-1. *Wireless e-mail basic setup*

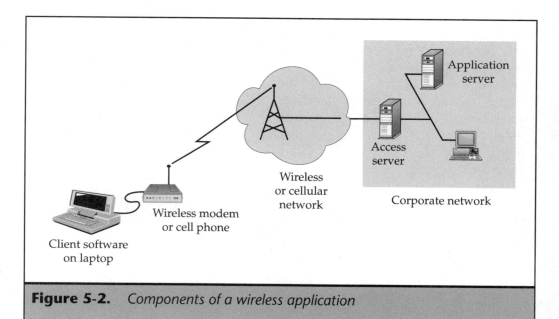

Figure 5-2. *Components of a wireless application*

client software to handle wireless connections, a remote access server, and server communications software to maintain and manage the wireless connections.

The shift in wireless usage from communications only (e-mail and, in some cases, fax) to accessing data and applications will take some time. But this is the direction many companies, like your own, are heading, so you must be aware of what is going on to provide such connectivity in the future. To give you an idea of the shift, consider that in the year 2000, 25 percent of cellular data users will only need wireless connectivity for personal communications (e-mail and faxing), according to McLaughlin & Associates (Chicago), a market research firm. The rest of the market for cellular data services will be split among several distinct types of users.

Figure 5-3 shows the breakdown for these different wireless applications. For example, one class of wireless users consists of service technicians at customer sites who need access to technician documentation or warranty information. Another class of cellular data users is made up of delivery and inventory people who need to transmit information gathered about packages or products. And then there are the true mobile professionals who require a full mobile office that provides access to applications, data, and personal communication services (again, e-mail and fax).

What's Hindering Wireless Connectivity?

For companies seeking to roll out wireless applications that access corporate applications and databases, there are, unfortunately, a number of obstacles. Wide-area wireless applications are still plagued by low-speed connections. Many wireless networks still only deliver rates of 4.8 Kbps, which is much lower than obtainable by use of a decent (28.8-Kbps) modem and an analog phone line. (Not to mention that wireless wide-area networks have a significantly lower performance compared with their LAN-based wireless counterparts that typically operate in the 1 Mbps to 2 Mbps range.) And even if you're willing to settle for the low throughput rates, there are still vast areas of the country where phone jacks are commonly available, but wireless services are not.

Another problem that has troubled potential users of wide-area wireless networks is that there's a lack of standardization among the types of services. That means corporations often find that they must use different wireless modems and develop multiple implementations of the same application just so it can access and ride over the different services.

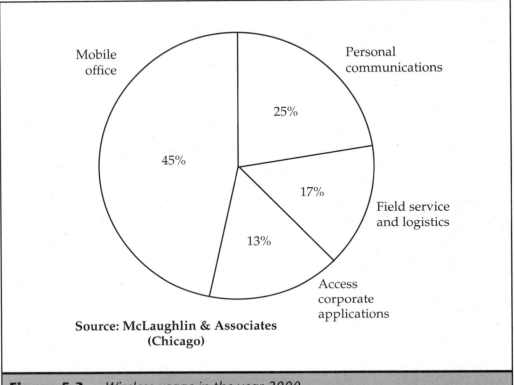

Source: McLaughlin & Associates
(Chicago)

Figure 5-3. *Wireless usage in the year 2000*

Stumbling Blocks to Deploying Wireless Applications

- Low throughput rates
- Service not ubiquitous
- Lack of standardization between services requires a different type of modem to connect to each service
- Complexity of applications that corporations want to run over wireless nets is increasing
- Wide variety of mobile platforms must be supported

This lack of compatibility is bad enough, but the difficulties of developing wireless applications are compounded by the wide variety of mobile platforms that must also be supported (everything from PDAs with limited memory and processing power to Pentium-based laptops that rival high-end desktop systems).

Further compounding the difficulties is that the wireless applications that companies want to roll out are increasingly complicated. Specifically, wireless nets primarily have been used to handle e-mail or message-based applications, but now many organizations would like to leverage the power of wireless wide-area networks so that users can access corporate databases.

One other factor to consider when looking at a wireless connectivity solution is the hidden costs. You might need to hire people with different skills than your current staff has accumulated working on your existing networks. Specifically, maintaining a wireless network requires a knowledge of the wireless services and hardware. It also requires a deeper knowledge of the relationship between the applications and the network they are running over. If there is a performance problem in your traditional networking environment, a technician can slap a diagnostic tool such as the Sniffer from Network General Corp. (or similar protocol analyzer tools from other vendors) on the network and look for problems. (Sniffer is the trade name for Network General Corp.'s network analysis and troubleshooting tool that captures data from a LAN and lets you examine the traffic. The Sniffer and other tools like it help diagnose problems by decoding the captured packets so you can more easily tell what is happening on your network.) Or, if a user cannot get access to a device, you can use diagnostic tools (such as pinging the device or performing a trace) that help you pinpoint the problem, or at least let you narrow down the type of problem you are dealing with. For example, when you ping a device, you send a packet over the network to the device using its IP address. If the device receives the packet, it returns a packet back to you, the sender. Receiving such a packet lets you know that the device is up and running and that it is connected to the network. Examining the round-trip time it takes the packet to go from your workstation to the device and back can be used to get a better understanding of the network conditions between you and that device. For example, a longer than normal round-trip time might indicate a congested link between you and the device or that the traffic had to pass over, for example, a slower-speed back link in the event a primary link failed.

All of that changes in a wireless network. You may not be able to notice a change in performance. And if you have a problem, you and your staff cannot use the traditional protocol analyzer tools, which attach to the network, to diagnose the problem. With a wireless network application, you are dealing with a very different set of problems, and you will likely have to hire staffers with expertise in the specific type of wireless technology and application you are using.

Some Reasons for Optimism

All of these issues have kept most organizations from deploying wireless applications in any wide-scale manner. (There are, of course, some exceptions—UPS and Federal Express, for example, developed and use wireless package-tracking applications.)

Fortunately, there have been some recent developments that should make wireless application development a little easier. To start, wireless network providers are boosting their maximum throughput rates. There's also a level of standardization being introduced with new digital cellular networks. And there are a number of middleware products hitting the market that make wireless database application development less of a chore.

Wireless service offerings have had two major shortcomings: they were not ubiquitous and they were very low speed. Today, the situation is not perfect, but it is improving.

Wireless services are now available in virtually every major city in the United States—up to 90 percent of major metropolitan locations have coverage, according to industry sources. And about 30 to 40 percent of the geographical area of the country has some form of wireless service available to users. That translates into about 80 percent of the U.S. population having a wireless networking service available. Some figures generated by wireless industry groups say these numbers are on the low side. When deploying a wireless application, you should check availability in the specific regions your users will need connectivity.

Two established wireless service providers, RAM Mobile Data and Ardis, have continually been expanding their areas of coverage into new sections of the country. And that trend is likely to continue at an accelerated pace thanks to increased competition from CDPD (Cellular Digital Packet Data) networks.

Fewer than a dozen cities had CDPD service by the end of 1994. As with ISDN, slow deployment of CDPD service has caused frustration for many network managers who would be interested in using the service, if only it were available.

In contrast to the established wireless providers, CDPD has some catching up to do. For example, Ardis, a two-way, store-and-forward, packet-based wireless network, is available in every state and now reaches more than 80 percent of the U.S. population, according to the company. By the second quarter of 1996, CDPD service reached slightly more than 45 percent of the U.S. population, according to the CDPD Forum, an industry association consisting of telecommunications carriers and equipment manufacturers interested in CDPD.

However, if you're trying to roll out a wireless application, don't get caught up in the numbers game. Even though the established service providers have more extensive coverage, it may not match the geographical regions your people will need access from.

Similar to the way cellular phone networks were deployed, wireless data networks have sprung up from within the core of many metropolitan areas and expanded outward. This scenario may not be the best for companies wishing to give users access to corporate resources from the field.

For instance, it's not hard to imagine a field service person needing access to online technical documentation from a customer's home or office in a rural area. This is an excellent use of wireless connections. However, for a company to rely on this method of communications for its technical staffers requires that wireless data services be deployed in the sparsely populated regions of the country—something that may not be the case for your area and the wireless service provider you use.

Speed Improves

Expansion of wireless services into more geographical regions will certainly help remove one obstacle to wide-scale deployment of wireless applications. But others remain.

For many users, the speed of a wireless connection is still an issue. Early users of wireless data services had to accept 4.8-Kbps connections. Many mobile users found such links frustratingly slow, especially if they were accustomed to higher-speed analog modem connections.

The wireless service providers recognized that speed was a limitation and have been improving their offerings. For example, Ardis offers speeds of 19.2 Kbps for users in most large cities (and 4.8-Kbps or higher service for smaller cities). Additionally, CDPD services and those offered by RAM Mobile Data also operate at 19.2 Kbps. Some service providers hope to carve out a niche market for higher-speed wireless services. For example, Metricom Inc. of Los Gatos, California, offers wireless connectivity up to 38.4 Kbps in several metropolitan areas including Seattle; Washington, D.C.; and the Silicon Valley area.

Transmission speed is an important criterion for a wireless connection. You most likely will want the highest-speed service available when connecting from the field. In some ways it's similar to using an analog modem and a phone jack. When making a hard-wired connection, your modem and the modem at the other end of the link negotiate the highest common speed that they can work at. Once this negotiation process is over, away you go.

Unfortunately, that's not the case in the wireless arena. Suppose you had a salesperson on the road who needed a wireless link with your company. If Metricom's 38.4-Kbps service were available, the traveling user could use it. If the service were not available, maybe a 19.2-Kbps CDPD would be available. And if the person got to a small town and neither service were available, he or she could opt for RAM Mobile Data or Ardis' 4.8-Kbps service.

Unless the person has a trunkload of wireless modems, the chances of accomplishing such a feat are small. That is because each type of wireless service requires a different type of modem. Even though all of the major wireless networks, such as Ardis, CDPD, and RAM Mobile Data, operate in adjacent parts of the 800MHz to 900MHz frequency bands, they each use different modulation and transmission methods. That means users tapping into these services must use a different proprietary modem for each.

The joke about having a trunkload of modems isn't that far off. And that's another problem that has slowed deployment of wireless applications. Wireless modems really do take up a lot of space. Until recently, wireless modems were about the size of a brick. So carrying several wouldn't be that practical (in many cases, carrying just one wireless modem wasn't that practical, either).

In March 1995, the first PC Card (at that time they were called PCMCIA) wireless modems were introduced at the Mobile '95 show held in San Jose. That's where IBM and Motorola introduced radio modems in the form of a Type III PCMCIA adapter. The device was a single unit that contained the antenna, as well as the power and signaling equipment to conduct wireless communications. (This was a vast improvement over the existing products. But even such a nifty product had one problem. It seems that it did not work with one of IBM's own laptops—the Butterfly version of its ThinkPad. If you installed the adapter in the slot of a Butterfly and then opened the lid, the keyboard, as it unfolded, caught the antenna and dislodged the modem from the card slot.)

The lack of standardization in access equipment is an obstacle to wide-scale deployment of wireless applications. As noted earlier, in the analog modem and phone jack world, one modem lets you make connections at any speed, and a single modem connects to all public switched-telephone networks regardless of the service provider.

While lack of compatibility is a problem with wireless modems, there is at least some effort toward standardizing the command sets of the modems for the various services. A common modem command set and some wireless APIs (application programming interfaces) are now under development. The Portable Computer and Communications Association (PCCA) has defined a set of common extensions to the traditional TIA-602 AT (Hayes) modem commands. These extensions would be used for wireless modems regardless of the service the modem is attaching to.

Additionally, the PCCA and the WINSock Forum are developing wireless extensions to the two most common network adapter drivers—NDIS (Network Driver Interface Specification) and ODI (Open Data-Link Interface). This effort is to specify common APIs for a wireless environment that would make it easier to run LAN-based applications over wireless networks.

The goal is to make applications networks independent so that users can attach to any of the wireless networks. That would mean that you could supply one user with access to several networks, or that your users in different parts of the country would have access to the regionally available services. In all cases, the same access methods would be used for any one application.

Tightening Integration

In that same vein, several vendors, including CE Software, Motorola, Oracle, Racotek, and Xcellnet, have concentrated on middleware that more tightly integrates existing applications with wireless networks.

The main point about much of the middleware for the wireless market is to take into consideration the low bandwidth of a wireless link. For example, Oracle Corp.'s Oracle in Motion is a network-independent tool that lets a company develop Windows-based wireless applications. The product uses agent technology to reduce the back-and-forth packet traffic that is common with LAN-based client/server applications. Specifically, Oracle in Motion uses an agent on the LAN to query a host.

Some middleware makes Windows applications compatible with the wireless networks. For example, RadioMail's RadioMail Connection for Windows (developed with ConnectSoft) is a wireless communications application that provides a Windows user with mobile messaging capability. (The product is a wireless version of ConnectSoft's E-Mail Connection.) With products such as these, development of wireless applications does not have to be from the ground up. Many existing applications can be left, for the most part, untouched and still be able to run over a wireless connection.

Such developments, along with standardization of APIs and modem command sets, as well as expanded geographical coverage (and higher speed) of the services, should make the move to wireless wide-area networking more manageable.

Matching Wireless Services to Your Applications

As noted earlier in this chapter, there is great potential for wide-scale deployment of wireless technology today. The idea of connectivity from anywhere, untethered, is very appealing.

Some segments of the wireless communications market—cellular phones and pagers, for example—have already been enthusiastically embraced and are considered necessary business tools. Wireless data connections for laptops and personal digital assistants (PDAs) are not nearly as common.

The stumbling blocks to widespread usage have included the lack of ubiquitous service availability, the cost of the services, lack of compatibility between the different wireless services, and the bulkiness and expense of wireless modems.

Even with these obstacles, some early adopters report they've been successful (see "Just the Ticket"). Typically, the early adopters have been companies that provide a service, such as hauling goods across country by truck or sending technicians into the field. And these companies say the productivity gains from using wireless technology yield a return on investment measured in months. Still, wireless faces a fundamental problem: no single major wireless data service is ideal for all applications.

Each of today's main wireless data service contenders (circuit-switched cellular, private packet radio, and Cellular Digital Packet Data) upon which wireless applications will run has strengths and weaknesses for different types of applications. In this section of this chapter I will go through each of the major wireless service offerings and discuss the strengths and weaknesses of each, relative to specific applications. If you cannot wait, Table 5-1 has a quick and dirty summary of the pricing structure, best applications, and advantages and disadvantages for each of the major wireless offerings. Such factors must be considered before selecting one service for a particular application. Choosing a service will not get any easier as new services, such as Personal Communications Services (PCS), bidirectional satellite, and enhanced specialized mobile radio (ESMR), become more widely available.

Type of Service	Data Rates (Kbps)	Pricing Structure	Best For	Advantages	Disadvantages
Circuit-switched cellular	1.2 to 28.8	Billed per minute (typically $.25 to $.40 per minute)	Sending large files and faxes	Available nationwide; reasonably priced for sending long messages	Slow call setup; expensive for sending many short messages
Cellular Digital Packet Data (CDPD)	19.2	Billed per kilobyte (typically $.15 to $.55 per kilobyte)	Transaction processing and database queries	Fast call setup; inexpensive for short messages	Expensive for large file transfers; limited availability
Packet radio	4.8 to 19.2	Billed per kilobyte (typically $.15 to $.25 per kilobyte)	E-mail and sending short, bursty messages	Available nationwide; often has links to commercial e-mail services	Expensive for large file transfers

Table 5-1. *A Look at the Major Wireless Services*

Selecting a wireless service will depend on the application designed to run over that service. For example, if the application primarily relies on the exchange of short, bursty messages, CDPD and private packet radio services such as Ardis and RAM Mobile Data would be your best bet. These services are economical for this type of data transfer, because you are charged by the kilobyte of data transmitted.

On the other hand, if the application requires the exchange of long text messages, large files, or faxes, circuit-switched cellular is a better choice, since a user is typically charged by the minute of connect time and not by the number of bytes transferred

That's a simple example of the considerations that must be examined before selecting a wireless data service. As noted, each service has its strengths and weaknesses for different mixes of traffic. The next three sections will look at the major service offerings in more detail to help you decide which is the best match for your applications.

Circuit-Switched Cellular

Circuit-switched cellular is the wireless service that's probably the most familiar to people. It's the same network that is used for cellular phones. To access the service, users simply connect a laptop with a cellular modem to a cellular phone and they're in business.

One of the biggest advantages to circuit-switched cellular is its availability. Business users in the United States essentially have access to the service nationwide. Another advantage to circuit-switched cellular is that you have both voice and data capabilities, since you're using a cellular phone and the cellular phone network.

The initial cost to outfit a laptop to connect to a circuit-switched cellular network is about $450 to $500. That includes buying a cellular modem (about $300 to $350) and a cellular phone (about $150) that has an adapter to connect the modem.

The cost to send data varies from service provider to service provider. These costs are the same as your cellular phone connectivity charges. Rates for circuit-switched cellular service range from $.25 to $.40 per minute (although volume discounts and long-term sign-up plans can drop this rate substantially).

The throughput rate for circuit-switched cellular, which depends on the speed of the modem, varies from 1.2 to 28.8 Kbps. Since you'll be billed by the minute and not by the byte of data transmitted, it make sense to invest in a high-speed cellular modem.

When selecting a cellular modem, look for one that supports one of the common error-correcting protocols, such as MNP-10 developed by Microcom or the Enhanced Throughput Cellular protocol from AT&T Paradyne. These protocols make the cellular link more efficient by performing services such as automatically lowering transmission speeds when a link is too noisy or when much data is being lost (a situation that requires many retransmissions). These protocols also up the transmission rate when a link is clearer. One note of caution: not all cellular service providers have equipment on their end of the link that supports these protocols. It's best to check with your provider first.

Under what would be considered good circumstances (14.4-Kbps throughput) it should only cost about $.25 to $.40 to send a 10K file. That's one of circuit-switched cellular's great benefits—you can send a large file for a small fee. Unfortunately, per-minute billing can also be a great disadvantage. A 100-byte file will cost about as much to send as a 10K file.

Additionally, in some applications, such as database queries or transaction processing (a wireless point-of-sale terminal or a package delivery service wireless pad), circuit-switched cellular may not be desirable because of the long setup time required for each connection. It takes about 30 seconds to establish a connection.

CDPD

If quick connect times are essential to an application, CDPD may be the answer. It takes about 5 seconds to establish a link. Such quick call setup is important in database query and transaction processing applications. That's not the only advantage of CDPD.

CDPD was conceived by a group of cellular service providers to address the high cost of sending short messages over cellular networks. It essentially transmits packets over unused portions of existing cellular network channels.

CDPD has several advantages over other wireless data services that might make it an attractive choice for many applications. First, it's based on TCP/IP. That means existing network applications that run over TCP/IP should be easily accessible over CDPD. However, modifications must be made to existing TCP/IP applications for them to economically run over CDPD. For example, broadcast and acknowledgment packets need to be filtered and kept off the wireless links.

Because CDPD is relatively new, modems to connect to CDPD networks had been priced significantly higher than their circuit-switched cellular counterparts. However, CDPD modem prices have been dropping, and there are several on the market that are in the $300 to $500 price range (which is comparable to the price of a traditional cellular modem).

Service charges to use CDPD networks vary from provider to provider, but typically it costs between $.15 and $.55 per kilobyte. A common way to pay for the service is to subscribe to a plan that allows you to send a set amount of data for a fixed price. Any additional data sent is charged on a per-kilobyte basis.

The way the pricing is structured, CDPD is most economical for sending many short messages. It can cost as little as $.01 to send an 80-byte file. (It would cost about $.15 to send the same file over circuit-switched cellular, because you're being billed by the minute, not by the kilobyte.)

On the other hand, a long file, such as a 10K spreadsheet, would cost between $1.50 and $5 under the different CDPD pricing plans. (Sending the same file over circuit-switched cellular would be significantly less—about $.25 to $.40.)

That means CDPD is well-suited for sending e-mail and for interactive database queries. That's a good fit for a large segment of the mobile work force. The problem to date with CDPD is the lack of availability of the service and of interoperability. In the second quarter of 1996, CDPD service was only available in about 60 percent of the major metropolitan service areas, according to the CDPD Forum. As noted earlier in the chapter, that translated into CDPD service only reaching about 45 percent of the U.S. population.

This lack of nationwide coverage has been one of the main stumbling blocks to CDPD. Recognizing this, CDPD proponents have come up with a way around the limited geographical coverage of the service. The solution: Circuit Switched CDPD (CS CDPD)—a hybrid service that gives remote users access to CDPD networks through the existing circuit-switched cellular network. The advantage of CS CDPD is that it extends the effective area of coverage of CDPD. As a manager, you can look at this extension in two ways. First, assume you are rolling out applications that run over a CDPD network and that some of your users travel to regions that do not have the service. These users can take advantage of CDPD services when they are available. In regions where the service is unavailable, they can still access the same applications using traditional cellular technology. A second way to look at this is that you can roll out a CDPD-enabled application to your entire company even if there are offices in locations where no CDPD service is available. The idea is that you can develop one remote access application that can be used by all of your remote users who need wireless access to your network.

To accomplish such levels of connectivity, CS CDPD uses two mechanisms to link remote users. First, there is the Circuit Switched Mobile Data Intermediate System (CMD-IS). Mobile users communicate into the CMD-IS through a modem bank, which supports circuit-switched data connections through the common cellular phone system. The modem bank also supports connection through your regular wired-telephone connections.

The second mechanism in a CS CDPD network is the Circuit Switched CDPD Control Protocol (CSCCP). In a hybrid cellular/CDPD system, CSCCP helps manage the call connection by transferring the call management data between the circuit-switched cellular and CDPD systems. The upshot is that circuit-switched cellular systems, which are fairly pervasive, can be used as an access point into CDPD systems when there are no regional entry points.

Packet Radio

Still, the main drawback to CDPD today is its limited availability. This can be a serious problem for an organization needing wireless data service on a nationwide basis. For companies that need such widespread connectivity, another type of wireless packetized data service—private packet radio—might be a good match.

There are two major private packet radio providers in the United States: Ardis and RAM Mobile Data. Users can connect to these services virtually from anywhere in the United States. Besides widespread availability, private packet radio has other advantages. It offers quick call setup time and is well-suited to applications that generate short, bursty traffic. This includes, for example, e-mail, database queries, and point-of-sale applications.

Because private packet radio has been around for several years, many vertical applications have been developed to ride over the network. For example, there are several sales force automation programs for Ardis and RAM that include messaging, scheduling, and electronic filing of expense reports. Additionally, there are applications that give real estate agents access to listing services, as well as applications that allow insurance agents to process accident claim forms at a customer's home or office.

Organizations rolling out wireless applications that run over Ardis or RAM find the pricing of the service is fairly attractive. It costs about $.25 per kilobyte to transmit messages. However, both Ardis and RAM offer volume discounts.

Developments in modems for private packet radio are also making the service more attractive. Previously, one of the biggest drawbacks to using any wireless data service was the size of the modems. The devices needed large amounts of power (compared with your traditional analog line modem) and thus were fairly large and bulky to accommodate the power equipment.

Just the Ticket

Most activities in service organizations revolve around paper-based *trouble tickets*. A worker goes into the office in the morning and a dispatcher hands him or her a piece of paper listing the first job of the day.

Once that job is completed, the worker calls into the office, and the dispatcher closes out the trouble ticket and directs the technician to his or her next assignment. Typically, the technician in the field spends 20 to 60 minutes on the phone each day conducting these chores.

Access into a trouble-ticket system is one area that seems ideally suited for wireless technology. Several companies with large service organizations—Sears, for example—have made the move to wireless.

Sears is equipping 14,000 of its service technicians nationwide with laptops and wireless modems. Using a wireless connection over the Ardis network, the service technicians will be able to peruse a parts database, send questions to other technicians in the field, and send and receive information about the current and next service call.

Sears' current system for handling service orders and dispatching technicians is paper-based and requires the technician to call a dispatcher after each service call. With the wireless laptop, the technician can close a service order once a job is completed and receive his or her next assignment. Sears believes productivity will increase 10 percent by virtue of the better scheduling afforded by use of the wireless units.

Thanks to some semiconductor developments for radio transmission equipment, wireless modems with much lower power consumption requirements can now be built.

In 1995, the first PC Card wireless modems for the Ardis network were introduced by Eiger Labs and IBM Networking Systems. At about the same time, Motorola introduced the first single-piece PC Card radio modem for Ardis, the Personal Messenger 100D, which is a self-contained Type 2 PC Card that runs on NiCd (Nickel Cadmium) or a 9-volt alkaline battery.

Such modems were among the first to support faster data rates. Previously, a major disadvantage of using private packet radio was its slow speed—typically 4.8 Kbps, but as low as 2.4 Kbps. Now, however, Ardis has started to offer 19.2-Kbps rates in many large urban areas.

On the Horizon

For companies developing large-scale wireless applications, waiting for higher-speed service to be deployed or for CDPD to be rolled out may not be an option. As such, some companies are evaluating new services that might be more rapidly deployed.

Among the newer services becoming available are enhanced specialized mobile radio (ESMR), bidirectional satellite, and a wireless spread-spectrum system based on Code Division Multiple Access (CDMA). Each of these services has strengths that other wireless services lack. However, the main disadvantage of each is lack of widespread availability.

For example, ESMR is an all-digital voice and data network that operates at 4.8 Kbps and is available primarily on the West Coast. With ESMR, a digital data stream is sent to a radio base station from which it is carried over the public network. And wireless CDMA, which will first be offered as a voice communications service, has the potential of offering very high data rates (up to 76 Kbps).

These alternatives are still a long way off (at least when it comes to wide-scale deployment). There are, however, wireless alternatives—bidirectional satellite, PCS, and wireless ISDN—that you should become familiar with and follow the deployment of, because they are poised to possibly take off.

Emerging Satellite Systems

There are two types of satellite-based systems—each of which fits a niche market for wireless connectivity. The first type of system uses *geostationary satellites* (satellites that orbit the Earth at the same rate as the Earth turns, thus giving the appearance of being "fixed" in a position at one spot above the Earth). Some satellite companies have developed data services using these geostationary satellites. However, even the best need an antenna about a foot or two in diameter to pick up the signal. For example, Hughes Network Systems offers DirectPC, a service that uses what some call an ultrasmall aperture terminal to send and receive data between a PC and a satellite. The "ultra" is in contrast to "very" as in VSAT (Very Small Aperture Terminal), which is on the order of several meters in diameter. Still, even the smallest antennas are impractical to use if a person is moving around. While antenna size is the disadvantage, the advantage to a geostationary satellite system is that one satellite can essentially give you coverage for the entire country. Three satellites can, in theory, provide global coverage.

Typically, a company uses such a satellite system to connect users in remote regions (really remote, meaning no phone lines), or it is used for temporary network connections (for a three-day conference, for example). Satellite-based connections are also good when other services are disrupted by severe weather or disasters. Such satellite systems are used infrequently.

Low-Earth Orbiting Systems

The second type of satellite-based system uses *low-Earth orbiting satellites.* There are several differences between such a system and one that uses geostationary satellites. The differences have consequences for you and your mobile users.

First, low-Earth orbiting satellites orbit the Earth in much less time than a geostationary satellite. Depending on the altitude of the satellite, a low-Earth orbiting satellite might complete one orbit of the Earth in anywhere from 45 to 90 minutes. That means the satellite is not always over the same point on Earth. Thus, to guarantee a mobile user can make a connection requires multiple satellites orbiting the Earth. One planned system, called Iridium (proposed by Motorola) requires 66 satellites in low-Earth orbit to provide worldwide coverage.

The practical consequence of this for you as a manager interested in this technology is that it takes time to deploy lots of satellites. So services based on a system such as Iridium will take time to become available and will not be ready for wide-scale use for a few years.

The large number of satellites required for a low-Earth orbiting data delivery system is definitely an inhibitor to such services becoming available. However, the potential benefits from a low-Earth orbiting satellite system make it interesting. For example, because the satellites will only be a couple of hundred miles above the Earth's surface (instead of many thousands of miles as is the case when communicating with a geostationary satellite), the signal from a satellite to a user on the ground is fairly strong compared with the signal coming from a geostationary satellite. A stronger signal means you can use a much smaller antenna to receive the signal. On the transmission part of a system, you can get away with a smaller transmitter—that means a smaller power supply. The combination of a smaller antenna and smaller power supply means the units used to send and receive data can be small compared with the antennas used to communicate with geostationary satellites.

PCS on the Way

Another wireless alternative that should be getting some attention soon is PCS (Personal Communications Services). PCS commonly is used to refer to the slew of wireless services that will be offered as a result of the U.S. government's auctioning of commercial licenses to use the higher (with respect to cellular) portion of the wireless spectrum. Typically, PCS systems will operate in the 1.5 to 2GHz portion of the wireless spectrum (in contrast, cellular operates in the 800 to 900MHz frequency range).

As these nationwide and regionalized services start to become available in the next year or two, the choice of a wireless data service will become even more tricky. Since no one service will be the perfect match in all cases, the best approach is to closely match the attributes of a particular wireless data service to the most commonly used applications.

There are two types of PCS services—*narrowband* and *broadband.* Narrowband services, as the name implies, offer limited bandwidth. But narrowband PCS services can be national in their coverage. Narrowband services would include such things as voice paging, two-way paging, and some data services. In fall 1996, AT&T became the first carrier to offer a nationwide, digital wireless service that offered narrowband PCS-type services. The AT&T Digital PCS offering included common digital phone services like caller ID, voice mail, text message, and alpha and numeric paging. (Technically, AT&T's offering is not PCS, since it runs over the company's cellular network, which operates in the 800MHz part of the wireless spectrum. However, AT&T said it planned to move these services to the typical PCS spectrum band of 1.9GHz in 1997.)

The other type of PCS service is broadband PCS. In contrast to narrowband, broadband services are intended to provide services that require higher bandwidth with regional, rather than nationwide, coverage. For example, one application of broadband PCS services would be to provide a wireless link for PDAs (personal digital assistants), where voice, data, and images could be carried over the PCS network. Doesn't this sound like Dick Tracy's wrist-radio?

Wireless ISDN

As I discussed in Chapter 3, one of the great limitations to using ISDN service is that deployment of the service has been particularly slow in some regions of the country. To provide ISDN service, a carrier or regional Bell operating company must upgrade old central office switches to support ISDN. And in some cases, this process has just not happened. Additionally, in Chapter 3, I mentioned that there is a distance limitation with ISDN service—your telecommuter must be within 18,000 feet of a telco's ISDN-enabled switches. That makes ISDN impractical (at least from a telecommunications service provider's perspective) in many rural areas.

One way around both issues—the lack of deployment by the telco and the distance limitation—would be wireless delivery of ISDN services. As luck would have it, some folks are actually working on just that. A new type of ISDN, called *ISDN Radio,* is starting to emerge.

There are two types of ISDN Radio service: satellite and radio. With the satellite version, a small office or home is equipped with a Very Small Aperture Terminal (VSAT) to send and receive traffic to and from a satellite over leased or call-based satellite channels. This type of service overcomes problems with RBOC deployment of ISDN service and the distance limitation issue. Additionally, such a satellite-based service is essentially available nationwide, even in remote areas where traditional phone service is not available.

A Line to God?

When I was an editor at *Byte Magazine,* Jeffrey Fritz, a telecom engineer, ISDN expert, and author, wrote an article about ISDN Radio and got one of the most interesting letters I have ever seen. A Brother from a monastery located in a desert in the southwestern United States wrote asking about this service. It seems the monastery was so far out of the way that electrical and phone lines did not run to the location. The Brothers used laptops (they used solar panels to recharge batteries and things like that) and cellular connections to check e-mail. But they needed higher-speed access to surf the Web (the monastery had a web site hosted at another location).

Your remote sites probably aren't that isolated, but you can see where ISDN Radio service would be quite beneficial if your sites are off the beaten path.

The radio version of the service is comparable to traditional radio broadcasting systems that provide drive-time traffic reports, sports coverage, and even an occasional song or two. Radio delivery of ISDN typically uses an antenna and a low-powered (one watt or less) transmitter. The use of a low-powered system means you (or the service provider offering the service) do not need an FCC (Federal Communications Commission) license, as would be the case for conventional radio systems. While the range of a satellite ISDN delivery system is nationwide, radio-based systems are limited to about 30 miles, depending on the height of the antenna used to deliver the signal and the terrain (radio systems are line-of-sight systems, so if you have something like mountains or many tall buildings between a remote site and the transmitting antenna, the signal would be blocked).

Both the satellite and radio-based versions of ISDN Radio would solve some of ISDN's nagging deployment issues. Such service can be established quickly—typically within 24 hours. So it can be used in situations where you might have needed ISDN's bandwidth, but would never have considered using the service. One such situation is to provide emergency connectivity to a site when there is a disaster, such as a hurricane or flooding, that wipes out terrestrial service. You could even use wireless ISDN for ad hoc networks, such as for a one-day event at a site that does not have ISDN service (or that would take too much effort to set up terrestrial service for one day).

Both forms of ISDN Radio systems have some disadvantages. They require more equipment than wired systems. And they require technicians with the knowledge of radio or satellite systems to maintain them. Additionally, satellite time can be expensive. And finally, satellite systems have inherent delays. A single hop from one user to a satellite and down to another station can introduce a delay of 260 milliseconds (ms) or 520ms for a complete two-way exchange. (The delay is due to the great distance the signal must travel to reach a geostationary satellite and then to send the signal back to the ground.) That's in contrast to 10ms delays in terrestrial domestic ISDN circuits and at most 140ms delays for international ground-based and underwater circuits.

A 520ms delay can be annoying for voice applications (if you've ever had a conversation over a satellite link, you know the delay can throw off the natural flow of a conversation). With data transmissions, the problem can move from annoying to disastrous. For example, the network protocol might believe that the link is down if the delay is excessive. Or, a slow network response might result in unneeded retransmissions.

Advanced Communications Technology Satellite (ACTS)

One of the more interesting demonstrations of satellite-based wireless communications technology is under way thanks to NASA. The agency's Advanced Communications Technology Satellite (ACTS), which was launched by the Space Shuttle in September 1993, is testing new communications technologies. One of the areas of tests involves delivery of ISDN services over satellite. NASA has connected ACTS and terrestrial ISDN circuits through a terminal in Cleveland. One experiment undertaken is between the Jet Propulsion Labs (JPL) and CBS Radio that is demonstrating the ability to deliver high-quality audio transmissions over ISDN. The North American ISDN Users' Forum (NIU-F) has been testing a PC-based multimedia teleconferencing system over a VSAT connection between NASA's Lewis Research Center, the JPL, and other sites. Other applications being tested include the ability to establish satellite-based ISDN service as a disaster recovery service.

Wrapping It Up

All of this might seem rather confusing. It is. There is no clear way to go when trying to link remote users through wireless communications links. The difficulties that have long prevented wide-scale deployment of wireless applications—low bandwidth, nonubiquitousness of the services, the difficulty of getting existing applications to work over wireless links, and the nonstandardization of equipment—continue to plague managers looking to deploy wireless applications on a nationwide basis.

While there has certainly been much progress in wireless service offerings and equipment in the last few years, there is still room for much more improvement. As a result, you will likely find that for the next few years, wireless is a niche solution for your remote connectivity needs.

Chapter Six

xDSL

The need to provide remote users with higher-speed access, particularly for surfing the World Wide Web, is causing a problem for many companies. As I have discussed in earlier chapters, traditional modem technology does not offer the speed needed for some applications. And while ISDN seems to be a very good choice when remote users need higher-speed access, the delay by the telcos in deploying the service and the difficulty of configuring ISDN termination equipment placed in a user's home or remote office have caused many companies to look for alternatives. For them, that alternative might come from a class of telecommunications access services called *DSL* (Digital Subscriber Line). DSL services promise to deliver data over your common two-wire twisted pair phone lines at rates of up to 6 or 8 Mbps.

Early demonstrations of DSL technology gave people a glance at the technology's potential. For example, one of the first public demonstrations of DSL technology took place in March 1995 at the CeBIT trade show, which is held annually in Hanover, Germany. At that show, Orckit Communications Ltd. (Tel-Aviv, Israel) transmitted video from an NTSC videotape player at 8 Mbps downstream (with a 640-Kbps upstream channel) using a pair of DSL modems. To put that into perspective, a 6.2 Mbps downstream DSL link would be able to support four channels of compressed MPEG video. That is quite impressive considering the system used copper wires.

There are several flavors of DSL technology, so I will refer to the class of services based on DSL as *xDSL*, where the *x* stands for one of the different types of service. Before I get into the types of offerings, I want to discuss xDSL technology, explaining what it is, how it works, and how it could be used to provide your remote users with high-speed access. Then I will go into the different types of xDSL services and discuss the types of applications and networking environments that are best suited to each.

What Is xDSL?

The basic concept with xDSL technology is that it offers high-speed data delivery by overcoming the inherent bandwidth limitations of an analog phone line connection. This is accomplished by encoding the signal and transmitting that signal in digital form between a telco's central office switch and a remote user's home or office. (Normal voice traffic, in contrast, passes over the same portion of the telephone network as an analog signal.) That segment of a user's connection is called the *local loop* or the *subscriber loop*—thus, the name of these technologies: Digital Subscriber Line (DSL).

As shown in Figure 6-1, to access DSL services, the typical setup in a remote user's home or office would require a DSL modem (some call it a "transceiver"). A user would need an Ethernet adapter card in his or her desktop computer and a cable to link the DSL modem to the Ethernet adapter card. The DSL modem in some cases would also have a telephone jack to which your remote users would connect their existing telephone or fax machines.

Sending the signal in digital format over the subscriber loop lets you achieve higher data rates than is possible with analog connections, because you can send data over a larger portion of the available spectrum—the spectrum your copper wires can support. Phone conversations and modem transfers use only a fraction of the spectrum—4KHz out of 1MHz—that can be used to send data over your common two-wire twisted pair copper phone line. The next section, "Breaking the Limit," explains in detail why the higher frequencies are not normally used. For now I will just say that the conversion of the signal to digital format lets you use a larger portion of the total available spectrum for transmitting data, and that allows xDSL systems to achieve much higher data transfer rates than you get with modems.

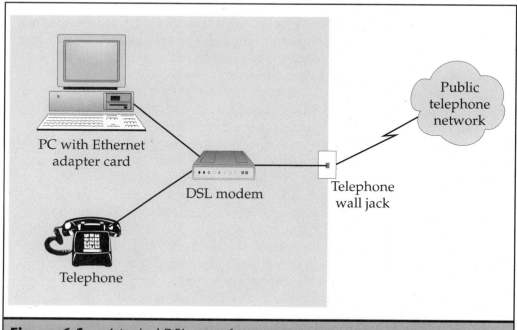

Figure 6-1.   *A typical DSL setup for a remote user*

xDSL technology is not new. It was developed several years ago by the telcos as a way to compete with cable TV companies. Specifically, the telcos were looking for a way to deliver video-on-demand. The telcos figured they would hit the cable companies in an area where huge amounts of revenue were anticipated. That market was video-on-demand—specifically, how to deliver video-on-demand services to homes. This led to many fiber-to-the-home trials by the telcos and the cable TV operators. Most of the trials showed that the technology to deliver high bandwidth to each home was there, but installing fiber to each house was not a cost-effective method. Bringing fiber to the home is still a hotly debated topic. Many fiber-based alternatives, such as fiber-to-the-curb or -pedestal, where fiber is deployed to a location near a home, and copper is used for the last few hundred feet of the link, are still being considered by both telecommunications companies and cable TV operators.

But even these systems require some expensive changes by the telcos. If there were only some way to use the existing infrastructure—the two-wire twisted pair copper wires that provide phone service to most homes and offices—the telcos figured they would not need to go to the expense of running fiber to or near every home. For video-on-demand, it was noted that there was an asymmetry—the user needed to send commands in one direction (upstream) to control a large downstream flow of data. (A similar asymmetry exists with Web surfing.) Thus began the search by the telcos for a way to deliver video over the existing copper phone lines that make up the bulk of the public telephone network infrastructure.

Note that the cable TV operators do not have a problem with delivering high bandwidth. Their predominately coaxial cable-based systems support much higher bandwidth than the copper wire used for telephone service. But the cable companies have problems giving users the upstream data path to control the delivery. Even today, you typically have to dial a phone number to get a pay-per-view video. The next chapter will discuss cable access to high-speed data and the ways the cable TV industry is trying to resolve its problems in this area so that a user may have two-way communications over a cable system.

As the telcos developed technology that would allow video-on-demand, the ability to offer other services became potentially more lucrative. Specifically, remote users needed high-speed access to the Internet and multimedia applications such as corporate videos (particularly videos and multimedia presentations for training, which are increasingly becoming important parts of business life).

Thus, the technology developed for video-on-demand to compete with the cable TV companies was seen as a revenue generator for the telcos. (Ironically, while all of this was going on, the cable TV folks moved into the data delivery arena—which, as noted earlier, is the subject of the next chapter.)

To date, there are five different xDSL services outlined in Table 6-1, being proposed by the telcos. The common thread among the different xDSL services is that they all offer the high-speed delivery of information over the same copper wires that carry your normal telephone traffic. That's the main advantage of xDSL—it uses the wiring infrastructure that exists today. (Some of the xDSL alternatives use a single two-wire pair, others use more. The specifics for each xDSL are discussed later in this chapter.) For most remote users, there will be no need to update the wiring to their homes in order for the users to take advantage of services based on DSL.

Type of xDSL Service	Typical Use	Maximum Data Rates
ADSL—Asymmetric DSL	High-speed access for remote user	Up to 8 Mbps downstream; up to 1 Mbps upstream
HDSL—High-speed DSL	High-speed link between two corporate sites	2.048 Mbps (more likely 768 Kbps)
RADSL—Rate Adaptive DSL	High-speed access for remote user	600 Kbps to 12 Mbps downstream; 128 Kbps to 1 Mbps upstream
SDSL—Symmetric DSL	High-speed access for remote user	160 Kbps to 2.048 Mbps
VDSL—Very-high-speed DSL	Video-on-demand (over limited distances)	Up to 51 Mbps downstream; up to 2 Mbps upstream

Table 6-1. *The Types of xDSL Service*

You might wonder how this can be accomplished. After all, we frequently hear that high-speed modems (at first "high-speed" meant 28.8-Kbps modems, and now it refers to 33.6-Kbps modems) are pushing the inherent limits of our analog lines. And there are indeed limits—specifically, there is a 4KHz bandwidth limit on analog phone lines. At least that's what we've all been told. Well, the limit is real, but the telcos have gotten around the limit by changing the fundamental assumptions.

Breaking the Limit

When I first heard about xDSL, I was puzzled. This idea of sending data at multi-megabit per second rates over copper lines seemed a bit odd to me. What I didn't understand was how it was possible to get 6- or 8-Mbps rates over a copper line, when I seldom get 28.8 Kbps with a modem. The explanation from most folks was perplexing. Rather than have you go through the same difficulty, I figured it was worth going into the details before I covered xDSL deployment issues and the cost of the services.

How It's Done

The copper wire running between a user's home and a telco's central office is capable of using a broader range of frequencies to carry data than the 4KHz typically used to carry analog voice traffic. Generally, the wire can support transmissions over frequencies up to about 1MHz for the wire lengths— between 12,000 and 18,000 feet—commonly used today. However, the problem with using the higher frequencies is that there is lots of signal loss, and the lines are susceptible to noise at the higher frequencies.

Because of the signal loss, noise, and interference problems, the telcos limit the portion of the spectrum they use to carry analog traffic to a 4KHz band. The way the telcos impose this 4KHz limitation of an analog line is derived from NyQuist's Theorem, which says that the sampling rate of an analog signal must be twice the highest frequency component of the system. The telephone companies use line cards within their central office switches to convert between the analog and digital signals in their system. The analog signal is carried between your home and the switch; the digital signal is carried over the telco's network. The analog-to-digital converter line cards sample the analog signal at a rate of 8,000 times per second (8KHz). That means the highest frequency supported is 4KHz (the NyQuist Theorem limit for analog lines).

xDSL technologies use higher frequencies to send data at a higher rate. To do this, an xDSL system does not use the analog-to-digital line card converters used for your normal telephone lines. Instead, the telcos use special line cards that employ sophisticated digital signal-processing techniques to squeeze more out of the line. Basically, the developers of xDSL equipment leverage the processing power of Digital Signal Processors (DSPs)—power that has increased significantly thanks to developments in microprocessor technology. (In a way, this is similar to the discussion in Chapter 2 on Intel getting more out of analog lines by leveraging the processing boost of its MMX technology incorporated into its Pentium processors so that a system using the chip can run videoconferencing over analog phone lines.)

The practical consequence of the telcos using special line cards is that xDSL services are suitable for stationary remote users—telecommuters and users in remote offices—but not suitable for mobile workers. The remote user must connect to a port on a telco's central office switch that is equipped with an appropriate line card. (I'll talk more about this later in this chapter's sections on deploying the various xDSL services.)

Besides tapping the processing power of DSPs, the other thing that is required to get data over a copper line at the higher rates is to use the available spectrum more intelligently. How you divide the spectrum and optimize its use is a matter of some debate. There are two main approaches: Carrierless Amplitude/Phase (CAP) modulation and Discrete Multitone (DMT) line encoding. CAP and DMT take different approaches to using the higher frequencies needed to send data at the higher effective transfer rates of xDSL systems.

DMT is similar to Frequency Division Multiplexing (FDM), where the 1MHz spectrum available over a twisted pair phone line is parsed into 4KHz channels. The basic idea is to divide the higher frequency part of the spectrum (the part above the 4KHz normally used for analog) into components (called *subchannels*) and send data over each component of the spectrum based on that component's ability to carry a signal. "Good" components get more bits to carry; components that are affected by noise get fewer (or no) bits to carry. (The "goodness" of a subchannel is measured by the signal-to-noise ratio.) That's how xDSL gets around the signal degradation and noise problems of using the higher frequencies. Bits of data are distributed over the different channels to overcome noise or interference problems that may plague that portion of the spectrum. In this way, channels that are susceptible to heavy noise are, in essence, avoided. This makes DMT more robust than CAP when noise is present on lines, according to DMT proponents.

CAP, on the other hand, is based on Quadrature Amplitude/Phase Modulation (QAM), which has been used in modems for more than 20 years. Rather than subdividing the 1MHz spectrum into discrete 4KHz channels, CAP uses the entire channel. CAP relies on the amplitude modulation and phase shift of a signal to take advantage of the higher frequencies (higher than your normal 4KHz used for voice) to deliver data at higher rates.

One bone of contention in the industry has to do with which of these two signal-encoding schemes to use. Many telecommunications carriers have opted for GlobeSpan Technologies Inc.'s (formerly AT&T Paradyne's) Carrierless Amplitude/Phase (CAP) modulation technique. But DMT is specified as part of an American National Standards Institute (ANSI) standard for some DSL technologies.

It comes down to the following: CAP is easier to implement, and CAP-based equipment has been used in many of the early field trials. However, CAP is based on proprietary technology and is more susceptible to noise. DMT, on the other hand, is more resilient when operating over noisy lines and is based on an ANSI standard. However, early on it lacked the support of the major telcos (something that has since changed).

So which is best for your users? Throughout this chapter, as I discuss each of the xDSL services, I will point out the differences in performance (if any) that your remote users would experience using equipment that supports CAP versus DMT. However, the issue may be moot for two reasons. First, some equipment vendors may support both methods in the same device. Second, and perhaps more importantly, it may not matter to you because of the way xDSL equipment will be sold. It may turn out that you will only be able to get xDSL modems (some call them transceivers) that connect to your phone jack from the provider offering the xDSL service. If that is the case, which encoding method used is the service provider's issue to deal with, not yours.

ABCs of xDSL

To get a better understanding of high-speed delivery over copper wire, we must first define the numerous xDSL technologies. Services based on these technologies are starting to emerge, are in field trials, or are already being offered on a limited basis.

As noted earlier in the chapter, there are five xDSL services. Some are more suitable for your corporate connectivity needs than others. Three types of service, ADSL (Asymmetric Digital Subscriber Line), SDSL (Symmetric DSL), and RADSL (Rate Adaptive DSL), are designed to give your remote users high-speed access to data (be it for Internet Web surfing, retrieving corporate data, or accessing multimedia presentations). Another service, HDSL (High-speed DSL), is aimed at providing high-speed alternatives to T1 and ISDN lines for linking corporate sites. And the last flavor of xDSL service, VDSL (Very-high-speed DSL), is aimed, at least for now, primarily at the consumer video-on-demand market. However, VDSL might also be used to provide high-speed Internet access.

ADSL

ADSL systems offer high-speed data rates by using more (compared with a normal voice signal) of the spectrum available to transmit data over a two-wire twisted pair copper wire phone line. With an ADSL system, a telecommuter or user in a remote office gets three channels over a single line. Essentially, the 1MHz spectrum available over a copper phone line is split into three channels. Figure 6-2 shows that the first channel is the traditional 4KHz band used for voice. Also in Figure 6-2, you can see that a second channel provides a low-speed upstream channel for data to travel from the user's location to a telco's central office switch or to an Internet service provider's (ISP's) point of presence (POP). A third channel is available to carry high-speed traffic downstream from the telco's switch or ISP's POP.

The data transfer rate that the upstream and downstream channels support varies with the encoding mechanism used and the maximum distance over which the signal must pass. For example, ADSL systems using DMT can support a maximum downstream rate of 8 Mbps, while a CAP ADSL system supports a downstream rate of up to 7 Mbps. Both encoding methods support a maximum upstream rate in the 640 Kbps to 1 Mbps range, depending on the implementation and the system's deployment. In other words, in the best-case scenario, ADSL offers a data transfer rate of about 235 times that of a 33.6-Kbps modem. That means a graphic-heavy web page that takes six minutes to display by use of a high-speed modem would take less than two seconds with ADSL. Thus, you can see the appeal of this speed boost for Web surfing.

An ADSL link is very sensitive to the distance between a remote user's home or office and a telco's central office. An ADSL system that delivers 6 Mbps downstream when the distance is 12,000 feet or less, will only deliver 1.5 Mbps downstream if that distance is extended to 18,000 feet. In the United States, only about 50 percent of all homes are within 12,000 feet of a telco central office. So that might be a consideration when you are planning to link users with ADSL. Obviously, in densely populated areas, such as the northeast

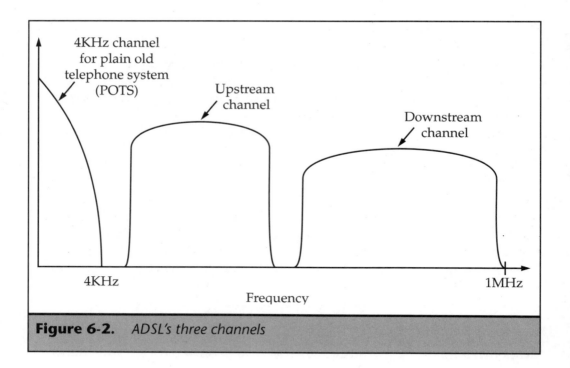

Figure 6-2. *ADSL's three channels*

corridor of the United States from Boston to Washington, D.C., and other metropolitan regions, this is usually not an issue. But in rural areas, the distance might be a factor, and ADSL systems in those regions might not be able to support the very high data rates (on the order of 8 Mbps). If that's the case, users in those regions might be better served by other access technologies. But as I have described in other chapters, your rural users might not be served by most new connectivity services. That is because other services, such as ISDN and wireless services, have typically been deployed first in the major metropolitan regions of the United States.

In Western Europe, where ADSL is also a hot technology, the distance limitations may not be as much of a concern. By some estimates, the number of homes within 12,000 feet of a telco's central office ranges from a high of 95 percent in Italy to 80 percent in Germany.

This discussion of the trade-offs between speed and distance may not concern you in the long run. You may find that, when using ADSL, your telecommunications service provider or your ISP will set the data rates based on the characteristics of their systems.

SDSL

Symmetric DSL (SDSL), as the name implies, gives users the same data rate in both directions. As with ADSL, your remote users get the higher speeds when telecommunications and Internet service provider companies exploit more of the spectrum available on copper lines.

Typically, an SDSL system will provide two channels for communications over a two-wire twisted pair copper phone line. Figure 6-3 shows that one channel would carry voice and would use the normal 4KHz frequency band. Also in the figure, you can see that the other channel would provide a bidirectional high-speed link using a large portion of the available spectrum (up to 1MHz) to transmit the data.

Similar to an ADSL link, SDSL connections are sensitive to the distances over which data must pass from a telco's central office switch to a remote user's home or office. For example, SDSL equipment from GlobeSpan Technologies will deliver 2.048 Mbps at distances of up to 8,000 feet; 400 Kbps

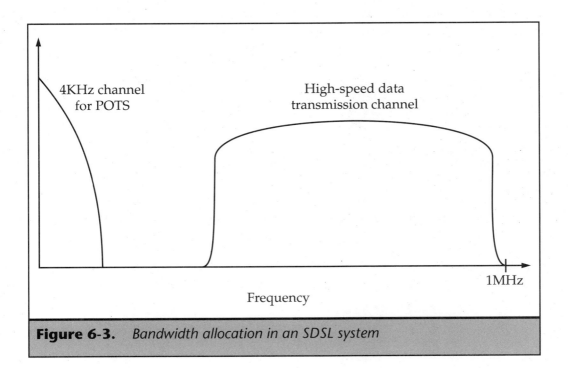

Figure 6-3. *Bandwidth allocation in an SDSL system*

at distances of up to 21,000 feet; and 160 Kbps at distances of up to 23,000 feet. These rate-distance combinations include the delivery of a normal voice channel and can be modified somewhat if the phone channel is not required. For example, a 2.048 Mbps rate can be delivered over 9,000 feet if your plain old telephone system (POTS) channel is not required. That is an additional 1,000 feet for that data delivery rate compared with a system that supports POTS.

The way these services are provisioned can give you some flexibility in the types of applications supported. For example, the 400 Kbps service might be provisioned as switched 384 Kbps service for videoconferencing and a POTS line.

RADSL

The next form of xDSL technology is called Rate Adaptive DSL (RADSL). In June 1996, what was then AT&T Paradyne (Largo, Florida) announced a technology it called GlobeSpan RADSL, aimed at providing high-speed Internet access along with a simultaneous voice service on a single telephone line. Since that announcement, AT&T Paradyne has become GlobeSpan Technologies Inc. and has provided more details about RADSL.

Like ADSL, GlobeSpan RADSL is an asymmetric service offering a downstream rate of from 600 Kbps to 7 Mbps (depending on the implementation) and an upstream rate of from 128 Kbps to 1 Mbps. In other words, in the best-case scenario, RADSL offers a data transfer rate of about 200 times that of a 33.6-Kbps modem. As was the case with ADSL, that means a graphic-heavy web page that takes six minutes to display would take less than two seconds with RADSL.

The difference between ADSL and RADSL is that with RADSL the highest attainable speed varies. In the case of the GlobeSpan RADSL technology, the transmission speed adjusts based on the signal quality and length of the telephone line that the signal is traveling over. RADSL equipment will be able to automatically select the highest practical operating rate (or this could be set by the service provider).

The greater the distance the signal has to pass over to go between the telco's central office and your remote user's home or office, the lower the maximum rate (and as is the case with any telecom situation, it is not the geographical distance between the central office and the user's location, rather, it is the length of the wire). A noisier line means the highest attainable downstream data rate is lower. However, the delivery rate can vary. In a way, this is similar to a traditional modem. Modems will automatically adjust their rate while establishing a session (and during a session with some modems) depending on the quality of the line between the two ends of a link.

HDSL

So far the discussion about xDSL services has focused on those services aimed at giving the remote user higher bandwidth over existing copper phone lines. This section discusses High-speed DSL (HDSL) service, which is geared to another market altogether. HDSL, which sometimes goes by the name "High bit rate DSL," is designed to provide a high-speed connection between two sites.

HDSL came out of some research work conducted by Bell Communications Research (Bellcore) in the late 1980s. At that time, the telecommunications carriers were looking for a better way to provision T1 services (and E1 services in Europe). Basically, the telcos wanted to reduce the number of repeaters required to deliver T1 service to users. The telcos also wanted to improve the way a T1 link was set up. The result of the research was a Bellcore specification for HDSL.

Bellcore developed a modulation technique that would allow you to carry data at higher rates by using a larger portion of the available spectrum. HDSL uses what is called "two binary, one quaternary (2B1Q)" modulation to transmit a signal at frequencies from 80KHz to 240KHz. That is in contrast to the 1.5MHz band of frequencies used by a traditional T1 link.

By use of this modulation method, HDSL gives a telecommunications company a way to offer you T1 service (1.544 Mbps) in the United States, or E1 service (2.048 Mbps) in Europe over multiple pairs of copper wires (more on this in the deployment section).

VDSL

While equipment vendors and telcos started rolling out ADSL, SDSL, RADSL, and HDSL products and services in 1996, work was also under way on Very-high-speed DSL (VDSL), a service that some consider to be the next generation of ADSL. VDSL promises to deliver even higher bandwidth than ADSL over existing copper phone lines.

Already, several semiconductor manufacturers, including Analog Devices and Motorola, have developed signal processing chips for a version of ADSL that would operate at either 25.6 or 51 Mbps. The higher bit rates of 51 Mbps or 25.6 Mbps for VDSL are possible because the encoding technology is only to be used over shorter distances. As noted earlier in the chapter, ADSL encoding technology for interactive multimedia via twisted pair copper wire telephone lines is now limited to about 8 Mbps downstream and up to 2 Mbps upstream for distances of up to about 12,000 feet (that is, the distance from the central office switch to the remote user's home or office).

With VDSL the 51-Mbps rates would be possible at distances of about 1,000 feet, while 25.6-Mbps operation would be supported at 3,000 to 4,000 feet. So while the current 8-Mbps ADSL encoding technology is being evaluated in field trials as an end-to-end system, VDSL will be used for niche applications that depend largely on the subscriber base and video services being delivered. Specifically, because of these distance limitations, the new VDSL technology, which some call "Very high bit rate DSL," will be used in conjunction with fiber-to-the-curb projects currently being deployed by the telcos to deliver multiple video-on-demand and cable TV-like services to the home. Such systems offer higher bandwidths by bringing fiber optic cabling to the curb of a residence or business and then, as shown in Figure 6-4, using existing copper connections to get from the curb to the home. In such a setup, VDSL is used over the last part of the connection—the segment that goes from a telco's fiber optic-based network to a user's home.

xDSL Deployment Issues and Costs

Now that I have described the basic characteristics of each of the xDSL services, I will go into deployment and cost issues. However, before I proceed, I want to point out one thing: xDSL is at a point where it could explode onto the scene, or it could be like ISDN and wireless services—services that were highly touted, held much promise, but never (at least up to now) really became as well-established and pervasive as many had expected them to be. For now, xDSL seems to be *the* technology of the next few years for providing users with high-speed access. Whether the promise of the xDSL technologies comes to fruition will depend on the ability of the telcos and Internet service providers to deploy these services and on the rates they charge for the services.

The next section of this chapter will look at the deployment and cost issues associated with the different xDSL technologies. It is still too early to tell how these services will do. Take a look at the issues that follow and decide for yourself if any of these technologies will help you give your remote users the type of connectivity they need.

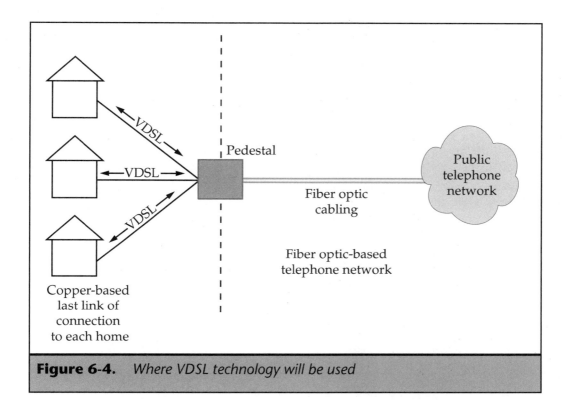

Figure 6-4. *Where VDSL technology will be used*

ADSL, SDSL, and RADSL Considerations

In this section I will look at the deployment and cost issues connected with the ADSL, SDSL, and RADSL. I have grouped these three DSL services together, because if you choose to use DSL technology to link your telecommuters or individual users in remote offices, you will use one of these three services. The next section discusses HDSL, which you would use to establish a high-speed link between offices.

There are several points to consider when deciding whether DSL is the way to connect remote users. I will go through the main points to consider. Keep in mind that DSL services are just emerging, so you may be frustrated by a lack of definite answers when you start posing "what-if" scenarios to see if DSL is the way to go.

Points to Consider when Deploying DSL Service to Remote Users

Type of applications to be supported Will you be using DSL to give a user high-speed access to the Internet, to applications on the corporate network, or both?

Availability of DSL services Does the telco in your area offer DSL? Does your Internet service provider (ISP) support DSL connections?

Which DSL modems to use Does the telco/ISP require a specific vendor's modem? Does the telco/ISP provide one? If so, must you purchase the modem outright? Or, are you required to lease it?

Cost of DSL service What is the fee to establish the service, the fixed monthly rate for the service, and the service's usage charge?

Changes to headquarters' network Do you need to make any changes to your remote access equipment in your main office to support remote users of DSL technology?

Which Applications Need DSL?

The first thing you must consider is what applications will need DSL. One way to think about this is to figure out which application will be the one that you say to yourself, "I need DSL for that…it's the only practical choice." For many of you, that first application that cries out for DSL will be Internet access for your remote users. As mentioned, DSL is ideally suited to Web surfing. That is because ADSL and RADSL both give the user a high-speed link downstream to carry all of those image-intensive web pages into their home or remote office. And both services give the user a more than ample upstream link, as well as a regular telephone line. SDSL provides much of the same type of service, with the trade-off being a slightly lower-speed downstream connection when compared with ADSL and RADSL (remember, though, that you do get a higher upstream connection).

Internet access may be the application that gets you to use DSL, but you may also want to tap the high-speed connection over copper phone lines to support other applications. For example, many companies are using videos and multimedia presentations to conduct training of new employees and to keep existing employees up-to-date about new policies, practices, or techniques they should follow or use. For employees within corporate headquarters, it is not that difficult to set up a workstation on a dedicated LAN segment so that the delivery of the data stream associated with these types of presentations is handled in a timely manner and does not clog the rest of the network. However, remote users would need high-speed connections to view the same presentations. Typically, a user would need to receive a video stream and send commands to control the presentation. Here again, ADSL, SDSL, and RADSL are well-suited to these types of applications.

You might say (and you would be correct) that there are other services that could also handle this type of traffic. Let's look at how DSL stacks up. ADSL, SDSL, and RADSL use special digital signal processing and multiplexing techniques to deliver between 6 and 12 Mbps of downstream data over existing copper phone lines (typical systems will offer about 6 Mbps). In contrast, V.34 modems offer 28.8 Kbps, and ISDN links offer 64 Kbps (or 128 Kbps if you combine the two B channels of a Basic Rate Interface line).

Cable modems offer comparable 10-Mbps data delivery rates. However, they require coaxial cable to run into the home or office. (The next chapter will look at cable modem technology and the current state of data delivery and offerings of high-speed services over cable TV systems.) ADSL devices will plug into a regular phone line like a modem.

You might also use ADSL, SDSL, or RADSL to give your remote users higher speed access to data on your corporate network. While this seems appealing, whether this was a practical use of DSL technology would depend on the nature of the applications your remote users needed access to. For instance, if your remote users only required occasional dial-in access to a mail server to send and retrieve e-mail, DSL might be overkill, since a regular phone line would be sufficient. If your users were doing collaborative work remotely, such as the shared editing of a document that requires some form of teleconferencing and an electronic whiteboard to illustrate points, DSL might be quite useful.

An added benefit (besides high speed) of using DSL for these types of applications is that the technology is capable of providing a user with a voice channel in addition to the high-speed data channel for SDSL or channels for ADSL and RADSL. That means, for instance, that a remote user can have a phone conversation while simultaneously downloading large files or surfing the Web. Or, the user might talk about changes in a document while remotely and jointly editing the document.

DSL Service Availability

ADSL, SDSL, or RADSL might be ideal for your remote users. But if the services are not available, you can't use them. After all, as noted in Chapter 3, ISDN was supposed to deliver high bandwidth to users, but the deployment of the service has been disappointingly slow. And as was also noted in Chapter 4, wireless services such as CDPD showed much promise when announced, but deployment of the services was a problem for years (and still is, in some people's opinion). Why should it be any different with DSL services?

At this point, no one knows if DSL will be different. But the analysts who study the market seem fairly optimistic about the deployment of DSL technology. For example, in fall 1996, Verona, N.J.-based Telechoice Inc., a telecommunications industry consultancy that specializes in broadband services, estimated that by the end of 1998, there would be about half as many ADSL lines deployed as there are ISDN lines. Essentially, ADSL would only take one year to reach half the number of ISDN lines—lines it took the telcos about 15 years to deploy. And Telechoice is not alone with such an optimistic view. The Yankee Group, a Boston-based consultancy, predicts that ADSL would hit the one million subscriber mark by 1999.

Again you might ask, why would DSL succeed when ISDN did not? Weren't there optimistic projections about ISDN (and CDPD) when the service was first introduced? Isn't this just the industry getting caught up in its own hype? Maybe. But there are a number of reasons to think that DSL will succeed where the other high-speed services have not.

First, it seems to be much less costly for a telco to make the necessary changes in its central offices to deploy xDSL than ISDN. To deploy ISDN requires that the telco must first upgrade the software on their digital switch. Such an upgrade costs, depending on the size of the switch, from $200,000 to $500,000, by some estimates. Additionally, the line cards in the switch must be changed to support ISDN. A typical ISDN line card costs between $150 and $400. So we are talking about an initial investment by the telco of something on the order of $750,000 to $1 million to get a central office switch ISDN-ready.

In contrast, it is supposed to be much less expensive to deploy DSL services. ("Supposed to be" is the key phrase here.) Details are sketchy, but the initial cost to upgrade a telco switch is not supposed to be in the $200,000 to $500,000 range it costs with an ISDN change. The main cost issue for the telcos is the expense of the line cards for DSL services. When DSL service trials were first under way in fall 1996, the line cards were estimated to cost from $2,000 to $3,000 per line. That estimate is probably on the high side. It is likely that the cost of the line card and a DSL modem together was, at that time, about $3,000.

The general opinion in the industry during the early DSL field trials was that the cost of the cards would drop substantially when they were produced in volume. The prevailing thought at the time was that the line cards would drop to about $500 to $1,000 in 1997. The telcos could easily make that investment back in a year or two through either the sale or leasing fee for a DSL modem, and through monthly service charges for the services delivered over the system.

In a typical DSL setting, the telephone company's central office will deliver video and data services to a home user while still providing that user with a line to dial out. To do this requires one more change in a central office. With a typical central office configuration for ADSL, SDSL, or RADSL, the line card would separate the voice traffic from the data traffic. Figure 6-5 shows that the voice traffic would then be handled as a normal POTS phone call, and the data would be passed to either a router or to an Ethernet switch and then a router. If the data traffic is Internet traffic, the router would be connected to the

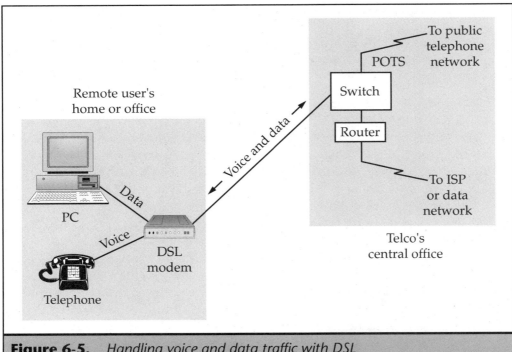

Figure 6-5. *Handling voice and data traffic with DSL*

Internet service provider. These changes are not considered major, since most central offices already have routers handling different forms of data traffic.

DSL service also seems to be easier to deploy than other services. Before DSL, all other approaches (including fiber-to-the-home, fiber-to-the-curb, and hybrid fiber-coax systems) to delivering high-bandwidth services, such as video-on-demand, posed high cost and high risk to the telephone companies. So the telcos did not deploy such systems in low-density areas or in areas where the telcos figured the "take rate" (the percentage of customers subscribing to a service) would be low.

DSL overcomes the risk to the telcos, since the service runs over the existing copper subscriber loop. If more lines are needed, installing plain old telephone system wiring is a low-risk, low-cost venture for a regional telephone company.

A final reason DSL might have a good chance of making it as a successful high-speed access technology is due to the competition between the cable TV operators and the telcos and between the various telecommunications providers. It seems that everyone wants to deliver video, Internet access, and other services. And thanks to the deregulation brought about by the Telecommunications Reform Act of 1996, there should be a fair amount of competition to deliver these services. In many ways DSL gives the telcos a way to compete with cable TV operators in delivering entertainment services such as movies-on-demand, and PC services such as Internet access and remote LAN access—all without the need to install the traditional hybrid fiber/coax systems used by cable TV.

Modem Selection

When considering whether DSL is the right technology for your users, you must also consider the DSL modem. Modems for ADSL, SDSL, and RADSL, are not like traditional modem technology where two people can each buy one and dial up each other. For a home or office to use these DSL services requires a DSL transceiver in the user's premises and the telco's central office. It is a one-to-one match between the telco and your user.

The practical side to this required matchup is that you may not have a choice in the DSL modem for your users. This can be looked at in several ways. First, standards, while greatly important with traditional analog modems, are not necessarily as important here. As long as the DSL technology supported on the line card in a telco's central office matches the technology in the remote user's DSL modem, the two can communicate. So the battle between the two encoding techniques (DMT and CAP) discussed earlier will not matter as long as the equipment you choose matches the technique supported in the central office. That will guarantee interoperability between the device in your remote user's office and the telco's equipment.

Because of this required matching of equipment, some telcos may not give you a choice of modem at all. Some telcos and ISPs will likely require that you either buy or lease a DSL modem directly from them. That is quite unlike a common modem connection. However, it is a similar approach to that taken by some ISPs who bundle a preconfigured (down to programming in the access telephone numbers), dial-up ISDN router with some high-speed Internet accounts.

Cost Issues

Okay, suppose you come to the conclusion that you have an application that would greatly benefit from DSL's speeds and assume you have a telco or ISP who has deployed the service; the next point to consider is the cost. First, you will need to determine the raw cost of using DSL services. Then you must figure if the higher-speed service is worth the price.

Pricing for DSL will vary greatly by ISP and telco depending on their costs to deploy the service and the cost of the DSL modems. The calculation of costs is similar to that performed in Chapters 2, 3, and 4. Specifically, you should consider the cost of the termination equipment (the DSL modem), the cost to establish the service, the monthly rate for the service, and any usage fees for the service.

One difficulty is that fees for DSL services will not likely be set until early to mid-1997. However, early implementers have proposed some rates that can be used for ballpark estimations of what it would cost to provide your users with DSL connectivity.

During the early field trials of DSL technology in late 1996, Bell Atlantic, while not quoting specific prices, said it thought that prices in the range of $30 to $50 per month would not be out of line. And U.S. West, which planned to offer services in the first quarter of 1997, said pricing for the service might be in the $50 to $100 per month range. Such monthly rates make DSL comparable to ISDN in cost. But note that these estimates do not include any estimate of usage rates.

It is difficult to come up with a good cost model based on these numbers. Because of this, I will use the only information available to me at this writing (early 1997) to perform my cost analysis. To figure your costs, simply use the following method, and substitute the pricing you get from your carriers and ISPs.

The first true commercial offering of ADSL was introduced in fall 1996 by InterAccess Inc., a Chicago-based ISP. InterAccess offered ADSL-based web access, with e-mail and access to Usenet news groups. The service provides a 64-Kbps upstream link and a 1.5-Mbps downstream link. The ADSL service for the InterAccess accounts was provided by Ameritech. Users of this service had to use a specific ADSL modem—the ADSL Worldvision modem—also from Ameritech. The modem had to be purchased from InterAccess and the price was $1,500. (InterAccess gave users the option of renting the modem for $125 per month.) This model of requiring a specific modem to be either purchased or leased directly from the service provider is likely to be the only way to get ADSL, SDSL, and RADSL services.

To use the InterAccess service requires a 10Base-T Ethernet card. InterAccess did not require that you buy this from them; however, the company offered one for $120.

It is likely your telecommuters will not have Ethernet adapter cards in their desktop PCs. So you must include the cost of this in your budget calculations. Some of your remote users might use a laptop instead of a desktop computer. If so, there are a couple of issues to consider. First, if these users have older laptops that only have one PC Card slot, it is likely that the slot is already used by a modem card. You can either buy such users a second PC Card that acts as an Ethernet adapter, or replace the modem card with a multifunction modem/Ethernet adapter PC Card.

Connecting Laptop Users

If your users have older laptops with only one slot for a PC Card, you have two choices. One choice is to buy a PC Card Ethernet adapter and have the user switch cards depending on the type of connection he or she needs. There are potential hidden costs associated with this approach—for example, the cost in labor charges for your staff to help the remote users if they have problems. And problems are highly likely, since PC Cards are not the easiest to install and configure.

The other choice, if your remote users only have one slot, is to consider using a single multifunction card that combines a traditional modem and Ethernet adapter. In that way, your users can use the Ethernet adapter to connect to the ADSL modem (and naturally to the ADSL service) and use the traditional analog modem to connect using a regular analog connection (either using a separate phone line or using an analog port on the ADSL modem—if one is available).

The bottom line is that you will likely have to buy an Ethernet adapter that plugs into a slot in a desktop computer, or either an Ethernet adapter PC Card or a multifunction Ethernet adapter/analog modem PC Card for users with laptops. So you need to add the cost of this hardware. A basic 10Base-T Ethernet adapter card costs between $110 and $150; InterAccess offers one for about $120. Let's use that amount for this pricing example.

Next, you must consider the price of the service. The InterAccess fee for an ADSL-based Internet account was $200 to establish the account and a $200 per month ($2,400 per year) fee for the service.

As is the case with any pricing calculation, you must use the dollar values for your particular service provider. I will use the same $200 startup fee that InterAccess uses. This seems reasonable for a high-speed service. As for the monthly pricing, I mentioned earlier that U.S. West had suggested its service would be priced at about $50 to $100 per month. The InterAccess monthly fee is $200, and that includes both the fee for the ADSL service provided by Ameritech and the fee for the Internet account. It seems reasonable then to use a monthly rate for service of $100 per month ($1,200 per year).

In the example I have just given you, based on the first available pricing for a DSL service intended for a single remote user, you can see that the total first-year cost, including the price of the equipment, the startup fee to establish the service, and the cost of using the service for a year, comes to $3,020 per user. This calculation does not include a very crucial component: the usage fee for a DSL service. And at this writing (early 1997) there was not even a hint of what a usage fee might be. (InterAccess, like many ISPs, offers a flat monthly rate for Internet access.) I will not even venture a guess at a usage fee for DSL services.

First-Year Costs to Connect a Telecommuter to a DSL-Based Service

Purchase price of ADSL modem	$1,500
10Base-T Ethernet adapter card	$ 120
Fee to establish the service	$ 200
Monthly fee ($100) × 12 months	$1,200
Total first year costs [1]	$3,020

[1] does not include usage fee for service

To put the cost into perspective, we can compare this to the first-year cost of another high-speed service: ISDN. If you look back to Chapter 3, you will see that it costs $9,880 for the first year of ISDN service. That figure includes the cost of the equipment, the startup fee for the service, the monthly rate for the service, and $8,640 for the ISDN usage fee the entire year. If we subtract this usage fee, we get some idea of the cost differences between the first DSL services and ISDN.

Performing the subtraction, I get a first-year cost for ISDN including the price of the equipment, the fee to establish the service, and the monthly fee for a year to be $1,240. That means (based on my numbers) it costs about 2.4 times as much for the DSL connection as the ISDN connection. Remember, my DSL numbers are based on the prices of the first services; when DSL becomes more available in late 1997 (or 1998, as many expect it will really be), the price may be lower. However, for now, let's use the numbers in the preceding example.

What you will have to determine is whether it is worth 2.4 times as much to use DSL versus ISDN. The answer will depend on the type of applications you run, but suppose your remote users use either ISDN or DSL strictly for Internet access. You could make a case that the time savings using the higher-speed DSL would be worth the extra cost.

ISDN BRI service offers at most (when combining the two B channels) 128 Kbps. DSL promises to deliver data downstream at a rate of 8 Mbps. That is a data rate of about 62 times faster. Even with the InterAccess offering, which delivers 1.5 Mbps, we are talking about a rate roughly 12 times faster than ISDN BRI service. We all know that Internet Web surfing time is not all taken up by waiting for information to be downloaded (there are the delays in establishing a connection with a site and getting a response from the site's server). But even if your users cut their connect time by one-third using DSL versus ISDN, you still have a case for using DSL.

The way the argument goes is as follows: Remote users will save a third of the time they have been spending surfing the Web by using DSL instead of ISDN. If a remote user is making $10 per hour (about $22,000 per year) and surfs the Web for six hours per week and 50 weeks a year, that user might have two additional hours per week he or she normally wouldn't have. If those hours can be translated into productive work (let's assume they can), the higher-speed link saves two hours per week or 100 hours per year. You can look at this number a few ways. One way is as the equivalent of $1,000 per year in savings.

Another way to look at it is as the costs you have saved your company. If your users had retained their slower-speed lines, your company might have had to hire more workers to get the same amount of work done. Or the extra work might not get done at all. With the extra two hours per week each user gets using DSL, he or she will be able to get more work done. So you might be able to cost justify the additional price of a DSL line based on the productivity gain of a remote user.

You may also be able to argue that the workers are not only more productive, but they also generate more revenue. For example, you might have order takers or travel agents working out of their homes. Such workers rely on their connections to corporate databases to perform their jobs. If the online part of such a person's job can be cut a third by use of a higher-speed link, not only are these employees more productive, but they also generate more revenue per employee. For instance, one order taker can handle more calls if it takes less time per call to look up the in-stock status of each item.

The additional cost of a DSL link might also be justified if you can demonstrate that such links are the only way to support a needed application. This argument will depend on the applications you are interested in deploying. For instance, if your company is service oriented and you have many remote users (if it's a travel agency, for example, or an accounting firm where associates work from small regional offices), you may need a way to provide these users with access to video presentations that show them how to perform basic procedures vital to your company's business or image. (Chapter 18 will go into more detail about the necessity of conducting such training and providing such information.) So, for instance, if your employees in small offices need to know the proper way to fill out a travel and expense report, they may simply click on an icon that starts the delivery of a prepared video presentation.

HDSL Considerations

While ADSL, SDSL, and RADSL are aimed at giving a remote user a high-speed link over copper phone line, HDSL is aimed at linking sites.

Some consider HDSL a simpler way of getting T1 or ISDN PRI-type connectivity. You will order HDSL service in the same way you order other high-speed services such as T1 lines or ISDN PRI lines. However, HDSL delivers T1/E1 bandwidth over copper wires at distances of up to 12,000 feet. Typically, two pairs of copper wire are needed for T1 services (as opposed to a single pair for ADSL, RADSL, and SDSL) that offer 1.544-Mbps data rates; three pairs are needed for E1 service that offers 2.048-Mbps data rates. There are trade-offs with HDSL. You can support slower speeds with different wiring. For example, you can get 784-Kbps rates up to 12,000 feet over a single two-wire pair of a copper phone line.

The advantage of using HDSL over comparable services like T1 or ISDN PRI service, is that it is easier for the telcos to deploy. An E1 or T1 link requires a repeater every 3,000 to 6,000 feet. With HDSL, the telco only needs to install an HDSL line card in their central office switch and can deliver the service over a distance of 12,000 feet without repeaters. This means HDSL links are easier to establish and can be installed much faster.

In your office location, you would need an HDSL transceiver. Figure 6-6 shows a typical HDSL configuration with the line card in the central office and the transceiver placed in front of your CSU (channel service unit) in your corporate site.

Like ADSL, SDSL, and RADSL, HDSL service is not widely available, so you will need to check to see if there are telecommunications carriers offering the service in your area before proceeding with a cost analysis.

If the service is available, you would need to look at the pricing structure from the specific carrier offering the service. In fall 1996, Anchorage Telephone Utility Telecommunications (ATUT) based in Anchorage, Alaska, offered the first tariffed HDSL service in the United States. At that time, ATUT rolled out its Anchorage Transparent LAN Service (ATLAS) Lite, an HDSL offering that provided 1.5-Mbps data rates over two pairs of copper wires. Users could also get 784-Kbps service over a single pair of wires. ATUT priced the service at from $160 to $200 per month (the pricing depends on the bandwidth the user

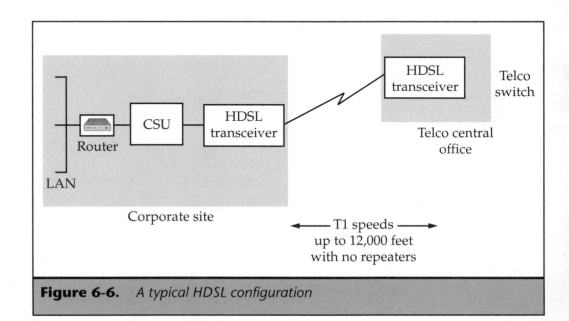

Figure 6-6. *A typical HDSL configuration*

company selects and the length of the contract a company is willing to agree to). That makes it quite attractive compared with your normal T1 service, which can be significantly higher.

There are two negatives with HDSL today. The lack of availability of the service is probably HDSL's major weakness. The second thing that you will need to examine for yourself is the ability of existing wiring to support HDSL's data rates. Just because the service is rated for 1.544 Mbps, doesn't mean every local loop can support such rates. Just consider your experiences with dial-up modems. Sometimes you get a 28.8-Kbps connection, sometimes you don't. You will need to determine whether the loop between your telco's switch and your company's site can support HDSL. In theory, it should. But in reality, you might have trouble if the line is very long or there are many sources of noise.

VDSL Considerations

Of all the DSL services, the impact of VDSL on a network manager is the hardest to figure. It is not clear whether VDSL will be strictly a consumer service aimed at the video-on-demand market, or if it will be used to support corporate video and multimedia applications.

The current state of the market has VDSL aimed solely at the consumer video-on-demand market. But VDSL might also be used by the telcos to offer high-speed Internet service. If that becomes the case, you might have to deal with ordering VDSL service for some of your telecommuters, and you might have to deal with the telcos for provisioning the service and getting the appropriate equipment.

Most likely, your choices will be limited. VDSL will be tied to the telco's deployment of some form of fiber-to-the-curb effort. While it is too early to get firm pricing from the telcos, it is likely the home user will be offered a package similar to a cable TV plan, where there are some basic services for a nominal monthly fee and some premium services (like video-on-demand and Internet access) for additional fees.

VDSL provides a financially sane way for the telcos to bring very high bandwidth to user's homes. That may make the service more attractive to the telcos and may speed up deployment. For years, the telephone companies have been trying to find a way to bring high-bandwidth into a home. Likewise, the telcos have looked at fiber-to-the-home as one way to accomplish this. Fiber optic cabling supports much higher bandwidths than copper. But a fiber-to-the-home system is quite costly for the telcos to deploy. One portion of the cost is replacing the telco's infrastructure of copper lines with fiber optic cabling. That, while costly, is typically viewed as economically feasible, since the telcos would be able to recoup the money by offering more lucrative services (like video-on-demand and high-speed Internet access). However, there is another portion of the cost to bring fiber to the home that is not financially feasible (at least not today or for the near future). A fiber-to-the-home system needs opto-electronics equipment, which converts the light signal into electrical signals, in every home. Such equipment is very costly, and the telecommunications companies have concluded that even if they offered lucrative services (lucrative to the telcos, that is), installing the opto-electronics equipment in every home would not be cost-effective.

So, we have a situation where the telcos can make a financial case to upgrade their wiring infrastructure from copper to fiber (assuming there will be more revenue from the services delivered over the fiber links), but it is not financially sound to install the necessary equipment in the home to access the fiber network.

This has led the telecommunications industry to pursue what some call fiber-to-the-pedestal or fiber-to-the-curb approaches for delivering high-bandwidth services. Essentially, both approaches rely on a fiber infrastructure to carry the high-bandwidth content (whether it's video-on-demand service to deliver movies into user's homes, multimedia Internet services, or live TV coverage of events, such as concerts, boxing matches, or political conventions). But unlike fiber-to-the-home, the signal travels over fiber only to the user's neighborhood. From a point close to the user's home, the signal is converted from light to electrical and then carried over copper wires into the home. This solves several problems. First, the telcos only need to deploy expensive opto-electronic conversion equipment in each neighborhood and not in every home. And second, the telcos get to retain their investment in the copper wires in the ground that go into each home.

NOTE: While you may not care whether a particular information delivery method is financially pleasing to the telcos, it definitely has an impact on the types of services the telcos make available to you and your users. If the telcos are to use fiber-to-the-curb for video-on-demand or Internet access, they will still need a way to stream data into a user's home at high rates. That is where VDSL technology comes in. Look back to Figure 6-4; it shows how a typical video-on-demand service based on VDSL might work.

Note that such a system is actually a hybrid fiber/copper system, and it offers the potential to deliver much higher bandwidths into a remote user's home than ADSL, SDSL, or RADSL. The trade-off in a VDSL system is distance. The other three services deliver their high bandwidth over lines that reach

12,000 to 18,000 feet from a user's home to a telco's central office. VDSL operates over much shorter distances. One of the first VDSL modems—the ORspeed VDSL modem from Orckit Communications—demonstrated at Telecom 95, was able to transmit over twisted pair copper wire data at 13-, 26-, or 52-Mbps downstream rates and 2-Mbps upstream over distances of 4,500 feet, 3,000 feet, or 1,000 feet, respectively.

56-Kbps Modems: A Possible Alternative

In fall 1996, as DSL field trials were popping up regularly and the first services were announced, a new twist was added to the high-speed connectivity over copper equation. Modem vendors, including Boca Research Inc., Cardinal Technologies Inc., Hayes Microcomputer Products Inc., Motorola Inc., Microcom Inc., U.S. Robotics, and Zoom Telephonics Inc., announced a new class of modems that would operate at 56 Kbps. The announcements came at the same time these companies (and many others) were rolling out their first 33.6-Kbps modems.

Was this a case of the modem manufacturers slitting their own throats? After all, who in their right mind would buy a 33.6-Kbps modem knowing that in a couple of months a 56-Kbps version would be available? Well, there was a catch with the 56-Kbps modems. 56-Kbps modems are not like your traditional dial-up modems. A system using 56-Kbps modems is, in some ways, more comparable to an xDSL system than to your normal analog dial-up access systems used today. A system built around 56-Kbps modem technology is a hybrid analog/digital system that operates at 33.6 Kbps upstream and 56 Kbps downstream. Basically, the user gets a 33.6-Kbps upstream analog channel and can get up to a 56-Kbps downstream analog link if certain conditions are met.

For a remote user to get the performance boost to 56 Kbps, several things must be in place. Your user must have a quiet, relatively noise-free local loop. And, as you can see in Figure 6-7, your corporation or ISP must have a remote access server that uses a digital service to connect to the public telephone network. This can be either an ISDN BRI or PRI link, or a channelized T1 connection.

With 56-Kbps modems, the user's end of the link is not changed, but the link between a telco's switch and your corporate site the remote user is connecting to must be digital. Similarly, the link between an ISP's equipment and the telco switch must be digital.

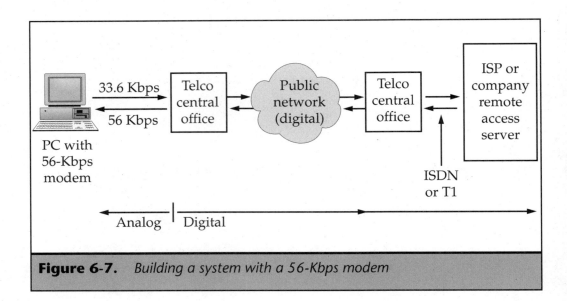

Figure 6-7. *Building a system with a 56-Kbps modem*

It is likely that the first uses of the 56-Kbps modems will be employed by ISPs to give users high-speed Internet access. Or, you might see companies setting up a remote access server for their users to dial in to. In either case, the ISP or the company would have to set up a system that is slightly different from your normal modem pool and remote access server that are used today to support remote user dial-in.

The first 56-Kbps modems will not be available until the middle of 1997. As this book was being written, there were still many issues that the modem manufacturers had to work out before units could be marketed. For example, the vendors needed to address whether all 56-Kbps modems would incorporate 33.6-Kbps technology. It seems to make sense to do this, and the consensus at the time was that all 56-Kbps modems would support 33.6-Kbps speeds. And then there is the issue of a standard for the 56-Kbps data rate. As was mentioned in Chapter 2, one of the reasons dial-up connectivity over analog modems will remain the dominant form of remote connectivity is that modems are based on international standards that ensure interoperability (the ubiquitous nature of analog phone lines was the other). It usually takes groups like ANSI and the International Telecommunications Union (ITU) a couple of years to formalize modem standards. The modem vendors submitted their standards proposals for 56 Kbps to these two organizations in October 1996.

Deployment Issues with 56-Kbps Modems

It is not clear how 56-Kbps modems will be marketed or how the services to use them will be offered. If the modem vendors include 33.6-Kbps modem technology in their 56-Kbps offerings, you might see them sold as a traditional modem that is 56-Kbps ready. But you will still need the service to a remote user's office or home to get the performance boost out of these devices that they are capable of providing. Most likely, an ISP will offer 56-Kbps downstream service and bundle a modem with the service.

Wrapping It Up

In fall 1996, DSL services were just starting to emerge. Many telecommunications companies, including the long-distance carriers and the regional Bell operating companies, were conducting field trials. At about the same time, 56-Kbps modems were being announced.

xDSL technology and the 56-Kbps modems offer a way to give telecommuters and users in remote offices a way to get high-speed access to corporate resources and the Internet. These technologies promised to deliver these services over the existing twisted pair copper lines used for conventional telephone service. Some xDSL services, like HDSL, give you a way to link remote offices, too. The best thing about using equipment based on these technologies and the appropriate services is that they all use the common twisted pair copper wiring that is extensively used in the public telephone network. Additionally, the telcos seem to have good reason to deploy xDSL services. The changes required in their central office switches are minor compared with the changes that must be made to deploy ISDN services. Hopefully, this will give the telcos enough incentive to deploy xDSL services more rapidly and to more users than was the case with ISDN. Additionally, the competitive nature of the telecommunications market today should also give the telcos some incentive to deploy these services quickly.

In 1997, there should be many xDSL service announcements. And we should see glimpses of where each technology is likely to head in the next few years. For instance, with ADSL, the issue is how to deliver other types of services, such as high-speed Internet and LAN access, over this high-speed conduit into the remote user's home or office. With VDSL we should be able to see if this service is strictly a consumer service for movies-on-demand, or if the service will be used by corporations to give them a way to deliver multimedia and video to their telecommuters.

One crucial element in the success or failure of xDSL services will be the price of the modems. According to industry analysts, the telcos say they need the price to be about $500 per user. Today, the price is three times that. We are in a chicken-and-egg situation where the suppliers of the modems say costs will drop if the telcos buy more xDSL modems; the telcos say they will buy more if the prices drop. This is common with any new technology.

While this round-robin of price versus demand runs its course, the likely impact on you is that it will be a while before xDSL services are widely available. Originally, the thought was that 1997 would be a huge year for DSL service deployment. It will be. But not on the order that many had hoped. Many analysts say that the big push in DSL services will come in 1998 and 1999. As noted earlier in the chapter, the consultancy firm, The Yankee Group, predicts that ADSL will get about 80,000 customers in 1997, and the market will hit the 1 million subscriber mark in 1999. You may be lucky and have it available in your area soon. But, like ISDN and the wireless services, xDSL may be a regional solution for your company.

Chapter Seven

Cable Access

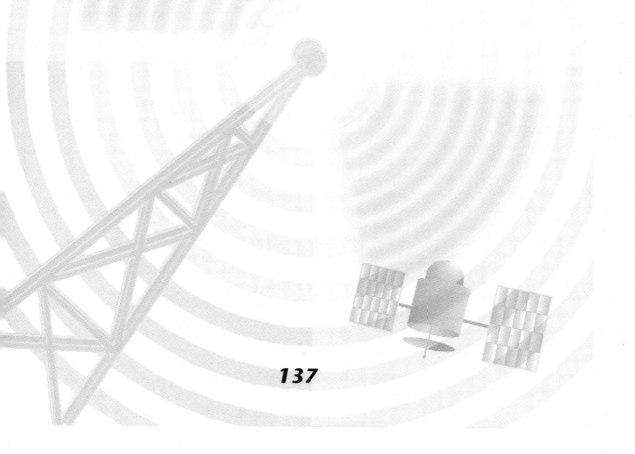

High-speed access to the Internet for remote users is driving many companies to look at connectivity alternatives that they would likely have never considered a year or two ago. One such alternative is cable access.

Cable TV providers, hoping to encourage users to ante up a monthly fee for something in addition to television programs, are looking at ways to offer users 10-Mbps access rates into online databases or the Internet. The way they plan to do this is to leverage the bandwidth of their cable TV systems to deliver high-speed data into the home.

It is likely that the delivery of high-speed data over cable will be more appealing as a consumer offering and not as a business tool for your telecommuters. But there is a chance your company could tap the high-speed link into a user's home for business purposes. In this chapter, I will discuss the general idea behind cable access; the way the first offerings are shaping up; and what it will take for cable access to become a useful, formidable business tool that you might call on to support the remote connectivity needs of your home users.

The common idea behind most cable-based data delivery systems is to offer users data rates of 10 Mbps—the same as if they were connected to an Ethernet LAN in the main office. That puts cable access well above the bandwidth options available with other connectivity options, such as analog phone lines, ISDN, wireless systems, and even most xDSL systems. To put that difference into perspective, in the time it would take you to receive one page of text over a 64-Kbps ISDN link, you could receive about 156 pages using a cable modem.

Thus, cable TV systems have the capability to deliver huge amounts of information into the users' home or office. They already do—delivering television programming into homes by use of more bandwidth than is available with other technologies.

While discussion about cable access systems has mostly focused on giving users high-speed access to the Internet, such systems might also be used to deliver other high-bandwidth services. For example, the 10-Mbps bandwidth is more than sufficient to deliver video conferencing services (there is still the issue of not having the bandwidth in the upstream direction with most cable systems). And the availability of a high-speed connection into a home or small office could also be used to connect users to a corporate network at the same data rates they would be accustomed to with a LAN.

How It Works

The basic idea behind cable data delivery systems is, at least for the near future, to offer high-speed Internet access and delivery of interactive multimedia applications (such as corporate training programs) to home users. Like some of the xDSL technologies, cable delivery systems can take advantage of the asymmetry in data transmissions that is common in most Web and interactive multimedia applications. Commonly, there is a need to have a high-bandwidth link downstream into the user's home for the graphical and multimedia-rich content of many web sites or interactive multimedia training presentations. And you also need a lower bandwidth upstream signal to control the surfing or presentation.

Most cable systems can handle the difficult part—the high-bandwidth downstream part of the system. Most cable systems are built using coaxial cable that can support higher bandwidths over greater distances while being less susceptible to noise than your common twisted pair copper wire. The idea is to use what is called a *cable modem* to terminate the coaxial cable entering the house. This modem would be used instead of a set-top cable box. The user would connect his or her PC to the modem using an Ethernet adapter card in the PC and normal Ethernet cable (most likely this will be the twisted pair cabling used in 10Base-T networks).

The part lacking in many cable systems is the upstream path. Most cable systems do not have the switching infrastructure in place to handle the routing of even simple upstream commands. This is evident in many existing cable TV pay-per-view offerings. Typically, you can select from about a half dozen movies and have any one of them delivered over the cable TV system to a specific channel on your cable TV system. The hitch is that you usually have to call a phone number to order the movie you want. Most cable companies aren't even sophisticated enough in their use of technology for you to select a movie from a menu using your telephone. Usually each movie selection has its own 800 number to dial.

Still, this system works fine for selecting an occasional movie. And there is some talk of using a similar type of out-of-band dial-up telephone connection to deliver high-speed Internet access over existing cable TV systems. Figure 7-1 shows how this might work. The home user would have a one-way dial-up connection into a cable TV system's head end server. This upstream channel would control the downstream channel. It might be used to start, stop, or rewind a video. Or, it might be used to answer questions in an interactive multimedia training presentation. Then again, it might be used to select a URL or hot link on a Web page.

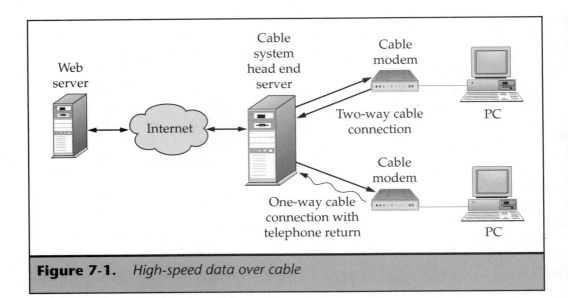

Figure 7-1. *High-speed data over cable*

Of these three scenarios, the control of a video is the one you will most likely see deployed. This application is geared more toward the consumer market and is of limited use in corporate environments. The next one of these scenarios likely to happen is the Internet access approach. While this approach is interesting, it seems unlikely to be deployed in any wide-scale way by cable system operators. Providing Internet services is a highly competitive market, and the economics might not be there for the cable operators. There are already many types of companies offering Internet access. Commercial online service providers like CompuServe, America Online, The Microsoft Network, and Prodigy all offer Internet access. And there are also Internet service providers. Additionally, the telcos, including the nationwide service providers and the regional Bells, offer Internet access. So the margins are likely to be pretty tight. This dial-in upstream channel approach requires a fair amount of administration on the part of the cable system operator. So, don't hold your breath waiting for this to be your corporate Internet strategy of choice.

The cable TV industry knows the one-way nature of their systems is a shortcoming that will impede the industry from getting into this and other types of interactive services. As a result, the industry is going to great lengths to improve its infrastructure to allow a two-way exchange of data over the cable system. If you look back at Figure 7-1, you will see conceptually how this two-way link would work. Such a system would be much easier for the remote user to work with, and it would be much easier for the cable system operator to administer.

For cable systems to operate in this two-direction link requires an upgrade of the traditional networks. The network needs a combination of very high bandwidth and some switching infrastructure to route signals in both directions. While there seems to be many different approaches to this new infrastructure, the common elements that seem essential are illustrated in Figure 7-2. In the figure you can see that one element is a fiber optic link between the cable TV operator's head end and the neighborhood. This gives the system the capacity to support the bandwidth needs of a group of users in one neighborhood. There is also a point in the network where the fiber line terminates and the coaxial cables that are already deployed to the homes in a neighborhood are used to deliver both the user's television programming and his or her high-speed Internet access. You also need some type of switching system in place to direct traffic in both directions.

Accessing Cable Services

The heart of any cable system offering high data delivery rates is the cable modem. Cable modems are devices that offer 10-Mbps data delivery rates over

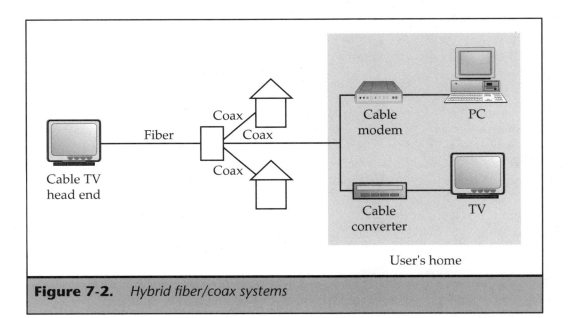

Figure 7-2. *Hybrid fiber/coax systems*

existing cable TV wiring. Such products, which include an Ethernet connection to which you attach your PC, connect to the coaxial wiring that delivers your cable TV signal. Most cable modems will in essence operate as a combination modem and Ethernet hub. Cable modems differ from traditional modems in that they are always online. Additionally, some cable modem vendors are also developing modems that operate at higher rates (more on this later).

There are several cable modems on the market today, and many more are on their way. These products come from vendors including Digital Equipment Corp., Intel, Hewlett-Packard, LANcity, Motorola, and Zenith Electronics. And you will soon see cable modem offerings from internetworking companies such as Cisco Systems and Bay Networks, who have acquired cable modem manufacturers. Commonly, the modems offer two Ethernet connectivity choices (10Base-T and 802.3) and require an Ethernet adapter card to be installed in the desktop computer. Several of the modems, such as the CyberSURFR from Motorola and the LANcity workgroup cable modem, offer advanced features such as being SNMP manageable.

To use these cable modems requires a cable TV operator who will deliver services. So they are not like your traditional analog modem that you can plug into any phone line. Virtually all of the large cable TV operators in the United States, including Rogers Communications, Time-Warner, Tele-Communications Inc. (TCI), and Continental Cablevision, have either already launched projects or are conducting pilot projects that will deliver high-speed data services to personal computers. Currently, it is too early in the development of cable delivery services to gauge the pricing structure for using the services.

Once these services get off the ground, users working from home will be able to enjoy a new level of remote connectivity. For example, access to the Internet at Ethernet rates would far exceed anything most users would ever have available in their office. Anyone who has browsed web sites via a 14.4-Kbps modem can see the appeal of cable modems, which would offer nearly 700 times the delivery rate.

Web site browsing aside, the market to deliver high-speed online services could prove to be a very fertile market. For example, Intel estimated that in 1994, there were 26 million homes that already had both a PC and cable service. And the number of homes with PCs has significantly increased since then.

Today, the bulk of the exchanges on commercial online services and the Internet are e-mail messages. With 10-Mbps bandwidth, service providers could start delivering multimedia applications into the home. For instance, such systems would be capable of delivering virtual reality and 3D entertainment. Or, the additional bandwidth could be used to enhance the types of information commonly available today. For instance, a cable TV provider might offer a live shot of a location linked to a weather or traffic report instead of a static, four-year-old photo of a city center with the temperature superimposed over the scene. Such applications offer more potential benefits to the consumer market, but there are ways these services could be used for business applications. And perhaps the most important thing about being able to deliver these extra services is that it might drive the market and make it more economical (we will only be able to tell if this is the case when they start to price the services).

One factor that will determine the success of high-speed cable access will be the price of the modems. Cable modems must cost about the same as high-end analog telephone modems (about $300 to $400), according to industry analysts. Like many technologies (networking or otherwise), cable modem manufacturers have been making strides in reducing the cost of their products as the products mature. Part of the cost saving is coming from the development of more sophisticated chip technology—again, something that is common in this type of technical arena. Specifically, cable modem manufacturers used three chips in their modems and are now reducing that to one. Many of the first cable modems would use one chip to handle the processing of the downstream data, one to handle the processing of the upstream data, and one to handle the MAC (media access control) layer functions required to connect to the cable network. Now, it is common for all three functions to be handled on a single chip. The advantage to this approach for the cable modem manufacturers is that their production costs are reduced—there are fewer connections between chips and circuit boards. This translates into lower direct costs for material. However, it also means lower labor charges and, perhaps more importantly, higher reliability because there are fewer connections. Higher reliability translates into more units passing quality control (higher yield rate). And the units cost cable TV operators less to support because they break down less often.

One of the reasons the early modems used different chips for different functions is because cable modems work differently on each part of a transmission. Usually cable modems send and receive data in different ways. Downstream data is modulated and spread over a single 6MHz cable channel. This channel is usually somewhere in the 42MHz to 750MHz range. As with xDSL modems, different vendors use different modulation schemes to move the data. The most common cable modem modulation schemes are QPSK, which delivers data rates of up to about 10 Mbps, and QAM64, which can deliver data rates up to about 30 Mbps (this is what the manufacturers of higher than Ethernet speed modems would use).

In the upstream direction, cable modems will need to include ways of sending data over a telephone or wireless link. In a two-way cable system, the upstream data is transmitted at a frequency range between 5 and 40MHz, which is often susceptible to noise and interference. Because of this problem, most cable modem manufacturers will use QPSK, because it is a more robust transmission scheme.

Hold Your Excitement

Such upgraded systems are currently being deployed throughout the country. A survey by Merrill Lynch found that between 1995 and 1997 the number of homes in the United States by which an upgraded cable system passed, more than tripled from about 16 million in 1995 to an estimated 50 million homes in 1997. Figure 7-3 shows that Merrill Lynch is bullish about the state of this market through the year 2001, when they believe there will be 85 million homes that will have an upgraded cable system pass by their door.

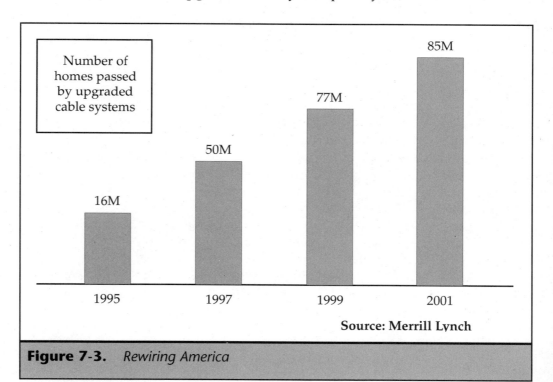

Figure 7-3.   *Rewiring America*

Those numbers seem pretty encouraging. After all, there are still only something like 500,000 ISDN lines in the United States (and that's after about 15 years of the telcos deploying the service). This seems too good to be true. You can give your users 10-Mbps downstream data delivery rates with cable versus 64 Kbps (or 128 Kbps if you aggregate the two B channels of an ISDN BRI link). Why would you even think twice about this choice? As bad as the telecommunications industry's reputation is for its slow deployment of ISDN, the cable industry faces an even bigger perception problem when it comes to its track record for service and reliability.

While there are many good cable TV systems, the perception of the industry as a whole will likely be a deterrent to you ever getting approval for any wide-scale corporate plan to use cable as the sole means of connecting remote users.

The cable TV industry is deemed by some to be unreliable. Users complain of service outages and of slow responses to outages. This criticism is perhaps unfair. But it is the common perception that many users have. And there's a saying: Perception is reality. Just imagine going to your boss and trying to convince him or her that the lifeline for your remote users is going to be a cable TV link into their home.

If you doubt that you will face resistance, ask some of your users when was the last time their cable went out. My bet is they will all have a recent date in mind. Then ask them how long it took them to get the problem fixed. They will likely tell you it took several days, and that they couldn't even report the problem until the next day during business hours. Ask the users the same questions about their phone service. They will likely be hard pressed to remember the last time their phone was out. I am not trying to bash the cable TV industry; I'm just trying to give you an idea of the resistance you will likely encounter if you opt for a cable access remote connectivity solution.

The cable industry has made strides to overcome this perception problem. And the upgraded systems will give them both a more resilient infrastructure and one that can more easily be managed. That should lead to even more improvements. All of this will be necessary, especially with the competitive environment that we are now entering.

One of the outgrowths of the increasingly competitive spirit between the telcos, cable systems operators, and Internet service providers is the possibility of cable operators offering phone service. In my opinion, when a cable operator provides a dial tone, that service has reached the point when cable access for high-speed connectivity moves from one of curiosity to one that is taken as a serious business alternative. The phone companies want to offer Internet and video services; it only makes sense that the cable operators should offer voice. And the deregulation brought about by the Telecommunications Reform Act of 1995 makes this possible.

The reliability factor can become a more serious problem when cable operators offer voice services. Imagine if a telecommuter's only business telephone line and only way to access corporate data are through a cable service. And imagine if the service goes out for days. Not a pretty picture. Telephone companies have done a much better job at keeping service up and running and making sure you get your service back if it does go out. Just think about it. When was the last time your home phone service was out? How long did it take the telephone company to restore it? In my case, the last outage was about four years ago, and the phone company had someone there the next day to fix it. (It was a difficult task in my case. A previous tenant had jury-rigged a connection to a phone jack box on the wall and had run an extension to another point in the apartment. The fault that knocked out my service was in this jury-rigged box.)

Reducing Complexity

Cable operators are aiming their high-speed Internet access services at the consumer market first. To reach this market, the cable operators want to make Internet access as easy as turning on a television. That means the cable modem, PC, and Ethernet adapter approach described previously simply won't do. This, while being primarily an attempt to reach consumers, might be useful for some of your users who want to simply surf the Web to conduct research for work from home. After all, even many sophisticated users would not know how to properly install and configure an Ethernet adapter card.

One approach being developed by cable TV operators features a keyboard (and no computer or Ethernet adapter card) for the user. The keyboard has a wireless connection to the set-top cable box. This type of setup requires a cable system capable of supporting two-way communications. The goal of this keyboard-only system is to reduce the complexity of the system. Such systems are obviously aimed at a consumer market that simply wants to surf the Web. It has no provisions for saving Web pages or printing information. And one downside that I would be concerned about is the wireless connection between the keyboard and the set-top box. The last wireless keyboard I used was on an IBM PC Jr. It was a great idea. I could move my keyboard to my lap and type at an angle that was (in my mind) perfect. The problem with this approach was that every once in a while the keyboard would get tucked in the angle of my body and my knee, or some other body part would block the signal and disrupt the connection. Maybe the technology used in these systems is more resistant to such obstructions, but I would check it out before using it.

To meet the needs of business users who might be technically more sophisticated, some cable TV operators would have you split the signal, directing one branch to your TV and the other to a cable modem and PC.

While the appeal of higher-speed access to online services is high, there are several roadblocks that might limit deployment of such systems. First, the cable TV operators must support such equipment, and at this writing there were no standards for cable modems. There were some industry-consensus types of agreements as to which modulation schemes to support, but there was no ruling body governing compliance to these agreed-upon schemes. A second obstacle is that cable TV operators must partner with Internet service providers and other information providers to make the system work. Given the competitive nature of the market, such cooperation might not be widespread.

The main point to remember is that cable access delivery systems have one large factor in their favor: bandwidth. But they also have a point or two that detract from their usefulness. I think it is important to look at the recent past when it come to cable TV systems. This is because many of the events that have shaped the market to date may come back to haunt it today. Specifically, cable TV has not had a stellar record when it comes to reliability and service. While the situation has improved and is likely to improve even more with upgraded systems, perception may make it hard to convince management to go along with a cable access plan. You can probably imagine the reaction of your boss when you tell him or her that the lifeline to your company's remote users, the link that allows these people to perform their duties for the company, is the same one that he or she just finished screaming about.

Chapter Eight

The Internet as a Backbone

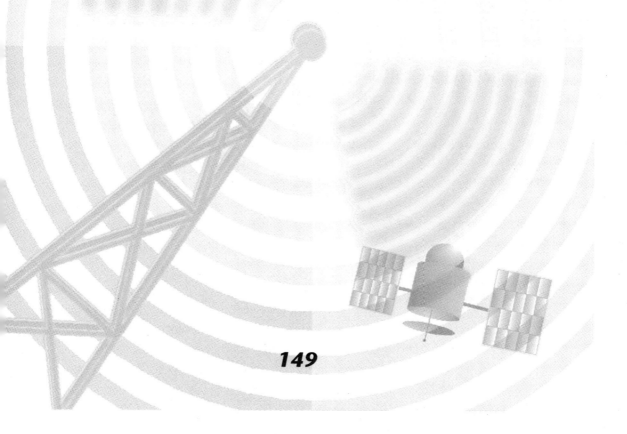

For many companies, the need for high-speed access to the Internet for users in small offices, for telecommuters, and for mobile workers is one of the major driving forces in their remote connectivity plans. In fact, all of the earlier chapters in this section have discussed ways to give users a cost-effective means of accessing the Internet.

Yet many companies have a limited view of the role of the Internet. For most companies, the Internet is simply something that provides their remote users with some basic, yet necessary services—they use it primarily for e-mail and as an all-encompassing encyclopedia/research tool. However, the Internet can play a much more important role. It can be used as an extension of your corporate backbone network to reduce the costs of communications and remote management.

As discussed in Chapter 1, the cost of connecting remote users goes beyond the purchase price of equipment and software. The two largest expenses to remote connectivity are the recurring telecommunications charges and the operational expenses to manage, diagnose, and fix remote user problems.

How can the Internet save you money? There are several ways. First, there is the potential savings when remote users send traffic over the Internet rather than over the public-switched or a commercial wireless network. There is also a potential to save money on telecommunications charges by giving remote users access to corporate databases and other applications through an Internet connection, rather than using a dial-in link. Perhaps the most important cost savings aspect of using the Internet as a backbone is the ability to reduce management costs. This chapter will discuss each of these topics.

However, one caution before I proceed. There are also some compelling reasons that might make the Internet-as-backbone an inappropriate connectivity solution. For many companies, the two major problems of using the Internet as a backbone are security and reliability. These issues will also be discussed in this chapter.

The Basics

For many years, corporations relied on their leased-line, private networks to cut their telecommunications charges by sending voice and data over these fixed-price-per-month circuits rather than over the public telephone network.

However, many companies could not reap the financial benefits from using leased lines, because they simply did not have the volume of traffic to make them practical. Or, they may have gained only a fraction of the potential savings, because they only used dedicated leased lines to link large regional data centers, not smaller regional offices.

Now you can essentially use the Internet as a substitute for leased lines with the advantage that these "lines" can be extended to small offices (as small as one telecommuter) that you cannot cost-justify using a leased line connection for.

As stated earlier, there are a number of reasons to use the Internet as a backbone to extend your corporate network to remote users. First, there is the cost-saving potential of sending traffic over the Internet. This applies to any type of traffic. It could be the exchange of e-mail, the transfer of files, or the transmission of commands to access and run an application. The potential savings come when you consider that the traffic, for the most part, rides free over the Internet. This approach has the most potential to save you money when you have remote users or small offices scattered throughout the country or even internationally. The basic idea is that rather than paying for long-distance connections, you pay for your remote users' local call into an Internet service provider. Also consider that for most long-distance calls you are billed based on the distance *and* the time the line is used. You often can get local service for a set monthly rate.

How much can you save? It depends on what you use the Internet for. Table 8-1 gives you some idea of the ways you can leverage the Internet to save telecommunications costs. At this point it might be useful to give an example to illustrate the cost savings.

E-mail

Take the simple case of using the Internet to send e-mail. If your company uses a dial-in mail server to give remote users access to, for example, cc:Mail, you might be able to save money connecting the remote users with a form of Internet mail. The more remote users you have, the more you save by switching from dial-up access to Internet mail. If you have international users, the savings can be that much higher.

If everyone had an Internet e-mail account, remote users would make a local telephone call, and the messages and the attachments to those messages could ride across the country (or between countries) without incurring the long-distance telecommunications costs. "Switching from Dial-up Mail Servers to Internet Mail" gives you an example of the potential cost savings such a switch might yield.

Application	Potential Savings or Benefit
Internet e-mail	Common way to save long-distance telecommunications charges over dial-up mail system
Voice over the Internet	Save money spent on long-distance phone calls
Conferencing over the Internet	Gives remote users a sense of unity with coworkers
Fax over the Internet	Save telecommunications transmission fees
Access to host data from remote locations	Lets you open up data to more remote users, customers, and business partners
Internet-enabled applications	Gives your remote users better access to information

Table 8-1. *How the Internet Can Cut Your Communications Costs*

One caveat to switching to Internet mail is that many companies have good reasons to keep their network-based e-mail systems and would not switch users within the company to something else. For example, many companies use a network-based e-mail package within the corporate headquarters. This might be something like IBM's Lotus cc:Mail, a mail system that runs on a minicomputer or mainframe like PROFs, or it might be the messaging portion of a groupware package such as Microsoft's Exchange, Lotus' Notes, or Novell's GroupWise. Such systems offer some safeguards that an Internet-only mail system might not include. For example, network-based messaging and e-mail programs give your users more features and give you administrative tools not available with a simple Internet mail account.

Companies with a large number of remote users often give these users the remote client portion of a network-based e-mail package and have the users dial into the network to retrieve and send their messages. That means you have lots of users making many (several times a day) long-distance phone calls.

It is most likely that you will not swap out an extensive internal network-based e-mail system and give everyone in the main office an Internet mail account as their only e-mail option. So you are faced with a situation where you could save significant money on telecommunications if your remote users used the Internet, but you want to retain the investment in the network-based e-mail system. If that is your situation, you are not alone. This is a very common scenario.

Switching from Dial-up Mail Servers to Internet Mail

Consider the case of an unnamed company based in San Francisco, with three small regional offices, which are located in New York, Atlanta, and Los Angeles. The regional sites are not connected to the main office by any private network. The main form of connectivity between the remote offices is dial-up e-mail. The users in the remote offices only have the capability to dial into a mail server located in the main office; they do not have the ability to connect to the corporate LAN in any other way.

This is a typical operation in many companies. The users in the remote offices each dial into the main site two or three times a day to check mail and send documents and spreadsheets as attachments to their mail messages.

The phone charges associated with just the dial-up e-mail for these sites are approximately $120 per month for the Los Angeles office, $350 per month for the Atlanta office, and $450 per month for the New York office. That is a grand total of $920 per month or $11,040 per year.

All the users in the remote sites also have an Internet account with a local Internet service provider. They pay a fixed rate per month for the accounts for unlimited usage. These accounts include access to news groups, web sites, *and* e-mail. They are already paying for e-mail.

What if they switched to using the Internet as their e-mail system? Since each user makes a local call to access the Internet service—and the company pays a fixed monthly rate for all local calls—there is no extra charge for the additional calls into the Internet. So the $11,040 per year spent by users dialing San Francisco from the three regional offices would be saved if the company were to switch to Internet mail. The same savings would apply if you had many telecommuters dialing long-distance to get e-mail.

There is a way to have the best of both worlds. You can keep your in-house users on their existing network-based e-mail system, give your remote users Internet mail, and use an e-mail gateway to connect the two. You could set up such a system so that the users do not see a difference between the two types of mail. For example, in your network-based e-mail directory you might make remote users appear the same as your network-attached users. Network-attached users would then simply address mail to internal and remote users in the same way—for example, by entering their last name in an address line or clicking on their name in a scroll-down directory. The fact that the remote users' address is an Internet mail address can be masked from the network-attached users.

When network-attached users send an e-mail message, it is routed to other network-attached users in the normal way, and those messages intended for remote users are passed on to the Internet through the e-mail gateway to an Internet service provider (ISP).

Similarly, you can configure the remote users' mail package to include a comparable corporate directory. A remote user selects the name of another employee from the directory and sends the message. The user would connect to a local Internet service provider and transmit the mail messages to that provider. The messages would be carried over the Internet to your corporate ISP, where they would be passed to your e-mail gateway. The gateway would then take the Internet address on the message and translate that address into the appropriate network e-mail address. The message would then be delivered in the normal manner over your network e-mail system. In this way, you only pay for your remote users' local call into their ISP and not for a long-distance call to the company's mail server.

Phone Calls over the Internet

One way to leverage an Internet connection is to run voice traffic over it. There are now many Internet phone products on the market that use the Internet to carry voice traffic. The idea behind the products is to bypass the public telephone network and use the Internet to carry the signal over long distances to save the phone charges. Remote users need an Internet account and Internet phone software. Each user also requires a sound card, microphone (or telephone handset connected through the sound card), and a SLIP or PPP link into the Internet.

Internet phone software now comes bundled with many applications and can also be purchased separately. The software usually relies on three algorithms: one for compression, one that handles packets that arrive out of order, and a third that smoothes out delivery based on Internet traffic loads to let users hold phone conversations over the Internet.

Early versions of some Internet phone kits were half-duplex, meaning only one user could speak at a time. It was a little like using a CB (citizen band) radio, where you would have to say "over" when you finished a sentence. Today, most Internet phone software packages are full-duplex, allowing normal two-way conversation.

Figure 8-1 illustrates how a typical Internet phone system would work. In the figure you can see that a caller wishing to place a call looks up a person in a phone directory maintained on a server. Some Internet phone software vendors maintain such directories for their users (you might also set up one for your organization). Once the person is found in the directory, the call can be "placed" to the other person. If that person is online (or has a dedicated Internet connection), he or she will be notified that an Internet call is coming in.

One drawback to using an Internet phone is that there are none of the higher-end features we are used to having with our normal phone systems. For instance, these systems do not usually have a way to handle a busy signal when the person you're calling is talking to someone else over the Internet.

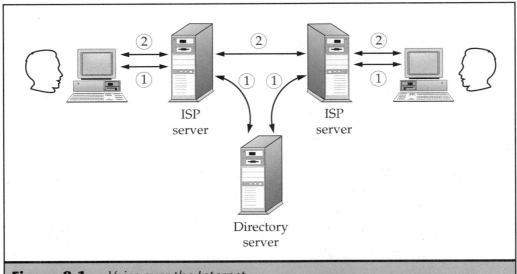

Figure 8-1. *Voice over the Internet*

And if the user on the other end of a connection is not online, the call is not completed. Some systems send intended recipients an e-mail message alerting them you tried to reach them, but that's about the extent of it—there's no voice mail to leave your message.

Another point to consider is that the quality of the phone conversations varies greatly and depends on the traffic on the Internet links that your voice traffic is traveling over. Typically, the quality is about that of a speakerphone, with some delays making the conversations choppy. However, many people say this is acceptable, especially since they're saving the cost of a long-distance phone call. Because of this voice-quality issue, you might not want to use this type of connection when conducting business with clients or with people in other companies. You would probably use an Internet phone connection internally, where remote users would talk to other employees of your company.

And one last issue to consider is that you need the people at both ends of a conversation to be equipped with the right setup. What if you want to reach a user who does not have an Internet account or the right type of sound card? Some progress has been made in this area. Some Internet service providers are trying services that let you connect to a regular phone. The idea is that you would use your Internet phone setup and be able to place a long-distance phone call to anyone with a telephone. The ISP would have to be set up to take such a phone call, direct it to its point of presence nearest the call recipient's location, and dial the person. The ISP would also have to act as an intermediary and take the digitized packets that comprise your part of the conversation, assemble them as they come off the Internet, convert them to analog, and send them down the phone line. Of course, it would also have to do the opposite— taking the person's analog voice signal off the line, digitizing and parsing it, and sending it over the Internet to you. These services are not widely available, but there is some work being done in this area.

Faxing

As stated earlier, many companies already use the Internet to send data around the globe, only paying for the cost of a local phone call and their monthly Internet access fee (combined, these fees are typically much lower than the cost of long-distance or international phone calls). Once you have the Internet infrastructure in place for things like e-mail and Web surfing, you can leverage this connection to your remote users to reduce the cost of sending faxes.

The cost savings of sending faxes over the Internet can be substantial. Today, faxing accounts for as much as 40 percent of a company's telecommunications charges, according to a 1996 Gallup survey done for Pitney-Bowes Corp. The survey found that the average Fortune 500 company spends about $15 million a year on fax transmission costs.

Sending faxes over the Internet is not as simple as sending e-mail. In any cost-benefit analysis, you will likely have to consider the labor charges to make the transition. You will have to choose between two methods to get your fax traffic on, over, and off the Internet.

The first method is to use a LAN-based fax server so that your LAN-attached users in small remote offices can send faxes from their normal applications. You would have to mask the difference between using the Internet and using a normal fax server approach. The idea is to have users send the fax from their PC in the normal way and have a fax server handle getting that fax to an Internet service provider (ISP). Naturally, this requires that the fax message be parsed into packets to be carried over the Internet. Then an ISP near the fax's destination must know what to do with the fax. At this writing there was one problem with this technology. How does the fax get off the Internet? You need a way to link a destination fax phone number with an ISP close to the location of the fax recipient. The ISP must understand that it is dealing with a fax, read a destination fax telephone number, dial that local number, and then transmit the fax to the fax machine.

This type of fax delivery over the Internet likely will not be available for several years. The best you can hope for in the near future is a fax server-to-fax server form of communication, where the faxes sent by one fax server are carried over the Internet to a fax server in another office, where faxes are delivered to LAN-attached PCs.

The other way you could send faxes over the Internet is more appropriate for faxing between corporate sites and small remote offices. The idea with this second approach is to use a device called a *fax router* that works with regular fax machines and converts the fax to a digital format, which then can be routed over a network, such as the Internet, as any other form of traffic.

This type of faxing between corporate offices costs companies a lot of money each year in telecommunications charges. An earlier Gallup poll found that 55 percent of fax traffic is internal to a company, meaning that it is destined for a fax machine within the organization. If you use the Internet for this traffic, the survey suggested that savings could be in the millions of dollars per year for large companies.

The leader in the fax router segment of the market is the Brooktrout Networks Group (Richardson, Texas). Brooktrout's IP/FaxRouter lets a company send a fax over the least expensive route—leased lines (when available), the Internet, or the public telephone network—meanwhile retaining the simple-to-use interface of a common fax machine. Figure 8-2 illustrates the key elements required to pull this off. Basically, all users do is dial the destination fax number as they normally would. The fax is then transmitted over the least expensive link based on information in the IP/FaxRouter's routing tables, which are constructed by a network administrator.

Brooktrout's FaxRouter first digitizes the fax signal and then transmits it in a store-and-forward manner to another FaxRouter, which, once it receives the entire fax, converts the digital signal back to analog for delivery to a fax machine. If you have a FaxRouter in each remote site, you would be able to send faxes between the sites over the Internet without incurring the long-distance communications costs. Some ISPs are eyeing this technology to offer international fax services, where they send faxes for you over the Internet at a fraction of the cost if you were to send them by phone.

Most likely, you will not set up such a system yourself, because configuring such a system can be quite tricky. But you may decide to look into this method because of the great cost savings. For example, one user of the FaxRouter, a mid-Atlantic Fortune 500 manufacturer with an international private network, says the payback period for the $2,500 unit is about two weeks.

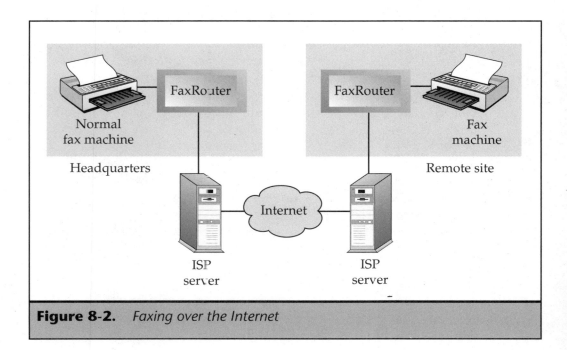

Figure 8-2.   *Faxing over the Internet*

Since the fax is converted to digital traffic, it can also be carried over traditional data networks. For example, Brooktrout, in conjunction with Cisco Systems Inc. (Menlo Park, California) has demonstrated that it can send digitized fax traffic over LAN internetworks. In one demonstration, fax data packets were sent over an Ethernet LAN to a Cisco 4000 router, which bridged the traffic over an internetwork. A second Cisco 4000 received the fax data packets and forwarded them to a FaxRouter, which converted the packets into G3 format and delivered them to a fax machine.

Accessing Data over the Internet

Is the web browser the ultimate corporate front-end? The hype about the Internet and intranets certainly indicates this. Trouble is, one vital component is missing from web technology: access to mainframe data. However, with some planning, browsers can give users a common front-end into mainframe data, thus extending another part of your backbone to remote users via an Internet connection.

Today, approximately 75 percent of all real-time transactions in the world still run on mainframe-based networks, according to Workgroup Strategic, a Portsmouth, New Hampshire, consulting firm. In other words, the data that corporate America runs on is currently inaccessible through browsers and Internets.

There are a couple of fundamentally different ways to give browsers access to IBM hosts. The two basic methods can generically be called *native 3270* and *HTML conversion*. Each method has technical merits and deficiencies.

With native 3270, you need to have a special browser. In this case, the browser needs some form of built-in 3270 terminal emulator and applets that know what to do with the 3270 data streams once they reach the desktop system. With conversion, 3270 screens are converted to HTML format and posted to a web server. The converted version of the screens can then be viewed by use of any browser.

With HTML conversion there are two flavors. One is a static approach— the user only has what amounts to read-only access to data that has been made available by an administrator. The other method is more dynamic (and similar to your typical transaction-oriented mainframe data access), where the user queries a database and views the results using a browser.

An example of the static approach would be where some mainframe data is made available to an organization. For example, a human resources department might, on a monthly basis, post to an intranet server the amount each employee has in his or her 401(k) plan. To do this, the 401(k) information would be pulled off of the mainframe and converted to HTML format. Then employees would be able to look up this information using the browser on their desktop computer by simply entering the URL of the web server. (Obviously, security is an issue here, and the information would need to be password protected.)

This approach to making mainframe data available through browsers is fairly static. While such access is fine in many situations, it does not suffice when users need access to data that changes more frequently. For example, you might have an inventory database that sales staffers frequently check when taking orders over the phone. For such applications you need an HTML conversion method that is more dynamic.

The way to accomplish this level of access to mainframe data is through embedded HTML scripts. (In a sense, this is the normal HTML process applied to 3270 data streams.) First, an SNA gateway into an IBM host pulls off a standard IBM host screen with embedded data. This screen is then converted to HTML format on-the-fly.

Figure 8-3 shows you how this might be done. From a common browser, the user enters the URL of an intranet server that is connected to the server performing the HTML conversion. Common gateway interface (CGI) scripts are used to generate the HTML pages based on user queries.

The possible downside to the HTML conversion approach is that you may not, in all cases, be able to support some of the more complex 3270 commands, such as creating built-in function keys that perform a series of operations.

An alternative to HTML conversion is to leave the data in its native 3270 data stream format and use a special browser. Such a browser would need 3270 terminal emulation features and would require an applet to handle the data. The browser would replace a terminal emulator and would include the underlying technology needed to maintain a connection with the mainframe (for example, by sending acknowledgments to the host to keep the session alive).

Using a special browser may seem idiotic. Would anyone actually do that? The answer is, probably—especially if the browser solves a specific problem, like giving users access to mainframe data. An alternative to a special browser is to use Java applets to, in a sense, make a common browser a specialty browser.

Using the native 3270 approach, a user establishes a session with the mainframe. Typically, the user would run a Telnet session into the host. The resulting TN3270 data stream would travel across the network to the desktop system. There, the browser would need embedded applets that would take the data stream and display it as a normal 3270 screen.

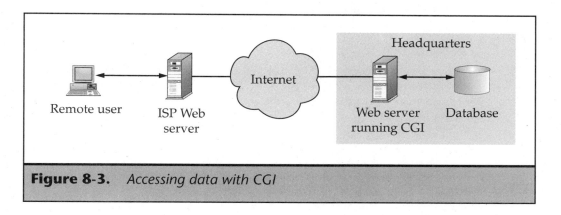

Figure 8-3.   *Accessing data with CGI*

The applets could be designed to handle even the most complex 3270 commands. This would overcome the shortcomings you might encounter with an HTML conversion approach. The trade-off, of course, is that you need a special browser that can perform emulation and handle the data. But, as noted earlier, that may not be a problem if you decide to use a common applet technology such as Java. If that's the case, then any of the major browsers will work, since virtually all the browser vendors either support Java or plan to.

Giving users access to mainframe data through browsers is a big start. But many users also want to extend this level of connectivity to other IBM environments—specifically, to AS/400 systems and LAN servers. The same Web-based access techniques can be applied in these areas.

Regardless of the method used to access mainframe data using a browser, there's one other issue that must be addressed before opening up access to the corporate treasures. That issue is security. What seems to be an issue is that many web browsers (including the Netscape Navigator) store onscreen images in a local cache and often in a server cache. After a user logs out of a session with a mainframe, these screen images can be viewed with the browser.

That means someone could come along after a session and have access to data that the original user gained access to only after entering a password and ID when logging onto the mainframe application. Peeking at the cached screen images also defeats any encryption that was used when the data passed over the network.

This is an area that is likely to be addressed quickly. Web browser vendors will probably add HTML extensions to tackle this security breach. It's at least something to consider before opening the doors to your mainframe data. But once that's done, you may have an easy way to give users a common interface into all your corporate data.

Modified Products

Another way to take advantage of an Internet connection to reduce communications charges is to look for Internet-enabled applications. Such applications are modified products that let you further exploit the Internet-as-backbone phenomenon.

The first wave of Internet-enabled client/server applications is under development. The early developers of this market came from group-scheduling companies. For example, in 1996, Campbell Service announced it was modifying its OnTime Enterprise group-scheduling system so it could be used for intercompany scheduling running over the Internet. The new product is implemented as a common gateway interface (CGI) application that will run on Windows 3.x, Win 95, and Windows NT web servers that support CGI.

Such intercompany group-scheduling tools have lots of potential for improving business relations. For example, a tool like this could help you coordinate meetings between an outside advertising agency and the marketing department of your corporation. Or, it could be used by an industry consortium so members could plan meetings.

The way group scheduling over the Internet would work is that one company would maintain a web server running a modified version of a scheduling program. Users pointing their browsers at that site would be able to view schedules in the form of HTML pages.

There are security issues to deal with in using such a system. Imagine what the stock market would do if someone got to a scheduling web site and saw that Bill Gates and Lou Gerstner were meeting for lunch five days in a row. For this reason, look for security systems offered with the packages. For instance, Campbell Service will use the existing security and access control features of its OnTime Enterprise product to prevent such abuse. Those features include management tools for adding, modifying, and deleting users, and the ability to tightly integrate the group-scheduling program with the Novell bindery.

Another way to use group-scheduling programs to save telecommunications charges is in intracompany scheduling, where users could pick up a revised schedule from any place they have Internet access. For example, a sales force within a company could dial into the Internet at night from a hotel room, select a URL that has the scheduling application running on it, and get a list of the next day's appointments that incorporates any last-minute changes entered by an assistant back in the home office.

Again, security and privacy are issues with this type of system. Many group-scheduling products have built-in security features that deal with these potential problems. For example, they let you import an e-mail user directory into a scheduling program so they can then determine who has access to the group-scheduling system (rather than building such a list from scratch). And some products let you hide a message or note—you can reserve a time slot so others can see that the slot is taken, but no one knows it's taken by you.

It's one thing to let users view meeting schedules over the Internet, but how about setting up those meetings in the first place? You'd need an Internet-enabled contact management program to pull off the meetings. One vendor who entered this market early is Elan Software. Its Goldmine product, a contact manager for workgroup products, already has many of the tools you'll need. For instance, one feature in Goldmine for Windows 95 is the ability to send and receive Internet e-mail. When a user receives a message from one of his or her contacts, the message is automatically linked to the contact's Goldmine record.

A user can compose messages offline, and these messages are queued up to automatically be sent when the next Internet connection is made. Additionally, users can now synchronize databases over the Internet.

For many corporate users, the real impact of Internet-enabled applications will come in the database management systems (DBMS) arena. Larry Ellison, Oracle's chairman and chief executive officer, has made it very clear that the Internet is the way to go for accessing corporate data. Ellison is one of the major proponents of the stripped down, networked PC that's geared toward retrieving information over the Internet.

Oracle's product line already includes web server software and a browser. But the company is also developing a server-based application suite that will include database and web server technology, systems management tools, and a messaging server with text search tools and e-mail. Many other database vendors are actively involved in this area.

The point is to make existing information available without having to do much extra work. For example, along those lines, Sybase lets you dynamically generate web pages from an existing database.

We're starting to see the first wave of products that have been modified to run over the Internet. Security seems to be the only potential obstacle standing in the way of an explosion in the use of Internet-enabled applications. Many of the application vendors who are modifying their programs to run over the Internet are addressing security up front by linking access control and user rights to existing security systems, such as user rights assigned for LAN access. How well the vendors do in this area will determine whether these types of Internet-enabled applications are embraced by large corporations.

Some people don't have time to wait for software developers to bring Internet-enabled products to market. If that is your case, you might want to do it yourself. Currently, the situation is quite interesting. Sun Microsystems' Java technology and Microsoft's ActiveX technology promise to make it fairly easy to build applets that run through a web browser, link to corporate databases, or embed dynamic links to information residing on databases or spreadsheets.

Reducing Management Costs of Remote Sites

Besides saving telecommunications costs, using the Internet to extend your corporate backbone to remote users can reduce the time (and therefore cost) to support remote users.

You will likely see a progression of web-based management tools starting with the ones available today—for example, the web-based interface developed by network management platform vendors such as Hewlett-Packard and Cabletron Systems Inc. (Rochester, New Hampshire). Such approaches give you an option of using a browser instead of that vendor's proprietary management console. There are also some web-based front-end tools that manage a single vendor's device, such as a router, hub, or other network device. One tool like this is the Web Assistant from Hewlett-Packard that lets a manager monitor and configure HP's PowerWise UPSes (uninterruptible power supplies).

Early in 1997, managers should see the first tools that use Java and ActiveX to make DMI (Desktop Management Interface) and SNMP (Simple Network Management Protocol) data of any network device (not just the devices of one vendor) available to a manager using a browser. Table 8-2 shows the types of web-enabled management tools you are likely to see between now and early 1998.

Extending the Reach of Your Helpdesk

In fall 1996, Intel Corp. demonstrated a web-based LANDesk management helpdesk that integrates a trouble-ticket/problem-tracking system, desktop and systems management tools, and a knowledge base for solving problems.

The integrated product, which has not been formally named, will cut the cost of LAN ownership by reducing the time it takes a manager to resolve a problem. It will also give the manager the information needed to diagnose problems without requiring a trip to a troubled PC, server, or other networking device.

Type of Tool/Management	Benefits
Web-browser front-end to access proprietary management platform data	Remote access to management platform data over Internet/intranet
Web-based access to DMI and SNMP data	Common interface to all management data through management services that sit on a network
Web-based access to standards-based management objects that define network elements and associations	True integrated, enterprise management

Table 8-2. *Web-Based Management Options Multiply*

Users will be able to submit problems to the helpdesk by using a web-based trouble-ticket form (they can also call in the problem). And users as well as managers will be able to track the progress of a problem's resolution using a browser. One early beta user of the technology was the coffee giant Starbucks, which plans to use this technology to support users in their international chain of coffee shops. Each Starbucks will have a PC with an Internet connection. Users will be able to get information about the corporation and will be able to view training videos that show how to do everything from make the perfect latte to how to properly grind beans. From the browser interface on each Starbucks PC, a user can generate a trouble ticket and send it to a central helpdesk. The helpdesk personnel can then use other Internet-enabled management tools, such as one that inventories the PC to see that it does not, for example, have the required driver to run a video. Using a software distribution tool within the helpdesk system, you would then be able to download over the Internet a new piece of software (the new driver) and then take remote control of the PC to install the new software.

The web-based helpdesk product from Intel will tightly integrate the tools, such as software and hardware inventorying, server and desktop performance monitoring, and remote control, in its LANDesk Management Suite with a helpdesk application that provides problem tracking and a knowledge base.

This should be a useful combination, since most helpdesk applications do not integrate systems management tools. Even those that do, often require that the manager launch a systems or desktop management application to get information.

Intel plans to link the questions in a knowledge base with the system management tools. So, when a user calls in with a performance problem running, for example, an Oracle database application, the knowledge base may have a list of questions about how much server memory is free, how much server disk space is available, and what the CPU utilization rate is. With the Intel approach, the LANDesk Management Suite tools will automatically pull this information from the network or over an Internet connection. This should help cut the time to resolve problems called into a helpdesk. And that should help you reduce the cost to support its end users.

Also in fall 1996, Novell Inc. enhanced ManageWise, its systems and network management offering. At that time, Novell demonstrated their new web interface to ManageWise that lets you use a browser to get real-time status information about your NetWare and NT server environments. Figure 8-4 shows you the type of information you can get using Novell's web-based management system. In this figure you can see that it is possible to view, through a browser, familiar management speedometer-like gauges showing the number of packets per second flowing in and out of a server.

Access to Existing Management Data

One level of web-based management that would be useful is simply being able to view existing SNMP (Simple Network Management Protocol) or DMI (Desktop Management Interface) information by use of a browser instead of a proprietary management tool or software package. The reason this would be useful is that it would mean that you could, in theory, take a look at any device on your network over an Internet connection.

Many network management programs let you link certain SNMP alerts to a pager. If you are paged, a web-based access to SNMP information would let you check out a situation without having to make a trip into the office. For example, you would be able to dial into the Internet and, as long as you had the appropriate Internet link into your company, would be able to view the SNMP data for the device sending the alert. Without a web-based approach, you would have to go into work to see what the problem was.

As you can imagine, there is growing interest in this type of web-based access to management data. You don't have to use such access just to avoid a trip into work at night. You could also take advantage of this type of capability

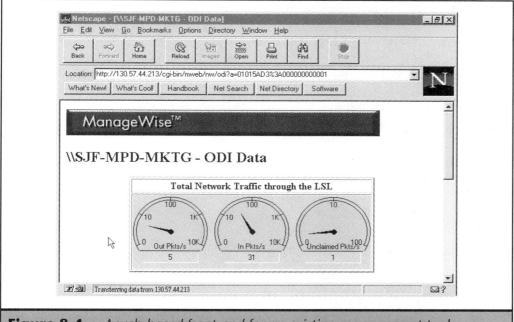

Figure 8-4.   *A web-based front-end for an existing management tool*

to support remote sites. Or, you could support users while you are traveling by dialing into the Internet from the road and checking the status of the network.

Until recently, the only way to get this SNMP data into a browser was to wait for a vendor to web-enable its management offering. This is happening quite a bit. A router vendor would, for example, give you web-based access into that one vendor's devices over the Internet using custom-developed Java or ActiveX management applications specific to that vendor's products. That is fine, but you might want much more. You might, for example, have a network with devices from multiple vendors. For instance, you might have an access router from Bay Networks and hubs from 3Com Corp.

To view SNMP data regardless of which vendor's products you use seems like a very basic requirement. Until recently, however, doing that required that you manually map SNMP information to HTML format. There are typically hundreds of SNMP MIB variables associated with every device on a network. And you really only need a few to get a sense of what is happening on your network. Basically, you would have to ensure that the MIB variables you wanted access to via a browser were somehow collected, mapped into an

HTML form, and made available to you. This is not my idea of fun, and I'm sure you have better things to do.

That is where the second type of web-based management tools mentioned earlier would really help. One of the first efforts to offer more than a simple web-based front-end to an existing management system was initiated by SNMP Research International Inc. (Knoxville, Tennessee) in fall 1996. At that time, SNMP Research Internet-enabled its SNMP management software program called Emante. This was accomplished by adding another piece of software, an agent called DR-Web, to the program. The idea behind the DR-Web agent was to provide an off-the-shelf product that eliminates the need to recode any data or to employ additional HTML (Hypertext Markup language)/SNMP interfaces to view network statistics on a web page. Basically, this application handles the conversion between SNMP and HTML. (Note that SNMP Research is not just your run-of-the-mill network management company. SNMP Research President Jeff Case has authored or co-authored many of today's network management standards.)

The DR-Web agent lets you browse the SNMP MIB tree and specify, by pointing and clicking, what SNMP MIB information you display on a web page. The DR-Web agent technology is not really aimed at individual network managers. It is more likely to be used by developers and OEMs (original equipment manufacturers) who want the ability to export their products' SNMP data to the Web. This technology will let these developers use the same management interfaces and existing SNMP access functions they have been using all along. And they will then make these products available to you.

Additionally, independent network management vendors are using Sun Microsystems' Java Management API (application programming interface) to develop management applications for the Web. Figure 8-5 shows you what you can get using these types of tools. In this figure, Aquas Inc.'s Java-enabled Bazaar Analyzer lets you view a web server's performance statistics (in this case the number of hits as a function of time) using a browser.

WBEM—The Ultimate in Web-Based Management

In July 1996, a new management initiative, called *Web-Based Enterprise Management* (WBEM), was put forward by Microsoft Corp. of Redmond, Washington; Intel Corp. of Santa Clara, California; Cisco Systems Inc. of Menlo Park, California; Compaq Computer Corp. of Houston, Texas; BMC Software Inc. of Houston, Texas; and about 75 other networking, computer, and management industry vendors.

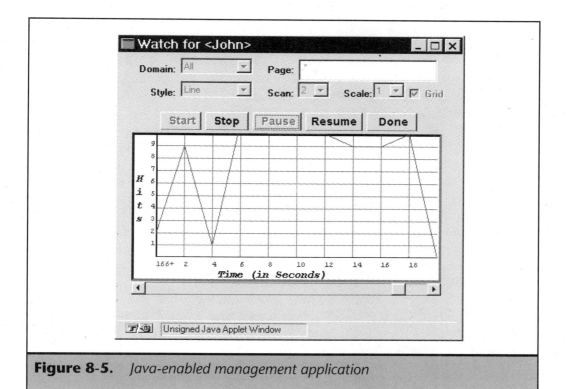

Figure 8-5. *Java-enabled management application*

The initiative promises to make it easier to manage networks by integrating network, systems, desktop, and applications management while making the browser the common tool to monitor networks. WBEM also promises to make life easier for network managers by using information about relationships between network elements to perform more intelligent handling of event alerts and alarms.

At the heart of the initiative are three new pieces to the management puzzle. First, there is the *HyperMedia Management Schema* (HMMS), a data model that represents each element of a network, including all hardware and software elements. The HMMS is the object representation of any element from a PC Card to a router, or a software driver for an adapter card to Lotus Notes. Basically, every hardware and software component of a network will be defined by use of HMMS.

Next, there is the *HyperMedia Management Protocol* (HMMP), which is a communications protocol designed to run over HTTP (HyperText Transfer Protocol). This protocol lets a browser access HMMS information over an intranet. And finally, there is the *HyperMedia Object Manager* (HMON), an object-broker based on Microsoft's OLE technology that manages network elements as objects, collects and manages the management data, and provides interfaces to other management data such as that contained in SNMP MIBs and DMI MIF files. Figure 8-6 shows you the WBEM architecture. In the figure, you can see that existing management data, such as SNMP, DMI, and CMIP, can be accessed by a management application by use of a service layer interface. HMMS data is directly available to the management application. Under the WBEM proposal, an object-broker called the HyperMedia Object Manager resides between the management application and the devices.

Users have mixed opinions about the value of this technology. If all the technology ends up doing is giving a manager access to management data through a browser, this is of limited value. As noted earlier in the chapter, there are other more simple ways to accomplish this. WBEM has great potential if it really delivers integrated systems, network, and application management along with more intelligent handling of alarms.

The effort's backers say they plan to do just that. For instance, one benefit of using HMMP instead of SNMP is that a manager with a common browser will be able to get status information about any device.

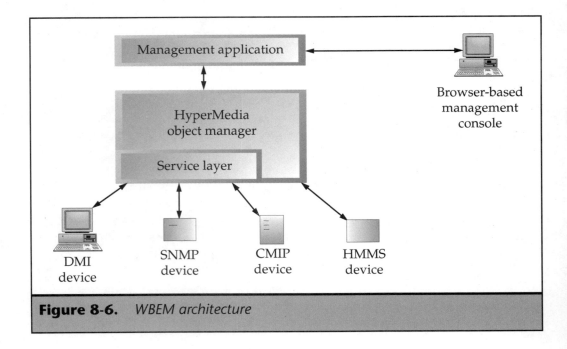

Figure 8-6. *WBEM architecture*

Another advantage to WBEM is the relationships or associations between elements that will be built into the schema. This makes the schema more useful than an SNMP MIB or a DMI MIF. A simple example of an association is relating a software driver for an adapter card to the physical adapter card. At a higher level, you might find an association between a database application, the server hardware it is running on, and the user's client workstation.

Having such associations, a management element application could then, in theory, take the information to better filter alarms. For example, today a manager might have a systems management tool that monitors a server's memory usage and a performance monitoring program to measure the time it takes an application to perform specific tasks.

With this scenario, the manager might receive an alarm telling him or her that the application's performance has dropped below an acceptable level and may get another alarm that a server has very little memory available.

Without knowing the link between the server and the application, the manager must put the two pieces of information together to determine that the two alarms are related. If that is the case, a manager would need to do mental correlation, looking here and there at different monitors and then drawing a conclusion about the nature of the problem. That is something a management application, using the association information in the schema, could do for an administrator.

This all sounds great, but let's be realistic. This ambitious initiative is in its very early stages. And we need only look to past all-encompassing management initiatives to consider taking a wait-and-see approach. The WBEM is not the first distributed management initiative ever proposed. Recall the Open Software Foundation's DME (Distributed Management Environment) of a few years ago.

Like DME, WBEM faces many obstacles. First, HMMS and HTTP must be approved. HMMS is being submitted to the Desktop Management Task Force (DMTF) for approval, and the HMMP is being submitted to the Internet Engineering Task Force.

While there is much solidarity today on this initiative, it doesn't take a stretch of the imagination to see that once the standards bodies begin deliberating, things may change. Look at SNMP—it is a widely accepted management standard, yet most vendors still add MIB extensions to give you that extra level of management for their products. Will the same be true of HMMS? Today, the answer from the vendors is no.

However, there are already some cracks in the initiative's armor. The heart of the initiative, the HyperMedia Management Schema (HMMS)—an object-based description of all network elements and the associations between the elements—will not likely be complete until late 1997 or early 1998. And it likely will incorporate other technologies not in the current schema.

In October 1996, a working group within the Desktop Management Task Force began work to define a common information model for network elements—a necessary component to any standards-based enterprise management technology. This effort got its start when the DMTF's technical committee took a look at the HMMS, which was submitted by the WBEM consortium.

At that time, the DMTF decided there were many technical details that should be looked at to properly define enterprise management objects, and the HMMS may not necessarily address all of them. Basically, everyone agrees that what is needed is a common way to represent management data and the associations between the various components of a network, and this may require an expansion of the schema.

Most agree that HMMS is a good start. However, to reach a common information model for network elements, three levels of tasks must be accomplished, according to DMTF Chairman Ed Arrington. First, you need to define rules—this is an object, this is what an association means. The next level is to define categories, such as systems or applications. The third and last task is to use these definitions and categorizations and come up with a standard schema. "This is the huge part," said Arrington.

This is where you have to develop names and attributes for devices, as well as the associations and relationships between devices. Such information is necessary to simplify management. For example, consider application management. Today, using the Desktop Management Interface (DMI), you can look at a software component on a workstation. But to get a true measure of application performance, you need to look at the application on multiple platforms. You need to view the whole network, rather than looking at one desktop at a time. That's where a common schema helps.

The first two steps in the process of developing a common information model for network elements were supposed to be accomplished by the time this book appears (first quarter 1997). It is not clear how long it will take to complete the third task, the definition of a standard schema.

One thing that may complicate the effort is what role Sun Microsystems' Java Management API will play in any web-based, industrywide, standards-based management initiative. Microsoft is the big proponent of WBEM, and the two companies (Sun and Microsoft) compete so heavily in the Web space that this has clouded the matter. But the one promising thing that might make all of this work is that the Java Management API and the HMMS are not mutually exclusive, and it may be a situation where we see a hybrid approach.

This is normal for the standards-setting process. However, there is one factor that makes it likely that some form of standards-based Internet-based management technology will come to fruition. Such a management approach, while being quite helpful to you, will also be very useful to networking equipment and management vendors. Today, vendors spend a fortune making their management services available to the numerous management platforms. It takes a lot of development resources to support the different platforms. Most network hardware vendors or systems management vendors spend a lot of time making the information their tools collect available to higher-level management platforms such as Hewlett-Packard's OpenView, Cabletron's Spectrum, IBM's Tivoli Management Environment, Computer Associates' Unicenter, and others. Often, a vendor needs to support integration with more than one of these platforms.

Basically, the companies are spending a lot of time putting data into the right format to be used by these management platforms. With a common representation for all elements of a network such as the WBEM schema the process would be much easier.

This means there is a potential cost-saving incentive for vendors to come together on this effort. The management platform vendors would be able to dedicate more of their resources to making better management applications. For instance, they could take advantage of the built-in associations between elements in the schema to make their management systems perform more intelligent alarm filtering.

A Word of Caution

As noted throughout this chapter, security is an issue when you extend your corporate backbone to remote users by using the Internet. Chapter 16 deals with security in remote connectivity. I'll discuss Internet security in that chapter.

There is, however, another issue when it comes to using the Internet as a backbone. That is reliability. The current state of the Internet, with its highly competitive, explosive growth and many small players entering the Internet service provider market, has made service an issue. There have already been several widely reported major outages of Internet service providers and commercial online service providers. Less reported but still a problem are so-called Internet brownouts, where service is not completely shut down, but is only available in, for example, a limited area for a few hours.

The main concern is that the reliability of your Internet connections may not suit your users. If you Internet-enable your applications and the Internet connection is the only way for your remote users to get their job done, you had better make sure you use an Internet service provider with a good track record and one who quickly remedies outages.

PART THREE

Connectivity Scenarios

This section looks at the different connectivity scenarios from a corporate perspective. In this section, I discuss the methods you should use to develop remote connectivity strategies for linking individual users to a corporate backbone or the Internet, linking small- or medium-size branch offices to the corpoarte backbone, and linking small sites to one another.

Many companies treat these different scenarios as separate entities where each type of connectivity is designed, deployed, and managed by separate staffs with little interaction between the groups. While this may be the norm, it makes more sense to look at all forms of corporate connectivity as one entity.

Chapter Nine

A Model for Corporate Connectivity

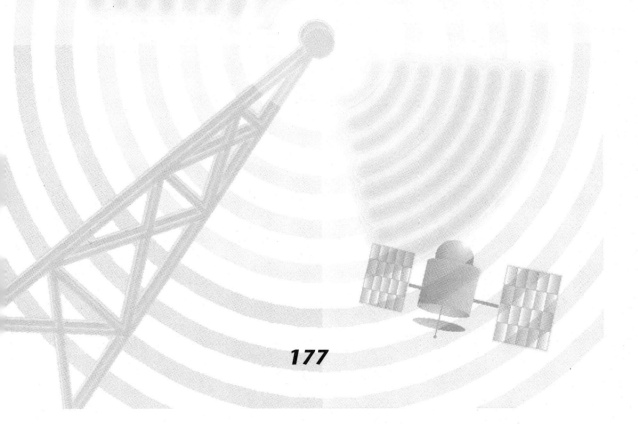

177

Corporations are riding out a major shakeup when it comes to connecting remote sites, telecommuters, and other mobile workers. The foundation upon which all corporate networks reside—the connectivity services offered by the telecom carriers—is undergoing a radical change.

Today, companies are using more public services to carry their data and connect their users. And new telecom services are making it easier to shift corporate traffic from private networks to public switched networks.

The nature of connectivity has changed dramatically. Corporations are much more decentralized, and that makes the old paradigm of private networks obsolete. Everyone wants more bandwidth, more performance, and more sites connected, all while paying less for the telecom services.

Some studies by market research organizations gives you an idea of the magnitude of the situation. For example, several years ago, Forrester Research, a market research consultancy in Cambridge, Massachusetts, estimated that Fortune 500 companies had over 225,000 branch offices with fewer than 25 people. Many of these offices run your typical LAN applications and need to exchange e-mail and transfer files with users in other sites, as well as to access data and applications residing on hosts in regional data centers. The Yankee Group estimates that there were 10 million telecommuters in the United States in 1996, and the number is growing at a compound rate of 15 percent per year.

To accommodate the connectivity needs of such widely dispersed sites and users is no mean feat. The trend in the industry is to use a mix of public telecom services that best meets the performance and economic needs of an organization.

The good news is that there are many services to choose from. The bad news is that some of the services are not ubiquitous, or their pricing structure makes them too expensive to use. Increasingly, companies are looking to the Internet to provide some form of connectivity.

The New WAN

For years, most corporate networks ran on a telecommunications infrastructure that was fairly stable. But in the last four or five years that has changed. The reason for this change is the widespread deployment and acceptance of ISDN and the growing acceptance of other public switched services including frame relay, SMDS (Switched Multi-megabit Data Service), and even ATM (asynchronous transfer mode). The availability and price of these switched services are turning corporate WANs into something quite different from the networks we had in the days when MIS controlled the network.

The new switched services came onto the scene at the same time there was a major shift in corporate structures. For many companies, organizational structure is shifting from a setting where most employees work in large central offices to one where employees increasingly work in many smaller, geographically dispersed offices.

The combination of this organizational shift, the growing demand to give users access to corporate databases, and the explosive use of e-mail within corporations requires new ways of thinking when it comes to corporate connectivity strategies. And increasingly, the network manager is being called upon to plan and provide this connectivity.

The result is a radical shift in the architecture of corporate networks. As Figure 9-1 shows, four or five years ago, you'd likely see a private backbone network of dedicated, leased T1 or T3 lines carrying voice and data traffic between, at most, a handful of large regional offices. Low-speed (9.6- or 19.2-Kbps) dedicated leased lines carried transaction-oriented data between dumb terminals in smaller offices (a bank branch office, for example) and mainframes in large data centers.

Today, it's more likely that this backbone architecture is supplemented with higher-speed links carrying LAN traffic from branch offices, dial-up and switched-circuit connections between the various branch offices, and dial-up access to the backbone for telecommuters and employees on the road. As Figure 9-2 shows, this new architecture makes more use of the public switched-telephone network.

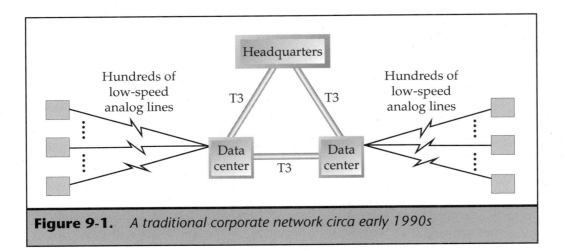

Figure 9-1.   *A traditional corporate network circa early 1990s*

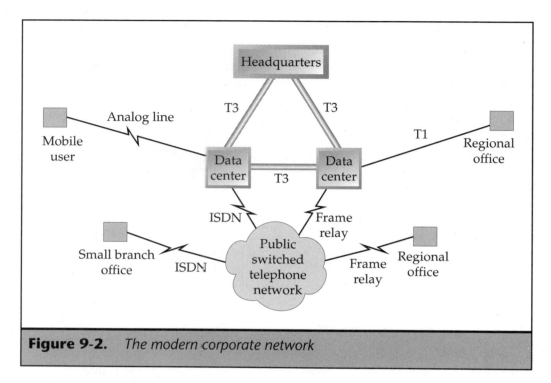

Figure 9-2. *The modern corporate network*

The shift is dramatic. It signals a change from the use of private corporate networks where most, if not all, of the traffic ran over dedicated, leased lines managed by the corporation, to a system where most traffic runs over the public switched-telecommunications infrastructure.

Making the Right Choice

The challenge most organizations face today is choosing the right service for their connectivity needs. Determining what exactly is the most appropriate service is often a juggling act.

The first step to selecting a WAN service is to understand the traffic that will be running over a link. Basically, you need to predict what the traffic volume will be for each link, the mix of protocols that will run over the link, and whether any of the traffic is time sensitive and mission critical.

For example, one office might have hundreds of telemarketers who need access to mainframe inventory databases. Another office might have many engineers who need to send large files with application source code they are developing or need to send CAD files to engineers in other locations. Or, users in another office might only need to occasionally check their e-mail or send a small document file a couple of times a day.

Second, there are performance issues to consider. You should ask yourself a couple of questions. Does the service provide enough bandwidth for my applications? Does the service let me set priority levels so that my most time-sensitive traffic gets through even when the network bogs down under a heavy load?

Third, there are the financial aspects of choosing a service. Pricing for the same service can vary greatly between regional Bell companies. ISDN is the perfect example of this. Users in Southern California have seen fairly low monthly fees and usage charges because of Pac Bell's aggressive ISDN campaign. Users in the NyNex region pay a higher rate for the same service.

Finally, there's the issue of availability. Sure, ISDN might offer the best performance characteristics and be reasonably priced, but if it isn't available in the town your accounting department's office is in, you need to reevaluate your choice.

One note about the pricing and availability of ISDN services. There may be many changes with ISDN service offerings in late 1996 and early 1997 because of the telecom bill passed by Congress in 1996 that basically did away with the regulations that prevented some forms of competition between the long-distance carriers, the regional Bell operating companies, local service providers, and even cable TV operators wishing to offer high-speed services. The general consensus among industry folks is that the effect of the bill will be increased competition. This will open up the ISDN market so that services will be available in more locations. For example, one result of the telecom bill that will likely have an impact in this market is that the long-distance carriers—the AT&Ts, Sprints, and MCIs of the world—can offer services in the local market.

Choosing a WAN Service

Examine the nature of the traffic that will run over the WAN.

Determine the technical specifications of the services, including bandwidth required for your applications and how much manageability you want over the service.

Establish the pricing of the service including any startup fee, installation fees, monthly charges, and usage charges.

Consider the availability of the service, particularly if you need connectivity in more than one region of the country.

The Basic Connectivity Scenarios

There are basically four connectivity scenarios that you will need to analyze: the backbone network, LAN-to-backbone connectivity, LAN-to-LAN connectivity, and single user-to-LAN connectivity. Each scenario has characteristics that will determine the best service to choose (see Table 9-1).

Backbone networks link large regional centers of an organization and carry both voice and data between the sites. Backbone networks have traditionally been built around dedicated leased lines that operate at either 1.544 Mbps (T1 speeds) or 44.736 Mbps (T3 speeds).

The backbone is a private network managed by the company using it. A manager can allocate up to 24 64-Kbps channels for each T1 line and up to 673 64-Kbps channels for a single T3 line (the equivalent of 28 T1 links). The way you allocate these channels depends on the needs of your company. For example, within a single T1 connection you might set aside four 64-Kbps channels (256

Connectivity Scenario	What's Linked Up	Traffic Characteristics	Traffic Volume	Protocol Mix	Type of WAN Service to Consider
Backbone network	Large data centers	Voice, data, and time-sensitive data such as SNA and transaction-processing traffic	Heavy	Multiple protocols such as TCP/IP, IPX, NetBIOS, SNA	Dedicated T1 or T3 leased lines, frame relay (ATM in the near future)
LAN-to-backbone	Regional offices linked to headquarters and data centers	LAN traffic and some time-sensitive traffic, such as SNA session traffic	Moderate	TCP/IP, IPX, some Appletalk and SNA traffic	Frame relay, Fractional T1, Switched 56, ISDN
LAN-to-LAN	Small offices linked to each other	LAN traffic from e-mail exchanges and file transfers	Moderate to low	IP, IPX	Frame relay, ISDN, analog
Single user-to-LAN	Telecommuters and mobile users dialing into a network	Access to server and host applications; e-mail, file transfers	Low to moderate	IP, IPX (usually just one)	ISDN, analog, wireless

Table 9-1. *Examining Corporate Connections*

Kbps total bandwidth) for voice, 12 64-Kbps channels (768 Kbps total bandwidth) for videoconferencing, and eight 64-Kbps channels (512 Kbps total bandwidth) for a data connection between mainframes in different sites.

To get traffic onto the network, you use a *time-division multiplexor* in each site. It aggregates numerous voice and data channels into one stream of traffic that goes out over the link. A device called a *channel service unit* (CSU) connects the multiplexor to the actual phone line.

T1 and T3 circuits are still the most commonly used circuits connecting large regional centers to form a core backbone network. But there are alternatives to consider.

Some companies use frame relay or SMDS to meet their backbone connectivity needs. Currently, frame relay is one of the hotter technologies. *Frame relay* is a packet-switching technology that allows you to send data between two intelligent devices—routers or frame relay access devices (FRADs), for example. Frame relay is more efficient than its predecessor X.25—it uses less error correction than X.25 to deliver a higher throughput.

With frame relay, the sending device parses the data into variable-length frames. Each frame has a header with addressing information. The sending device transmits the frames intermittently over a link, and the receiving device reassembles them.

Data travels between two sites over a logical link called a *virtual circuit.* There are two types of virtual circuits. One is called a *permanent* virtual circuit (PVC), where you define the path and the endpoints of a link once, and they always remain the same. The other is called a *switched* virtual circuit, where, as the name implies, the frame-relay hardware assembles and tears down the logical link between two points for each transmission.

You can use public or private frame-relay circuits to build backbone networks. You order service by specifying the minimum guaranteed throughput you would like over a particular PVC. This minimum figure is called the *committed information rate* (CIR).

One of the appealing factors in using frame relay is its flexibility when it comes to designing a network. You can select a CIR with speeds ranging from 64 Kbps up to T1 rates so you have some room to maneuver when trying to match the actual performance needs of a connection with a telco service offering.

Another appealing thing about frame relay is that it accommodates bursty traffic, such as the traffic generated by your typical LAN applications. Even though you order frame-relay service based on the CIR, traffic loads above this amount can be accommodated (at no extra charge) if the telco's network has the capacity to handle the traffic. How often and how long you can exceed the CIR is something that must be negotiated with the carrier before the service is installed.

Frame relay is a hot technology these days. Vertical Systems Group, a market research firm based in Dedham, Massachusetts, estimates that low-speed (56/64 Kbps or lower) frame-relay ports will grow from about 72,300 in 1995 to over 243,000 by 1998 (more than a 236 percent increase). Such low-speed ports account for most of the corporate frame-relay connections, according to a report commissioned by the Frame Relay Forum.

For the most part, frame-relay networks only support data. However, a number of companies run their voice traffic over their private frame-relay networks. And it is even possible to carry voice traffic over a public frame-relay network.

Similarly, companies have traditionally used SMDS as a data service. It's a public high-speed packet-switched service aimed at interconnecting LANs at T3 rates. But it, too, can carry voice if you have the proper equipment. For example, some multiplexors allow you to combine voice, data, and video traffic so that it can be carried over a single SMDS link.

The advantage of running voice traffic over your data network with either SMDS or frame relay is that you only require one link between sites and therefore you save money. In essence, the voice traffic between the sites gets a free ride.

One of the great attractions of SMDS is that it is the only high-bandwidth public network available today (at least until ATM becomes more widespread). That makes it attractive to organizations that must send large files between companies—for example, when an automaker wants to send CAD files to a parts manufacturer. If both companies use SMDS, they can communicate through the public network without the hassle of setting up private lines.

ATM is another possible service to consider for a backbone technology. But today, its availability is fairly limited. However, that could change in the next few years.

When trying to select one of these WAN services over another, you should consider the nature of the traffic that will be carried over the links and the pricing structure of the services. Some of the factors you should consider when looking at WAN service costs are the startup fee to use the service, the installation charge, the monthly fee, and the usage fee.

Most services have an initial fee that must be paid for the privilege of using that service. In addition to a startup fee, you will likely have to pay another one-time charge: the fee to install the service.

Once the service is installed, you will be billed monthly for the service, and there may be an additional usage fee, which may depend on the amount of data sent over the link, the distance between sites, or the length of time the circuit is used. Each WAN service has a different pricing structure (see Table 9-2). Leased lines, for example, carry a set monthly fee and there are no additional payments for usage. With SMDS you pay a monthly fee based on the bandwidth you have selected for the connection. There may also be an additional usage charge based on how many megabytes of traffic pass over the link. ISDN carries a monthly charge and a usage fee based on the total time the connection is up and running.

Branching Out

Often the choice of a backbone wide-area networking service dictates the service choices for connecting branch offices. For instance, if you're using frame relay for the core network, you'll likely use frame relay to bring in the traffic from your branch offices. However, there is a degree of flexibility.

In a typical LAN-to-backbone connectivity scenario, you will have to support multiple networking protocols, handle time-sensitive traffic to and from legacy systems (such as IBM hosts), and support high-volume LAN traffic.

Many private networks use fractional T1 service between sites. As the name implies, this service is offered in fractional units of a T1's link—usually

WAN Service	Monthly Billing Structure
Leased lines	Pay fixed price for set amount of bandwidth (for example, T1 or T3); no additional fee for usage
Frame relay	Pay fixed price per month for a connection and a flat rate for a circuit based on the bandwidth
ISDN	Pay fixed price per month for service and usage fee based on connect time
SMDS	Pay monthly fee based on bandwidth of link; may also pay usage charge based on megabytes of traffic sent over link
ATM	Pricing normally quoted on a case-by-case basis

Table 9-2.   *WAN Service Cost Factors*

in increments of 64, 128, 512, or 768 Kbps. Typically, you would select the bandwidth based on your peak traffic loads between sites. That's the safe way to do it. But it can also be uneconomical. You might only generate the peak traffic once a week—for example, when marketing and engineering are having a teleconference to discuss a new product's rollout, or while engineering is sending CAD files to headquarters.

The ideal solution would be to select your service based on average loads and somehow get some extra bandwidth when it's needed. Frame relay does that to some extent, allowing you to exceed your CIR when you have a burst in traffic load.

But if you are using leased lines between sites, there's another way to design your networks to save money: use switched services to supplement leased lines. Suppose your average traffic loads are below a T1 line's capacity, and your peak loads are somewhat above that. Using traditional communications options, you might opt for a second T1 line just to be on the safe side.

A better choice would be to use a T1 link that satisfies your average traffic loads, and then simply add bandwidth as needed by use of dial-up ISDN lines. Once a leased-line link is saturated, a router in a branch office simply establishes an ISDN connection to the main office. This process, illustrated in Figure 9-3, is called *bandwidth-on-demand* (BOND). (Most of the major router vendors have incorporated bandwidth-on-demand features into their router management software.)

Use of ISDN like this gives a link some elasticity to accommodate peak traffic. Most routers can add a single 64-Kbps B channel. To add more bandwidth requires the use of an *inverse multiplexor,* which allows you to aggregate the bandwidth of additional B channels into a single higher-bandwidth link. For example, with an inverse multiplexor you could easily merge the two B channels of an ISDN BRI (Basic Rate Interface) connection to form what appears to be a single 128-Kbps pipe to carry desktop videoconferencing traffic between users in two sites.

Another way you can use ISDN connections with existing leased lines is as a backup link in case the main link fails—a feature called *dial backup.* This, too, can save money on WAN service charges. For example, many companies install redundant leased lines between sites in case the primary one fails. Typically, the secondary, or backup, line remains idle unless there's a failure. All the while, you're paying monthly charges for this additional line.

The way dial backup works is that once a branch office router detects a failed link, it brings up an ISDN connection to the main office to carry traffic. Additionally, you can use ISDN in LAN-to-backbone connectivity as the sole

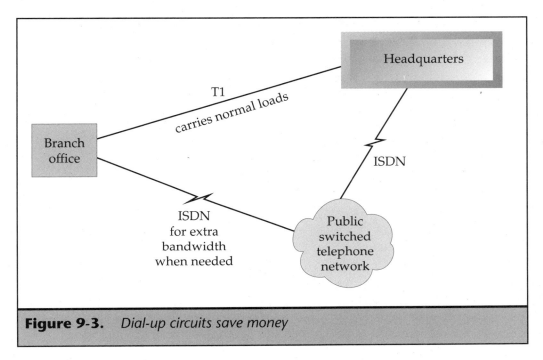

Figure 9-3.   *Dial-up circuits save money*

connection. Basically, an ISDN router attached to a LAN in a remote site dials
up a connection when it receives traffic destined for a LAN in another location.

If you want to connect a number of smaller offices to a regional office using
ISDN, you can equip the regional office in one of two ways. One way is to
have multiple ISDN BRI lines coming into the facility. This approach requires
one piece of line-termination equipment for each line coming into the central
site. Or, you could choose ISDN PRI (Primary Rate Interface) service for the
central site. With PRI service, the telecommunications carrier multiplexes the
signals coming from the various sites onto a single access line into your
facility. This reduces the amount of equipment needed in your larger office,
and it saves some management time (it's easier to manage one piece of
equipment than several).

ISDN has been around for a long time, and its popularity has grown with
its wider availability. Frame relay, in contrast, is a relative newcomer, and its
popularity in connecting remote sites is due to its melding of performance
characteristics with user demands.

Besides its ability to accommodate an occasional burst of traffic, frame
relay is also gaining favor because it can handle time-sensitive SNA (Systems
Network Architecture) session traffic between an IBM host and end nodes,

such as 3270 terminals or PCs running 3270 terminal emulation programs. When it comes to handling SNA, frame relay has given many companies a way to replace numerous dedicated, point-to-point low-speed leased lines (which operate at 9.6 or 19.2 Kbps).

It should be emphasized that despite the attention devoted by trade journals to downsizing applications from mainframes, there is still a large installed base of mainframe-based applications and data. And there are many users who need access to these applications. That means you will likely have to deal with the issue of handling SNA traffic.

There are several advantages to using frame relay, and many of them are ideal for handling SNA. A company can replace hundreds of point-to-point low-speed links with frame relay connections at a lower cost and get a performance boost (see the special section, "A Network Make-Over").

A Network Make-Over

Before:

- Bridged network that outgrew itself
- Remote sites costly to connect, equipment expensive to maintain
- Mainframe-based, corporatewide, e-mail supported only text messages and could not handle binary files, graphics, and images that many users want to exchange
- 250 point-to-point analog connections between remote sites and data center

After:

- Migrate to a collapsed backbone router-based network
- Use access routers in remote sites to provide connectivity for both PC-based LAN traffic and SNA session traffic
- Higher-speed, lower-cost frame-relay connections
- Migrate to LAN-based e-mail system

Linking Small Offices to Small Offices

Interbranch office connectivity needs are different from the needs you will typically see when linking a branch office to a corporate backbone. They are so different that you will need to pay special attention when selecting the service you will use.

For example, it is usually impractical to have dedicated links from each office to all other offices. Such meshed networks were common when you only needed to link a handful of large offices. But today, it is quite common for a large organization to have hundreds of smaller offices. The more typical network pattern is a star structure, where smaller offices feed into larger data centers. In this scenario, a person in Boston might send a file to a coworker in Pittsburgh by way of the company's headquarters in New York. However, there are often times when it makes sense to let two branch sites connect directly (see Figure 9-4).

Determining whether the link between two smaller offices should be dial-up or dedicated is not a simple matter. With a leased line you pay a fixed monthly rate. You can fill the link to capacity for every second of the month, or not send a single byte of data over it, and you still pay the same amount. With a dial-up ISDN link, you typically have a small, fixed monthly fee and a usage fee based on the time the connection is up.

There are no hard-and-fast rules of when to use a dedicated line versus when to use an on-demand dial-up connection—it largely depends on the

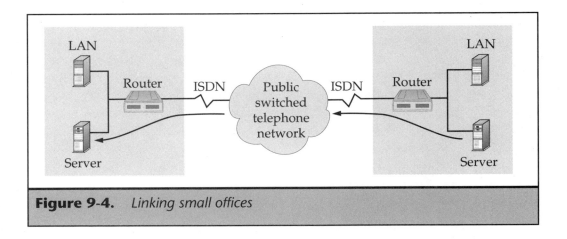

Figure 9-4. *Linking small offices*

pricing of the service offerings. Generally, if you need more than three to four hours of connectivity per business day, you should use a dedicated line. Anything below that, and you can get by with a dial-up line. Most routers support a function called dial-on-demand for this type of LAN-to-LAN connectivity between smaller offices.

For many years Switched 56 service was an attractive alternative for linking small offices. Switched 56 service is a dial-up service that lets two sites exchange data at 56 Kbps, but it uses a DSU/CSU (data service unit/channel service unit) instead of a modem to place the call. With Switched 56 you pay a monthly fee plus a usage fee that is based on the time the circuit is up. That made it economically practical for what some call casual connectivity, where one site simply needed to open a link to another site for a short period each day. Switched 56 is well-suited to applications such as videoconferencing and telemedicine, where large image files must be transferred.

But the use of Switched 56 is likely to drop off as ISDN becomes more available. ISDN offers more bandwidth (two 64-Kbps channels in a PRI circuit versus 56 Kbps for a Switched 56 link). And many carriers are pricing ISDN so that it makes better economic sense to use it, rather than Switched 56 services.

ISDN is also starting to gain ground in the single user-to-LAN connectivity area. Today, most telecommuters and mobile workers still rely on modems and analog phone lines. However, as ISDN BRI service becomes easier to get and the price for ISDN terminal adapters drops, more telecommuters will switch to ISDN because of its higher speeds.

The subsequent chapters in this section go into greater detail for three of the connectivity scenarios mentioned in this chapter: LAN-to-backbone connectivity, LAN-to-LAN connectivity, and single user-to-network connectivity.

Chapter Ten

LAN-to-Backbone Connectivity

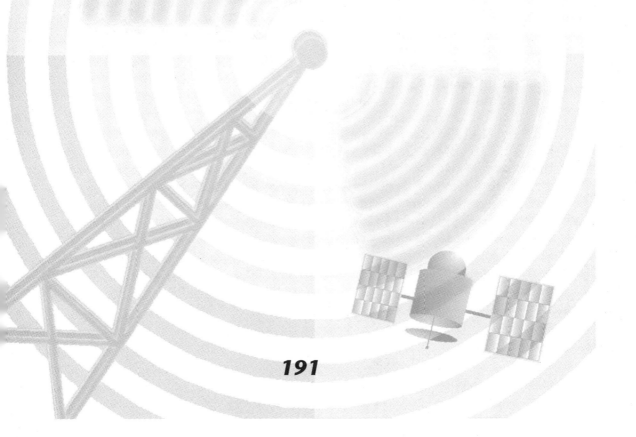

User connectivity requirements have changed radically in the last decade. Today, the combination of corporate decentralization and the reliance on LAN-based applications for business productivity has altered the connectivity landscape. What it all comes down to is that there are more users in smaller regional and branch offices than ever. And those users need access to corporate applications and databases, which often still run on mainframe computers in data centers at the corporate headquarters. Additionally, these users need a way to share the work they are doing—be it documents, spreadsheets, or presentations—with fellow employees located in other branch offices.

For a network administrator, a branch office represents a management challenge. There are typically many sites, all geographically dispersed, and most have little, if any, on-site technical support. With tightening budgets, the cost to manage and maintain internetworking equipment in remote sites is a primary concern for corporations. Additionally, the recurring telecommunication charges to link these branch sites are under scrutiny.

The need to connect many users in branch offices is a fairly recent phenomenon. In the past, the typical corporate networking scenario centered around a small backbone network that linked large data centers. Two or three regional data-processing centers were connected together by use of dedicated T1 or T3 lines leased from a telephone company. In many cases, these lines carried both voice and data traffic between sites.

Users in smaller branch offices needed access to mainframe-based applications running in the data centers. The traffic was time-sensitive, terminal-to-mainframe, host-type traffic. Most often the traffic was carried over an SNA (Systems Network Architecture) network. Under this scenario, the physical connections between the users in branch offices and the data center were usually either dedicated low-speed lines (9.6 or 19.2 Kbps links were fairly common), or dedicated fractional T1 links. Internetworking bridges carried the traffic from a branch office to the data center's site.

There has obviously been a shift from the old data center days, thanks in part to the decentralization of many organizations, along with the growing use of LAN-based applications. Today, a user in a branch office needs access to the centralized databases of an organization (that still run in large data centers), but these users also need to exchange e-mail, documents files, and spreadsheets with colleagues scattered throughout an organization.

Routers Take Over

To meet the connectivity needs of users in remote offices, many companies have turned to what can be called *mid-level routers* and *access routers* to carry the mix of LAN and SNA traffic between the branch office and the large regional data centers.

Mid-level routers and access routers are designed with the connectivity needs of the branch office in mind. They connect LANs in a branch office to a central site router using either leased lines, dial-up switched circuits, analog phone lines, or a combination of these three. Mid-level routers would be used to connect moderate-sized branch offices to the corporate backbone, while access routers would be used in smaller remote offices.

Mid-level routers and access routers offer moderate performance and a limited feature set compared with the higher-end routers used to build backbone networks. For example, a mid-level router might support the same protocols as a high-end counterpart, but may offer fewer LAN and WAN ports. Or, such routers may not offer the high packet-forwarding and filtering rates of the backbone routers.

Similarly, access routers may only support one or two networking protocols—most support IP and IPX, while some only support IP. That's not the case with higher-end routers, which may support a dozen or more protocols. The limited protocol support is usually not a problem, since most sites run either IP, IPX, or both. Access routers are designed to handle one or at most two LAN connections.

These restrictions in protocol support, number of LAN ports, and number of WAN ports are not that bad when you consider the offices these routers are intended for. Most small offices only run one or two networking protocols, and you wouldn't imagine these sites having more than a couple of LANs. If they did, a mid-level router would be a better match. It turns out there are many small offices that need access routers. Fortune 500 companies alone have over 225,000 offices with fewer than two dozen workers, according to Forrester Research (Cambridge, Massachusetts). The workers in these offices need to be able to exchange e-mail with other company employees, transfer files among departments, and access corporate databases.

Vendors, seeing the growing demand for connectivity, have eagerly introduced mid-level and lower-end routers to meet the connectivity needs of small- to medium-sized offices. Mid-level routers typically come from the same vendors who offer backbone routers. This comprises a fairly small set of vendors and includes such companies as Cisco Systems, Bay Networks, 3Com, Proteon, Ascom Timplex, RAD Network Devices (RND), Retix, and CrossComm. These vendors offer both the routers used to build the backbone networks and the routers that would be placed in branch offices.

Access routers are another matter. There are over 90 vendors selling access routers. Most of these vendors do not offer higher-end routers. This has made interoperability a key concern for users of access routers. As such, vendors have addressed this issue by offering products that link their access routers to another vendor's central site router by use of the Point-to-Point Protocol (PPP).

PPP, which was derived from the Serial Line Internet Protocol (SLIP), lets routers from different vendors exchange data over a serial link. When two routers use PPP to link up, each router basically tells the other what features it has implemented. For instance, each router determines which networking protocols the other is running. The routers then agree to use a common set of features to pass data between the two sites.

Cutting Lifetime Costs

Many network managers are starting to look at the lifetime costs of using mid-level and access routers. They are looking specifically at the labor charges associated with installing and managing the router, as well as the telecommunications charges to link the router to a central site. And for good reason.

A study by the market research firm Dataquest (San Jose, California) found that the purchase price of the router only accounts for one-third of the lifetime costs of owning an access router. The other two-thirds of the expense of using an access router goes toward paying, primarily, the telecommunication line charges and, secondarily, the wages of the people managing the devices.

Router vendors have taken different approaches when trying to reduce the cost of router ownership. Most have tried to make installing the routers easier. After all, a company may have only a few high-end routers, so it's not such a big deal if a high-end router needs some special attention to set up. But a company may have hundreds of mid-level and access routers in branch offices. So a company deploying hundreds of routers may not be too keen on spending lots of time on each router, especially when they are at sites that may not have the technical expertise to configure a router.

One approach to simplifying the installation of routers is to use a platform that is familiar to people in the remote sites. Namely, a PC. PC-based routers are built using a communications card and Multiprotocol Router software from Novell. PC-based routers are, in theory, easier to install and configure because they have a familiar look and feel to the people in the remote sites.

Specifically, a PC is more familiar to some managers than the proprietary box-type routers. PC-based routers use the same onscreen interface as a NetWare management screen. Using a familiar interface, as the PC routers do, means a manager does not have to learn cryptic command-line instructions that are required to configure a traditional router. An added advantage to using NetWare-like configuration instructions is that there's a better chance of finding someone in a remote office with NetWare experience than of finding someone with router experience.

Proprietary box-router vendors have used UNIX-like commands for configuring the devices. However, most vendors have simplified the procedure to configure their routers. Many offer Windows-based and menu-driven configuration tools to make configuration and installation easier.

3Com and RAD Network Devices (RND) took this simplification a level further several years ago when both companies tried to make the access router a plug-and-play device by modifying their routing software. 3Com and RND adopted a strategy where they centralized the routing intelligence, moving all routing decisions into the central site router. That allows the companies to make the access router a simpler device that requires little, if any, configuration.

Making installation and configuration easier is only the tip of the iceberg when it comes to keeping operating costs down. After a router is configured, the unit has to be maintained and managed. For instance, routing software updates must be installed on every mid-level or access router. And this is an area where many vendors are trying to make things easier so that companies can reduce the amount of labor involved.

In the past, every time a new version of routing software came out, a technician would have to go to each router and replace a chip, which stored the router instructions, with a new chip. Or else the technician would have to go from router to router with a disk containing the new software and manually install the new algorithms on each machine.

Chip replacement and disk-based updates were not a major problem when a company only had a handful of routers. But with companies linking dozens or even hundreds of sites, this process is at best tedious, and at worst a financial drain because of the labor charges incurred sending staff running to every remote site. Today, virtually all routers use Flash EPROM (erasable programmable read-only memory) to store routing software. The advantage to using Flash EPROMs is that they allow updates to be downloaded to the router over the network.

Cutting Telecom Charges

Besides reducing labor charges to install and configure routers, vendors are offering a number of ways to keep telecommunication line costs down. One of the most important changes that has occurred in recent years is the growing use of public switched services, such as ISDN and frame relay, to cut the cost of using dedicated leased lines to link sites (see Figure 10-1).

As you can see in Figure 10-1, dial-up switched circuits can supplement leased-line connections to save money and in some cases can be used in place of dedicated links. For instance, one way to use such switched services is to supplement a leased line's bandwidth—a process called bandwidth-on-demand (BOND). Bandwidth-on-demand reduces telecommunications costs by allowing a company to use a lower-speed leased line, which can accommodate normal traffic loads, rather than using a higher-speed line that would handle peak traffic.

With bandwidth-on-demand, a leased line would be the primary connection between a remote office and a central site. When traffic loads

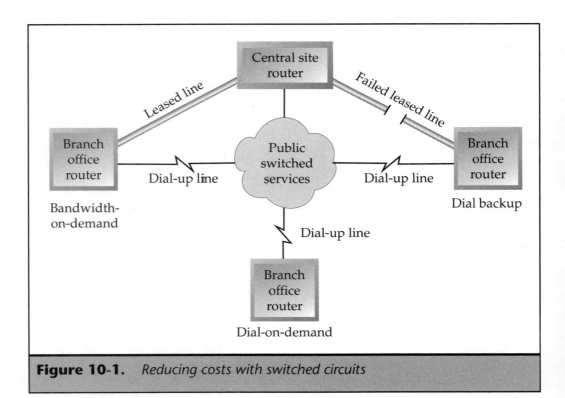

Figure 10-1.   *Reducing costs with switched circuits*

exceed a preset limit, the router can automatically dial up a switched circuit to provide additional bandwidth. Therefore, you can pay for a slower-speed dedicated line and still ensure you can carry traffic during peak periods.

Some network managers want to take advantage of dial-up lines for another purpose. Many would like to use these links for emergency backup. As you can see in Figure 10-1, dial backup allows a company to use switched circuits to provide links between the remote site and central office when a primary link fails. This feature saves money over the traditional backup method, where spare leased lines sit idle most of the time and are only used when a connection goes down. By relying on switched circuits for emergency connections, companies can reduce the number of leased lines to each site and only pay for emergency dial-up links as needed.

Still others want to save money by eliminating all leased-line connections. This capability is useful for offices that need what is called casual connectivity. Such offices primarily need to exchange e-mail and to occasionally transfer files or access host databases and applications. Dial-up routing will save money if a site requires less than two to four hours a day of connectivity to a central location. The break-even point in terms of the number of hours of connectivity per day can be calculated by comparing the monthly cost of a leased line to the hourly charge for switched circuits.

Dial-up Versus Dedicated: Calculating the Crossover Point

There are no hard-and-fast guidelines for determining the crossover point that makes a dial-up connection more economical than a dedicated, leased-line connection. However, here is a way to roughly estimate the transition point.

1. Take the monthly rate for a dedicated link, subtract the monthly rate for a dial-up line, and divide this number by the hourly rate for the dial-up service.

For example, suppose you pay $700 per month for two 64-Kbps dedicated links. Also suppose it costs $40 per month for an ISDN BRI line, which has two 64-Kbps channels, and it costs $0.25 per minute ($15 per hour) for connect time for the ISDN link. The calculation is as follows:

($700–40) per month / $15 per hour = 44 hours of connect time/month

2. Divide that number by the number of business days in a month, and you will get the number of hours of connectivity per day.

In this example, that is

44 hours of connect time per month / 20 business days per month = 2.2 hours per day

If the users in a site require more connect time than this, a dedicated line will be more economical. If they require less, a dial-up line is better.

By adjusting the rates in the preceding example to your specific rates, you will be able to calculate the crossover point that makes a dial-up link more economical than a leased line.

Look for Higher-End Features

There are other ways to save money when linking branch offices. For example, some router vendors offer higher-end features that may cost more up front, but may pay for themselves over the lifetime of the product. Advanced features, such as data compression, spoofing, and traffic prioritization, offered by router vendors can save money by using bandwidth more efficiently (see Figure 10-2).

Data compression lets you squeeze the most out of a low-bandwidth line connecting remote sites. Most of the routers that use data compression use a proprietary implementation of compression algorithms. Most use a variant of the Lempel-Ziv algorithms, which identify redundancies in data and only send information over a WAN link once. Depending on the type of data being sent between sites, these algorithms can typically compress data to half its original size or less (many vendors claim a 4-to-1 compression ratio with their software).

The drawback to data compression is that it is strictly a proprietary offering. The Internet Engineering Task Force has developed some standards for data compression over a PPP connection. However, such efforts have not been widely embraced by the router community. So a company must use routers from the same vendor to reap the cost-saving benefits.

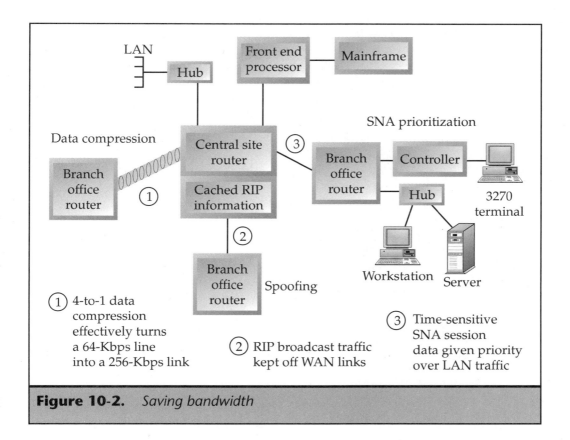

Figure 10-2.   *Saving bandwidth*

Another method to save bandwidth is to keep nonessential traffic off of low-speed links. The filtering capabilities of routers have always been used to keep traffic from chatty protocols, such as NetBIOS, off of wide-area links. But there are other ways to reduce traffic. Specifically, network managers should consider a router that performs spoofing, where routing path updates are cached at a central site.

Spoofing is essential when you use any type of dial-up link, such as an ISDN line. The reason is that router-to-router protocols, such as the routing information protocol (RIP) and Open Shortest Path First (OSPF), were developed when routers only used dedicated links that were always up. Both protocols pass information about routing paths and the state of the network between routers—RIP does so every 30 seconds, and OSPF, every time there is a change.

Spoofing holds RIP and OSPF information in the central site router. Many router vendors also offer a caching of NetWare's Service Advertising Protocol (SAP) information. When a branch office router makes a connection, the RIP, SAP, or OSPF information is passed along. Without spoofing, your routers will bring up the link every 30 seconds (if you are running RIP). This essentially defeats the purpose of using a dial-up connection to save telecommunications charges.

Another way to save telecommunications charges is to look for features that keep performance high without the need for adding more bandwidth. There is one area in particular where this is key: handling time-sensitive SNA traffic. In the past, companies have maintained two independent networks—one for their LAN traffic and one for the SNA traffic that linked terminals, either local or in remote sites, to mainframe computers. But the cost of maintaining two networks is high. This has led many companies to combine their network where the SNA traffic, called SDLC (Synchronous Data Link Control) traffic, is carried over the same WAN links that carry their LAN traffic. This is usually accomplished either by encapsulating the SDLC traffic into IP frames or by converting the traffic to LLC (Logical Link Control) traffic that is passed over the network as any other LAN traffic would be.

The problem most companies face in this scenario is that the SNA traffic is very time sensitive. Typically, an SNA session times out after ten seconds, requiring the user to restart the session (LAN traffic does not have this problem). Old SNA networks were very deterministic. A manager could predict the performance of such networks. Internetworked LANs, on the other hand, are not deterministic. LAN traffic is by nature bursty. One moment, there might be a fairly underutilized link between a branch office and a central site. The next moment, several users might flood the link by transferring large files between the sites.

When that happens, network response times can decrease significantly. Oftentimes, SNA traffic can find itself stuck in a router queue waiting for a large file to be transferred. One way around this is to use higher-performance routers and higher-bandwidth links between sites. But that goes back to the mentality of buying bandwidth for peak situations and not normal loads. Basically, you ensure the SNA traffic will get through by paying for a high-bandwidth link just to cover those times when LAN traffic exceeds a certain level.

A better solution is to look for routers that offer traffic prioritization. Specifically, this would be a router that lets you give a higher priority to traffic based on the protocol type, destination address, or source address. The idea behind traffic prioritization is that time-sensitive SNA traffic gets priority over less time-critical LAN traffic. In that way, you pay for the bandwidth you need for average conditions without worrying about those times when a network can get congested.

Integration Cuts Costs

Besides saving money on recurring telecommunications charges, there are ways to cut the recurring labor charges required to maintain and manage equipment in branch offices.

One cost-cutting approach is to buy products that integrate into one unit all the products needed to connect branch office end users. Such products might incorporate a router, hub, and DSU/CSU (data service unit/channel service unit), into one box. Some vendors also include an SDLC converter in their all-in-one approach. The all-in-one approach saves money in several ways.

First, installation is much simpler. A person at the branch office can take the unit out of the box and have it up and running quickly. If there are any problems, there is only one vendor to call. If separate devices—each from a different vendor—are used, it would require much more setup time, because you might need a representative from each company to travel to the branch office.

Second, devices can be managed better as one unit than as separate units. When devices are purchased separately, each device has its own management system. So you may end up with four management consoles—one each for the router, hub, DSU/CSU, and SDLC converter—in a central site (see Figure 10-3). It takes more effort to resolve problems with four management systems. At best, the manager must mentally consolidate four pieces of information to solve a single problem. An integrated device will typically let you manage all four devices from the same management console using a single interface.

Third, integrated units extend the management further into the remote site. Usually, network administrators can only manage the LAN side of their networks, but not the WAN side. Using an integrated product, net managers can assess the situation at any point on the network.

For example, vendors typically offer loopback testing and diagnostics of the DSU/CSU—something that is usually not available on a stand-alone DSU/CSU. Additionally, most DSU/CSUs are configured by manually setting *DIP switches* (tiny toggle switches that usually require a pencil or pen to flip on or off).

An integrated unit is often configurable through software. This allows a network manager in a central site to perform the task, rather than sending a

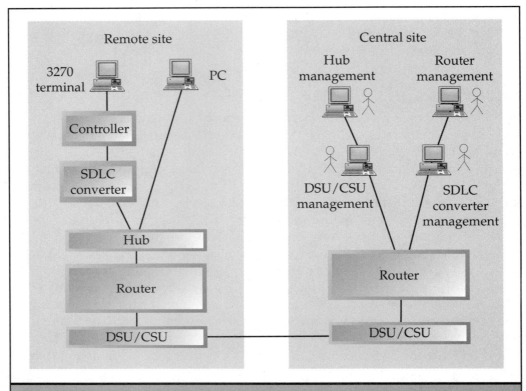

Figure 10-3. *Connecting branch offices—traditional approach*

person to the site. Additionally, the loopback tests can be performed from a central site to isolate the source of a network anomaly—a downed WAN link that is the responsibility of the telephone company, for example. This can also save a trip to the remote site.

Fourth, even the simplest things can save money. If separate units are used, they must be connected by cables. Each cable is a potential source of failure in a network. Thus, an integrated product makes the remote site internetworking equipment more reliable (see Figure 10-4).

Changing Role of Hubs

It has been the router vendors who have bundled hubs and DSU/CSUs into their existing products. But hub vendors have also taken note of this area and

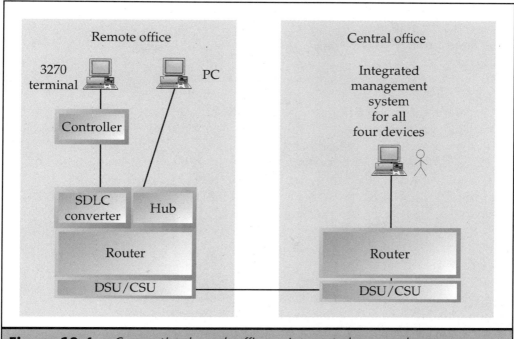

Figure 10-4.   *Connecting branch offices—integrated approach*

beefed up their WAN offerings to offer an integrated unit where all components are managed through one management system.

The advantages of integrating hubs and WAN access devices like routers and DSU/CSUs include simplified management, enhanced management functions, improved reliability, easier installation, and easier problem resolution.

For most network administrators, these benefits are required as they try to meet the changing connectivity needs of their users. Specifically, managers are trying to satisfy the growing demand to connect LAN-based users at different sites and to provide users with dial-out access to commercial e-mail services. Additionally, there is a need to provide mobile users (people traveling with laptops or those who work at home) with dial-in access to network resources.

In the past, these levels of connectivity would be handled by use of stand-alone routers, terminal servers, communication servers, modems, and other line-termination devices such as ISDN terminal adapters, multiplexors, and DSU/CSUs. These devices were typically purchased separately—a Forrester Research survey of 50 large U.S. businesses found that 60 percent of the companies bought these components individually.

However, purchasing patterns are changing. Forrester Research found that 54 percent of network managers said they will buy WAN access products from their hub vendors. The reason for the shift is that a hub with WAN access integrated into it is easier to manage compared with the use of stand-alone solutions. Responding to this demand, virtually all of the major hub vendors, including 3Com, Cabletron Systems Inc., IBM, Optical Data Systems, and Bay Networks, have introduced products to provide WAN connectivity. Many other vendors who have expertise on the WAN side, including Shiva Corp., Xylogics, and Xyplex, have been enhancing their offerings and partnering with the high-end hub vendors.

All of these developments mark a fundamental shift in the role of the networking hub from a departmental wiring concentrator to that of the single point in a network that gives users both LAN and WAN access. With this changing role, there is a need to change the way WAN access products are managed. In the past, managing this mix of equipment has not been easy, because each piece of equipment had its own proprietary management systems.

The integrated approach allows all devices to be managed by one system, typically the hub's management system. This reduces the complexity of managing the network. Besides simplifying management, integration most often provides better management capabilities. That's because stand-alone WAN access devices, such as communications servers, DSU/CSUs, modems, or ISDN terminal adapters, have lacked even the most basic management utilities.

Vendors who are integrating such products into their hubs often provide enhanced management tools for remote management. For instance, many are adding SNMP (Simple Network Management Protocol) support to these products. With SNMP, management of the WAN devices is easier. For instance, products, such as modems or ISDN terminal adapters that have lacked management functions, can now include SNMP agents that can send alerts to higher-level management systems like Hewlett-Packard's OpenView, Sun Microsystems' SunNet Manager, or Cabletron's Spectrum.

Extending a Manager's Reach

Two trends—decentralization of organizations and the growing use of LANs—have created a challenge for network administrators. They find themselves responsible for keeping LANs in many remote locations up and running.

A big part of the problem is that many smaller sites do not have and cannot afford full-time technical staffers to handle even the simplest problem. After all, you can't expect a person who can barely use a computer to attach a protocol analyzer, such as a Network General Notebook Sniffer Analyzer, to the network and diagnose the problem on his or her own. (That's not to disparage the protocol analyzer folks who have been making their products easier for networking professionals to use.)

Recognizing that managers need to somehow see what's going on at distant locations, the IETF developed specifications for a *remote monitoring* (RMON) *system* that keeps tabs on the state of distant networks. RMON is an extension of the IETF's Simple Network Management Protocol (SNMP), which is commonly used to manage large networks. With SNMP, a central console polls devices on the network that have SNMP agents. With RMON, some management intelligence is moved out onto the network, where the RMON probes alert a centralized console whenever a threshold, like number of packets, is exceeded.

The idea behind RMON is to distribute, throughout a network, probes (called RMON agents) that collect information about the traffic on that network (see Figure 10-5). In a typical use of RMON technology, one probe would be located on each LAN segment. The probe would monitor data transmission on that segment and organize the information it collects into a format that makes it easy for a manager at a central site to analyze traffic patterns and diagnose problems at remote sites. Because of these features, RMON is taking off. Virtually all router and intelligent hub vendors either are offering RMON capabilities in their products or say they soon will.

While RMON has great potential to help network administrators better manage remote-site LANs, there is some confusion about what role an RMON probe plays in traditional network analysis and troubleshooting. The major point of confusion is that there's a belief that RMON probes will obviate the need for traditional *protocol analyzers.*

That is simply not the case. In fact, most networks would do well to employ both RMON technology and protocol analyzers. The two perform

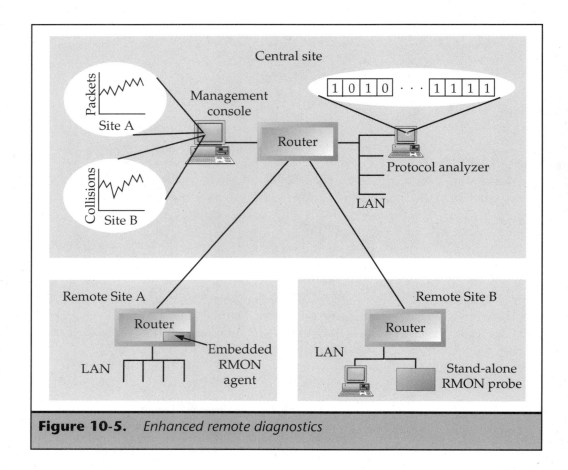

Figure 10-5. *Enhanced remote diagnostics*

complementary, not competing, functions. One analogy might help explain the difference between an RMON probe and a protocol analyzer. In general, it's the difference between knowing that the editor of this book got 50 letters about the book and knowing what opinions were expressed in those letters.

Analogously, a network RMON can provide a manager with good statistical and trend information about the number of packets passing over the network, while a protocol analyzer can take a captured packet and decode all seven of its protocol layers.

Naturally, there is some overlap in the functions of an RMON probe and a protocol analyzer. For example, many a protocol analyzer can perform trend analysis on the data it collects. The way the two technologies can work to complement one another is to use RMON to baseline networks, study usage trends, and identify potential problems before they cause problems for users.

This will help reduce the number of trips to remote sites that technicians must make to solve problems.

When there is a problem that requires higher-level diagnostics to be performed, use the protocol analyzers. For example, you could dispatch a person with a laptop running protocol analyzer software to a troubled site. The type of information an RMON probe might collect is how many packets and what size packets are transmitted on the LAN segment. It will also look at the number of packets broadcast and collisions. Among other things, this information could be used to spot a defective adapter card on the segment that is bombarding the LAN with bad packets, causing poor performance.

RMON probes can also collect a trace of the traffic on the LAN segment over a given time. This can be used to study traffic patterns and perform trend-analysis of the bandwidth demands of the users on that segment. One of the most important features of RMON is that it can also be used to send alerts and alarms to network management systems when a preset threshold of some network parameter has been exceeded—for instance, if collisions exceed a level that is considered normal for a particular segment.

The benefit of RMON is that it automatically collects information about the traffic on a LAN segment that is in a remote location. For a manager responsible for many LAN segments that are not all in the same location, that can be a great cost-saving benefit. For example, without RMON, any problem called into a helpdesk or network troubleshooting center that cannot be solved over the phone, requires a trip by a technician to the site.

The cost implications of such an approach to network troubleshooting are high. First, there's the technician's time. Even if it takes him or her 15 minutes to solve the problem, there's the round-trip travel time to consider. And that's a best-case scenario.

Oftentimes, it's hard to know just who to send to the remote site. In many cases of network outages, it's hard to determine (remotely) whether it is, for example, a router that has failed, or if it is a DSU/CSU, or if it is simply a matter of trouble with a dedicated line between the sites. Without being able to diagnose the problem remotely, a company may first send the wrong person to the site. Then the problem still requires another person to go to the site, thus wasting one technician's time for the travel.

Adding to the cost of problems at remote sites is the fact that even if the right person goes to the site the first time and solves the problem instantly, the people in that site must still sit by doing nothing while waiting for the technician to arrive. If it takes a technician two hours to get to a site, people at that remote site are sitting idly by for a quarter of their business day.

Using RMON throughout a network can help reduce the number of "emergency" trips to remote sites. By virtue of letting a manager preset performance threshold levels, he or she might be able to spot a problem in the making and let the manager take corrective action before the users on your network notice anything has happened. For example, a manager might notice that traffic on a LAN segment is increasing at a steady pace and is getting very close to the maximum percentage bandwidth utilization that is acceptable before performance noticeably drops. Having noticed this trend, a manager can segment the LAN so that traffic on each new segment is well below the level where performance suffers.

In this way, the users never see any performance degradation. And the network manager does not receive a call from screaming users saying it's taking forever for their applications to run. That's just one example of how RMON will make it easier to automatically collect information about the state of remote networks. With networks getting increasingly decentralized, network managers will need all the help they can get. Table 10-1 will help you determine what you will need to consider to keep your connectivity and management costs down.

Nature of traffic	Multiple protocols. Time-sensitive SNA session traffic. High volume between sites.
Approaches to cutting telecom costs	Use public switched services to supplement dedicated links. Use advanced features such as data compression, spoofing of RIP and SAP broadcast traffic, and traffic prioritization.
Approaches to reducing management costs	Look for branch office routers with Windows-based or menu-driven configuration tools. Look for integrated devices that are easier to install and manage. Look for remote diagnostic capabilities to reduce trips to remote sites.

Table 10-1. *Points to Consider for LAN-to-Backbone Connectivity*

Chapter Eleven

LAN-to-LAN Connectivity

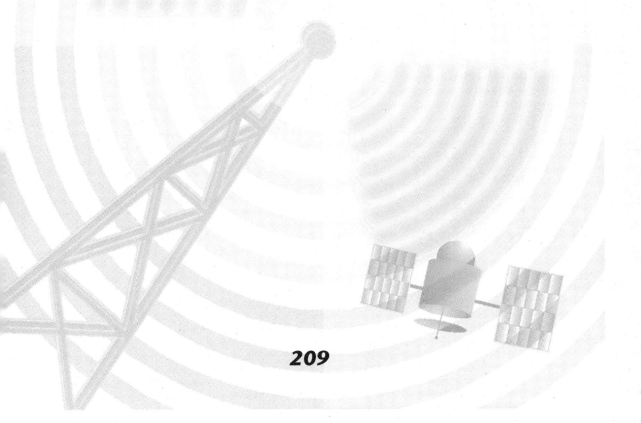

Network managers increasingly find that they must provide connectivity for users in many small offices. This connectivity between multiple offices is known as LAN-to-LAN connectivity. The challenge to you is how to provide users in these sites with the connectivity they need to perform their jobs and how to manage the equipment at these sites. This chapter will look at ways to economically provide the needed connectivity and how you can cost-effectively support the users in such offices.

A LAN-to-LAN connectivity scenario involves many small offices that are fairly autonomous. The users in each office need to share resources in their office and occasionally need access to resources in other offices. The LAN-to-LAN connectivity scenario is similar to the LAN-to-backbone scenario discussed in the previous chapter. However, there are a couple of important differences. The amount of traffic between sites is much different in this LAN-to-LAN scenario than in the LAN-to-backbone scenario discussed previously.

With LAN-to-LAN connectivity, it is common to have light traffic loads between sites. You can satisfy the connectivity needs of the users in the many small offices by using analog and ISDN lines. That is in contrast to some LAN-to-backbone cases where dedicated, high-speed lines are needed.

Another difference between the LAN-to-LAN and LAN-to-backbone scenarios is the nature of the traffic that passes between the sites. For LAN-to-LAN connectivity you will most likely only be dealing with one or two networking protocols—IP and IPX. Typically, there will not be any time-sensitive traffic (as is the case with a LAN-to-backbone scenario when users need access to mainframe applications that require a session be established between the mainframe host and the user's computer acting as a terminal).

The combination of lighter traffic loads, fewer networking protocols to support, and the lack of time-sensitive traffic means the connectivity equipment in a LAN-to-LAN scenario can be much simpler than that used for LAN-to-backbone connectivity.

Office-to-Office Connectivity

In the LAN-to-LAN networking scenario, the typical office will have anywhere from a handful to a dozen or so users. Figure 11-1 shows what these small offices will probably look like from your perspective as a network manager. As you can see in the figure, there will likely be a simple LAN consisting of one server, one hub, a printer or two, and PCs or Macintosh computers linked to the server through the hub.

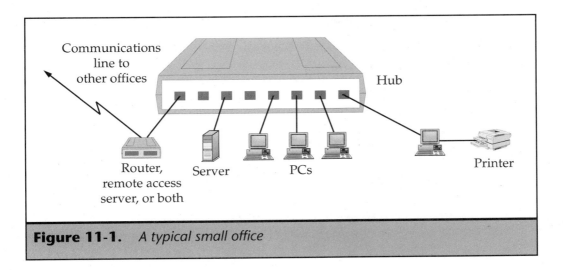

Communications
line to
other offices

Hub

Router,
remote access
server, or both

Server

PCs

Printer

Figure 11-1. *A typical small office*

These small offices will also need some type of device to communicate with users in other offices. The organizational structure of your company, the type of applications your users run, and the data acquisition needs of the users in the remote offices will determine the type of network connectivity equipment you need to connect these users. If your company is highly centralized—many of the remote users need to access data from several applications running in your corporate headquarters—the type of connectivity you need is more akin to the LAN-to-backbone scenario discussed in the preceding chapter.

For the LAN-to-LAN connectivity scenario discussed in this chapter, your remote sites must be fairly autonomous and must not need constant access to corporate data in a single site. Instead, the small offices would operate, in essence, as mini business units. Users in the offices might occasionally need access to data or applications running on servers in another office, might need to transfer or share a document or spreadsheet with a coworker in another office, or might simply need to exchange e-mail.

Again, the difference between a LAN-to-backbone and a LAN-to-LAN scenario will depend on your corporate structure. The LAN-to-backbone scenario is common in, for example, a banking environment where every branch office will have a small LAN, and the users in these offices constantly need to access information about customer accounts, bank mortgage rates, and the latest interest rate the bank is paying on certificates of deposit.

In contrast, an accounting firm might have small local offices where tax specialists can perform most of their duties using a server-based tax program and a printer. However, occasionally there is a need for a user in one office to connect to another office to, for example, get the past records of a client who has moved. Or, a person handling an out-of-state tax return might need to get the tax rate information from one of the company's offices in that state. This is the classic LAN-to-LAN connectivity scenario. In Figure 11-2 you see what this office-to-office connectivity would look like architecturally.

One common scenario is to retain the office-to-office connections for most things, but to centralize some services. For instance, it is common to see a company use a single e-mail server in one office. Figure 11-3 shows that users in all offices connect to this one server to exchange mail with other users—this is a hub-and-spoke architecture that is very common in the LAN-to-backbone scenario. However, we are not talking about having a high-end router in the central location through which LAN traffic from all remote sites passes.

Types of Connections

The way you provide the link between the offices will depend on the nature of the traffic between the sites and the amount of traffic. If you must plan, deploy, and support the typical LAN-to-LAN scenario, you will find that you have three types of connectivity to concern yourself with. Table 11-1 summarizes the three types of connectivity. First, there is the need to give a user on one LAN in one office access to an application (and its associated data) running on a server in another office. The second type of connectivity needed for each office is a

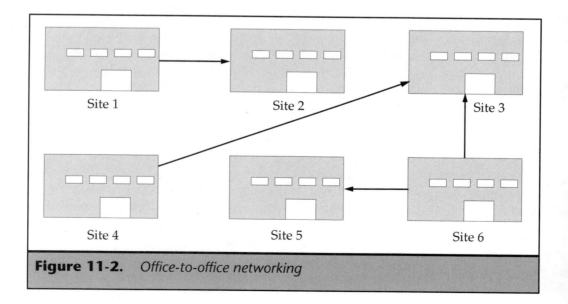

Figure 11-2. *Office-to-office networking*

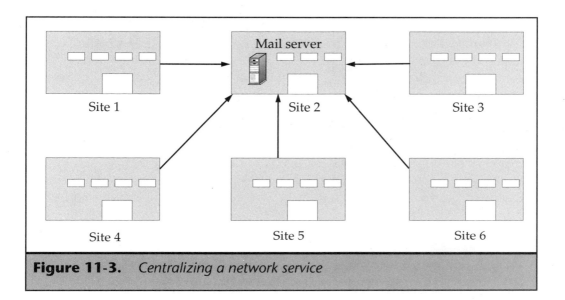

Figure 11-3.   *Centralizing a network service*

dial-out capability so that users can connect to online services and the Internet. The third type of connectivity needed is a dial-in capability for each small office so that users can access the LANs in those offices from home or when they are on the road.

Type of Connectivity	Example
User in one office needs access to an application (and its data) in another office	Access a database running on a server in a different office
Dial-out capability	Access to Internet or other online service
Dial-in capability	Give telecommuters and travelers access to their office LAN applications and data

Table 11-1.   *The Different Types of Small Office Connectivity*

Providing these three types of connectivity could require a mix of equipment. For example, you might use a dial-up router to give a LAN-attached user in one office transparent access to a server in another office, a stand-alone modem for the user to dial into an online service, and a remote access server to give users dial-in access to the LAN from home or when they travel. If this is the case, you would need to support each type of access equipment (a router, remote access server, and modems) in each small office.

However, in contrast to giving users access to a backbone network, the equipment needed for such LAN-to-LAN connectivity is more modest. For instance, you can get away with a lower performance, fewer function router since the traffic loads are lighter, there are fewer protocols to support, and it will not need to support time-sensitive traffic. Also, a communications or remote access server would not need to support as many incoming or outgoing lines.

Depending on the connectivity needs of the users in the small offices, you might be able to use an even less expensive, simpler approach than using lower-end routers and remote access servers. The key is that the three types of connectivity needed by users in small offices are not mutually exclusive. You may be able to use a single product that delivers all three types of connectivity.

For example, if the traffic loads between sites are modest, you might be able to forego the stand-alone, dial-up router and use a communications or remote access server with built-in routing capabilities. This would give your users routed access to LANs in other locations, as well as provide dial-in (and in some cases dial-out) capabilities. Such servers provide software-based routing on top of the other communications functions they perform. Using software for routing makes the devices lower performing than a stand-alone router, but the performance level is usually adequate for the low traffic volumes ordinarily generated by small offices.

The advantage of combining the LAN-to-LAN routing functions in the same remote access server that provides dial-in (and in some cases dial-out) capabilities is that one device is easier to manage than two. If you buy a router from one vendor and a remote access server from another, the two products would have different configuration, administration, and management tools. That means someone on your staff (or you) would have to learn two different software packages for installing and maintaining the units. A combined unit would use the same interface and command structure to configure the device for both types of connectivity. The management commands and tools would be the same for both.

Cutting Communications Costs

Another type of shared unit, a *shared network modem,* can lead to substantially lower communications charges for each small office.

Usually, you will have to provide your users in the small offices with some form of dial-out access so they may connect to online services or the Internet. These users might also need to dial up one corporate site to get e-mail. And some users may need to dial up vendor bulletin board systems to get updates and fixes to programs they are running for their job.

One way to provide such dial-out access is to give each user a modem and a phone line. Figure 11-4 shows how this would look. Basically, every user who needs to dial outside the company would have a modem (either a stand-alone external type or an internal plug-in card) with their PC.

Multiple modems mean multiple pieces of equipment to buy and support, and multiple access lines. And that means more labor costs to install and manage the modems, and as you will see shortly, higher telecommunications costs.

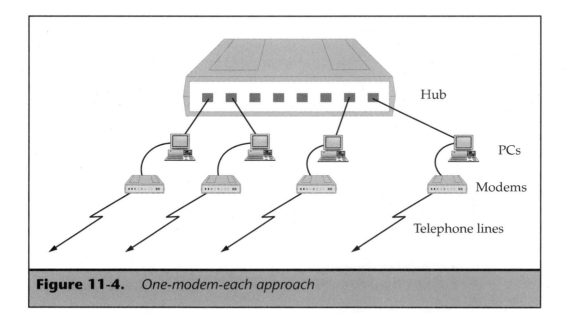

Figure 11-4. *One-modem-each approach*

When it comes to the management costs, just consider that you must configure every communications software application each user runs with the proper comm port and IRQ that the modem is using. With each application, you must also typically select the modem from a list of models the package supports. In some cases you will need to install a modem driver. Older communications packages might not list a newer modem; this might require that you go to each PC and install a driver specifically for that modem. (Some, but not all, of the configuration problems go away if you use Windows 95 and plug-and-play modems.)

The other way to provide dial-out access to users in small offices is to let them share network-attached modems. Figure 11-5 shows how this shared modem approach would look. Each LAN-attached user would have access to a modem over the LAN. There are several advantages to this approach when it comes to installing and managing the modems.

First of all, since the users are sharing modems, you would have fewer modems to deal with. Second, you would only have to configure the modems themselves once for all users to access. You will still have to help the users adjust the parameters in their communications programs so these programs can access the network-based modems. However, supporting and managing

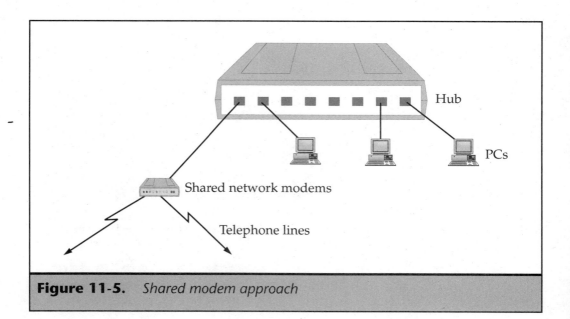

Figure 11-5.   *Shared modem approach*

the modems after the initial installation will be easier with the shared approach, since you have one unit on the network to maintain and not numerous modems sitting on each person's desk.

Still, you might argue that the installation and configuration of the network-attached, shared modems requires a more highly skilled technical person. This might make the shared modem approach less attractive to you. Before you dismiss the shared modem approach for such a reason, there is another issue to be considered that might tip the scales in favor of the shared approach. A shared approach will significantly cut your recurring telecommunications costs.

Take, for example, a case where you have ten users in a small office who need dial-out access. You could give each of them a modem and a telephone line. Or, you could let them share, for example, two network-attached modems. I will now go through the cost calculation to show how much you can save on telecommunications charges by taking a shared modem approach.

For the purposes of this calculation I will retain the ten-to-two separate modem-to-shared modem ratio. You will have to determine what the best ratio is for your users based on their connectivity habits. If you have many users who will dial into the Internet over an analog phone line and surf for hours or more at a time, you may need more shared modems. If, however, your users are simply dialing into a mail server at another site a few times a day, and they take only minutes for each call, you might be able to have more users sharing fewer modems. If you have a different ratio, simply change the numbers in the following example to reflect your usage patterns.

Reducing Lines, Cutting Costs

Here's how to calculate the cost of the two dial-out approaches. The calculations are based on ten users needing dial-out access. I will begin by calculating the first-year costs to give ten users each a modem and a phone line, and to pay the phone bill for those ten lines for the year. Then I will do the calculation for a shared modem approach.

Assume that the first case has ten users, each with a modem and each of the ten averaging about half an hour a day of connect time, five days a week, for 20 business days per month. This half hour per day average takes into account that some users will only need a few minutes of connectivity a day to check e-mail, while others will spend a couple of hours per day surfing the Web. As with all the calculations in this book, use your own numbers in place of mine to get a better understanding of your costs.

To calculate the cost of this ten-modem for ten-user scenario, you must first take into account the price of the equipment. Let's assume you will use standard 28.8-Kbps (or 33.6-Kbps by the time this book is in print) modems. These cost about $250 each, so it will cost you $2,500 for the ten modems. Again, if you believe your modem costs are significantly different than these, use your own figures here.

Next you need to calculate the telecommunications fees. First there is the fee to establish the service. This varies, but let's take a fee of $100 per line for a total of $1,000 for the ten lines. Then there is the fixed monthly fee for using the analog service. This too varies, but let's take a rate of $25 per month. That comes to $250 per month for the ten lines or $3,000 for one year. And finally there is the usage fee for the service. Again, this varies quite a bit among telephone companies. For this calculation, let's assume it costs $0.10 per minute for connect time. I said earlier that each user averages half an hour per day. That means for the ten users you will spend $30 per day, $600 per month (based on 20 business days per month), and $7,200 per year. As Table 11-2 shows, the grand total to buy the ten modems, establish the telephone service, and pay the phone bill for this service is $13,700.

	Ten-Modem Ten-Line Approach	Two Shared Modems Approach
Equipment	$ 2,500	$ 2,100
Fee to establish phone service	$ 1,000	$ 200
Total monthly fee for one year of service	$ 3,000	$ 600
Total usage fee for service	$ 7,200	$ 7,200
Grand total for first year	$13,700	$10,100

Table 11-2. *Comparing Dial-out Approaches*

Next I will calculate the fee for having two shared network modems. I will work in the opposite direction on this one. Presumably the usage fee for the phone lines will be the same; the users are simply sharing the lines. If a user needs his or her e-mail and gets a busy signal, I'm assuming he or she will try dialing out again.

That means the usage fee is the same as for the ten-line case. You still have ten users who need an average of half an hour per day connect time, for 20 business days per month. So the $30 per day, $600 per month, and $7,200 per year usage fee is the same.

The monthly charge for the lines is different. In this case we have two lines versus ten in the first example. So the $25 per month per line fee comes to $50 per month or $600 per year. And the cost to install the two lines would be the same $100 each, for a total of $200.

That was the easy part. Now let's consider what type of equipment you will need to buy so the users can share a dial-out capability. You have several choices. You can buy two LAN-attached modems and connect both to your network. Or, you can buy a unit that offers multiple modems in a single unit. You might also want to get a higher-end system that does more than give your LAN users the ability to dial out. You might, for example, select a remote access server that gives LAN-attached users dial-out capabilities, as well as giving telecommuters and travelers a way to dial into the network and, in some cases, a way to route LAN traffic to a LAN in another office.

Chapter 12, "Single User-to-LAN," will discuss the higher-end products mentioned earlier and discuss when one is more appropriate to use than another. For the sake of this calculation I will choose a simple two-modem network-attached unit. When I was writing this chapter, you could buy a LAN-attached shared modem unit with two 28.8-Kbps modems for about $2,100 (for example, Global Village Communications Inc. (Sunnyvale, California) offered a 28.8-Kbps two-modem unit for $2,099).

That brings the first-year total for ten users sharing two network-attached modems to $10,100, which is $3,600 less than the first-year cost of the ten-modem approach. Table 11-2 compares the costs. As you can see in the table, the equipment costs are about the same, and by my assumption, the usage charge is the same. One difference is the higher fee to establish service for ten lines versus two lines. That is a one-time expense, so you might feel that is not a good way to compare the two approaches. Even discounting this difference, the two-line approach is less expensive by virtue of the lower fixed monthly fee you will have to pay for each line.

The fixed rate for the service costs $250 per month for ten telephone lines versus $50 per month for two. So you save $200 per month on this fee alone. That amounts to a $2,400 savings per year per site. If you have ten offices with similar connectivity needs, we are talking about a $24,000 per year savings on your company's phone bill by use of the shared line approach.

Managing Remote Offices

Building network systems that let users in small offices share connectivity equipment and services can reduce the operational costs of running those offices. As many of the chapters in this book have discussed, the other way to reduce the cost of supporting remote users is to find ways to extend the reach of your support staff so they do not have to make as many trips to the sites to resolve any problems they may have.

Some of the earlier chapters in this section have discussed internetworking and connectivity equipment that use SNMP and RMON to reduce your support costs. The same holds for LAN-to-LAN connectivity equipment. You should look for products that incorporate SNMP and RMON to make it easier for you and your staff to understand what is happening to the equipment in the small offices. When developing a LAN-to-LAN connectivity strategy, you will face many of the same issues as was the case with LAN-to-backbone connectivity. For instance, you will need to keep unnecessary traffic off the lines between the offices by using filtering and spoofing techniques.

Beyond the management of the connectivity equipment, you may also need to be concerned about managing the other equipment in those offices. The extent of your involvement in managing and maintaining equipment such as printers and servers in the remote sites will depend on your company's philosophical approach. If you find yourself responsible for keeping the users in small offices up and running, you may have to also manage printers and servers. Chapter 14, "Server Tools," looks at some of the ways to keep a check on servers in remote offices, so I will not go into the details here. In the rest of this chapter I'll discuss how you can keep your support costs down if you have to manage those many small office networks.

Printer Management

One of the key pieces of equipment in a small office is the printer. Because printers need consumables (paper and ink or toner) and have more mechanical parts than other LAN-attached devices, you will need to consider ways to remotely manage them. Otherwise, you will be spending a lot of money sending support staff to remote sites to take care of printer problems.

Fortunately, we're on the cusp of a major change in the way printers are managed. This change is necessary because of the way printers are being used—more printers are networked than ever before. Increasingly, network managers find they must support printers from multiple vendors in mixed network environments that move beyond NetWare to include Windows NT, intranets, and the Internet.

Managing printers is of great concern to network administrators, because it costs a lot to support printers. The majority of calls to helpdesks are printer-related, and network administrators spend 20 to 30 percent of their time on printing issues, according to the consultancy BIS Strategic Decisions (Norwich, Massachusetts).

The way most managers hope to reduce the time they dedicate to supporting printers (and therefore reduce the cost of printer ownership) is to take advantage of the network connection to get better information about the physical printer devices and about the status of print jobs submitted to these devices.

When it comes to printer management, administrators face two obstacles: there are no printer management solutions that work in every environment, and good printer management requires a two-way flow of information between printers and the management programs.

Fortunately, there has been a lot of activity in the last two years in trying to address both issues. Printers capable of bidirectional communications are increasingly making their way onto networks. And there are a number of proprietary and standards-based printer management efforts aimed at managing printers from multiple vendors in mixed networking environments. This has led to a number of approaches to managing network-attached printers. Table 11-3 gives you an idea of the various types of printer management applications and techniques that are available or that are being developed by the printer vendor community.

Printer Management Approach	Points to Consider
Printer vendor supplied management software	Makes detailed information about printer device and print job status available. Only supports that vendor's printers, although some vendors offer limited support for a second vendor's product.
SNMP-based management	Printer problems reported to SNMP-based network management consoles. Some departmental LANs do not have SNMP management tools.
Desktop Management Task Force's Desktop Management Interface Printer MIF	Makes detailed information about hardware and software configuration of any vendor's printer available to DMI-compliant management programs. DMI-enabled printers just starting to appear.
Novell Embedded Systems Technology (NEST) and NetWare Directory Print Services (NDPS)	Makes it easier to install and manage printers from multiple vendors by tapping NetWare directory, security, and authentication services. Both approaches are NetWare-centric.
Management over an intranet or the Internet	Offers a common user interface (a web browser) for managing any vendor's printers. Few printers support this approach today, and there may be security issues to deal with.

Table 11-3.   *Managing Network-Attached Printers*

The best printer management programs to date have been supplied by printer vendors for their own line of printers. All the major printer vendors, including Canon U.S.A. (Lake Success, New York), Xerox Corp. (Rochester, New York), Hewlett-Packard Co. (Palo Alto, California), IBM (Armonk, New York), Tektronix Inc. (Beaverton, Oregon), QMS Inc. (Mobile, Alabama), and Lexmark International Inc. (Lexington, Kentucky), offer proprietary management systems that give network managers detailed information about the status of their printers on networks, as well as information about the print jobs submitted by users.

Normally, these vendor-supplied printer management packages, which require an upstream flow of information from the printer (that is, the printers are capable of bidirectional communications), are Windows-based and give a manager a graphical view of all the printers on a network. You would need to dial up the LAN in the small office to which the printer is attached to take advantage of this approach.

Printer management utilities, such as JetAdmin and JetPrint from Hewlett-Packard, CrownNet from QMS, Document Services for Printing (DS/P) and CentreWare from Xerox, and MarkVision from Lexmark, let a network manager get details about a printer's operation. For example, a manager who clicks on a printer icon will get an image on the management console screen depicting the printer's paper trays, paper feed paths, and toner cartridges.

This seemingly low-level amount of information is in fact quite handy, especially when you consider that many companies are consolidating management and the routine servicing of their printers. For example, many companies are centralizing all aspects of their printer operations. That means some companies send technicians to an office just to diagnose and fix printer problems like a paper jam.

Reducing such service trips is even more important when a company is managing printers located in many sites. This has forced some companies to look into printers with bidirectional communications capabilities. Such printers pass information up to printer management utilities. This information gives you a clear view of what's going on, down to the exact location of a paper jam. In this way, you can, for example, bring up a printer on a management console in one office and talk the user in another office through something like clearing a paper jam.

Within the last year, the major shift in the proprietary printer management packages has been the incorporation for support of other vendors' printers. Already several vendors, including Hewlett-Packard, Xerox, Canon, and Lexmark, have printer management software programs that support bidirectional communication printers from other vendors. Typically, the support for other vendor's printers is minimal. For example, there might not be a visual display of the other vendor's printer on a screen. Instead, a manager might simply get an alarm that a printer is down or a paper tray is empty.

The move by printer vendors to incorporate other vendors' printers into a single printer management offering is just the start. Within the last year, there has also been much more emphasis on standards-based approaches to managing multivendor print environments.

Novell has taken the lead in offering multivendor printer management on NetWare LANs. Novell's main efforts are Novell Embedded Systems Technology (NEST) and NetWare Directory Print Services (NDPS). NEST-enabled printers can connect directly to a NetWare LAN and can take advantage of NetWare services such as directory, security, and authentication services. As such, NEST-enabled printers are easier to install and manage. For example, a manager sets access rights to a printer by defining such rights in the printer's NDS object. In that way, existing access rights assigned to users or groups of users are easily mapped to the printer.

Novell's other effort, NDPS, which was developed with Xerox and Hewlett-Packard, is a print services architecture that can be incorporated into printers or used with existing printers (see the next section for more information about NDPS). NDPS, like NEST, makes it easier to add printers to networks since its architecture taps NDS. In addition, NDPS improves on the traditional queue-based printing found in today's NetWare LANs by combining the functions of printers, printing queues, and print servers into one entity that can be managed from NWAdmin or an SNMP management console.

While Novell's efforts are aimed at the NetWare environment, other standards efforts are aimed at incorporating printer management into traditional network management platforms. For example, several years ago, the printer vendor community, through the Internet Engineering Task Force, developed a Printer MIB (management information base) so printers can be managed through SNMP.

It took a while for SNMP-manageable printers to gain favor—most printers were running on NetWare LANs, and often managers did not have SNMP management programs available. Now SNMP management of printers is more widespread. Companies want to control their printer support by managing all printers within an enterprise as a collective group, rather than trying to manage each department or site's LAN printer on its own. As a result of this change within user organizations, most printer vendors offer built-in SNMP management in their higher-end network printer lines.

An SNMP-manageable printer passes event alarms—for such things as a printer being down—to network management platforms such as Hewlett-Packard's OpenView or Cabletron's Spectrum. Thus, the printer is depicted as any other SNMP-managed component of the network. And like other SNMP efforts, printer vendors have developed proprietary MIBs for their products that, using the vendor's management system, make more detailed information about the printer available to a network administrator at a management console.

Another standards-based effort, which is several years old but just now gaining hold, comes from the Desktop Management Task Force (DMTF). A working group within the DMTF has developed a Printer MIF (management information format) that specifies the type of information needed to manage printers as any other Desktop Management Interface (DMI)-enabled device on a network. In February 1996, Lexmark was the first vendor to offer a DMI-enabled printer.

The Printer MIF gives a manager information about the printer such as the model and serial number, the printer's status (for example, whether it is idle, printing, or in a warm-up state), and information about the hardware and software configuration of the printer.

Network managers can access this information through DMI-compliant management applications such as Novell's ManageWise and Intel's LANDesk Management Suite. With DMI-enabled printers, a network manager can diagnose complicated printer problems from the same application that he or she is using to manage a LAN. For example, a user might call complaining that a document isn't printing correctly. The network manager can use the DMI information to find out if the printer has the correct software fonts and print drivers.

As with many other forms of network management, there are some efforts to offer printer management over the Internet or an intranet. The basic idea is to have a common interface—a browser—to manage printers. This interface would be used by network administrators to manage remote printers and print jobs submitted to those printers over an intranet or the Internet connection. Users would also be able to use the simple interface to submit print jobs.

The field of printer management through a browser is in its early stages. For example, in June 1996, Xerox announced a broad printer management strategy that, when the actual management software becomes available, will let network administrators manage Xerox Document Centre printing systems, Xerox DocuPrint network laser printers, and Hewlett-Packard LaserJet printers.

Through a browser interface, network managers will be able to get printer status information as well as print job status. Some printer companies plan to build Java-enabled applications that will automatically update the information on a user's screen.

Other printer vendors are also working on management of printers through a browser interface. For example, in late 1995, Tektronix announced plans to build a web-based printer management application into its printers' ROM. The application, called PhaserLink, will let network administrators configure printers using an HTML (Hypertext Markup language) form.

The idea with such efforts is to make printer management universal, where all it takes is a common web browser to access information about a printer and to send commands to the printer to adjust its configuration or printing parameters. Such browser-based approaches may be the ultimate solution to your nightmares when it comes to managing multiple vendors' printers in mixed networking environments.

NDPS

In the early days of networking, NetWare LANs gained popularity because they offered file and print services. Over time these services have remained virtually unchanged as other services, such as security and directory services, have been added to NetWare.

With the release of Green River (NetWare 4.1) and IntraNetware in 1996, Novell offered network managers a new print services architecture, called the NetWare Directory Print Services (NDPS), which makes printer management easier by integrating printers with security and directory services. Specifically, NDPS reduces the time a network administrator will spend setting up printers, establishing user access rights to printers, and troubleshooting printer problems.

Managing printers and the printing process is easier with NDPS because it improves on Novell's traditional queue-based print service architecture, which requires creating and linking printers, print queues, and print servers.

Under the queue-based system a user first has to capture a printer port, then the client redirects the data to be printed to a file in a print queue. There the data is spooled until a print server sends it to a printer. Under NDPS, queues have been eliminated—users send a print job straight to a printer. This simplifies the process for a user and should reduce the number of printer-related calls to a helpdesk. Additionally, with NDPS a network administrator can monitor all network print devices from within NWAdmin or an SNMP management console.

NDPS is a distributed client/server print architecture based on the ISO 10175 Document Printing Application standard. It was developed by Novell in conjunction with Hewlett-Packard Co. and Xerox Corp., and virtually every printer vendor says they will support the standard.

The way NDPS simplifies the printing process is by combining the print queue, print server, and the print spooling functions into one entity called a *printer agent.* A printer agent is a software module that runs on a server that front-ends a printer connected to that server or that is embedded in a network printer. Each printer incorporated into the NDPS environment must have an associated printer agent.

The agent manages print jobs, carries out printing security by validating client requests for services, and generates event notifications when there are problems with a print device or job. If a printer is capable of bidirectional communications, a print agent can tell users whether a printer is available and provide information about the status of the device or the printing job. For example, a printer with bidirectional communications can tell a user that toner is low, a paper tray is empty, or that paper is jammed. Such printers can also provide information about the unit's configuration and which software fonts are loaded.

NDPS-aware printers with built-in printer agents also advertise that they are available as soon as they are connected to a network. A printer agent, thus, is the main component of NDPS. These agents are created, configured, started, and stopped by use of what is called the *NDPS Manager,* an NLM that can be accessed through the NetWare Administrator or a server console. Managers can configure the agents to be a *public-access printer,* which is available to anyone on the network, or a *controlled-access printer,* which taps the security and access control features of Novell Directory Services.

NDPS provides printing security in a number of ways. For example, by using NDPS, managers can deny users or groups of users access to specific controlled-access printers. Also, a manager can deny unauthorized users access to a printer that has company letterhead or even blank check forms. Or, NDPS might be used simply to let users match the characteristics of a print job with a printer's features. Finally, you might give a drafting group access to a high-resolution film printer and a marketing department access to a printer that generates color transparencies.

In the past, assigning such rights was a tedious task. It required that a manager set up printing queues and assign access rights almost on a user-by-user level. The process is particularly painful with many remote printers.

With NDPS, such tasks are somewhat simplified. A manager creates a printer agent in such a way that the printer is added to the Directory Services name space and appears as an object in the NDS tree. Such controlled-access printers no longer are available to users directly as public access printers.

Instead, users with appropriate access rights to the printer can access it through the NDS object list.

The first printers with NDPS printer agents embedded within them appeared in fall 1996. But even if the market were flooded with NDPS-enabled printers, most companies would still use their existing printers and retain their queue-based printing environments for a while.

Recognizing this, Novell, HP, and Xerox built in some backwards compatibility, offering limited support for existing printers and clients that remain in a queue-based printing environment. For example, a client in a queue-based system cannot take advantage of the bidirectional information provided under NDPS, such as printer availability or status information about the printer's paper or toner levels. However, a client in a queue-based system can submit a job to a printer with an embedded NDPS controller.

NDPS Points to Consider

Benefits

- Manages printers from multiple vendors and improves on queue-based print services previously available with NetWare.

- Adding printers is easier because managers use existing access rights assigned within NDS to give users or groups of users access to printers.

Drawbacks

- NetWare-centric approach.

- Like most higher-end print management systems, requires printers capable of bidirectional communications to exploit all the features of NDPS.

Uninterruptible Power Supplies (UPSes)

Keeping networks up and running is tough enough, but keeping remote networks going is even harder. One of the simplest things you can do to help reduce the number of trips you need to make to remote sites is to install uninterruptible power supplies (UPSes) in each site for your network equipment and servers.

UPSes perform a range of functions. Low-end models simply provide battery backup when the electrical power at a site fails. Mid-range systems include power monitoring and management systems that protect equipment from power spikes, surges, and dips. Some UPSes come with server shutdown software, which is software that recognizes when the power has failed and the UPS has kicked in. The software then starts shutting down applications. When power is restored, the software automatically brings the server back up.

Depending on the equipment in the remote sites, you can buy a UPS tailored to the needs of a particular office. If one site experiences occasional power outages or temporary power brownouts, you might want to put in a UPS just to keep the server going during these infrequent outages. If another site needs the server up even if the power is out for hours, you might look for a UPS with a high-capacity battery.

The one trouble with UPSes is that, like printers, they rely on an exhaustible component: batteries. You could periodically send a staffer from site to site, office to office to check the UPS batteries. But that seems silly. You might spend more money in the time and travel expenses for this person to go office to office than you would save by keeping the equipment up and running during power outages.

If you can't get someone onsite to properly and constantly check and maintain the UPSes, you will need the capability to perform these tasks remotely.

Managing UPSes

UPSes have long been used to keep servers running in case of power problems. Now, with more servers in remote sites—sites with little, if any, technical staff—the role of the UPS is changing to also provide a remote reboot capability and the graceful shutdown and restarting of servers, hubs, and other network devices when power is disrupted.

As such, UPS management tools have been extended to work remotely and to tightly integrate with network management systems. And there is a move to make these tools more web-friendly, so UPSes can be monitored over the Internet or an intranet.

Increasingly, companies are putting UPS systems into small offices with no onsite technical staff. Administrators want to be able to control and monitor their UPSes as they do all other devices on their networks. UPS vendors, such as American Power conversion (APC, West Kingston, Rhode Island), Best Power Technology Inc. (Necedah, Wisconsin), Exide Electronics (Raleigh, North Carolina), Liebert Corp. (Columbus, Ohio), Minuteman (Dallas), Tripp Lite (Chicago), have taken a couple of approaches to the remote

Ways to Manage UPSes	What It Does
Proprietary management software from UPS vendor	Offers detailed information about the status of the UPS and electrical power statistics through a graphical user interface (GUI).
Manage UPS through server management tools	Lets a manager get UPS status information using a server management tool such as Compaq's Insight Manager.
SNMP-based management	UPS status information made available to network management platforms.
Web-based management	View UPS management information through a web browser.

Table 11-4.   *The Types of UPS Management*

management of their products. The major ways to remotely manage UPSes are shown in Table 11-4.

Additionally, some vendors, such as APC, Exide, and Tripp Lite, offer shutdown software that runs on the server and that works with management software running on the UPS. This type of software gracefully shuts down a server when a power failure occurs. Typically, the software alerts managers and users to the problem, and closes applications running on the server. When power returns, the server is restarted.

Usually, software that gracefully shuts down and restarts a server runs locally, so a remote manager does not get too involved in the process. Still, you might want to know when such a process has taken place. And you might want to check on the status of the remote UPSes from a central location.

That's where integration of UPS management software with existing management tools comes into play. At first, UPS management consisted of giving managers a way to check the status of the batteries in remote units. Over the years, UPS vendors have beefed up their management software offerings to cover a much wider range of features.

First, managers have the option of using the basic, proprietary management software offered by most UPS vendors. This software commonly offers a graphical display of the UPS and uses, for example, a change in color on the screen to note that a battery's power is below a certain level. Such software also provides a network manager with statistics about the line current and voltage into and out of the UPS.

Next, there are UPS management programs such as APC's Powerchute that link with server management programs such as Compaq Computer's Insight Manager. With this form of management, a manager is able to gather statistical information about a UPS' performance over a LAN.

Another form of UPS management involves using SNMP agents on the UPSes to integrate with traditional network management platforms. The Internet Engineering Task Force has developed a UPS MIB for those who want to manage their UPSes using SNMP. This form of management can take two forms. The UPS vendor might simply let a manager set threshold levels for alerts and alarms to be handled by the management platform. In this way, the UPS is managed in the same way as any other SNMP-enabled device on the network. There is a UPS SNMP MIB (management information base) that specifies the type of information and the format the information must be in so that it can be used within an SNMP management program. Table 11-5 lists the MIB groups and what aspects of a UPS each group covers. For example, the MIB has groups that describe the physical device and characteristics of the input and output electrical power.

In a somewhat different approach to SNMP management, a UPS management vendor might offer a graphical user interface that plugs into a management platform such as HP's OpenView or Novell Inc.'s ManageWise. This would give the manager a visual way to discern alarms and alerts. For example, without a plug-in GUI, a UPS that has a problem may simply appear as a red icon on a map of the network displayed on a management console. With the plug-in GUI, the manager could click on the icon and see a graphical representation of the UPS that might, for example, depict the batteries in red if they are not holding a charge.

In the future, there are two areas where you can expect to see some enhancements to UPS remote management systems. The first involves extending the UPS' role in reducing network downtime. Currently, the role of the UPS is to reduce server and network equipment downtime caused by power disruptions and glitches (most UPSes smooth out the effects of power surges and dips). There are, however, other things that cause network downtime—for example, high temperatures in a wiring closet. Some UPS vendors are now starting to offer an additional piece of hardware that monitors the environment around the UPS.

MIB Group	What It Contains
Device Identification Group	Information about the UPS hardware and software
Battery Group	Information about the battery or batteries in the UPS
Input Group	Information about the power entering the UPS
Output Group	Information about the output power of the UPS
Bypass Group	Information about the bypass lines used in the UPS
Alarm Group	Information about the number and type of alarms used by the UPS
Test Group	Lets you initiate a test of the UPS and have the results of that test returned to the management console
Control Group	Lets you shut down the UPS or the UPS output power
Configuration Group	Includes the basic information about the normal operating parameters of the UPS

Table 11-5. *SNMP Management of a UPS*

Such probes can alert you when, for example, a fire alarm goes off, or the temperature and humidity reach an undesirable level in a small remote office. The probe can also send an alarm to you when a door opens—something that might be helpful if you suspect someone is tampering with equipment.

The other area that is already getting attention is to use the Web to get status information. The idea is to make available to a manager with a web browser in one office the information collected by a UPS running in another office. This trend mimics a management trend that is being tackled by most systems and device management vendors, including network printer and internetworking product vendors.

A Quick Summary

As you can see from this chapter, you might find yourself dealing with many forms of communications and management issues when linking LAN-based users in small offices to LAN-based users in other small offices—the LAN-to-LAN connectivity scenario.

Although the situation is different than the LAN-to-backbone connectivity scenario in the previous chapter, many of the issues are the same. Specifically, you must look for ways to reduce the recurring communications charges, and you must keep the support costs down. In this chapter I showed that the best way to reduce communication costs is to have users in small offices share communications resources such as modems and especially, phone lines. When it comes to keeping support costs down, the most important thing you can do is find ways to reduce the number of trips you and your staff must make to the many remote sites. The basic approach here is to invest in LAN equipment that incorporates remote management capabilities.

Chapter Twelve

Single User-to-LAN

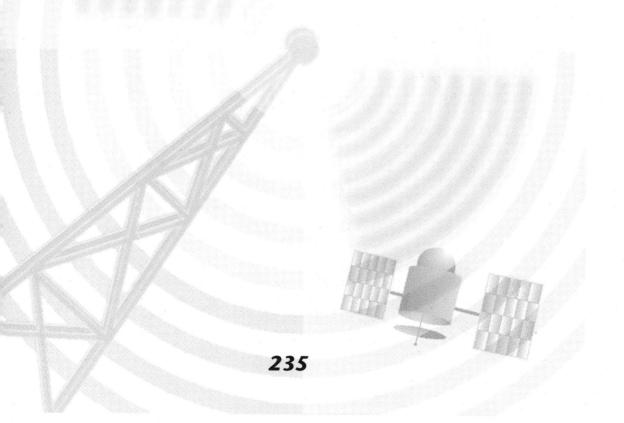

The most common remote connectivity scenario is connecting a single user to a network or LAN. Many of the chapters in Part 2 discussed the connectivity services you would use to accomplish this. Those chapters also discussed the types of equipment you would need for a telecommuter or mobile worker to make such a connection possible.

This chapter looks at the scenario from a different perspective—from the central site—examining the various approaches you can select to connect all of your remote users to your LAN. Specifically, this chapter discusses general approaches and strategies you might take to give remote users access.

The basic considerations you must deal with when connecting many remote users to a network are what type of access speeds and what type of access your users need. For example, can everyone get by with 28.8-Kbps rates using dial-up modems and analog lines? Will some users need higher-speed access such as that offered using ISDN BRI lines? If they use ISDN, will one B channel, which offers data rates of 64 Kbps, be enough? Or will they need to aggregate the bandwidth of the two B channels of a BRI link to get a higher data rate of 128 Kbps? These choices will dictate what type of equipment and which approach you will need in your central site.

Components of a Connection

While there are many ways to connect single users to a network, there are some common elements among the various approaches. The key elements are the client software, an entry point into the LAN, and communications equipment that connects to the telecommunications services.

There are several generic types of client software. Each type is used for different forms of access to network resources. Table 12-1 lists the three main categories of remote access software.

Remote Control

The three types of connectivity software give your users different types of access to your network. Remote control software, as the name implies, lets a user remotely control another machine. Using remote control software, a remote or mobile worker dials into a PC or server on the network. Typically, as is shown in Figure 12-1, this network-attached machine is some form of application server or high-end server running a specific application. The machine within the company may also be a stand-alone PC.

Type of Client Software	What It Does
Remote control	Gives a remote user control of a PC or server on the network
Remote node	Lets a remote user's PC become a node on the network letting the user perform all the functions available to network-attached users
Terminal emulation	Lets a remote user access host applications and data

Table 12-1.   *The Basic Choices for Remote Connections*

Remote control access to a corporate PC or server can be used in several ways by remote users. The traditional use of remote control access has been to give users access to an application not running on their PC. By using remote control, a user runs the program on another computer, entering commands as if he or she were sitting in front of the PC or server. The remote user sees the same display on his or her PC as the one on the centrally located computer.

Remote control is used when an application requires great processing power, huge amounts of memory, or lots of storage. One way to think of

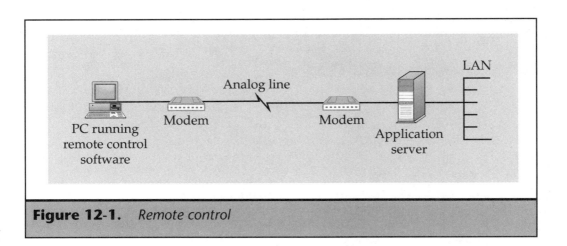

Figure 12-1.   *Remote control*

remote control is that you can give users with a lower-powered PC access to an application that would not run on their machine (there are other ways to accomplish this, such as using Citrix's WinFrame technology, which will be discussed in Chapter 14, "Server Tools").

A classic example of where to use remote control is when you want to give a user access to something like a Computer-Aided Design/Computer-Aided Manufacturing (CAD/CAM) application that requires lots of processing power and memory. You could set up a high-end PC in the main office running the CAD/CAM application. Users within the company could go to that PC and access the program, and remote users could dial into the PC. This gives a remote user with a modest PC the ability to run a high-end application such as the CAD/CAM program. This saves your company money, because you do not need to furnish everyone who needs access to the one power-hungry application with a high-end system.

Another application that lends itself to remote control is the processing of database queries. For example, suppose you have a large corporate database of 200,000 customers. Each entry has detailed information about a customer's account, including billing information, a history of that client's orders, and a record of payments. To run this database, you might need a system with a large amount of memory, lots of storage, possibly a RAID system to improve disk access speeds when performing queries, and a backup tape system to ensure that the data is safe.

This is not the type of system you are going to give to every telecommuter or mobile worker. If you want remote users to be able to do queries against this database, you need to give them access. Remote control is often the preferred way to do this. Remote users dial into the server and run the database program just as they would if sitting in front of the computer.

Cut Management Costs

As discussed earlier, remote control gives you a way to provide remote users with access to higher-performance computers from their homes or from the road when traveling. Remote control also lets you give users access to data that needs special safeguards. For instance, in the preceding example, the customer database has great value to the company, and you had to make sure it was properly backed up.

There is another use of remote control access that can dramatically reduce the cost of supporting remote users. The idea is to use remote control to troubleshoot a remote user's problems. For example, suppose a telecommuter calls and tells you that his or her printer is no longer working. Or he or she is simply experiencing very poor performance all of a sudden. With a remote control package, you could dial into the user's computer from your office, from the road, or even from your home. Once you dial into the user's computer, you could, for example, run a diagnostic program that resides on that user's computer to detect the nature of the problem.

Suppose the user is having a serious performance problem. You might run a utility and find that the user's hard disk is severely fragmented. Once you have identified this as a potential source of the problem, you could then run a defragmentation program. In this example, I am assuming that the diagnostic utilities reside on the remote user's PC. If this solves the problem, you have saved a trip to the user's location. And that means you saved money by reducing your labor costs. If the person having the problem is far away, you also saved the travel expenses, such as the cost of gas, tolls, food, and so on, to send a person to the user's location.

A more sophisticated use of remote control in cutting support costs takes the process just described a step further. Suppose a user calls to tell you the external CD-ROM drive you sent does not work properly. Again, you could dial into the user's PC using a remote control package. Since it is an external CD-ROM that isn't working, you might suspect that the user did not load the driver properly. If you were to ask the user to help you, it could be frustrating for both of you. It might go like this:

You: Please look in the autoexec.bat file and tell me if there is a line that says

"IF Exist BPCDDRV$ \BPCDROM\MSCDEX /D:BPCDDRV$"

(that's the real line my external CD-ROM adds to my autoexec.bat file when loading the drivers for the device).

User: Autoexec what?

You: You know, the autoexec.bat file. You just go to File Manager and look in the root directory.

User: File Manager?

You get the point. And I'm sure you have been in a similar situation. Remote control can help make this an easier process. Many remote control packages, such as Laplink from Traveling Software, Norton pcAnywhere from Symantec, and Close-Up from Norton-Lambert, let you transfer files in addition to running a program remotely. So, once you connect to the remote user's PC using a remote control package, you can transfer files between the two systems. In this case, you would want to copy the user's systems files, including the autoexec.bat, config.sys, and win.ini, to your system to look at them. If the user has not properly installed the drivers for the CD-ROM, you can simply download the driver installation program, take control of the user's PC, and run the installation process yourself to ensure it is done properly.

This way of using remote control packages can save you many trips to a remote user's site and can cut troubleshooting time. All you need to do to take advantage of this type of support is to make sure the remote user's PC has remote control software installed and that each remote user's PC is configured to take an incoming call. For that minimal amount of effort and cost, you can potentially save your company a great deal on support costs.

Let's look at the cost-analysis of this process. Your remote users will have modems (they are telecommuters or remote workers dialing into your network). You basically have to pay for the user's remote control software. The typical price for a decent remote control software package varies from about $100 to $300 per user. Most companies offer volume discounts on their software, so for the sake of this calculation I will use a per-user cost of $100. As is the case with all of the calculations in this book, if your price is substantially different, insert your own numbers into my calculations.

Assume you have 50 remote users at small sites with no technical support, ten full-time telecommuters, and a dozen nontechnical professionals who frequently travel. If you buy each one a copy of a remote control product, that comes to 72 copies times $100 per copy, or $7,200. Let's, for the sake of this calculation, assume you can troubleshoot and correct all problems using remote control software (this assumption may be overly optimistic, but let's just see what the cost trade-offs are in an ideal situation, and then we can take it from there).

Now let's look at how much it would cost you if you did not use remote control software. Assume that without remote control software you had two calls per month where you could not fix the problem over the phone by talking with the user. In these cases, the user would need to send his or her computer by overnight delivery to you. If your company is like any I've worked for, you would also have to send a loaner computer by overnight delivery for the user to work with until his or her computer is repaired and returned. So we are talking about twice a month paying overnight delivery fees for two computers each time. Considering that you have to insure the computers, we are talking about a shipping fee of between $20 to $30 each way. I am going to use $25 per computer each way. That means you will pay $200 per month, or $2,400 per year just in shipping fees.

If remote control software allowed you to solve all of these problems, you can see in Table 12-2 that in three years ($2,400 x 3 = $7,200) you have recouped the cost of the software.

As you can see, the price of sending PCs and laptops back and forth can really add up. You might not have the luxury of sending PCs back and forth in this manner. It might be your corporate policy to send a staffer to the user site to fix the problem. This is more common when you have users in a small office with no technical staff. If that is the case, you might find you are spending much of your travel budget to send technicians to user sites.

	Cost of Not Using Remote Control Software	Cost of Using Remote Control Software
License fee for 72 users		$7,200
Three-year cost to overnight-deliver two broken PCs per month (includes insurance)	$3,600	
Three-year costs to overnight-deliver two users a loaner PC per month (includes insurance)	$3,600	
Total three-year costs	$7,200	$7,200

Table 12-2.   *Cost Analysis of Using Remote Control Software*

Remote control software could reduce the number of these trips. And even if you cannot fix the computer, you might be able to adequately diagnose the problem to guarantee you send the right technician to the site. For example, if you could remotely diagnose that a remote user's problems stem from device configuration problems, you can hold back your application specialist who might not be able to help the user and send your technician who is a wizard at resolving hardware conflicts. This would at least eliminate wasted trips.

Some companies are taking remote control support a step further. The idea is to aid diagnosis by giving the user a voice in the process. Suppose a remote user or traveling user calls you with a problem. If the remote user is a telecommuter, he or she might have a second phone line. If that is the case, he or she can be on the line with you as you try to remotely troubleshoot the problem with remote control software.

But what happens if users have only one telephone line? The users have to hang up and let you dial into their PC, effectively cutting off verbal communications. This is frustrating because you may want to be asking the users questions as you try to find the source of their problem—"When did this problem start to occur? Does it happen all the time? Which application were you using when you noticed this?" These questions go unanswered when the users have only one telephone line.

There are two ways around this. You can either use a software-based line-sharing approach, or buy modems equipped with hardware that lets you share a line. In Chapter 2, I talked a little bit about these types of products. The software approach lets you maintain a telephone and data connection with the remote user. The software handles data in the normal way until it detects a voice signal. At that time, the analog line is switched to handle the voice traffic. This means you could be transferring the remote user's systems files and ask him or her a question. The file transfer would be suspended while voice traffic is carried over the line, and then would resume once the line is clear. Such software is typically bundled with modems and is often preinstalled on many computer systems.

With the hardware approach to line sharing, the basic thing to look for is a DSVD (Digital Simultaneous Voice and Data) modem. Such modems, which in late 1996 started to be included with many computer systems, offer a way to simultaneously handle voice and data traffic on a single analog phone line. If you and your remote users have DSVD modems, you can dial into the remote user's modem, start transferring systems files, and talk to the user at the same time. When voice traffic is passed over the link, the data transfer rate is reduced a bit. And when the conversation ends, the data rate kicks back up to the normal speed. Such shared-line techniques are ideal for traveling users dialing in from the road, where there is likely to be only one phone line in a hotel room. With a shared-line approach you and the remote user can discuss the problem as you try solving it.

The shared-line technique can also help with training when combined with remote control software. If users do not know how to run a program, you can talk them through a procedure while showing them how to perform a task. For example, if a user has just received a new accounting package and is having trouble using it, you can dial into the user's computer and launch the application. With a remote control package, you will see the same screen as that on your remote user's monitor. As you move through the application, you can tell the user, "This is how you open a file, this is how you add an entry, this is how you save your work." If the user has a question, you can answer it on the spot, or you can demonstrate again how to perform an operation or task within the program.

Remote control combined with a shared voice/data access technology will let you cut your support costs and help reduce your training costs for remote users. To summarize how remote control reduces these costs:

- Speeds troubleshooting by launching diagnostic utilities from the central site

- Transfers remote user's systems files to look for telltale signs of problems

- Cuts training costs by taking control of applications and showing the user how to perform tasks

- Uses shared-line techniques to talk the user through problems while diagnosing the situation

Remote Node

Next we will look at remote node access to a network. Remote node connectivity lets a user dial into a network and become a node on the network.

Figure 12-2 shows you the typical networking setup you will need to provide remote users with remote node access to your network. In Figure 12-2 you can see that the remote user must run a remote node client program. This program must support a SLIP (Serial Line Internet Protocol) or PPP (Point-to-Point Protocol) connection. Similarly, your central site must have a communications server into which users dial. This server must also be running either SLIP or PPP (for more information about SLIP and PPP see "Sending LAN Traffic over Serial Links").

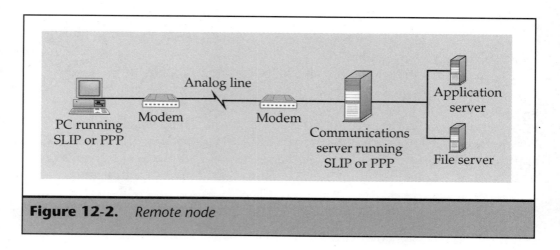

Figure 12-2. *Remote node*

Also in Figure 12-2, I have indicated that the connection is over an analog phone line and uses modems at both ends of the connection. This is probably the most common way used today to provide remote users with remote node access. However, the link can just as easily be an ISDN BRI line with ISDN terminal adapters at each end of the line.

With a remote node connection into your LAN, a remote user has the same level of access as if he or she were sitting in the office connected to the network. For example, remote users can view network directories or drives as they would if they were in the office. Such users can, for example, use File Manager or Windows Explorer and copy files from a network drive to their hard disk drive (and vice versa). And the remote users can access network-based applications as they would in the office. For instance, if you have a server running a database program, the user will be able to click on an icon on his or her laptop from the road or on a desktop computer in his or her home and launch the program.

Sending LAN Traffic over Serial Links

For a remote user to dial into a network and connect as a remote node, the user must run a special protocol on his or her computer. The reason is that analog phone lines and digital ISDN lines operate as serial connections over the switched-circuit telephone network, while network links are packet-based and connectionless.

To get network and LAN traffic in the form of packets over the switched-circuit telephone network, the remote node connectivity software running on the remote client must use either the Serial Line IP (SLIP) or Point-to-Point Protocol (PPP).

SLIP was developed in the early 1980s to connect network devices over serial links. By use of SLIP, IP packets are put into frames that are passed over the serial line to the remote user. At the user's end of the link, the same algorithm reverses the process and takes the packets out of the frame.

PPP is a follow-on to SLIP and includes support for IP and IPX packets (SLIP only supports IP). Additionally, PPP is more robust in that it offers data compression and security features, such as Password Authentication Protocol (PAP) and the Challenge Handshake Authentication Protocol (CHAP), lacking in SLIP.

As a manager, you can set user access rights for remote users dialing into your network using remote node connections just as you would for a network-attached user. That means, for instance, if a user on the LAN must log into a server before getting access to an application, you can have the same system in place for the remote users. Or, you might set levels of access to data for remote users just as you would if they were sitting in the office. For instance, you might give all supervisors read-and-write access to a particular database, but give staff members of a department read-only access to the same data. It would not matter if the user were on the LAN or in his or her home, the access levels would be the same for a particular user.

For remote users, remote node connectivity is the next best thing to being there. There is, however, one major difference—the speed of the connection. If a user is attached to an Ethernet network, the data rate is 10 Mbps. That is about an order of magnitude faster than the 28.8 Kbps a remote user with an analog phone line connection can achieve. Basically, if I drop-and-drag a moderate-sized file from a network drive to my hard disk, it might take a second to copy when attached to the network, while it would take tens of minutes (depending on the size of the file) over a dial-up connection. Many remote users can live with this wait to get the level of connectivity offered with a remote node connection.

With this in mind, now is a good time to point out that there are certain applications where a remote node connection is the best bet and other applications where it is better to use remote control.

Choosing Between Remote Node and Remote Control

To decide which is the best connectivity solution for a user—remote node or remote control—look at the traffic generated by the application.

For example, with a remote control application, the screen display of the computer within the company walls appears as the display on the remote user's PC. If you have an application that is graphics intensive, all of that information displayed on the one screen must be sent over the phone line before it is displayed on the remote user's PC. That could take a long time. So for graphics-intensive applications, a remote node connection is best.

If the application is a spreadsheet or database program, the size of the file being accessed makes the difference as to which remote access method is best to use. Suppose the file is large, say 20MB. If the user comes into the network as a remote node, running the application on his or her PC, the file must be downloaded over the phone line to the user's computer before he or she can start working on it. To transfer a file that size would take about an hour and a half with a 28.8-Kbps modem and analog phone line—tying up the phone line for the entire time. It's hardly a productive way to work.

Contrast that to a remote control connection. The file remains on the server or PC within the company walls. The user simply runs the application from afar. What needs to be transferred down the line is simply the screen image and commands. The manipulations and queries are processed on the machine within the company walls, and the results, as displayed on that computer, are seen on the remote user's PC. So, for this type of application where manipulation of a large file is involved, remote control is best. The determining factor when choosing between remote control and remote node is the amount of traffic that needs to be exchanged between the remote user and the networked computer at work, when running an application in each connectivity mode.

Making a Choice

Remote node is best for:

> E-mail
> File transfers
> Graphic-intensive applications
> Working with small data files

Remote control is best for:

> Handling e-mail attachments
> Working on large spreadsheets
> Working with large data files
> Applications with minimal graphics

Often your remote users will need both types of connectivity, because they will have a mix of applications they need to access. One question that you must ask is, "Are my users knowledgeable enough to know when to choose remote node versus remote control?" My bet is they are not. And that is not to denigrate your users. Sometimes it is difficult to make the proper choice. For instance, as discussed earlier, when accessing an application means you must transfer a large file, you might opt for remote control rather than remote node. But where is the cutoff point? How large a file makes the wait too long? And what about choosing remote node over remote control for graphics-intensive applications? Where is the dividing line? How intensive do the graphics have to be to cause a user to use remote node?

Those are tough decisions to make. And your users might have trouble with the easy decisions, too. You could leave the choice up to the remote users and hope that they choose the right connectivity method in every case. Or, if you believe your users will need a lot of help, you could look at one of the more interesting products introduced in 1996.

There's a saying that the best choices are those that don't have to be made. Why not apply that logic to your remote access solutions and take the decision of whether to use remote control or remote node out of the hands of your users? WorldDesk Applink, a rules-based software package introduced in July 1996 by Cubix Corp., Carson City, Nevada, selects the most efficient way for a user to come into a network, based on the applications a user is running.

This can save your company money by optimizing each dial-in connection for the application the user has selected. Essentially, WorldDesk Applink tries to overcome the common problem of a user not knowing when it is best to use remote node versus remote control.

If you're like most managers responsible for remote connectivity, you probably already know how hard it is trying to explain the difference between the two remote access technologies (remote control and remote node) to users. WorldDesk Applink, which runs on a Citrix Systems Inc. WinFrame Application Server, can automatically make this decision for the dial-in user by using a set of manager-defined rules. Applink can also switch a user from remote node to remote control without the user having to log off the network and dial back in.

With WorldDesk Applink, managers create connectivity rules using simple if/then statements that reflect the best choice between remote control and remote node. As discussed earlier, the rule of thumb is that remote node is best for e-mail, file transfers, and applications that use small files; remote control is best for running database and spreadsheet programs that use large data files.

You can fine-tune these general rules with WorldDesk Applink. For example, you might choose to build rules based on file size. If that is the case, you can designate that whenever a user needs access to a file, such as a Microsoft Corp. Excel spreadsheet file larger than 300K, to use remote control (called "remote application" in a WinFrame environment), rather then remote node. That would save the time needed to download the file to the dial-in user.

Similarly, you can set rules based on application names. If the user wants to run Lotus Development Corp. Lotus cc:Mail, for example, you would opt for remote node mode. Again, the user does not have to know the difference between entering the network in remote node versus remote control mode. The application selects the most appropriate connectivity method.

Rules can also be based on time of day, the origin of the call, and the type of user. You might, for example, want to associate an engineer with a CAD program that runs on a high-end server and automatically select remote control.

One of the main reasons users often don't know the difference between remote node and remote control is due to a lack of supervisory support for remote workers, according to the Gartner Group Inc. in Stamford, Connecticut. Part of the problem with many companies is that they do not have the resources to properly train all of their remote workers. Or, they might train people on how to use applications when connected to the corporate network, but give the same users no guidance when it comes to the applications these users would run while traveling.

Why don't companies train their users? One reason is the cost. Gartner analysts have found that support and training costs for remote users are higher than LAN-based users—Gartner claims the total cost of ownership for supporting a full-time remote user can be as much as 52 percent more than supporting a LAN-based user.

Another reason companies do not spend the time to educate their remote users is that it is not easy. For instance, how do you teach a remote user how to use a new e-mail package? You can send the user a manual for the application. But realistically, how many applications have you learned by reading a manual? Trying to teach a user something as subtle as when to use remote node versus remote control is much harder than having the user learn an application. That's why a program such as Cubix's is interesting.

There are, however, other ways to reach your remote users to give them some guidance as to which type of connectivity they should use. A common approach is to create a cheat sheet for your users based on the applications deployed throughout your company. For instance, you might have a simple two-column table where one column lists the applications for which a remote user is to use remote node and the other column lists applications for which the user is to kick into remote control mode.

Cubix claims that WorldDesk Applink can make this type of training a moot point. Remote users run their application as they normally would. Once the call is placed, Applink analyzes the user's selection and makes the connectivity choice based on the rules you have set up. WorldDesk Applink works with Cubix's remote-node servers, WorldDesk Comlink and Commuter. It also works with other vendor's remote-node servers, including those from Novell Inc., Attachmate Corp., and Shiva Corp.

Host Access by Terminal Emulation

Remote node and remote control are the most common types of access your users will probably need. However, you might have some users who need a simpler form of access—namely, access to mainframe data from a remote location.

Such host access can be achieved through a remote node connection with the user running a terminal emulation program. But if all your users need is host access, you can provide a lower level of access that will be easier for you to maintain. This form of access is often called *host access.* Figure 12-3 shows the basic network configuration to give users host access. The user runs a communications package that offers terminal emulation which matches that required by the host computer. If the host is a mainframe, your users would need a 3270 terminal emulation package. If your company is using an AS/400 minicomputer, you would need to supply 5250 terminal emulation software. There are about a dozen terminal emulation formats, one for each of the major minicomputer systems.

A communications software package usually includes terminal emulators for most of the major systems. So you might not need to buy anything beyond a communications package for the remote user. The user would then dial into the network over an analog phone line using a modem. The connection could also be through an ISDN BRI line using an ISDN terminal adapter.

On the other end of the connection, you must install a *terminal server.* Such a device lets many terminals connect to a single host—a mainframe or minicomputer—over a network connection. Terminal servers go back to the early days of networking, when most users sat in front of a dumb terminal and accessed applications and data that resided on a mainframe computer. The

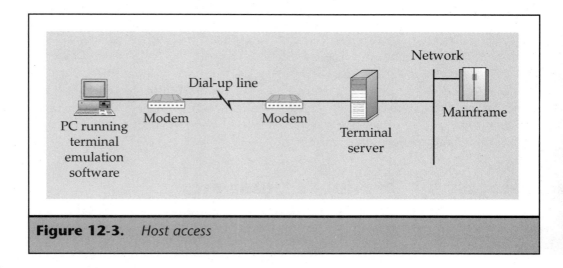

Figure 12-3. *Host access*

new terminal servers simply support terminals in remote sites that dial in over phone lines.

The host access-only approach is losing supporters these days. A remote user who needs to connect to a mainframe typically also needs to connect to other network-attached devices within the company walls. For that reason, most managers choose a remote node approach and make host access one option when the user connects to the network. However, if your remote users only need host access, this method offers a basic level of connectivity that should satisfy them. If you are unsure which form of remote access is the best to use, Table 12-3 gives you some examples for remote control, remote node, and terminal emulation.

Connectivity Service Options

All three forms of remote access have similar components. There is a remote computer running some special software for the type of connection to be

Type of Remote Access	Example of Usage
Remote control	Lets a remote user with a slow PC run an application, such as a CAD/CAM package, on a higher-performance PC located within the company.
Remote node	Lets a remote user have access to network file directories and printers, letting a user perform such tasks as dropping and dragging files from his or her PC's drive to network drives and queues.
Terminal emulation	Lets a remote user access mainframe applications, such as an order entry system, so the user can perform transaction-oriented tasks.

Table 12-3.   *How to Use the Different Types of Remote Connectivity*

made. And there is an entry point into the network. The entry point into the network can be either a terminal server, a communications server, or a remote access server. The distinction between these three types of devices often blurs, since they all perform some common tasks. Chapter 13 will discuss the differences and what to look for in each type of device.

The other components to a remote connection are the link between the remote site and the main site, and the line termination equipment used to make the connection. The most common form of connectivity remains the analog phone line. Typically, a user has a modem, and the connection is dialed up over a phone line. However, you might have some users connect over an ISDN BRI line using ISDN terminal adapters at each end of the link. As was discussed in Part 2, an ISDN BRI line offers higher bandwidth than an analog connection, and in many cases, depending on where you are, ISDN service is reasonably easy to get. In terms of price, ISDN service is more expensive than analog service (see Chapters 3 and 4 for some comparisons), but many companies can justify the costs based on the productivity gains afforded these remote users when higher-speed connections are available.

You will likely have a mix of ISDN and analog phone lines. This requires that the remote access server support both analog and ISDN connections. For the users in the remote sites and those working at home or dialing in from the road, there is no difference in running the programs (except, of course, for the speed of the connection).

The basic configuration to support a mix of analog and ISDN connections is shown in Figure 12-4. Both types of remote users would dial into a single network entry point. In the figure I have used a remote access server, but it could also be any type of communications server.

Probably you will need to support more than one remote user. So instead of a single modem and a single ISDN terminal adapter in the central site (as Figure 12-4 shows), you would have a modem pool and a pool of ISDN terminal adapters. Such pools can be configured in two ways. You can either dedicate a telephone number to each access line, or you can use what is called a *roll-down system.*

The first approach is very straightforward. Each modem or terminal adapter is attached to a phone line, and each has its own number. If a remote user calls in and the line is being used by someone else, the caller gets a busy signal and must retry the same number later. Or, the remote caller can enter a different phone number to connect to a modem or terminal adapter that is not busy. To try that second phone number, some applications make the user

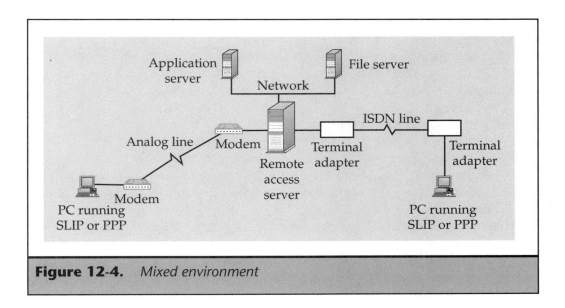

Figure 12-4. *Mixed environment*

reconfigure the communications settings of the application and enter the different number. While this is fairly easy for a person experienced with communications packages, it might be more than some of your remote users want to learn. Some applications, cc:Mail for example, let you enter multiple numbers in the session setup and if one number is busy, the software automatically tries another number.

An alternative is to set up what is called a roll-down system for your users. With a roll-down system you request the same number of telephone numbers from the telephone company, but you instruct the telco to roll-down the numbers if a user gets a busy signal. In this way, everyone has one telephone number to dial into the system. If that line is busy, the telephone company detects this and automatically connects the user to the next number you have designated for your modem or terminal adapter pool. If, for example, you have ten modem lines with associated telephone numbers (212) 555-1000, (212) 555-1001, (212) 555-1002, up to (212) 555-1009, remote users need only set their communications program to dial the first number. If that number—(212) 555-1000—is busy, the users are automatically connected to (212) 555-1001. If that number is busy, the telco rolls down to the next number and continues to do so until a free line is found. This process is transparent to the remote user, and it does not require any attention from you (except, of course, setting up the system with the telephone company when the lines are ordered).

Managing the Central Site

If your company is like most, the number of remote users you will need to support will grow with time. As more remote users are added, the complexity of managing the central site grows. This is part of the operational cost of supporting remote connectivity. And as was noted in Chapter 1, the operational costs associated with supporting remote users are substantial—representing 50 percent of your total remote access costs.

The recurring operational charges for remote access include the telecommunications charges and the labor charges to support the remote users. In a single user-to-LAN connectivity scenario there are a couple ways to reduce these costs.

First, let's look at the recurring telecommunications charges. You might do like many companies and simply install more lines into your central site as you add users. You don't need to add one line for every user, but you will need more access lines as you add large numbers of remote users. Chapter 13 will look at some of the trade-offs in sizing your remote access server so that you have an adequate number of lines, yet not too many. The basic consideration is how many hours per day your users are connected to the central site. If most remote users simply dial in for e-mail and disconnect, you can have a higher ratio of users to access lines. If your users enter the network in remote node mode and spend hours at a time connected to the network, you will need to take that into account and provide more lines for the same number of users.

However, no matter what the ratio of users to access lines is, there is a way to save money. You can consolidate your incoming traffic onto a single higher-capacity line such as an ISDN PRI line or a T1 circuit. Basically, all of the incoming traffic is aggregated onto one line by the telephone company. Figure 12-5 shows what a network design like this would look like. As you can see in the figure, remote users each have their own ISDN BRI or analog lines. The traffic sent from their homes, remote offices, or hotel rooms while traveling is carried over the public switched telephone network and combined onto a single access line to the company site.

It doesn't take many connections to make this consolidated-traffic approach a cost-effective alternative. In Chapter 4, I gave an example where a company had ten remote users who dialed in over analog phone lines, five users who had ISDN BRI lines, and three remote sites with routers that used ISDN BRI lines to connect to the corporate network. In that example, I showed that one T1 or ISDN PRI line into your central site would be less expensive after one year than the alternative of using ten analog lines and eight ISDN BRI lines at the central site.

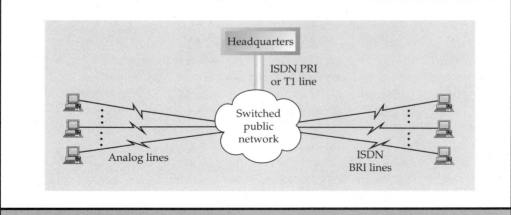

Figure 12-5. *Consolidating traffic*

Ways to Cut Recurring Operational Costs

Central Site Tactics

- Use roll-down telephone number system from telco to simplify access.

- Consolidate numerous central site ISDN and analog access lines into a single high-speed line.

- Train staff in ISDN equipment management, or outsource the management of these devices.

Remote Site Tactics

- Use intelligent communications software that automates access.

- Standardize access equipment to simplify support.

- Train users how to use access software and equipment.

This adds complexity to your central site network entry point. Usually, the direct impact on you and your staff is that the higher-end ISDN or T1 termination equipment is harder to install and configure. In Chapter 3, I talked about some of these difficulties from the remote users' perspective, and many of these same issues apply to the central site. Specifically, ISDN termination equipment requires more information to set up than does a modem. You must have information about the telephone company switch to which you are connected, and you need ID information furnished to you by the telephone company.

Having a remote user configure ISDN terminal adapters requires lots of hand-holding. Presumably, the process in the central site will be easier due to familiarity. You should have at least one support person on your staff proficient in the use of ISDN equipment who knows what information is needed to configure the devices and how to carry out the installation. If such a person does not exist, you might consider sending one of your support staff to training seminars. Many ISDN equipment vendors offer seminars for their customers. There are also independent training programs where you pay for a member of your staff to attend.

You might decide that you would rather not have your staff take time away from their existing duties to perform this type of service. If that is the case, you might consider hiring a value-added reseller (VAR) or systems integrator to install the equipment for you. Some VARs and integrators specialize in ISDN connectivity systems, and hiring such a firm could make it more cost-effective to offload this responsibility from your staff.

Additionally, you might decide that the installer should also manage the equipment. Outsourcing the management of your remote access equipment will have to be based on your corporate philosophy. For some companies, the idea of not having a person on staff who is directly responsible for the day-to-day management of the remote access system is not acceptable. Such companies want control over the remote access process. Some managers like to be able to pick up the phone and get someone from within the company to answer their questions when there are problems. This has a lot to do with corporate politics and procedures. Some companies just believe they have more control over an in-house person—meaning they can threaten these people more effectively than an outsider.

In some companies, the outsourcing of the remote access portion of a network operation is not an issue. If you can make a business case that your staffers are needed for other tasks and the outsourcing company can handle the support duties in a cost-effective way, it may be the best solution.

Chapter Thirteen

The View from Headquarters

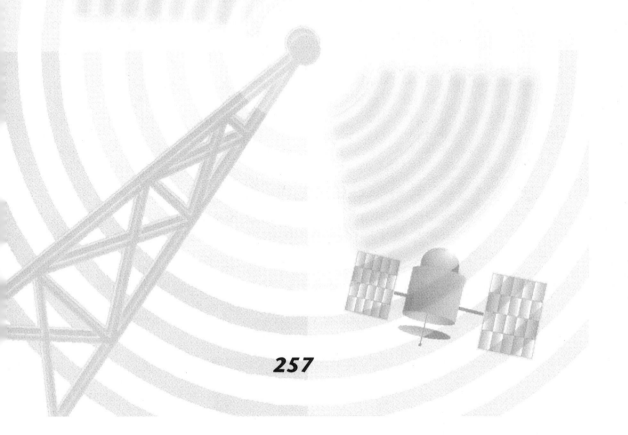

Now that you are familiar with the different types of remote access, as well as when and where each is appropriate, it's nearly time to start talking about how to implement them. However, before I do that, I need to prepare you for shopping for remote access equipment. I also need to prepare you for a little sticker shock.

Generally speaking, remote access usage starts off slowly, with only a few users taking advantage of it. However, it usually doesn't take long for its popularity to explode. Keep in mind that remote access on a small scale is relatively inexpensive, but expanding to meet the needs of the masses can be very costly. Therefore, before you launch into an implementation project, I recommend that you

- Determine exactly which segments will benefit from remote access, as detailed in Part 3 of this book

- Select an appropriate remote access service, as described in Part 2 of this book

- Carefully estimate the costs of implementing remote access for the selected service for the appropriate number of users

To help you "put a pencil" to these potential expenses, I have prepared worksheets that outline the major cost components of remote access and describe how to calculate the cash outlays associated with each. These worksheets appear at the end of the chapter. The actual prices for each of the specific services are discussed in Part 2. However, before you make your final calculations, you'll want to check with service providers and vendors to make sure that the pricing hasn't changed.

Who Will Benefit from Remote Access?

Before you can estimate costs, you'll need to determine to which segments of your user population you want to give remote access. This can be your most difficult planning task because you'll want to offer remote access to every user who can effectively increase his or her productivity, but not make it available any more widely than you'll really need due to both the high costs and the security issues associated with it. Here are a few guidelines to help you develop a good scope for your remote access implementation project:

■ **Add enough remote access capacity to see you through the next 18-24 months.** Upgrades intended to last less than that amount of time will be outdated nearly before they are complete. Remote access technology and services are advancing rapidly, so you won't want to lock yourself into outdated technology.

As well, the future beyond 24 months is too unpredictable. Under *no* circumstances should you claim that no further upgrades and expansion will be required for more than two years; the networking industry in general—and remote access in particular—is changing too fast to make such dangerous assertions!

■ **Upgrade the busiest 20 percent of your network.** The 80-20 rule usually applies in networking as well, so upgrading the top 20 percent of bandwidth-starved segments should cover most of your problem areas.

NOTE: A little remote and a lot of management go a long way. As you'll read later in this chapter, there are many things you can do to prevent traffic jams on your remote access server that don't *involve adding more equipment.*

Hardware Worksheet

The cost of equipment is probably the first and most obvious expense related to installing a remote access system. What may not be so obvious, however, are the many costs directly and indirectly related to installing new hardware. The Hardware Worksheet outlines the equipment and related costs you will have to consider, along with the quantity and the cost of each.

Remote Access Servers

When installing remote access servers, be sure to contact your NOS vendor to find out exactly which remote access software and peripherals are fully certified for the version of the NOS you now have. Remember, integrated remote access is relatively new, so the version of the network operating system you currently have installed may not support all versions of the remote access server software you have selected. If it doesn't, a NOS upgrade—with all the attendant heartache—will be in order. Furthermore, a new version of the operating system or a new driver for the remote access service interface may require other hardware upgrades, such as increased memory or disk space. Be sure to ask your vendors about system hardware requirements, and figure any upgrades into your cost estimate.

Remote Access Server Interfaces

A remote access server interface can be as pedestrian as a stand-alone modem or as sophisticated as frame relay interface to your network routers. The number and type of remote access service interface boards you require depends on:

- The type of remote access service you select
- How many users will be using your remote access system
- The port density of the remote access interfaces you want to purchase

If you are using dial-up lines for remote access, you will need one or more modems. These can be either standalone external modems, or modems rack-mounted into a communications server chassis. If you have or are planning to purchase a chassis-based unit, the smallest unit will be a chassis module. In either case, be sure to include the cost of special cables and connectors required to attach the remote access ports to your existing network.

Finally, remember to include the cost of any changes that you'll need to make in your wiring closet to accommodate the remote access service, such as additional racks and patch panels.

ROUTERS   Your routers may require new physical interfaces, either internal or external, as well as software and firmware upgrades to work with the remote access service interface. They may even have to be replaced altogether. In either case, some manual configuration will be necessary, so be sure to include all the associated costs.

SWITCHES   Some switches offer remote access service interfaces as an option. If you choose to implement your remote access via an interface in a network switch, you may need to upgrade your existing switches or purchase new ones. Upgrading your switches may involve high-speed interfaces or firmware upgrades. Be sure to quiz your vendor to make sure you know everything involved in preparing your switches for remote access.

Remote Client Workstations

Implementing remote access on users' workstations involves many of the same considerations as upgrading servers. Contact your workstation vendor to make sure the modems you have chosen are supported by the remote access software. Also, make sure the workstations are running a version of the operating system that supports both the modem and the remote access client software, and that they have sufficient memory and hard disk storage to accommodate the operating system, remote access client software, and drivers. And remember to get the desired performance, you may need to replace the workstation altogether.

Service Cost Worksheet

Now that you have chosen a remote access service, it's time to determine your network's remote access requirements. What kind of speed, security, and flexibility do you need in your remote access system?

The Service Question: How Much Access?

Before you do anything, you'll have to get some idea of how much your remote access system is going to be used. Obviously, the more traffic that will be traveling over the network, the more bandwidth you will need on the remote access system to provide acceptable availability and performance.

NOTE: *Remember that the wide-area network links on which your remote access system will run simply don't support the high-bandwidth protocols that local area networks do.*

How Much?

The best way to estimate the traffic that will be running over your remote access system is to take a sample of your current remote access traffic. Your current telecommunications carrier should be able to do a traffic study of your remote link to see exactly how much bandwidth or how many minutes of wide-area telecommunications service you use during which times of the day. Be sure the report includes at least one full month's worth of traffic. An analysis of a single day or even a single week of wide-area network traffic simply isn't enough to reveal usage patterns.

Analyzing your telephone bill is another way to calculate usage, but this is only valid if you are currently using a usage-based service. A usage-based service charges you for only the amount of service you use, measured either in minutes or bandwidth. If you are currently paying a flat fee for your telecommunications service, your telephone bills really won't give you accurate information on actual telecommunications service usage.

For First Time Remote Access Managers

Of course, using a traffic sample and analysis is a viable option only for those of you who already have a remote access system. If you are trying to build your first remote access system, you'll need to estimate the traffic. One of the best ways to do this is by conducting a survey of your users. Ask all the network users just how often they would be using the remote access facility—how often they would be dialing in to the network to communicate with people and resources. Then ask them what they will be doing during that communication—file transfers? document preparation? electronic mail? or, (shudder) videoconferencing?

And When?

Don't forget to ask the users the times of day and days of the week or month that they will be using the remote access system. This will not only help you determine how much bandwidth the remote service should provide at any given time, it may help you save money. That's because telecommunications companies—just like airlines and hotels—price their services cheaper during off-peak periods. Therefore, you may be able to arrange for the heaviest usage to occur during off-peak rate periods.

Figure 13-1 shows a sample traffic survey form that you may want to adapt for use in your own traffic survey.

Turning Survey Data into Traffic Figures

Suppose the traffic survey you conduct reveals the usage detailed in Figure 13-2. Notice how easily you can identify weekends and holidays because there's hardly any remote access traffic on those days. You can also guess which days are month-end from the heavy telecommunications traffic. The sales people must be turning in their expense accounts, and the accounting department is probably pulling billing information from the remote offices.

Don't Design for the Average Day

You may look at the traffic analysis and assume that all you have to do is divide the total amount of traffic captured for the month by the number of days in that month. You might think that if you simply take an average of the heavy traffic days and the light traffic days, throwing out the weekends and holidays, you'll hit a happy medium figure for service that will meet the needs of your company's average business.

Remote Access Usage Survey

We are preparing to install a wide area network link to connect our local area network with the local area network in our _____[Fill in location]_____ office. To ensure proper performance, we need to know approximately how often you will be sending and/or receiving information from the ___[Fill in location] network. To help us estimate this, please take a moment to answer the questions below.

Please return this form to the Director of Information Services, M/S [Fill in mail stop] by [Fill in Date].

How many of the following types of information will you be sending to the remote office each day? at what time of day (if you can predict)?

	No.	Time of Day	Size of Document
Spreadsheets	_____	_____	_____
Word processing documents	_____	_____	_____
Databases	_____	_____	_____
Facsimile documents	_____	_____	_____

What will be your primary means of communication with the remote office after the remote access system link is in place?

	No.	Time of Day	Size or Length
Electronic mail	_____	_____	_____
Overnight document delivery	_____	_____	_____

Do you foresee using the following means of communication with the remote office? If so, what time of day and how frequently?

	Time of Day	Purpose	Frequency
Electronic mail	_____	_____	_____
Groupware/Group Discussion databases	_____	_____	_____
Videoconferencing	_____	_____	_____
	_____	_____	_____

Figure 13-1.   *A sample traffic survey form*

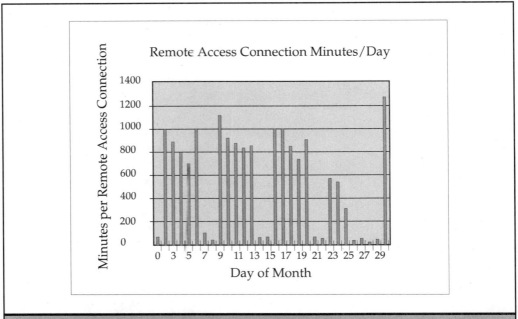

Figure 13-2. *The first step in bandwidth planning on the remote access system measuring call minutes/day*

Wrong.

If you design a remote access system to carry only the average service required throughout the month, during the heavy traffic periods, fully half of the users are going to be unable to access the corporate network. However, you don't want to build the network to handle all the traffic on your busiest days with top performance, because that means most of the time you would have idle remote access facilities. The trade-off between performance and cost wouldn't be satisfactory. Therefore, you're going to have to design your remote access system to accommodate all traffic on all but the busiest days. To figure out how to do this, you'll have to identify and quantify your remote access system's busy days and busy hours.

For most businesses, some days of the week are regularly much busier than others. For example, airline reservations centers are much busier on weekdays than on weekends. This means you can't simply use the average business day traffic as your remote access system's minimum daily requirement of bandwidth. Instead, you should calculate your *remote access busy day remote access average*, which is the average traffic of the five highest-traffic days of a typical month.

Next, it's time to look at how your remote access requirements will vary throughout a typical day. Suppose again that the results of your traffic survey look like the usage in Figure 13-3. Just as you can easily spot holidays and weekends in Figure 13-2, in Figure 13-3 you can see when people check their e-mail for the first time each day, when they are out on appointments, go to lunch, and when they stop working for the night.

If you analyze your remote traffic over a month or more, you'll probably find that there are two busy periods per day—one in the morning and one in the afternoon—that are just about equal in both length and traffic density. Take the average traffic of these two busy periods and divide it by the total number of hours included in the busy period.

> **TIP:**   *Professional traffic engineers have found that a single busy hour represents between 12 percent and 16 percent of the total traffic for the day. Therefore, if you can't get detailed hourly call information for your remote access system, you'll probably be safe assuming that one busy hour of traffic equals about 14 percent of the total traffic for the day.*

Protocol Analyzers: Tool of the Trade

Next, it's time to translate these minutes and hours of traffic into actual packets sent and received. This means you will need to calculate the average packet size of your local area network. Currently, the average packet size for the typical local area network is 512 bytes. However, using a protocol analyzer, you can determine the average size of data packets traveling across *your* particular network. A protocol analyzer can be configured to monitor packets for the specific topology and protocol of the segment, letting you monitor the traffic on the segment to which it's connected. A protocol analyzer will help you determine not only the average bandwidth utilization on the segment, but also the average packet size and composition. As well, a protocol analyzer can assist in spotting trends in traffic, peak traffic periods, and devices that are generating bad packets or acting as network bottlenecks.

If you don't have your own protocol analyzer, you can rent one or even hire someone to bring in a protocol analyzer and do the traffic monitoring and protocol analysis for you. Most network integration firms offer protocol analysis services. In any event, *don't proceed with plans for implementing a remote access system until you have monitored your network with a protocol analyzer and are familiar with packet sizes and traffic patterns on the LAN.*

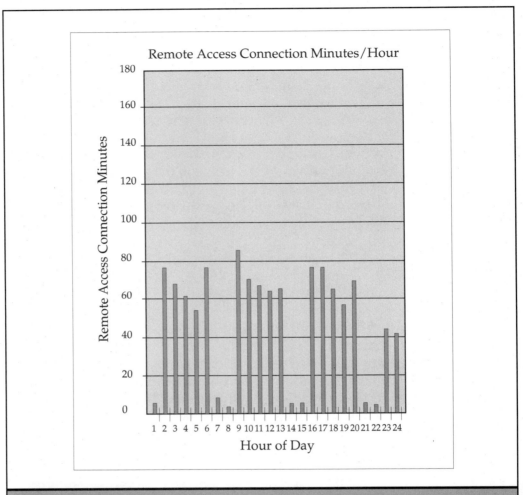

Figure 13-3. *A typical distribution of calls (minutes/day)*

TIP: *When you calculate your remote access service needs, you need to consider the packet size of the wide-area protocol you'll be using. This will vary from protocol to protocol. Therefore, when you narrow your selection of protocols to two or three choices, you may want to recalculate your bandwidth needs for each individual protocol using the packet size of each.*

What This Means in Bandwidth

Now that you have all the measurements, it's time to see how they add up. I had originally planned to launch into an exhaustive methodology of calculating erlangs and performing regressions until you found the perfect bandwidth amount to meet your remote access needs cost-effectively. Then I realized this couldn't be done without also launching into a crazed dissertation on queuing and probability theories, and giving pages of recursive equations with their attendant "do loops."

However, none of this is really necessary for you, the network manager. After you have calculated the busy day and busy hour loads, you have a general idea of the service and equipment you will need to accommodate your wide-area network traffic comfortably. This will let you know whether you should be shopping for high-speed remote access services or more pedestrian services.

Once you have selected a remote access service, however, it's wise to ask your telecommunications service provider to perform some traffic engineering analysis to determine the ideal amount of resources (whether they be measured in circuits or committed information rates) to support your wide-area networking needs cost-effectively. Telecommunications service providers have entire departments dedicated to this type of *traffic engineering*, and you should take advantage of their knowledge to ensure the best, most economical service level for your remote access system.

For your clarification, the following section contains an extremely brief definition of the terms and equations used in traffic engineering. Don't worry—there won't be a quiz.

NOTE: *Everything I know about traffic engineering I learned from* Reference Manual for Telecommunications Engineering *by Roger L. Freeman, now in its second edition (New York: John Wiley & Sons, 1989). I don't recommend undertaking serious traffic engineering work without it.*

For Those of You Who Really Have to Know: What's an Erlang?

An *erlang* is a measure of telecommunications traffic. One erlang equals one transmitting station using 100 percent of single transport resource 100 percent of the time. The erlang was developed as a measure of telecommunications traffic in 1917 by Danish mathematician A. K. Erlang, and it has been the standard measure ever since. The formula for calculating the erlang load on a data telecommunications link is

(No. of packets/sec.) × (no. of bytes/packet) × (no. of bits/byte)/(bits/second)

This equation yields a measure of load on a single transport circuit of a given bandwidth. The key is that the number of circuits provided must be equal to or greater than traffic erlangs. Otherwise, packets will start queuing for transport at a far greater rate than the transport circuits can carry them, and consequently they will be lost.

CALCULATING THE PROBABILITY OF CIRCUIT BLOCKING   The equation for determining the probability of blocking is called the *Erlang-B* equation, and without launching into the aforementioned crazed dissertation on queuing and probability theories, let's just say that this is recursive form of the equation:

$$B(a,k) = (a \times B(a,k\text{-}1))/k{+}a \times B(a,k\text{-}1)$$

where

a = erlangs
k = number of resources (circuits)
B(a,k) = probability of circuit blocking

CALCULATING THE PROBABILITY OF A PACKET BEING LOST BECAUSE A CIRCUIT IS BLOCKED   The equation for determining the probability of a packet being lost due to its circuit being blocked is called the *Erlang-C* equation:

$$C(a,n) = (B(a,n))/(1\text{-}a/n \times (1\text{-}B(a,n)))$$

where

a = erlangs
n = number of resources (circuits)
B(a,n) = Erlang-B equation
C(a,n) = probability of losing packets due to circuit blocking

FINDING THE AVERAGE DELAY TIME   With the two preceding calculations, you can determine a packet's average delay time under any given traffic load this way:

$$T = L/C + (C(a,n) \times L)/((1-a/n)) \times n \times C)$$

where

> a = erlangs
> L = packet length (in bits)
> n = number of resources (circuits)
> C = line speed (in bits/second)
> $C(a,n)$ = probability of blocking
> T = average message delay time

FINDING THE AVERAGE QUEUE LENGTH   Finally, you can find the average amount of time a packet will spend waiting in a queue under any given traffic load by using this equation:

$$q = (C(a,n) \times a/n)/(1-a/n)$$

where

> a = erlangs
> n = number of resources (circuits)
> $C(a,n)$ = Erlang-C equation
> q = average number of packets in a queue

ERLANGS IN HAND, WE CONTINUE   Therefore, to find the most cost-effective type of service for a given traffic scenario, for each type of protocol or service you are considering:

1. Calculate the erlang.
2. Round the erlang to the next integer and use this number as the number of resources.

3. Run the equations for average delay time and average queue length, varying the number of resources (circuits) until the average delay time queue time is less than the transmission time of a single packet (in bits per second), and the average queue length is less than a single packet in length (in bits).

4. Multiply the number of resources (circuits) times the cost per circuit.

Voilà! You have the most cost-effective amount of bandwidth to meet the traffic needs of your wide-area network. See why I recommended that you let your telecommunications service provider do this?

Get Out Your Pencil—There Are Lots of Variables

If you choose to run the preceding calculation yourself, you may find that you'll have to run it several times because, as you have read in earlier chapters, there is a wide variety of wide-area networking services and protocols from which to choose. In the U.S., the most popular tariffed telecommunications services are the following circuit-switched offerings:

- 56-Kbps circuit
- Multiple 56-Kbps circuits
- One DS1 (1.544 Mbps) circuit

Furthermore, you'll remember that there is a variety of wide-area network protocols available through negotiated contracts with telecommunications carriers that are even better-suited to high-speed wide-area packet-based traffic such as local area network traffic. These services include:

- ISDN (Integrated Services Digital Network)
- isoEthernet with ISDN
- Asynchronous transfer mode (ATM)
- Asymmetric Digital Subscriber Line (ADSL)

Flexibility

If your remote access network traffic varies widely from day to day or hour to hour, you'll need to investigate the flexibility of the service or protocol you're considering. Many services and protocols are designed to let you pay for only the traffic you use, while others accommodate traffic bursts in excess of the bandwidth for which you have subscribed. Frame relay, for example, lets you commit to an average bandwidth, the committed information rate, while allowing your WAN traffic to burst above this rate when total traffic over the resource allows.

Recommendations

After all this discussion of determining your particular requirements for a wide-area network protocol or service, I think I owe you a few pointers. The following are my personal recommendations—based on my own experience as well as research—for the appropriate protocols and services for each type of wide-area function.

File Transfer

If you're just doing a batch transfer of files from remote computers to the corporate network, my recommendation is to use a traditional circuit service. If the file transfers are light and/or intermittent, a switched-circuit service will suit you just fine. If the file transfers are constant and/or lengthy, and are from a fixed location such as a remote office to headquarters, a dedicated circuit service may prove more cost-effective.

Multimedia and Videoconferencing

Those of you who are contemplating using multiuser multimedia and videoconferencing over the wide area network might want to look into using a combination of ISDN and isoEthernet.

Wide-Area Workgroup

For workgroup applications, such as Lotus Notes, over the wide area, my favorite is again traditional circuit services. They're solid, stable, relatively inexpensive, and easy to install and maintain.

Internet Access

Frame relay is rapidly becoming one of my favorite technologies for Internet access. This is because it is flexible, inexpensive, and easy to install and maintain. Chapter 9 gives you the details.

Figuring the Cost

You may need help with all of this. Use the Service Cost Worksheet when considering the cost of any outside service providers you may retain to help you with your remote access system implementation. This will include contract programmers to help you enhance applications, and network integrators to help you upgrade your servers and network operating system, as well as your switches and routers. Don't forget PC maintenance companies that can help you upgrade your remote workstations. Finally, you may need to hire cabling contractors to help upgrade racks, risers, and patch panels in your wiring closets.

Staffing and Staff Development Worksheet

Hiring and/or training a staff to install and maintain a remote access is a significant expense. Because, as I have mentioned earlier, remote access networking technologies are relatively new, chances are your current staff hasn't been adequately trained in them. Therefore, before you dive into a remote access system implementation, you'll need to make sure that your staff has acquired the necessary skills both in troubleshooting and management. This means they need to learn not only how to physically connect devices to the remote access system, but also to optimize drivers and operate management applications for the system.

Preparing your staff to handle these responsibilities includes sending them to courses and seminars, purchasing books and other reference materials, and possibly hiring temporary staff to keep your network running while your regular staff acquires expertise in high-speed networking.

Sometimes developing existing staff isn't enough. You may even have to hire additional staff that are already experienced in remote access. If that's the case, be sure to include recruiting and hiring costs into your implementation budget. The Staffing and Staff Development Worksheet can help you estimate your budget.

Time Estimate Worksheet

One of the hardest figures to estimate is that of time. Using the Time Estimate Worksheet, come up with an estimated time to upgrade each server, router, workstation, and switch, then multiply that by the number of units of each piece of equipment you will convert.

Don't forget, the cost isn't limited to just time spent on the actual installation and configuration of your remote access system. A major expense of remote access is managing equipment and software, as well as training and supporting users. There may also be a period of reduced productivity for remote access users while systems are being optimized and the inevitable implementation problems are being solved. And don't forget the reduced productivity of your staff while they become comfortable with the new equipment, software, and systems. Also, don't forget the opportunity cost associated with a new implementation: the things that won't get done well, or get done at all, while your staff is concentrating on implementing the remote access system.

Applications Worksheet

You will need to install or upgrade the remote access client software applications as well as hardware. Further, if you will be upgrading the network and/or desktop operating systems, application upgrades may be necessary or desirable to get the required performance and support of the operating system.

Now That You Know

Okay, you've figured in the cost of equipment, staff, applications, and services. Despite it all, a remote access system still seems cost-effective. Although the number crunching can be tedious, the results are worth it. You are now ready to face your management, your staff, and your users with a sound plan and a relatively firm budget.

Hardware Worksheet

Remote Access Servers:

Equipment	No. of Units	Cost per Units	Total
Network adapters			
NOS upgrades			
Memory upgrades			
Disk upgrades			
Other hardware upgrades			
Total			

Remote Access Interfaces—Number of ports to upgrade:

Equipment	No. of Units	Cost per Unit	Total
Modules			
Chassis			
Patch cables			
Connectors			
Terminators			
Racks			
Patch panels			
Total			

Routers:

Equipment	No. of Units	Cost per Unit	Total
New routers			
Router interfaces			
Firmware upgrades			
Software upgrades			
Total			

Hardware Worksheet (*continued*)

Switches—Number of switched ports needed:

Equipment	No. of Units	Cost per Unit	Total
New switches			
Remote access interface modules			
Switch upgrade modules			
Firmware upgrades			
Total			

Remote Client Workstations:

Equipment	No. of Units	Cost per Unit	Total
New			
Operating system upgrades			
Modems			
Memory			
Disk space			
Total			

Cable and Media:

Equipment	No. of Units	Cost per Unit	Total
New drops			
Upgraded (additional pair terminated) drops			
Patch cables			
Total			

Service Cost Worksheet

Service	No. of Hours	Cost per Hour	Total
Contract programmers			
Client applications			
Server applications			
Management applications			
Network integrators			
Server upgrades			
Network operating system upgrades			
Cabling contractors			
Wiring closet upgrades			
Racks			
Risers			
Patch panels			

Total

Staffing and Staff Development Worksheet

Staff Development Costs:

Seminars	No. of Enrollees	Cost per Enrollee	Total
Management systems			
Cabling			
Switches			
Routers			
General protocol			
Total			

Courses	No. of Enrollees	Cost per Enrollee	Total
Management systems			
Cabling			
Switches			
Routers			
General protocol			
Total			

Books and Reference Materials	No. of Units	Cost per Unit	Total
Management systems			
Cabling			
Switches			
Routers			
General protocol			
Total			

Staffing and Staff Development Worksheet
(*continued*)

Temporary Staff Costs	No. of Hours	Cost per Hour	Total
Network management			
Programming/ analyst			
Hardware maintenance			
Network administration			
Total			

New Staff Recruiting Costs	No. of Positions	Cost per Position	Total
Advertisements			
Search firm fees			
Orientation costs			
Total			

Time Estimate Worksheet

Installation Time	No. of Hours	Cost per Hour	Total
Remote access server hardware			
Remote access server software			
Workstations			
Remote access client software			
Routers			
Switches			

Upgrades and Optimization	No. of Hours	Cost per Hour	Total
Servers			
Routers			
Switches			
Workstations			

Application Upgrades	No. of Hours	Cost per Hour	Total
Workstations ($\times$ no. $\times$ cost =)			
Servers			
Network management			

Total

		Downtime:		
Segment	No. of People on Segment	Avg. Cost per Hour for Person on Segment	Estimated Downtime in Hours	Total Cost
What won't get done				

Total downtime

Applications Worksheet

Client Applications	No. of Licenses	Cost per License	Total
Upgrades			
New			

Server Applications	No. of Licenses	Cost per License	Total
Upgrades			
New			

Management Applications	No. of Licenses	Cost per License	Total
Upgrades			
New			

Total

Chapter Fourteen

Server Tools

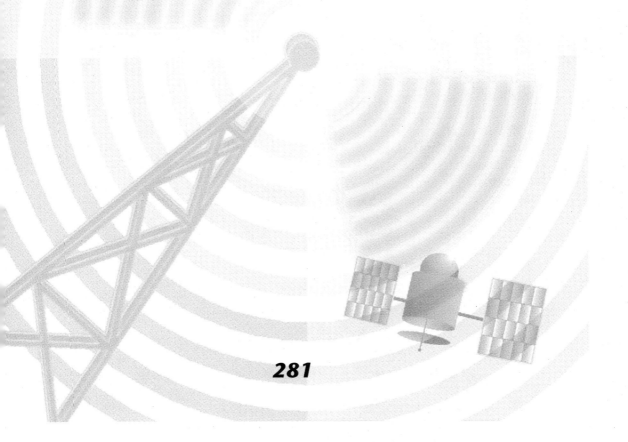

As I have discussed earlier, essentially there are two basic types of remote access systems:

- Remote control systems, which give users the same feeling as sitting at their desks

- Remote access systems, which essentially extend network resources over the wide area

Both types of systems have their unique advantages, disadvantages, and appropriate deployments. Typically, they also use different types of hardware. You'll want to evaluate both solutions to determine which is right for your network.

Remote Control Systems

These systems are either a desktop PC or a modem and processor sitting in a rack that act as a desktop PC. Either is controlled by a remote PC dialing in with appropriate client software and "taking over" the function of the PC.

The simplest remote control system is just a desktop PC, complete with modem and network interface card, loaded with a remote control server program such as Symantec's pcAnywhere. It sits ready to receive a call and be controlled by the remote client. If you have just one or two remote users, this configuration will probably work just fine for you.

However, chances are you have dozens of users who want to access the network from remote locations. In this case, you will want to consider a *consolidated server*, which is a rack of modems and processors mounted in a single chassis. Some vendors of consolidated servers are Cubix Corp. of Carson City, Nevada, and Chatcom Inc., of Chatsworth, California. The consolidated server has several advantages over stacks of stand alone modems. These advantages include:

- Less space required
- Ability to manage the box as a single unit
- Ability to troubleshoot modems as a group rather than separately

Even when you use consolidated servers, you'll find that remote control systems are essentially limited. Rather than supplying two processors for each remote user (one in the user's remote PC and one in the consolidated server), you'll eventually find that it makes more sense to configure the remote user as simply another node on the local area network. In this case, you'll want to employ remote access technology.

Remote Access Systems

As I stated, remote access servers don't supply a separate processor for the remote client to "take over." Instead, it provides a wide area connection to the remote PC, over which the remote client logs into the network and functions as any other node on the LAN. Remote access server hardware falls into three categories:

- Terminal servers
- Communications servers
- Remote access servers

Terminal Servers

Terminal servers are inexpensive remote access servers with limited intelligence and generally support only the IP protocol. They were designed to provide wide area access to dumb terminals, and usually don't support PCs. However, for many mainframe shops that have remote users working from home on dumb terminals, a wide area terminal server is enough to fill the bill.

Communications Servers

A communications server is something of an intelligent terminal server. It was designed to provide wide area access to a local area network for PCs. It supports multiple protocols, including both IP and Point-to-Point Protocol (PPP).

Communications servers, as well as terminal servers, aren't necessarily intended for corporate network use. They are more commonly found in public remote access systems, such as those built by Internet service providers (ISPs).

Remote Access Servers

Remote access servers are really the heart of the corporate remote access system. They are designed to limit the amount of traffic generated between the remote user and the network by handling most of the computing at the remote access server, and sending only the minimum amount of information to the remote client. Essentially, only keystrokes and screen information is exchanged between the remote client and the remote access server.

Remote access servers also offer more sophisticated tools for managing the system, such as better security and integrated SNMP agents.

The Tie That Binds

One thing that both remote control systems and remote access systems have in common is a strong need for management. The number of users and their needs will largely determine which type of system you select. However, there are also a few server management and administration issues you need to consider when selecting remote access server systems.

Network Operating System Support

Select a remote access server package that is integrated with your network operating system. Choose one that takes advantage of existing LAN user logins and profiles to prevent repetitive data entry. As well, a remote access package that supports your network directory services can give you greater management reach and flexibility than one that has to be administered separately from the directory services.

Network Management Tool Support

Select a remote access server package that can be administered with your existing network management tools. This is related to the previous tip. If you can manage your remote access system using standard management tools, you have both time and money. For example, remote access server tools that have SNMP agents, and even support RMON2, are available and can let you use the same tools for managing both local and remote access devices.

Internet Protocol Support

Select remote access products that support Internet protocols. While you may feel that you have more control when using dial-up or ISDN lines, having a "back door" through the Internet can save you in case your primary access service goes down.

Multiple Client Support

Select a remote access server that can support several different client types. For example, Microsoft Remote Access Server supports both Novell and Microsoft client stations.

The Outsourcing Alternative

Lately there's been a great press toward outsourcing the remote access server function. With a public remote access service, you don't have to mess with equipment or support, or worry about keeping up with the latest in remote access technology. Furthermore, many providers have entered this market, including MCI, Sprint, and AT&T, along with several Internet service providers (ISPs), offering you a wide variety of potential outsourcing vendors. This makes the market far more competitive, giving you an opportunity to get top service at a reasonable price.

Management: The Ultimate Determining Factor

Selecting the remote access server platform will determine the rest of the requirements for your remote access system: client platforms, training, management tools, and support needs. It will also determine the number of dollars and hours that will be needed to implement and maintain your system. Therefore, as I have emphasized in this chapter, the remote access server's manageability is the foremost selection criteria.

Chapter Fifteen

Client Software

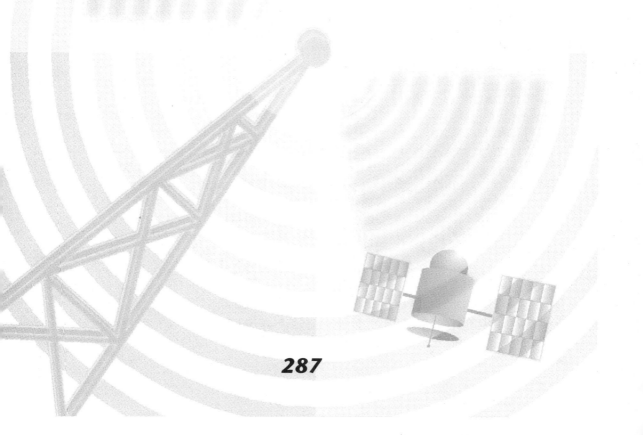

Increasingly, remote users need an IP stack on their computer to connect to your corporate network and the Internet. These users can be telecommuters dialing into the network as a remote node. Or, they can be LAN-attached users in small remote offices who need access to resources in a main office.

The most common way to give such users access to network resources and the Internet is to use a Serial Line Internet Protocol (SLIP) or Point-to-Point Protocol (PPP) connection and to establish a session between each remote user and either your remote access server or an Internet service provider's communications server. To accomplish this requires that the remote users have a network protocol stack running on their machine. For a SLIP connection you must use IP; for PPP you have more flexibility since it supports other protocols.

While you may use a variety of network protocol stacks (IP, IPX, DECnet, and so on), today the most commonly used one for remote access is the IP stack. This wide use probably has more to do with the Internet than anything else. IP does not have inherently better features than say, IPX, when it comes to remote access—it is just the protocol used on the Internet. Some companies support remote users who need a mix of protocols. You may see a remote user or small remote site running at most two or three protocols, with IPX and IP being the most common. However, for the most part your remote users will require an IP stack on their computer for connectivity.

Because IP is becoming the de facto remote access protocol, this leads to the question of which IP protocol stack to use. One issue that is becoming more important as more users need a PPP connection is whether a company should use the free IP stack that now ships with Windows 95 and the Macintosh's System 7 operating system, or if it is worth buying a stack from a vendor such as FTP Software Inc. (Andover, Massachusetts); Walker, Richer & Quinn Inc. (WRQ) of Seattle, Washington; or NetManage Inc. (Cupertino, California).

On the surface it seems like a no-brainer. You can either use an IP stack that comes bundled with each remote user's computer operating system at no extra cost, or you can pay several hundred dollars for a third-party IP stack. The free IP stack seems like the best choice. You would not have any trouble convincing upper management that this is the right choice. After all, it costs nothing beyond the price of the operating system that you will be spending money for anyway—you get the stack even if you do not need it. Why would you ever consider paying for an additional protocol stack?

There is more to this issue than purchase price. The basic argument for using third-party stacks is that they are easier to manage since they come bundled with more powerful troubleshooting and diagnostic tools. You may be able to exploit these management tools to cut the total cost of supporting your remote users.

Getting Started with an IP Connection

Sometimes you need more IP power than the IP stack offered with Windows or the Mac OS provides. Apple and Microsoft now bundle IP stacks with their operating systems. Does this mean you'll never need to consider a third-party stack? Maybe. The built-in stacks have a lot going for them, not the least of which is that they're free. But there are still those who need something more—say a particular type of terminal emulation or a specific network management function. And that's what third-party IP stacks have to offer.

Before proceeding, I want to make it clear that the arguments that follow are not just applicable to IP stacks. I am not picking on Microsoft or Apple for their choice of IP offering. The main point in this chapter is that the operating systems vendors have been making an effort to give users more than just an operating system. For example, with Windows 95 you get many accessories including games, a fax capability, system diagnostic tools, a built-in word processor, and a calculator. For some people, the fax system with Windows 95 offers enough features for their requirements so they do not need anything else. For others, a more sophisticated fax software package might be needed. Similarly, some people will be content to play Solitaire, Hearts, and Minesweeper (all of which come with Windows 95), while others will go out and buy the latest adventure games complete with high-end graphics and multimedia features. Some will never need more utilities than, say, the hard disk defragmentor included with Windows 95, while others may want a richer set of tools such as Symantec's Norton Utilities.

The same goes for IP stacks and the connectivity they provide. For some remote users, the bundled IP stack is all they will ever need. For others, a more sophisticated offering will be necessary. Table 15-1 lists some of the reasons you would choose a third-party IP stack over the one that comes bundled with your remote users' operating system. Your role will be to decide which users can get by with the bundled stack and which users will need something else.

The basic IP stack packages Apple and Microsoft offer are just that: basic. For most of your users, these packages are enough—they enable them to do basic functions such as configure IP addresses manually or use DHCP (Dynamic Host Configuration Protocol), and the IP stacks bundled with Windows 95 and the Mac OS include such standard tools as FTP and Telnet, which will let your remote users connect to IP hosts.

Why Choose a Third-Party IP Stack?	Usefulness
Richer features	More mature tools from third-party IP stack vendors may be easier to use.
More utilities	Third-party offerings go beyond the basics, providing more connectivity choices.
More diagnostics	Geared for enterprise networks, third-party offerings include more sophisticated management tools.
Tighter integration between utilities and IP stack	Allows third-party vendors to offer more robust management tools.
Heart of their business	IP stack and related offerings are the primary sources of income for third-party vendors.
Support issues	Operating systems vendors charge for support; many third-party IP stack vendors do not.

Table 15-1. *Making the Case for a Third-Party IP Stack*

Windows 95's TCP/IP stack has a lot going for it. First off, it's easy to install. While Windows 95 will not automatically detect a TCP/IP network as the Setup Wizard does for Novell and NT nets (where it will select such things as the right protocol and Ethernet frame type), you can use Microsoft's Windows Internet naming service or the DHCP to automatically configure your workstation for TCP/IP connectivity. Lacking these services on your network, you'll have to enter configuration information, such as an IP address and subnet mask, manually. That may be a problem for a nontechnical user in a remote site.

Some third-party IP stack vendors offer easier configuration, so that may be an issue. But for the most part, even third-party stacks need this initial configuration process to be carried out. If that is the case, you may need to perform the configuration for each remote user before he or she receives his or her machine. If users already have their systems and you decide to take advantage of the Windows 95 IP stack approach, you will need to send someone to each remote site to perform the configuration. That could cost your company a lot of travel money, especially if your users are geographically dispersed.

You might be able to eliminate the need for your staff to travel for such a task if you have the right set of circumstances. Some companies find that their mobile or remote users gather at least once or twice a year. For example, sales staffs get together for annual sales meetings, marketing folks meet to plan product rollouts, systems engineers come together to get trained on new products. If the bulk of these users use laptops, you simply make it a requirement that they bring their system to the centrally held meeting. Some companies make it a formal requirement that their sales staff drop off their laptops at the start of the first day of an annual sales meeting. Other companies take a less formal approach and simply get to each user during these meetings and perform whatever tasks are necessary. In either case, you could probably take advantage of such meetings to configure the IP stack on the majority of your remote users' computers.

Once an IP stack is installed, there are many issues to consider that will help you decide if the bundled IP stack or a third-party offering is best for your remote users. For example, there are the utilities that come with the stack. Microsoft includes a number of useful utilities with the Windows 95 stack. Users running Windows 95 have Telnet, Ping, and an FTP (file transfer protocol) client available. Additionally, with Windows 95 you have Microsoft's Internet Explorer, the company's Internet browser.

The Macintosh TCP/IP stack is part of Apple's Open Transport networking architecture. Beyond the basic stack, the newer versions of Open Transport offer automatic configuration via BOOTP or DHCP. Internet access is also straightforward. That's because Apple includes MacPPP and MacSLIP, which allow you to make a PPP or SLIP connection into an Internet service provider. Apple does not include a browser with its operating system. However, an Apple Internet connectivity kit (sold separately) provides many tools used for Internet access, including a Netscape Navigator and Newswatch browsers, the Apple Internet Dialer, Adobe Acrobat, Fetch FTP (File Transfer Protocol), and NCSA Telnet.

Is a "Free" IP Stack Enough?

With the major OS vendors throwing in a TCP/IP stack and Internet access tools, you'd think third-party IP stack vendors would be posting "going out of business" signs on their front doors. But that doesn't seem to be the case. Most third-party vendors will concede that the level of IP connectivity offered by OS vendors is fine for home users. But they'll argue that it's not enough for corporations where TCP/IP is, no pun intended, the backbone of their business.

Third-party IP stack vendors say there are several reasons people will pay for something the OS vendors are giving away. First, they say that by virtue of their years of experience with IP, the basic TCP/IP utilities bundled with their stacks offer richer feature sets than the ones bundled with OS vendors' stacks. Second, they say they offer more TCP/IP LAN utilities and better administrative and management tools than the OS vendors. And third, they typically don't charge for support—something you usually pay for from the OS vendors.

Will any of these touted benefits make any difference to you? For instance, does maturity make a difference? It seems the answer is yes: many of the TCP/IP utilities offered by third-party stack vendors have had several years to mature and it shows.

More Functions

Let's look at the first point, the richness of features. Microsoft offers a character-based FTP utility for transferring files. It requires you to be familiar with the FTP syntax we all grew to know (and, perhaps despise) from UNIX. The text-based syntax, while not difficult, sometimes defies logic (at least to me). For instance, I always want to type "exit" instead of "quit" when I want to exit a session. Some third-party offerings have simplified matters to avoid this type of thing. For example, Walker, Richer & Quinn (WRQ) employ a drag-and-drop Windows-based FTP program that's similar to the Windows File Manager. And many of NetManage's basic tools included with its Chameleon suite are Windows based. That is in contrast to the command-line utilities from Microsoft that have to be run from a DOS window.

When trying to decide between an operating system's IP stack and a third party's, you should also consider configuration utilities. FTP Software's IP configuration program lets you fine-tune low-level TCP/IP parameters, enabling you, for example, to adjust the size of the TCP/IP window. You can also do this with Windows 95, but you must perform the change with the Registry Editor (REGEDIT)—something I am not fond of doing, and I'm sure you aren't, either.

Macintosh users can also get richer utilities from third-party IP stack vendors. For several years, the Wollongong Group's PathWay Access TCP/IP suite for the Mac has offered scripting features in its Telnet and FTP clients that allow you to automate repetitive tasks. (In 1996, Wollongong was acquired by Attachmate.) Scripting can come in handy in several ways. For example, you might use a script to automate backup where you transfer important business data files from a remote user's PC to a UNIX server every day.

More Utilities

Besides providing richer functionality in basic utilities, third-party IP stack vendors offer utilities that make a lot of sense in a setting where TCP/IP is the backbone of a corporation. If you're just looking for Internet access, these utilities probably don't make quite as much sense. But if you are connecting remote users to corporate IP networks, you might want the added utilities and diagnostic capabilities offered with third-party IP stacks.

If you have remote users in small remote offices who need both Internet access and IP access to LAN-attached hosts within their site, a third-party stack might be more useful. For example, most IP stack vendors include Network File System (NFS) client software. Typically, the users who would need NFS capabilities work in a networking environment where TCP/IP is the backbone protocol.

Additionally, third-party vendors usually offer more choices for host connectivity by providing a fuller set of terminal emulators. Sure, Windows 95 has HyperTerminal, but HyperTerminal doesn't support connections over network protocols—only over serial links. The story is the same on the Mac: there is no emulator for a network connection. Third-party stacks, on the other hand, tend to include a high-quality emulator. For instance, Frontier Technologies includes TN3270 and VT320 emulators with its SuperTCP Pro product for IBM and Digital host connectivity. Pacer Software also offers an extensive suite of emulators for Mac clients, and Attachmate's TN3270 emulator for the Mac includes support for AppleScript (for automating routine tasks) and drag-and-drop file transfer capabilities to an IBM host. If all your remote users need is Internet access, these emulators will not be needed. However, if your remote users (particularly those LAN-attached users in small sites with no technical staff) need access to a variety of host computers, third-party offerings may be a better choice.

Extras like NFS and terminal emulators can often ride over any IP stack, thanks to Winsock (in the Windows arena) and the APIs in Apple's Open Transport. As a result you will see some IP stack vendors selling their utilities as an add-on to your Apple or Microsoft TCP/IP stack.

The Windows Socket (Winsock) specification was developed to simplify the use of TCP/IP protocol stacks. The specification provides a way to separate a Windows application from the protocol stack.

Before Winsock, an application developer who wanted to use a TCP/IP protocol stack as the conduit to the network would need to know the intimate details about the specific stack used. Then the developer would have to tightly link communications-related activities of the application to the specific program calls required by the stack's vendor. Many of the calls are standard, but for a TCP/IP stack, there is room for a protocol vendor to include some proprietary features.

Basically, before Winsock, application developers had to be very aware of the network and the nuances of the protocol stack that served as the link through which a user interacted with the application. Winsock removes much of the necessity of a developer being a communications expert. And, more importantly, it allows any Winsock-compliant Windows application to run over any vendor's TCP/IP stack.

Essentially Winsock uses a layer of software that fits between a TCP/IP protocol stack and a Winsock-compliant application. Figure 15-1 schematically shows the relationship between an application, the Winsock layer, and the protocol stack. This software is commonly loaded in the form of a Dynamic Link Library (DLL) called winsock.dll or wsock32.dll.

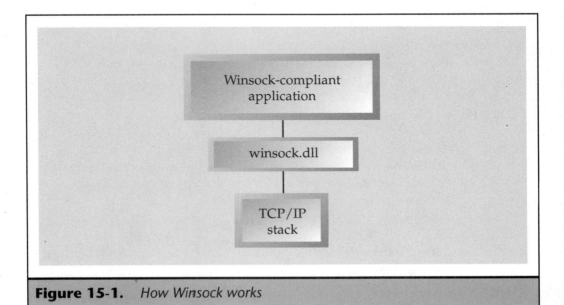

Figure 15-1. *How Winsock works*

In theory, a single winsock.dll or wsock32.dll is all that is needed to run any Winsock-compliant application. In reality, you will frequently find there are problems with this. One of your users may have an Internet access account that uses the Windows Internet Explorer. When selecting the Internet Explorer as the browser of choice, the user will, in configuring the connection, make use of the wsock32.dll or winsock.dll file in the C:\Windows\System subdirectory or folder. The user may later subscribe to a commercial online service that happens to include Internet access with the service. The online service might use another browser that requires a different DLL file. This is something that the user will not know and that you will not know about if the user adds this on his or her own.

While Winsock is a standard, there are still variations in vendor implementations where the winsock.dll is tied to that vendor's IP stack. This can lead to problems. Typically, the users might install the software for the new service and have everything work fine. Then, when they try to access the original communications application, the program fails. The remote users might not realize that the loading of new software is related to the failure of an existing, previously working communications package. When the remote users call you, this piece of information might never surface, making the problem very difficult to diagnose remotely.

What has probably happened is that the new communications application uses a different winsock.dll. And when it was installed, the new file was installed over the original in the C:\Windows\System subdirectory or folder. When the original application accesses the DLL file, it is not compatible with the application, and the protocol stack and the link cannot be established.

This situation occurs more often when there is a mix of 16-bit and 32-bit Windows applications. For example, a remote user might have been upgraded to Windows 95 and 32-bit remote access client software. But the user may still be using a Windows 3.x, 16-bit communications package for his or her online service access. Figure 15-2 illustrates this point by showing you how one vendor's Winsock implementations may not work with another's. When you install a different vendor's TCP/IP software onto one computer, it is common to write over another vendor's device drivers and DLLs.

eyond Winsock—Tighter Integration

Many people look at Winsock and say, "that's a solved problem, let's move on." But there are many higher-level applications that require specific hooks into a stack and that do not go through Winsock.

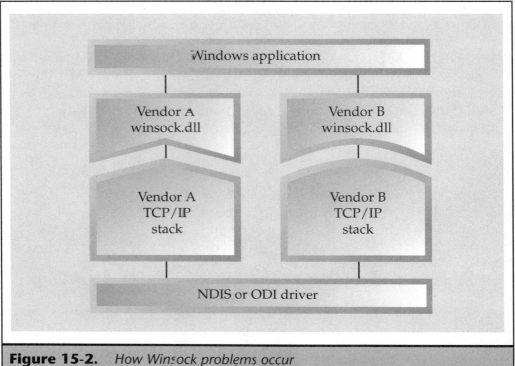

Figure 15-2. *How Winsock problems occur*

There are, for example, some utilities that will never break away from their parent stacks. Specifically, some network management programs are intimately bound to the kernel of the IP stack and cannot run over Winsock or Mac APIs. This is another issue to consider when deciding between a free stack in an operating system and a third-party stack. Some in the industry call this linking of the stack with a utility the "Above/Below the Winsock Line" issue.

For example, there's no API within Winsock to pass summary statistics about network traffic to an SNMP management system. For the home user, this is irrelevant, so the stacks from Apple and Microsoft are fine. For the corporate TCP/IP network, however, SNMP statistics can be important to problem diagnosis.

Examples of this type of integration include WRQ's SNMP-based network management statistics tool, which is tied to its stack. Similarly, FTP Software has its own IP diagnostic tool that gathers information about TCP/IP packet traffic. And many third-party IP stack vendors offer their own APIs for connecting their stacks to different services—the "below" in "Above/Below the Winsock Line."

For example, FTP Software's stack allows automatic switching between serial and Ethernet connections. Usually, you have your stack configured so that a LAN connection is the default. When you want to access the Internet over a SLIP or PPP connection, you have to reconfigure to a serial connection. With MacTCP or Win 95's IP stack, this process is manual. FTP Software's switching function detects when you fire up a dialer program to make your Internet connection and automatically changes the settings for you. When you terminate the call, it restores the LAN connection.

As stated earlier, for remote users who only require Internet connectivity, many of these things are not important. However, for users who need Internet access and connectivity to your network, the ability to use advanced management tools may be an issue that sways you to a third-party IP stack.

There is one other factor that plays to corporate audiences: support costs. Most TCP/IP stack vendors offer free support for the life of the product. Contrast that to Microsoft, which charges corporate users for support by the hour.

Again, this is something that might not be important to a user who just needs Internet access. Often the Internet service provider will help resolve configuration and connectivity problems. However, in a TCP/IP LAN environment, where connectivity is essential, free support is worth a lot, especially if you are dealing with many remote users in geographically dispersed sites.

Basically, view the free IP stacks from OS vendors as a good start. Many users won't need any more. Corporate types with large IP networks, on the other hand, will appreciate the fuller-function utilities, advanced network diagnostic capabilities, and free support offered by third-party stack vendors.

Reducing the Cost of Remote Client Software

The most important thing to consider when selecting remote connectivity client software is the total cost of ownership. Some organizations think that once you've connected every PC to a LAN, your network should run itself. That's hardly the case. As anyone who's managed a network knows, networks and the needs of users attached to them are constantly changing.

Keeping up with these changes is a labor intensive, and thus costly, proposition. And unfortunately, many of the costs associated with keeping a network running are hard to quantify. By carefully selecting PC connectivity products that address some of the hidden costs of remote connectivity, you potentially can cut the total cost of ownership associated with supporting remote users.

The Hidden Costs of Managing Software

Network management has always been labor intensive—routine tasks such as providing user support and troubleshooting, adding users to the network, changing user's access rights, and keeping track of hardware and software were all performed manually.

For many years, the true costs of managing networks were unknown. That's because many of the costs are hidden—basically, they are hard-to-quantify support costs. As such, companies seldom had a sense of what it was costing them to keep their networks up and running.

Compounding the difficulty of measuring support costs was the fact that LAN management was decentralized. That meant the recurring labor charges for network staffers to provide user support were often absorbed in many different operating budgets. However, as LAN management functions became centralized, companies could begin to assess the magnitude of the situation.

Still, it's hard to quantify the costs of connectivity. In the last few years, there has been some help, thanks to several studies by market research firms. All of the studies, while using different metrics, have come to the same conclusion: the costs to perform routine management tasks are staggering.

For example, LAN support costs $778 per user per year on NetWare LANs, according to a survey of 180 large user organizations conducted by Business Research Group (Newton, Massachusetts). And a Forrester Research Inc. (Cambridge, Massachusetts) study of LAN support costs found that, for a 5,000-user network, it costs three times more to support LAN users compared with the cost to support an equal number of users on an SNA network.

Another study estimates that, on average, the support costs per node in a LAN environment come to about $1,200 per year. For a network of, say, 250 users, that's about $300,000 a year just to keep the network up and running.

And the cost to handle other administrative tasks, such as user moves, adds, or changes, is just as staggering. Annually, American businesses spend about $1.3 billion moving, adding, and changing user's access rights on networks, according to the consultancy Datapro.

These studies point out that over a three- to five-year life cycle, the support costs of connecting a PC to a network can easily exceed the money spent on equipment itself. And the cost to support remote PCs are even higher, according to the Gartner Group.

For example, today you can buy a 133MHz Pentium-based PC, with 16MB of RAM, a 1Gb hard disk drive, a CD-ROM, a 15-inch color monitor, and bundled with Windows 95 all for about $2,000. If you add in a $250 10Base-T adapter card or a high-end modem, you've got a very decent desktop system for $2,250.

Taking the most conservative estimate of support costs (the Business Research Group's $778 per node annually for a NetWare LAN), it takes less than three years for the support costs to exceed the price of the desktop system. As you can see, the recurring costs of using products can easily exceed the purchase price of the products themselves. While this is certainly the case with hardware, it is even more so with software.

Software licensing fees account for only 14 percent of the cost of using software, according to a study by the Gartner Group. The largest portion of the cost associated with using software is the cost of supporting users, which amounts to 45 percent of the total cost of ownership. And administrative tasks, such as ensuring that concurrent licensing agreements are being properly enforced, account for another 13 percent of the total cost.

Additionally, the cost to distribute and install software is even higher than the fee to license programs. The Gartner Group study found that software installation and distribution accounts for about 17 percent of a company's total software costs.

Reducing the cost of software ownership starts with making intelligent purchasing decisions. In many organizations, software purchases are made based on a one-node, one-license basis. That's fine if all software acquisitions are centralized. But in most organizations, departments buy software as they need it.

This decentralization of purchasing, combined with a lack of up-to-date information about what is on every desktop, has led many organizations to over-buy software. The Personal Computer Asset Management Institute, an organization of end-user companies and vendors dedicated to looking at the costs of managing network assets, estimates that in 1994 U.S. companies, government, and military organizations spent as much as $2 billion on software they already owned.

Such situations can be avoided when a network administrator knows what software is sitting on the network and the local drives. That's something that a good connectivity package can help with. For example, with this information, a network administrator could easily size up the situation and reduce the number of licenses in a purchase.

And these savings can be quite substantial. For example, if 10 percent of the users in a 1,000-user network already have Microsoft Office, a company could save the purchase price of those licenses. That amounts to a savings of about $48,000 based on a retail price of $480 for Microsoft Office.

Such savings are what will cut the lifetime ownership costs associated with network connectivity and reduce the cost to access information. Another way to save money is to buy software that reduces distribution and installation costs. Specifically, select connectivity software that is installed on the server. And to cut the administrative costs associated with managing software licenses, you should select a vendor who offers a blanket licensing agreement for all of your connectivity needs. That way, you only need to worry about the number of PCs and will not have to juggle different types of licensing agreements for each part of your connectivity solution.

Hidden Costs of Host Connectivity

Reducing such costs greatly helps a company's bottom line. But it's still the recurring end-user support costs that form the largest portion of the total cost of connecting a remote PC to a network.

Network managers have been stymied in trying to reduce support costs because of nonstandard desktop configurations. Some network managers estimate that nonstandard configurations can triple the helpdesk staff's workload.

Unfortunately, nonstandard configurations are quite common. When companies try to give their users access to data on host computers, they often use a protocol stack from one vendor and a terminal emulator from another. When the same users need access to an additional host, yet another vendor's terminal emulator may be used.

Selecting products in this manner can lead to problems. There may be conflicts that prohibit the products from working together. And using such a mix of products on a single desktop may require rebooting the computer when switching between the products. Table 15-2 summarizes the main advantages to choosing a single-vendor approach for remote connectivity client software.

Choosing a single vendor for all connectivity needs simplifies such matters in several ways. First, it eliminates any conflicts. Thus, a company can save time troubleshooting problems. And if there is a problem, going with a single vendor means there is no vendor finger-pointing (the stack vendor blaming the terminal emulation vendor and vice versa).

A second advantage of the single-vendor connectivity approach is that it reduces end-user training costs. That's because products from one vendor all use the same interface for connectivity. If users currently are accessing an IBM

Issue	Benefit
No finger pointing between vendors when a problem occurs	Saves your staff time troubleshooting problems
Ensures that different access tools, such as terminal emulators, will work together	Eliminates many common conflict problems
Users get a common interface for all tools	Reduces end-user training costs

Table 15-2. *Benefits of Using a Single-Vendor Client Connectivity Approach*

host and need to connect to a Digital Equipment Corp. host, they are presented with the same look and feel on their screen.

A common user interface is a key in many organizations. After all, the goal is to give end users access to data, not for them to learn how to use multiple connectivity software packages.

Another way to cut administrative costs is to choose connectivity software that is intelligent. Look for software that can identify what is already installed and that can identify a user's network configuration. Some connectivity software even has enough built-in intelligence to alert the user to potential trouble spots, thus avoiding conflicts. For the most part, you should look for software that is smart enough not to create new connectivity problems.

Besides looking for software that won't cause problems, you should also look for software that makes it easier to diagnose problems when they do occur.

Look for built-in features that aid helpdesk staffers. For example, some connectivity software will allow you to view a user's settings and configuration. This can be quite helpful in the event the user has changed the configurations from a standard setting. Being able to quickly identify such a change, a helpdesk staffer can easily rectify the situation.

To reduce this type of problem even further, you might want to select connectivity software that lets the network administrator (if he or she so chooses) prevent users from changing their configuration.

What it all comes down to when trying to reduce the support and administrative costs associated with software is to know what is on the network. You can't manage connectivity if you don't know what you have installed. Yet many companies still rely on once-a-year inventories where a network staffer travels from PC to PC to perform an audit.

Such inventories are expensive. It takes, on average, about a half hour per PC to conduct a software inventory. For a network with 250 PCs, that's 125 hours, or the equivalent of three networking staffers working solely on inventory for one full week. And if your organization has 1,000 PCs, an inventory will take three people four solid weeks.

Most organizations do not have the luxury to dedicate staffers to such tasks. And even if they did, the inventory information is quickly outdated—to properly deliver support, you need to have up-to-the-minute information about the programs and files that reside on hard disks throughout the organization.

For example, users might call your department saying they're having trouble connecting to a particular host. They connected yesterday, but they just can't get it to work today. With all of the moves, adds, and changes that daily take place on a network, such problems are common. You need to know what users have running on their machine when they call for help.

The way to cut end-user support costs is to give helpdesk personnel accurate configuration data. One way to do this is to provide helpdesk staffers with access to configuration and systems files on each desktop. For example, by quickly identifying that a caller to a helpdesk is automatically installing an old version of a network driver program in his or her autoexec.bat file, a helpdesk technician can save lots of time.

That's just an example of a benefit derived from using good network connectivity software. An organization using connectivity software can reap other benefits.

Some connectivity software products help you reduce recurring labor costs by virtue of their enhanced troubleshooting and management tools, such as Telnet and FTP capabilities. Additionally, use of such connectivity software can help reduce the cost to distribute and install other software, perform administrative tasks (such as software management, handling access rights, mapping applications to drives, and so on), and can help diagnose problems on the network.

Good connectivity software helps in all of these areas. It frees up network staffers' time so that they can spend it on more urgent tasks, such as troubleshooting network problems.

Additionally, having access to information about each PC on a network can be used by an organization to become more proactive. Support costs can be reduced further by alerting the network manager to a potential problem before it has an effect on the users attached to the network.

In this proactive mode of operation, a network administrator can identify a problem in the making and correct the situation before users are bothered. This will allow network staffs to operate more efficiently, since they can turn their attention to preventing problems rather than spending all of their time fighting fires.

Selecting one vendor for all your remote PC connectivity needs will save time and money, because there will be far fewer conflicts to resolve. That means users will be able to quickly get up and running on the network. And it means a single PC connectivity vendor approach will save an organization money because it won't be wasting staffer's time resolving the conflicts.

You can estimate how much you will save when standardizing on a single PC connectivity vendor by using the following formula:

Cost of multivendor approach =

Direct labor costs to resolve conflicts
+ Lost productivity of workers affected by conflict
+ Lost revenues those people would have been generating if there were no conflicts

The direct labor costs can be derived by taking the hourly wage of the network staffer solving the conflict and multiplying that by the number of hours to troubleshoot the conflict. That's the cost to take care of one PC. You will need to multiply that figure by the number of PCs experiencing different conflicts.

The salary of a technical support person will vary within your organization. Keep in mind that it will require a fairly sophisticated level of technical expertise to resolve a conflict between say, one vendor's protocol stack and another vendor's terminal emulation program. That means you will have to dedicate one of your more highly skilled (and highly paid) staffers.

Suppose your mid-level to upper-level technical staffers make between $40,000 and $50,000 per year. That breaks down to about $20 to $25 per hour.

If it takes six hours to troubleshoot and resolve a connectivity problem, that means your company will spend $120 to $150 per PC. If 5 percent of a company's PCs have conflicts of different natures, the cost to resolve conflicts between different vendors' products will be between $15,000 to $18,750 in an organization with 250 PCs and between $60,000 and $75,000 in an organization with 1,000 PCs.

Table 15-3 summarizes these calculations and can be used as a quick guide to calculate the direct labor costs for various hourly wages, hours to resolve conflicts, and numbers of PCs affected. The numbers in this table are based on the assumption that it takes six hours to resolve each conflict and a labor cost of $20 per hour (approximate hourly rate for a staffer making $40,000 per year).

Lost productivity due to network downtime when there are program conflicts can also be estimated in the same manner. Take the average hourly salary of the employees affected by a network connectivity problem multiplied by the number of PCs involved and then multiplied by the number of hours it takes to resolve the problem.

Table 15-4 gives some examples of the costs of lost productivity. The numbers in the table are based on the assumption that it takes six hours to resolve each conflict and an average hourly rate of $10 per hour (approximate hourly rate for a worker making $20,000 per year) for all employees affected by the outage. These numbers are probably a good measure of the cost of lost productivity for your typical office workers. They would be much higher for, say, employees in a remote office that provides a service such as a travel agency or insurance company. As is the case with all the cost calculations in this book, use this model as a guide, and substitute your own numbers to calculate your lost-productivity costs.

Number of PCs in Organization	5 Percent of PCs Affected	10 Percent of PCs Affected	25 Percent of PCs Affected
200	$1,200	$2,400	$6,000
500	$3,000	$6,000	$15,000
1,000	$6,000	$12,000	$30,000
2,000	$12,000	$24,000	$60,000

Table 15-3.   *Cost to Resolve Multivendor Conflicts*

Number of PCs in Organization	5 Percent of PCs Affected	10 Percent of PCs Affected	25 Percent of PCs Affected
200	$600	$1,200	$3,000
500	$1,500	$3,000	$7,500
1,000	$3,000	$6,000	$15,000
2,000	$6,000	$12,000	$30,000

Table 15-4.   *Cost of Lost Productivity*

The total cost of a network connectivity problem due to incompatibility between different vendors' products would be the sum of the network staffer's time to resolve the problem plus the lost productivity due to the problem. Table 15-5 takes the information in the two preceding tables and calculates this total cost.

Estimating Less-Quantifiable Losses

It's straightforward to calculate what it costs an organization in direct labor charges to resolve problems from using products from multiple PC connectivity vendors. It is harder to calculate the cost due to lost productivity and lost revenues.

Number of PCs in Organization	5 Percent of PCs Affected	10 Percent of PCs Affected	25 Percent of PCs Affected
200	$1,800	$3,600	$9,000
500	$4,500	$9,000	$22,500
1,000	$9,000	$18,000	$45,000
2,000	$18,000	$36,000	$90,000

Table 15-5.   *Total Cost of Connectivity Problems*

For example, while it may take six hours of a network staffer's time to resolve a conflict, that period may be spread over several days. Most conflicts will require calls to at least two vendors. There will certainly be finger pointing between the vendors, each placing blame on the other. Even if it only takes one vendor to resolve the problem, it is not uncommon for it to take two days to get a return call from some vendor's technical support people.

Perhaps a person whose PC is having a connectivity problem might not be able to access a database residing on a networked host for two days. That means this person cannot perform one aspect of his or her job for that period. That's a loss of productivity.

And if the person's job involves any form of customer service, billing, handling invoices, and so on, the inability of this person to do his or her job can translate into lost revenues for the company. Take these factors into account when selecting PC connectivity software.

Some Final Considerations Before You Choose

In addition to considering the technical advantages of using one vendor's connectivity software offerings over another's, there are several other issues to think about before selecting a product.

You should look for a vendor who can provide helpdesk training of your staffers. The vendor should also be willing to make onsite network troubleshooting visits. Additionally, you should look at the vendor's total connectivity line. Select a vendor who offers all the pieces of the connectivity puzzle that you need.

Make sure the vendor supports a broad range of connectivity options. You may only need one type of connectivity today, but with corporate acquisitions happening all the time, you may find yourself with vastly different host connectivity needs tomorrow. Such unpredictability about future connectivity needs makes it imperative to consider the long-term costs of using any product. You don't want to waste vast amounts of technical resources resolving various conflicts between different products every time your organization adds another division or business unit.

Because networks are such dynamic environments, you must take all of the hidden cost issues into account before purchasing products. Choose the ones that will help reduce the total cost of ownership when it comes to PC connectivity.

Chapter Sixteen

Remote Security

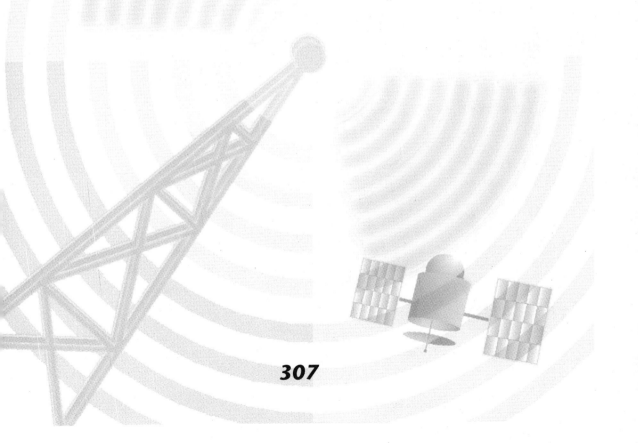

Ｉf you think protecting the data on your personal computer can be confusing, imagine how difficult it can be to protect data while promoting remote access. The complexity increases exponentially! And since remote access by definition lets users share data and access applications over long distances, how do you draw the line between being "open" and "vulnerable"? This chapter isn't meant to scare you into implementing proper security measures, but rather to help you determine where to draw that line, which will vary from business to business. But to do so, you must know two things:

- The value of your data (that is, the cost of downtime both in dollars and goodwill)
- Your data's enemies

With this information, you can establish a plan to protect your valuable data, and keep your network—and hence your company—up and running.

Nuts and Bolts of WAN Security

Security in a computing environment consists of three primary ingredients—*confidentiality, integrity,* and *availability*. These form a very appropriate acronym: *CIA*. These ingredients will be covered next.

Confidentiality

Keeping strategic information out of the hands of competitors can be key to the survival of your business. The subject of information ownership and who has permission to access certain computer files is explained here.

Integrity

Data integrity means that when you input a figure into the computer, that figure remains unaltered. Data integrity can be compromised by computer glitches, a weary typist, a hacker, or a delete command gone awry.

Availability

Is there such a thing as being too secure? Yes—if those intended to work with the data can't access it, the purpose of security is defeated. This also encompasses disaster planning and business-resumption plans. A natural disaster or even an act of terrorism could make your data unavailable.

Security Planning

To determine the value of your data, you must conduct a *business impact analysis,* in which you assess potential threats, their consequences, and their likelihood of taking place. Potential threats include theft, sabotage, viruses, dumb errors (we've all made our share), hackers, disgruntled employees, natural disasters—the list goes on and on. Computer output can also pose a risk, as anyone willing to rummage through your garbage can find the first draft of that confidential report you printed in the wrong typeface and then threw away.

With each potential threat, you must also determine the consequences— for example, loss of equipment, loss of data, interruption of business, loss of goodwill. Once you have a list of potential hazards and have assessed their risk, you can assign an associated cost and priority. This is a good place to include a plan of action for each possibility.

Physical Security

Securing your LAN starts with securing the hardware. This means keeping your hardware in working order and from being stolen. Losing a file server costs more than just the price of the server. This holds true whether someone steals it or if the janitor spills a bucket of water on it. The lost or damaged computer might contain critical data whose confidentiality, integrity, and availability would be sacrificed. Critical systems should be kept behind locked doors in a server closet. This includes file servers, routers, hubs, and other high-priority hardware. Such high-priority hardware should also be protected from power irregularities and outages. An *uninterruptible power supply* (*UPS*) that can issue an orderly system shutdown in the event of an extended power outage should be used on every file server. And don't forget to protect routers, hubs, and your telephone equipment with a UPS. Just because the power at your site is out, doesn't mean that the power's out at one of your remote offices which accesses files from your server.

Equipment that must be left in work areas should be secured with physical-restraint devices. Difficult-to-replace items, such as specialty cables, should either be secured or extras kept on hand. Easily removable media also requires special attention, especially floppy disks. Floppies can contain considerable amounts of data, and their small size makes it easy for your sensitive data to walk right out the front door.

Password protecting each computer is also a good idea. Most computers sold today support *BIOS passwords,* which prevent the computer from even booting up until the correct password is entered. This kind of password protection is great for restricting access to powered-down computers, but it can be overcome if access to the motherboard is possible.

The next level of password control is *application-level* passwords. Applications can be password protected through a menu system, or password security might be built into the application itself. Such passwords are sufficiently effective for most users, but for them to withstand attempts to gain access by more advanced users, access to the DOS prompt must be prohibited. *Network access* also requires a password. Security on a network is typically very secure as long as access to the server console is not allowed. Once a hacker has access to the server console, there is little that can stop him or her.

Access Control

Another aspect of physical security is regulating who has access to your site and when such access is allowed. The simplest method is probably the one you employ at your house—a lock and key. But for tighter control there are other methods, ranging from magnetic stripe cards to smart cards. By using electronics, you can now specify *when* as well as *where* each person can gain access. You can also electronically audit access, tracking how long a certain person was in the building, or in a certain room.

The problem with these systems, like the lock and key, is that they don't require that the card be in the possession of the rightful owner. Available today, but not yet widely used, is a technology that uses *biometrics* to positively authenticate a user to his or her access privileges. These products include fingerprint, hand, voice, signature, and retinal scanners. Such systems leave it up to you to enforce that those who are given privileges don't abuse them.

Secure Networks

The very nature of a remote access system introduces security problems for network administrators. LANs are nightmarish enough, with their constant growth and changes. They allow valuable information to be accessed from the desktop. Remote access makes that data available even from outside the office.

This means that there are more possible points-of-attack, leaks, and damage that can occur. A hacker can attack from any workstation, dial in to any modem, plug into any hub, or gain access through any router on the network. And the rewards are usually much greater for breaking into a file server than for accessing a single stand-alone system, as the server is where the data vault is stored.

Data copied from a secure server to a local workstation drive poses a security risk, as most workstations do not have barriers to prevent a hacker from walking out the door with your sensitive data. Windows 95, with all its wonderful built-in networking features, still lacks simple security to protect even itself. Windows NT Workstation, on the other hand, offers stand-alone security that is nearly impossible to bypass. Having protected workstations on your network protects the network all the more. For this reason, this chapter started out placing and continues to place great emphasis on protecting individual workstations.

For a secure network, you must protect the workplace, the computer, and the files the computer can access. You also must ensure that the computer is reasonably capable of manipulating data on the network without affecting the data's integrity. In addition, the communication between networked computers must be protected, and the identity of the sender and receiver verified. If sensitive data is passing across a wire, you must protect it as aggressively as you would files on the server. As data or even passwords are transmitted over the wire, they are subject to distortion or even theft.

Most network protocols perform error handling for you, ensuring that what is transmitted is what is received. But ensuring the integrity of the data doesn't guarantee that it won't be received by unauthorized users. To make sure that anyone "listening" to your wire can't steal the data being transmitted over it, the best defense is making sure the "listeners" can't understand the "language" of the data. This is achieved by use of *encryption,* and encryption schemes ensure that no one can understand the language but the intended listener.

Start with the LAN

A LAN provides three primary functions, which will be covered next:

- Distributed file storage
- Remote computing
- Messaging services

Each of these functions brings with it issues that relate to information availability and security over the wide area, so the LAN is the logical place to begin your security measures.

Distributed File Storage

With network file servers, users can access various parts of the file system. Typically this is done by allowing a user to attach a certain file system, or directory, to his or her workstation to be used as though it were a local disk. This presents two potential problems. First, the server might provide access protection only to the directory level, so that a user granted access to a directory has access to all files contained in that directory. To minimize risk in this situation, proper structuring and management of the LAN file system are important.

The second problem is caused by inadequate protection mechanisms on the local workstation. For example, a personal computer might provide minimal or no protection of the information stored on it. A user who copies a file from the server to the local drive on the PC loses the protection afforded the file when it was stored on the server. For some types of information, this might be acceptable; however, other types of information might require more stringent protections. This requirement points to the need for access controls in the PC environment.

Remote Computing

In this context, "remote computing" refers to the ability of one computer to run application software that resides on another computer, as opposed to simply using the other computer's data storage. A WAN allows you to remotely run an application on one or more components, while having the appearance of running locally. This allows you to utilize the processing power of the WAN as a whole. However, remote computing must be controlled so that only authorized users can access remote components and remote applications. These requests also might call for the local and remote servers to authenticate to each other. The inability to authenticate can lead to unauthorized users being granted access to remote servers and applications. The integrity of applications utilized by many users over a WAN must be ensured.

Messaging Services

Today, many organizations and a good many users could not survive without e-mail. It is one of the most commonly used applications on LANs. Unfortunately, the messaging services add additional risk to information that is stored on a server or that is in transit. Inadequately protected e-mail can easily be captured, altered, and retransmitted, affecting both the confidentiality and integrity of the message. This especially holds true as the Internet has become the most common messaging transport.

Network Security Policies

A weak or nonexistent security policy contributes to the risks associated with a LAN. A formal security policy governing the use of LANs should be in place to demonstrate management's position on the importance of protecting valued assets. A security policy is a statement of the upper management's position on information values, protection responsibilities, and organizational commitment. A strong LAN security policy should be in place to provide direction and support from the highest levels of management. The policy should identify the role that each employee has in ensuring that the LAN information is adequately protected.

The LAN security policy should stress the importance of, and provide support for, LAN management. At the same time, LAN management should be given the necessary funding and resources. Poor LAN management can result in security lapses. The resulting problems could include security settings becoming too lax, security procedures not being performed correctly, or even the failure to implement the necessary security mechanisms.

Lack of user awareness regarding the security of the LAN also can add risk. Users who are not familiar with the security mechanisms and procedures might use them improperly and perhaps less securely. Responsibilities for implementing security mechanisms and procedures and following the policies regarding the use of the PC in a LAN environment usually fall to the user of the PC. Users must be given the guidance and training necessary to maintain an acceptable level of protection in the LAN environment.

LAN Threats

The following section contains possible threats to and vulnerabilities of LANs. It categorizes each one and describes the impact it can have on the LAN.

LAN TRAFFIC SPOOFING An example of spoofing is if a message appears to have been sent from a legitimate, named sender, when actually the message came from elsewhere. Data that is transmitted over a LAN should not be altered in an unauthorized manner as a result of that transmission, either by the LAN itself or by an intruder. LAN users should be able to have a reasonable expectation that the message that was sent is received unmodified. A modification occurs when an intentional or unintentional change is made to any part of the message, including the contents and addressing information.

Messages transmitted over the LAN need to contain some sort of addressing information that reports the sending address of the message and the receiving address of the message. Spoofing of LAN traffic involves the ability to intercept a message by masquerading as the legitimate receiving destination, or to pose as the sending machine and send a message to a destination. For an unauthorized machine to pose as a receiving machine, the LAN must be persuaded into believing that the destination address is the legitimate address of the machine. Unauthorized reception of LAN traffic also can be done by listening to the messages as they are broadcast to all nodes.

Masquerading as the sending machine to deceive a receiver into believing the message was legitimately sent can be done by faking the address or by means of a *playback*. A playback involves capturing a session between a sender and a receiver, then retransmitting that message. The spoofing of LAN traffic or the modification of LAN traffic can occur by exploiting these vulnerabilities:

- Transmitting LAN traffic in plain text
- Lack of date/time stamp
- Lack of message-authentication code mechanism or digital signature
- Lack of real-time verification mechanism

INAPPROPRIATE RESOURCES ACCESS An example of inappropriate resource access would be an individual, authorized or unauthorized, gaining access to LAN resources in an unauthorized manner. Resources on a LAN might include file storage, applications, high-end printers, modems, scanners, data, and so on. However, not all resources need to be made available to each user. To prevent compromising the security of the resource, only those who require the use of the resource should be permitted access to it.

Unauthorized access occurs when a user, legitimate or unauthorized, accesses a resource that the user is not permitted to use. Unauthorized access might occur simply because the access rights assigned to the resource are not assigned properly. However, unauthorized access also might occur because the access-control mechanism of the privilege mechanism is not granular enough. In these cases, the only way to grant the user the needed access rights or privileges to perform a specific function is to grant the user more access than is needed or more privileges than are needed. Unauthorized access to LAN resources can occur by exploiting these vulnerabilities:

- Use of system default permission settings that are too permissive to users
- Improper use of administrator or LAN manager privileges
- Data that is stored with an inadequate level of or with no protection assigned
- Lack of or improper use of the privilege mechanism for users
- PCs that utilize no access control on a file-level basis

As LANs are utilized throughout an organization, some of the data stored or processed on a LAN might require some level of confidentiality. The disclosure of LAN data or software occurs when the data or software is accessed, read, and possibly released to an individual who is not authorized for the data. This can occur when someone gains access to information that is not encrypted, or views monitors or printouts of the information. The compromising of LAN data can occur by exploiting these vulnerabilities:

- Improper access-control settings
- Data that has been deemed sensitive enough to warrant encryption being stored instead in unencrypted form
- Application source code stored in unencrypted form
- Monitors viewable in high-traffic areas
- Printer stations placed in high-traffic areas
- Data and software backup copies stored in open areas

LAN DISRUPTION LAN disruptions are threats that block LAN resources from being available in a timely manner. A disruption of LAN functionality occurs when the LAN cannot do the job that it was designed to do in an acceptable manner. A disruption can interrupt one type of functionality or many. A disruption of LAN functions can occur by exploiting these vulnerabilities:

- Configuration of the LAN that allows for a single point of failure
- Inability to detect unusual traffic patterns, such as spamming
- Improper maintenance of LAN hardware
- Inability to reroute traffic or handle hardware failures

UNAUTHORIZED SOFTWARE MODIFICATIONS This problem arises when someone modifies, deletes, or destroys LAN data and software in an unauthorized or accidental manner. Because LAN users share data and applications, changes to those resources must be controlled. Unauthorized modification of data or software occurs when unauthorized changes (additions, deletions, or modifications) are made to a file or program.

When undetected modifications to data are present for long periods, the modified data might be spread through the LAN, possibly corrupting databases, spreadsheet calculations, and various other application data. This can damage the integrity of most application information.

When undetected software changes are made, all system software can become suspect, warranting a thorough review of all related software and applications. These unauthorized changes can be made in simple command programs, such as batch files or utility programs in multiuser systems. They can be made by unauthorized outsiders, as well as by those who are authorized to make software changes.

These changes can divert information to other destinations, corrupt the data as it is processed, or harm the availability of LAN services. Unauthorized modification of data and software includes viruses. Currently viruses have been limited to corrupting personal computers and generally do not corrupt LAN servers, although viruses can use the LAN to infect many workstations. The unauthorized modification of data and software can occur by exploiting these vulnerabilities:

- Lack of virus-detection tools
- Write permission granted to users who require only read permission to access
- Lack of a cryptographic checksum on sensitive data
- Undetected changes made to software

UNAUTHORIZED LAN ACCESS   This threat involves an unauthorized individual gaining access to the LAN. LANs provide file sharing, printer sharing, file storage sharing, and so on. Because resources are shared and not used solely by one individual, there is a need for control of the resources and accountability for use of the resources. Unauthorized LAN access occurs when someone who is not authorized to use the LAN gains access to the LAN (usually by acting as a legitimate user of the LAN). Three common methods used to gain unauthorized access are password *sharing,* general password *guessing,* and password *capturing.*

Password sharing allows an unauthorized user to have the LAN access and privileges of a legitimate user with the legitimate user's knowledge and acceptance. Password guessing is a common means of unauthorized access when proper password policies are not enforced. Password capturing is a process in which a legitimate user unknowingly reveals the user's log-in ID and password. This might be done through the use of a Trojan horse program that appears to the user as a legitimate log-in program. However, the Trojan horse program is designed to capture passwords and store them in a file. Capturing a log-in ID and password as they are transmitted across the LAN unencrypted is another method used to ultimately gain access. The hardware and/or software to capture LAN traffic, including passwords, is readily available. Unauthorized LAN access can occur by exploiting these vulnerabilities:

- Non-password-protected single-user PCs
- Lack of disconnect for multiple log-in failures
- Password sharing
- Lack of identification and authentication scheme
- LAN access passwords that are stored on PCs
- Poor physical control of network devices
- Lack of a time-out for log-in time period
- Unprotected modems
- Poor password management
- Lack of "last successful log-in date/time" and "unsuccessful log-in attempt" notification

DISCLOSURE OF DATA   This problem involves an individual accessing or reading information, and revealing the information either accidentally or intentionally in an unauthorized manner.

DISCLOSURE OF LAN TRAFFIC   This problem involves an individual accessing or reading information, and revealing the information either accidentally or intentionally in an unauthorized manner as it moves through the LAN.

LAN Security Services

A *security service* is a collection of procedures, controls, and other mechanisms that is implemented to help spot the security risks just described. For example, the authentication and identification service helps reduce the risk of the unauthorized user. Some services provide protection from threats, while other services provide for detection of the threat occurrence. Some types of WAN security services are described next.

User Identification

The first step toward securing the resources of a LAN is the ability to verify the identities of users. The process of verifying a user's identity is referred to as *authentication*. Authentication provides the basis for the effectiveness of other controls used on the LAN. For example, the logging mechanism provides usage information based on the user ID. The access-control mechanism permits access to LAN resources based on the user ID. Both these controls are effective only under the assumption that the requester of a LAN service is the valid user assigned to that specific user ID.

Identification requires the user to be known by the LAN in some manner. This usually is based on an assigned user ID. However, the LAN cannot trust that the user is who he or she claims to be without it being authenticated. The authentication is done by having the user supply something that only he or she has—a *token,* and something only the user knows—a password or other unique identifier such as a fingerprint. The more of these that the user has to supply, the less risk in someone masquerading as the legitimate user.

A requirement that specifies the need for authentication should exist in most LAN policies. The requirement might be directed implicitly in a program-level policy that stresses the need to effectively control access to information and LAN resources, or it might be explicitly stated in a LAN-specific policy that states that all users must be uniquely identified and authenticated. On most LANs the identification and authentication mechanism is a user ID and password scheme.

Password Selection

Proper password selection has always been an important issue. Passwords produced by generators that create passwords consisting of pronounceable syllables are more likely to be remembered than those created by generators that produce random characters. Password-checker programs can be used to help the user to determine whether a new password is considered easy to guess and thus unacceptable.

Smart Card- or Token-Based Mechanisms

Password-only mechanisms, especially those that transmit the password unencrypted, are susceptible to being monitored and their passwords captured. This can become a serious problem if the LAN has any uncontrolled connections to outside networks. If, after considering all authentication options, LAN policy determines that password-only systems are acceptable, the proper management of password creation, storage, expiration, and destruction becomes all the more important. However, because of the vulnerabilities that still exist with the use of password-only mechanisms, more robust mechanisms might be preferred. Considerable advances have been made in the area of token-based authentication and the use of biometrics.

A smart card-based or token mechanism requires that a user have a token and additionally might require the user to know a *PIN* (*personal identification number*) or password. These devices then perform a *challenge/response* authentication. Use of real-time parameters helps prevent an intruder from gaining unauthorized access through a log-in session playback. These devices also can encrypt the authentication session, preventing the compromise of the authentication information through monitoring and capturing.

Physical Locking

Locking mechanisms for LAN devices, workstations, or PCs that require user authentication to unlock them can be useful to users who must leave their work areas frequently. These locks allow users to remain logged into the

LAN and to leave their work areas for a reasonable amount of time without exposing an entry point into the LAN. Some screen savers under Windows 3.x or Windows 95 have such a feature, or Windows NT Workstation can also be secured.

Modem Protection

Modems that provide users with LAN access might require additional protection. An intruder who can access the modem might gain access by successfully guessing a user password. The availability of modem use to legitimate users might also become an issue if an intruder is allowed continual access to the modem.

Access Control

A variety of access-control mechanisms and access-privilege mechanisms can protect against the unauthorized use of LAN resources. Most file servers and multiuser workstations provide this service to some extent. However, PCs that mount drives from the file servers usually do not. Users must recognize that files used locally from a mounted drive are under the access control of the PC. For this reason, it can be important to incorporate access control, confidentiality, and integrity services on PCs to whatever extent possible.

Access controls can be categorized as *discretionary* or *mandatory*. Discretionary access control is the most common type of access control used by LANs. With discretionary security, an individual user or a program operating on the user's behalf is allowed to specify the types of access other users or programs can have to information under the user's control. Discretionary security differs from mandatory security in that it implements the access-control decisions of the user. Mandatory controls are driven by the results of a comparison between the user's trust level or clearance and the sensitivity designation of the *information.*

Access-control mechanisms can support access granularity for acknowledging an owner, a specified group of users, and all authorized users. This allows the owner of a file or directory to have different access rights from all other users and allows the owner to specify different access rights for a specified group. In general, access rights allow read, write, and execute access. Some LAN operating systems provide additional access rights that allow updates, append only, and so on.

A LAN operating system might implement user profiles, capability lists, or access-control lists to specify access rights for many individual users and many different groups. Using these mechanisms allows more flexibility in granting different access rights to different users, which can provide more stringent access control for the file or directory. Access-control lists assign the access rights of named users and named groups to a file or directory. Capability lists and user profiles assign the files and directories that can be accessed by a named user. User access can exist at the directory level or the file level. Access control at the directory level places the same access rights on all of the files in the directory. For example, a user who has read access to the directory can read any file in that directory. Directory access rights can also provide an explicit negative access that prevents the user from any access to the files in the directory.

Some networks control how a file can be accessed, in addition to controlling who can access the file. Implementations can provide a parameter that allows an owner to mark a file *sharable* or *locked.* Sharable files accept multiple accesses to the file at the same time. A locked file will permit only one user to access it. If a file is a read-only file, making it shareable allows many users to read it at the same time.

These access controls also can be used to restrict use between servers on the LAN. Many LAN operating systems can restrict the type of traffic sent between servers. There might be no restrictions, which implies that all users might be able to access resources on all servers, depending on rights. Some restrictions might allow only certain types of traffic, and further restrictions might allow no exchange of traffic from server to server. The LAN policy should determine what types of information need to be exchanged between servers. Information that is not necessary to be shared between servers then should be restricted.

Privilege mechanisms enable authorized users to override the access permissions or, in some manner, legally bypass controls to perform a function, access a file, and so forth. A privilege mechanism should incorporate the concept of *least privilege.* The principle of least privilege should be implemented to perform the backup function. A user who is authorized to perform the backup function needs to have read access to all files to copy them to the backup media. The user is granted a privilege to override the read restrictions on all files to perform the backup function.

The more granular the privileges that can be granted, the more control there is, without having to grant excessive privilege to perform an authorized function. For example, the user who has to perform the backup function does not need to have write override privilege. The types of security mechanisms that could be implemented to provide the access-control service are

- Access rights: defining owner, group, and world permissions
- Access-control lists, user profiles, and capability lists
- Mandatory access control
- Granular privilege

Data and Message Confidentiality

The data and message confidentiality service can be used when the secrecy of information is necessary. As a front-line protection, this service can incorporate mechanisms associated with the access-control service, but also can rely on encryption to provide further secrecy protection. In this way, if the access-control service is circumvented, the file can be accessed, but the information still is protected by being in encrypted form.

It is very difficult to control unauthorized access to LAN traffic as it is moved through the LAN. For most LAN users, this is an accepted problem. The use of encryption reduces the risk of someone capturing and reading LAN data. Only the authorized user who has the correct key can decrypt the message once it is received. A strong policy statement should dictate to users the types of information that are deemed sensitive enough to warrant encryption. A program-level policy can dictate the broad categories of information that need to be stringently protected, while a system-level policy can detail the specific types of information and the specific environments that warrant encryption protection.

At whatever level the policy is dictated, the decision to use encryption should be made by the authority within the organization charged with ensuring protection of sensitive information. If a strong policy does not exist that defines what information to encrypt, then the data owner ultimately should make this decision. The types of security mechanisms that could be implemented to provide the message and data confidentiality service are

- Use of routers that provide filtering to limit broadcasting
- Physical protection of physical LAN medium and devices
- File and message encryption technology
- Protection for backup copies on tapes, disks, and so on

LAN Hardware Security

Installing a LAN involves combining a number of computers with additional hardware and software. Some network hardware opens new fronts for security attacks, while other hardware actually can provide increased security. At the most basic level, hardware purchased to create a network adds a further area of potential loss from theft. However, the right combination of network hardware can make data on a network harder to steal or corrupt than if it were stored on a stand-alone system. The main hardware components of a LAN can be grouped as follows:

- Cables carry signals between the computer's network interface and the rest of the LAN.

- Interfaces and connectors make the connection between the network cabling and the main circuitry of the computer.

- Expanders or peripherals supply shared facilities like printing, facsimile transmission, and connections between networks or to remote computers.

- Security components provide backup, redundancy, and access control.

Cables

As you know, the cables used to form a LAN range from simple telephone wire to coaxial cable to optical fibers. The installation of LAN cables can be a very expensive and disruptive undertaking. Some office buildings are now constructed with cables already installed to avoid the time and expense of retrofitting. The value of the cable itself usually is not so great as to make it a tempting target for thieves, but the installed cable does represent a significant asset that needs proper protection. Cables should be installed professionally, in such a way as to minimize the risk of accidental cutting, abrasion, or other damage. If data is the lifeblood of the organization, then network cables are its arteries. The most common threats to cabling are

- **Interference** The data traveling along the cable is altered by electrical fields. These fields might be generated by power cables for heavy machinery, or by radio and microwave equipment. Metal cables normally are shielded to prevent such interference, while fiber optic cables are not affected by interference.

- **Cable cutting** The connection made by the cable is broken, preventing the flow of data along the cable. This can happen when equipment is moved, or the structure housing the data is altered.

- **Cable damage** Normal wear and tear can weaken the shielding that preserves the integrity of transmitted data, or damage the cable itself, leading to unreliable communications.

For most organizations, these problems come under the category of natural hazards, similar to those faced by a lot of other office equipment. However, they also could be seen as a means of attacking a network to disrupt its operation. Network cable also provides a new front for attack by the determined interloper seeking access to your data. Cable does not have to be physically penetrated for the data that it carries to be revealed, thanks to EMI. Because it does not emit electromagnetic radiation, fiber optic cable is relatively impervious to eavesdropping. However, fiber and copper cables alike can be tapped. Even bending fiber optic cable sharply will allow light to escape, as will slight cracks in the insulation. While it is more difficult to tap fiber than coax, it is still possible.

Interfaces and Connectors

Despite the growing acceptance of LANs as a way of increasing the productivity of personal computers, many personal computer models still do not come standard with a network interface. This means that for most machines, a network adapter must be added. Network interfaces do not pose much of a security threat. External interfaces can be seen as one more piece of equipment that can go missing, but securing them to desks is easy enough to do. Network interfaces even can be given a positive security role. By providing a locking network connection, you can control a workstation's use of the network independent of the network software or workstation access control.

Expanders and Peripherals

One of the reasons for networking computers is to spread the cost of acquiring expensive peripherals that could be shared by many users. These peripherals include laser printers, typesetters, optical drives, facsimile transmitters, modems, and gateways to other networks or mainframe systems. Some of these components present potential security problems. For example, several users on a network might share a single laser printer. This often leads to a situation in which one or more users are having their documents printed at a printer that they cannot see from their workstation.

Obviously, printed documents are a very vulnerable form of data. For example, there is no point using password protection on a payroll database if payroll reports sit in a print tray where those who should not read them can. Access to network devices designed for communication beyond the network, such as gateways, mainframe connections, network modems, and network fax machines, needs to be controlled.

Security Components

For the interloper seeking access to data on a network, the two most promising lines of attack are remote access and a network workstation. This means that workstations must be protected very carefully. There must be systems in place that prevent unauthorized users from logging on to the network, copying information off it, or even printing data from it. The network administrator might want to classify network users to impose the appropriate level of security, which might look something like the following:

- **Administrative level** Those who design, maintain, and run the network. This might be the administrator alone, or a small group of support staff.

- **Trusted users** Those who are competent, stick to the rules, and whose work benefits from greater freedom of access to the network.

- **Vulnerable users** Those who lack competence, are excessively curious or belligerent, or are for any other reason not to be trusted.

Network Access Control

You must know the value of the data you are protecting, the needs of the users, and the sophistication of potential problems to know which of the following methods to employ for protection:

- Restrict access to workstation areas and to workstation power-up through keys, ID cards, smart cards, or biometrics.

- Password protect network login.

- Password protect all sensitive data areas and restrict programs on a need-to-use basis.

- Log all workstation activity and identify it by user ID.

- Password protect or lock out all copy-to-floppy operations on workstations.

■ Monitor all copy-from-floppy operations on workstations.

The Diskless Workstation

There is a need both to prevent the copying of programs and data off the network onto floppy disks, and to eliminate the possibility of viruses and other programs being copied from floppies onto the network. On the other hand, the person responsible for running the network needs wide-ranging access to all drives. One answer is to provide vulnerable users with diskless workstations. These units essentially use the same architecture as an ordinary personal computer, but with the important difference of no floppy or hard disk drive. The user stores data on the network server's hard disk. By eliminating the disk drive, the diskless PCs make it difficult to introduce viruses on the network. Diskless PCs also prevent users from stealing corporate information or software.

If you're wondering how a PC can work without any disk drives to load the operating system, it's fairly simple. The operating system is placed in ROM, which cannot be infected by viruses or foolishly deleted or formatted. Most NICs can be fitted with network ROM so that when the diskless PC is turned on, everything loads from ROM, and the connection to the network is made. Operating system details specific to individual workstations can be stored in batter-backed CMOS, allowing each one to be configured with its own password.

Protecting the Server

The most important part of the network is the server. The concentration of data on the server, in terms both of quantity and sensitivity, makes it essential to protect it from all eventualities. You should store your server in a lockable, well-ventilated server closet. No one, with the exception of the MIS staff, should have access to the closet. All printers and other shared resources needed by others should not be stored in the server closet.

The data on your server should be backed up regularly. Backup tapes should be kept locked up, and a set of backups should be kept offsite, and rotated regularly. Your backup administrator should be someone you trust.

LAN Fault Tolerance

Networks must function when you need them to. *Fault tolerance* is the ability of your network to continue functioning in the event of a major problem or catastrophic breakdown, with no damage to data and with no perceptible change in operation. Most commonly, fault tolerance entails a redundant piece of hardware that automatically takes over in case the primary component fails. However, fault tolerance can mean as little as storing duplicate file allocation tables and directory entries on separate areas of the same disk or simple read-after-write verification to ensure that data is never written to a bad sector on the disk.

Not every network will require the same degree of fault tolerance. Fault tolerance usually involves additional costs, so you will want to weigh these against your uptime requirements. The basic question to answer is, what happens if the network goes down? If you stand to lose serious money or goodwill from such an event, then you need to consider investing in a certain level of fault tolerance.

Fault tolerance has several levels. At the ultimate level, every hardware component is duplicated to ensure nonstop network performance. The most common form of fault tolerance is at the low end of the spectrum, where the only replicated component is the one responsible for most network failures: the server's hard disk. This is the part of the network most prone to failure.

Duplexing and Mirroring

The first fault-tolerant systems were implemented with a second disk drive that was a mirror image of the first. Any data that was written to the first drive also was immediately written to the second. If the primary drive failed for any reason, the secondary disk would take over automatically, allowing the first drive to be replaced without disrupting network service. This is still a widely employed method for providing fault tolerance and is included with many NOSes.

Even within the area of disk mirroring there are different levels of redundancy. *Mirroring* infers the use of one controller card for both drives, while *duplexing* provides each drive with its own controller. This adds another level of security against the possibility of a controller failure, which would still defeat a mirrored setup. Duplexing drives also improves network performance, because with two separate controllers the system has a split-seek capability. Not only can users read files simultaneously, but the server can determine which disk can service a read request more quickly. Duplexed disks can also have one disk reading and the other writing.

Later RAID came to the scene. Six RAID levels were initially defined, levels 0 through 5. The most common are RAID levels 0 (data striping) and 5 (where an extra "parity" drive is used so that a failure of any one drive would not cause data loss). RAID systems typically incorporate multiple, hot-swappable drives and power supplies. RAID systems can get pretty expensive, but their ability to keep a server up continuously, despite a drive failure, make them worth the investment for many.

Uninterruptible Power Supply (UPS)

Every piece of computer equipment on your network should be protected with at least a surge protector, while file servers, hubs, routers, and even your telephone system should be connected to UPSes. Any UPS you connect to your file server should have the capability to issue an orderly shutdown in the event of an extended power outage.

Tape Backup

Even if all your drives are mirrored, that still doesn't eliminate the need for a tape backup. They offer different levels of protection. A tape drive allows data to be backed up and taken offsite, and tape drives are a common companion to most RAID systems.

Backing up today's networks is no easy task, with the quantity of data rapidly increasing. You must decide whether to back up from a workstation or from a server. A tape drive attached directly to a server can receive data much faster than if it must be transferred across the network. The amount of data you have and the amount of time you have to back it up determines which route to take. A large, multiserver network might require Fast Ethernet in order to allow all file servers to be backed up overnight. Dedicated backup servers can increase backup performance even more.

Business Resumption Plan

If your business depends on being accessible across the country, you had better have a *business resumption plan.* If your office is destroyed, the tape backup that you keep offsite won't do you a bit of good if you have nowhere to restore the files. A business resumption plan includes the necessary hardware and a designated meeting place so that you can get back up and running as quickly as possible. With tapes in hand you can quickly restore your most recent set of tapes kept offsite and be back in business—maybe not at 100 percent, but at lease back up.

Summary

Companies are becoming increasingly dependent on their networks, and network downtime can be costly in terms of dollars and goodwill. You can choose the appropriate levels of security by understanding the possible eventualities and their associated risks. A proactive approach to system security can help you be confident in the integrity of your data, and that it will be available to those who need it, when they need it.

Chapter Seventeen

Software Distribution and Asset Control

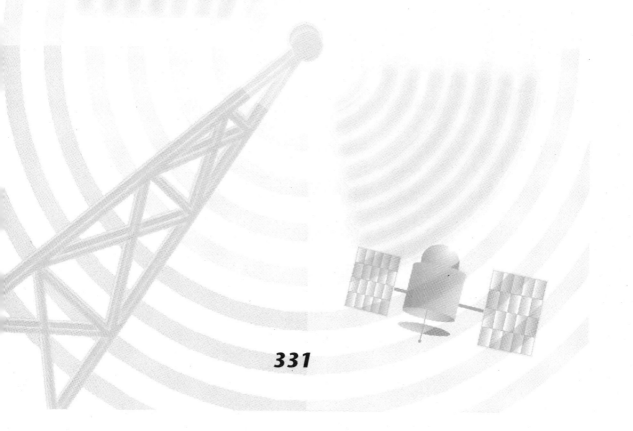

Throughout this book a common theme has been to look for ways to cut the total cost of remote connectivity. This chapter looks at asset management, which has the potential to save your company great amounts of money when done properly, but which also is one of the more difficult areas to control.

Asset management includes the ability to inventory the hardware and software installed on computers, control access to applications to ensure compliance with licensing agreements, and to automatically distribute software. These tasks are fairly difficult in controlled networking environments where all users are attached to a network. And they are even more challenging when you are dealing with remote users.

This chapter will explore each of the asset management areas, starting from a very general perspective, to show where the cost savings potential lies with each type of management. In these discussions, I will point out the issues you will face when trying to apply asset management principles to include your remote users.

The Basics of Asset Management

In general, a good asset management strategy helps you in several ways. Here are the most common ones:

- Cuts support costs (knowing what's on a desk makes it easier to quickly resolve problems)

- Reduces money spent on support by managing warranty information to ensure that products covered by warranties are serviced by vendors

- Helps you intelligently plan migrations and upgrades

- Lets you make smarter purchasing decisions when buying new hardware and software

- Reduces labor costs when you install new software

- Saves money on labor and parts for emergency repairs by using equipment service histories to become proactive in managing equipment

First, a good inventory of installed hardware and software can significantly reduce troubleshooting time by giving your support staff more information to work with when a problem is called into a helpdesk. This means you could possibly use fewer staffers to support the same number of users. But more likely, it will let you solve more user problems with the same level of staffing. If your company is like most, the ability to support more users per network staffer will become increasingly important, since market research studies indicate that corporate networks are growing at a much higher rate than network operations budgets.

The second way a good asset management strategy can help is that it reduces software acquisition costs. Many companies give departments the responsibility to make their own software purchases. A centralized software purchasing strategy lets you reap the benefits of volume purchase discounts and site licensing agreements that offer cut rates per license over buying the same software department by department.

A third way a good asset management strategy helps is when you are planning major software upgrades or migrations. Such changes require planning and purchases beforehand to ensure that the users will have the proper equipment to run any new software. For example, if you are planning to move everyone from Windows 3.x to Windows 95 or Windows NT, you would need to know which PCs need to be replaced, which need more memory, and which need more hard disk space to run the new operating system.

Still another way that a good asset management strategy helps reduce costs is by reducing the labor needed to install new software. Part of this ties in with intelligently planning migrations mentioned earlier. If an upgrade has been properly planned, when it comes time for the actual software installation, you know that the hardware sitting on a user's desk is capable of running the application. But that is just the tip of the iceberg. The real cost savings when installing new software occur when you use the network—be it a LAN in a small, remote office or a dial-up connection into the corporate network—to distribute software to your remote users.

The rest of this chapter will discuss these areas in much more detail.

Reducing Support Costs with a Good Inventory

To get an idea of the importance of having good, up-to-date asset information available, let's take an unrelated example to illustrate the issue.

Suppose it is time to plan your summer family vacation. You call Human Resources to see how many vacation days you have coming to you and they don't know exactly—they tell you it's between 10 and 20. Makes it kind of hard to plan, wouldn't you say?

Well, when you and your staff try to support end users, you are probably in the same situation if you do not have good asset information available. Without an up-to-date inventory, you must provide end-user support while lacking accurate information about the hardware and software your users are working with.

As a direct result of this lack of information, support costs are much higher than they need to be. After all, it's very difficult for a helpdesk staffer to troubleshoot a problem over the phone when he or she doesn't know the type of equipment the caller is using, the configuration of that equipment, or what software (including applications, operating system, and drivers) is in use.

This has made asset management a key issue in many organizations. The idea is that support costs can be reduced if a better hardware and software inventory exists. On top of that, many companies find that there are additional benefits to having accurate information about what they own. For instance, a good inventory can be used to make smarter purchasing decisions and can help you better plan when purchases need to be made.

Recognizing the need for such inventory information, the vendor community has responded with a multipronged approach. Software utility product vendors, such as Seagate, Horizons Technology, McAfee, Microsoft, Symantec, Intel, and Tally Systems, offer asset management software (essentially, programs that perform hardware and software inventory of network-attached PCs, Macs, workstations, and servers).

An industry consortium called the Desktop Management Task Force (DMTF), which is comprised of many hardware and software vendors, has developed a specification that provides a standardized way for computer equipment to be inventoried over a network and remotely.

Server and PC manufacturers, such as AST, Compaq, Dell, and NEC, are beefing up their products by adding firmware that performs a hardware inventory and then makes this information available to network and systems management programs.

Outsourcing firms, such as Hewlett-Packard's service organization and others, which specialize in network management, now also offer configuration and asset management services, performing an inventory for you and furnishing you with the results.

These alternative approaches to asset management all offer an organization the same benefit. They help managers get an accurate picture of the hardware and software deployed throughout their organization by collecting detailed inventory information. Traditionally, such inventories have been performed manually by going from desktop to desktop. But such manual inventories have always had drawbacks.

First, there is the labor required to perform an inventory. It typically takes a half hour per PC to perform a hardware and software inventory, according to the PC Asset Management Institute (an organization of users and vendors interested in asset management).

For a modest-sized organization of 2,000 PCs, that translates into 1,000 hours of labor. That's the equivalent of dedicating one full-time IS staffer to doing nothing else but inventory for half a year. In large organizations with 10,000 PCs, it's the equivalent of paying two or three people just to perform inventories. And these numbers get worse when you are dealing with many remote users. If you have several small sites with a handful of users attached to a LAN in each site, you must send a staffer to each location just to perform an inventory. And when you have to support a large number of full-time telecommuters, the difficulty of performing manual inventories quickly gets out of hand.

A second disadvantage to a manual inventory approach is that the collected information quickly becomes outdated, and thus the value of that information diminishes. For example, if an inventory is performed once a year, people could easily add components and software that might cause conflicts (for example, a user might install a sound card in a PC).

Most organizations have no inventory or use an outdated one. As a result, they find that they are constantly performing ad hoc inventories for specific reasons. For example, a company buying memory to upgrade PCs so they'll be able to run a new application would need to take a quick inventory of the amount of installed RAM on each PC. Another reason for an ad hoc inventory might be something as simple as needing configuration information to troubleshoot a problem with a single PC.

No matter what the reason, companies spend 40 hours per month, on average, performing asset and inventory management, according to a survey of 106 network managers conducted by Infonetics Research (San Jose, California). That means an organization is paying a week's salary every month to an employee just to take such spontaneous inventories.

For these reasons, it makes sense to automate as much of the inventory process as possible (thus reducing the labor charges incurred when performing manual inventories). That's what the products from software utility vendors do. Typically, asset management software programs provide a way to automatically collect detailed hardware and software inventory of servers and nodes on a network.

Hardware inventory programs from such systems management vendors collect information about a wide range of components within a PC. The programs get all the basics such as processor type, number and type of disk drives, type of BIOS, number of serial and parallel ports, and the amount of RAM installed. Other types of information about installed hardware is also collected. For example, you can determine what type of network adapter card is in use and whether a mouse or game port is installed.

Software inventory programs also collect information about the systems files, drivers, and applications installed on machines. The inventory programs can often collect other information such as the version number of an application, and the date and time the application was created. Some software inventory programs use dictionaries of applications suites so that the program can tell the difference between a user running, for example, Microsoft Word, Excel, and PowerPoint as separate applications, and a user running the same applications as part of the Microsoft Office suite.

Automatically collecting hardware and software inventory information has usually required proprietary approaches. Quite often hardware inventory software vendors use a custom-developed TSR (terminate and stay resident) program to run on each PC. The program queries the machine's hardware and passes this information along to a server-based inventory program.

For software inventory information, most vendors take a brute force approach and simply build lists (with information about common applications) that ship with the inventory program. The information typically includes the name of the executable file for hundreds to thousands of common software programs, as well as the size and date associated with each application's executable file.

Software inventory programs then simply look for executable files and compare the name, size, and date to the information in the master list to determine what programs are installed and what versions of the programs are in use. There are a number of tricks employed to make sure the version numbers are correct. Most often, a quick check can be made by looking at the time a program was created, since many application vendors set the time to correspond to the version number. For example, the executable files for Norton Desktop for Windows version 3.0 carry a time stamp of 3:00 A.M.

These techniques to collect inventory information can be used to instantly inventory equipment attached to a network. For laptops and stand-alone PCs and Macs, vendors usually provide a separate program that the user runs on each machine. This extra program collects inventory information and stores it on a floppy disk. The information on the disk can then be incorporated into a database of all the networked equipment and software.

Handling Remote Users

Such an approach works well for collecting information from LAN-attached users in remote sites. For telecommuters and mobile workers with laptops, the process of collecting inventory information is a little more difficult. You have three choices. First, you can teach your telecommuters how to run an inventory on their own. You might ask users to perform an inventory once a month. Many of the inventorying software packages offer a way for a single user to do just that. The user must then send you a floppy with the inventory information, and you must incorporate this information into a common database of all inventory information. While this may not seem ideal, it is better than having no inventory information at all. And since hardware is less likely to change, it gives you a decent starting point when troubleshooting a problem over the phone.

Another way to get asset information from remote users is to take advantage of their connections to the network. If telecommuters enter the network as a remote node, they are, in essence, network attached. When a user makes such a connection, you might take the opportunity to collect asset information and store it to a central database. To accomplish this requires that you install on each telecommuter's computer a software agent associated with the asset management application. Figure 17-1 shows how this process might work. The agent collects the inventory information and, when polled by the asset management application upon connecting to the network, passes the information up to a server in the central site.

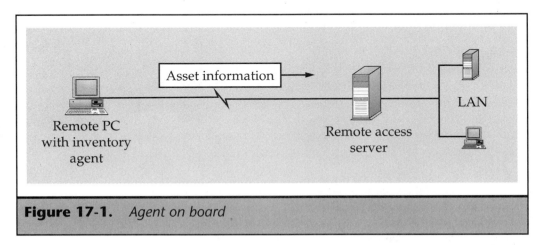

Asset information

Remote PC
with inventory
agent

Remote access
server

LAN

Figure 17-1. *Agent on board*

In some cases, the remote user's computer may never connect to the network. For instance, a mobile user may never connect his or her laptop to a network docking station in the office, or he or she may never remotely connect to the network in remote node mode. Thus, there is no chance to automatically extract inventory information. Such a situation requires a more imaginative solution.

Some companies have decided to require inventories of laptops at predetermined times of the year. For example, you might have a highly mobile sales force where everyone uses a laptop while on the road. You might set a corporate policy that all salespeople must bring their laptop with them to the twice-a-year sales meeting. At each meeting, the users must check in their laptops before the morning sessions begin. This gives you and your staff a day to perform a quick inventory of each laptop. So at least twice a year you have an accurate account of the hardware and software each salesperson has on his or her computer.

An alternative to having your remote users gather information or having people bring their systems to you is to hire a firm to perform the inventory for you. As mentioned earlier, some outsourcing vendors (such as Hewlett-Packard and Comdisco) who have provided network management services are gearing up to provide inventory and asset management services. Such companies say they will charge from $3 to $8 per device per month for inventory services. For an organization with 2,500 PCs, that translates into $90,000 to $240,000 per year.

That's quite a substantial amount of money to pay an outside firm just to take inventory. You might ask why anyone would pay so much for something that simple. Because it's probably going to save an organization money in the long run.

The purchase price of a typical PC only accounts for 12 percent of the total cost of ownership of the product over its lifetime, according to the Gartner Group. The other 88 percent goes toward administrative factors, such as inventory, training, and auditing costs. Additionally, support costs over the three- to five-year lifetime of typical computer products are three to seven times the purchase price of the equipment, according to studies by several consultancies including the Business Research Group, the Gartner Group, and Forrester.

It has only been within the last few years that such recurring management costs have become an issue. For many years, the true costs of managing PCs and LANs were simply buried in numerous departmental operating budgets. As organizations have tried to rein in control of departmental LANs over the last few years, these costs have been consolidated into one operating budget, and the magnitude of the expense has struck home.

Still, many companies have no idea what they are paying to support their end users. A 1994 survey by the Help Desk Institute of its members found that 82 percent of survey respondents didn't know what the average cost of a support call cost their organization. And for those who did answer, the amount ranged from $1 per call to $75 per call.

A number of studies have tried to quantify the costs of supporting users. For example, LAN support costs $778 per user per year on NetWare LANs, according to a survey of 180 large user organizations conducted by Business Research Group (Newton, Massachusetts). And a Forrester Research Inc. (Cambridge, Massachusetts) study of LAN support costs found that, for a 5,000-user network, it costs three times more to support LAN users compared with the cost to support an equal number of users on an SNA network.

These studies point out that there is often a real lack of understanding of support costs by most companies. When it comes to supporting remote users, the costs are even harder to estimate (as well as being higher). As was discussed in Chapter 1, the operational costs to support remote users is 50 percent of the total cost of ownership for remote users. And the hidden costs for supporting remote users was another 35 percent of the total cost.

Asset management information is crucial to reducing these costs. Troubleshooting a problem requires accurate information about a system's software and hardware. One network administrator at a Texas oil company says he is able to cut, on average, one-third of the troubleshooting time off of each phone call to his helpdesk by simply knowing what program (and version of the program) is running on a caller's desktop. Without an inventory program, many companies will have trouble keeping track of who has the latest fix or patch. This will make it harder to provide support. It will take longer to troubleshoot problems and therefore be more expensive.

This problem of tracking who has which patch or fix will become increasingly important as more and more users get access to online resources, such as CompuServe, America Online, and the Internet. Specifically, users will most likely see online notices that new patches are available, and simply download and install them themselves. Thus, your department will lose control of a process that they customarily managed. And more importantly, if you do not have an inventory program, you will not know when a user has taken the initiative to install his or her own patch or fix.

Many companies find that a good inventory also helps cut costs indirectly. For example, you can reduce money spent on support by managing warranty information better to ensure that products covered by warranties are serviced by vendors. Warranty information can easily be stored in a hardware inventory database.

Another way to use asset management information to reduce the recurring costs of ownership is to look for trends in this data and head off problems before they occur. For example, a company can reduce the amount they spend on labor and parts for emergency repairs by using equipment service histories (stored in an asset management database) to become proactive in managing equipment. Specifically, you can use service histories to schedule preventive maintenance on hardware identified as being likely to fail in use within a certain period of time. For example, by studying repair histories, you might notice that one brand of laptops experiences hard disk failures at a higher rate than other brands. For instance, you might notice that with one brand of laptop, the hard disk fails, on average, after one year of use, while all the other brands do not have a history of hard disk drive failures. You might take this information into account and make sure your remote users who have the same brand frequently back up their data (especially when they are approaching that one-year mark). You may also take this information into account when purchasing new equipment, avoiding this brand of laptop. And you might also use the information to do preventive maintenance and replace the troubled disk drive with a more reliable model.

The bottom line is that the recurring costs to support software and computer equipment dwarf the purchase price of the products. The way to reduce these costs is to have accurate inventory information to cut troubleshooting time when problems occur, to ensure that equipment covered under warranty is serviced by vendors and not internal staffers, and to head off problems by analyzing service history trends. All of these require accurate hardware and software inventory information.

Moving Toward More Automated Inventorying Systems

The current methods for performing hardware and software inventory work well in many cases. But life would be easier if programs and hardware components could somehow tell asset management systems more about themselves. For example, it would be simpler if hardware components could identify themselves to an asset management system, rather than you having to run a proprietary TSR that comes with an inventorying program on every PC.

Two industry initiatives are starting to tackle this issue. For software inventory, there's the Licensing Service application programming interface (LSAPI), which includes a series of program calls that provide licensing services from within an application.

LSAPI provides a common way for applications to pass licensing information to an inventory or metering program. The inventory function can either be built into a network operating system, or it can be performed by a third-party utility program. Microsoft and Novell plan to include LSAPI in their operating systems. Other vendors who have either already adopted or say they'll adopt LSAPI include Apple Computer Inc. (Cupertino, California), Banyan Systems Inc. (Westborough, Massachusetts), Digital Equipment Corp. (Maynard, Massachusetts), IBM's Lotus Development Corp. (Cambridge, Massachusetts), McAfee & Associates (Santa Clara, California), and Oracle Corp. (Redwood Shores, California). As with most standards, adoption of LSAPI has been slow. However, once LSAPI is commonly deployed in applications, it will be easy for administrators to identify software on their networks.

On the hardware inventory standards front, the Desktop Management Task Force (DMTF) is leading the way. The thrust of the DMTF effort is the Desktop Management Interface (DMI), which specifies a common way of accessing the hardware and software components in a desktop PC. The main function of the DMI is to provide a way for management systems to access the information about a PC's internal components. The way the DMTF accomplishes this is through the use of a common application programming interface (API) that will make it easier for third-party network management software vendors to write applications to access information about a desktop PC's components (see " Looking Under the Hood").

The founding members of the DMTF included some of the industry's biggest players: Digital Equipment Corp., Hewlett-Packard Co., IBM, Intel Corp., Microsoft Corp., Novell Inc., and SunConnect. Most of the major PC manufacturers, including AST, Compaq, Dell, Hewlett-Packard, IBM, and NEC, have embraced DMI and are incorporating DMI-compliant components into their PCs.

Most recently, the DMTF has tackled the issue of DMI for remote computers. The latest version of the DMI specification uses Remote Procedure Calls (RPCs) to retrieve inventory information from remote computers when they connect to a network. The rationale for using RPCs is that most operating systems now include native support for RPC technology. For example, operating system vendors such as Microsoft, Novell, Apple Computer, and Sun Microsystems include RPCs with their offerings. The DMTF's DMI 2.0 specification supports three types of RPCs, including RPCs for DCE (distributed computing environment), ONC (open network computing), and TI RPC (transport independent RPC).

Looking Under the Hood

The Desktop Management Task Force (DMTF) has developed a set of specifications that, once adopted by equipment manufacturers, will make hardware inventory easier. The specifications, called the Desktop Management Interface (DMI), were finalized early in 1996. Over 150 vendors have pledged support for the standard.

The DMI defines a format of a management agent for desktop systems. Figure 17-2 shows that the DMI architecture is a layered model that allows a wide range of software and hardware components to pass along information about themselves to an asset management system. The layers of the DMI architecture include a management interface (MI), a service layer, a component interface (CI), and Management Information Files (MIFs).

The management interface resides between an asset management system and the devices. This interface is used to pass requests for data about a device from the management system to the device. Each component has a vendor-supplied MIF that describes the device. The service layer uses the information stored in a MIF database to interpret what exactly is being requested. The CI makes calls to component management software routines, which when run, yield the information requested by the asset management program.

Reducing Support Costs: Hardware Issues

You'd think that something as straightforward as keeping track of computer equipment would be a snap. It's far from it. One Fortune 100 company that purchased 250 laptops for its sales force in 1989 could account for fewer than 60 percent of the machines four years later, according to the Personal Computer Assets Management Institute (an organization that studies the issues of controlling the operational costs associated with using large numbers of PCs in corporations).

These laptop computers were not stolen, they simply are unaccounted for. As people changed jobs within the company, they either took the laptops with them to their new job or left the laptop for their replacement to use. If a LAN staffer needed to find a particular machine to service it or to replace a part under warranty, it could take numerous phone calls to locate the laptop.

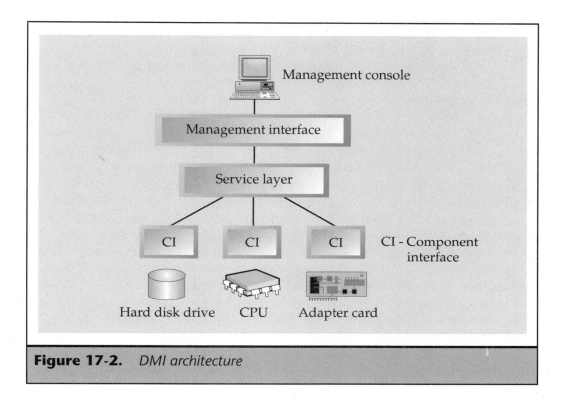

Figure 17-2. *DMI architecture*

Many companies find it difficult to keep track of mobile computers and computers and equipment in remote sites and in the homes of telecommuters. (Many companies have the same difficulties tracking onsite equipment.) And that can be a problem when it comes to supporting users. You can't provide effective support if you don't know what is installed in remote sites and users' homes.

As was the case with performing a software inventory, one way to collect information about the hardware is to send staffers around to every PC and have them tear open each machine to examine the contents. In this asset inventory process, they will also have to run a utility program to determine the amount of memory the PC has, which processor is used, the storage capacity of the hard disk, and other parameters along those lines.

Such manual tracking of assets takes time—an estimated 30 minutes per PC. That can add up to considerable time for a network of even modest size—one LAN staffer can spend an entire week inventorying as few as 80 PCs, and that is if the PCs are in the same location. If you add travel time to visit small remote sites and each telecommuter's home office, you are talking about significantly more time required for each computer.

While you may decide it is worth the investment in your LAN staff's time to perform such an inventory, the benefits you can derive from this information will be short lived. The information will only be valid for a short time, since computer systems are not static.

Departments are constantly adding users and equipment. A small remote site that had five users and two printers last year might now have two more computers, a networked CD-ROM drive, and an additional printer. Your remote users also might upgrade frequently, adding components inside each PC over time. For instance, some of your telecommuters might have added sound cards and more memory to their PCs. Thus, the information gathered by a manual asset audit will quickly be outdated.

Furthermore, a manual audit will not alert your staff to changes that occur. For instance, you might set up a small remote office with networked applications, such as a word processing program, to use specific printers for output. If one of the printers is moved or taken off the network, you will only know that this change has occurred when users call to complain that they can't get a printout of their document.

Increasingly, the information gathered in an asset inventory is crucial to network support and to planning enhancements and changes. For example, your company may decide to standardize on a particular application, such as Microsoft Word. Upper management will ask you, as the network administrator, to estimate what it will cost to move everyone over to that application. To figure the costs, you will need to know how many people have machines on their desktop with the processing power, hard disk space, and memory to run Windows and the application.

If you have an up-to-date inventory of hardware stored in a database, you can determine how many older PCs—286s and slow 386s—will need to be replaced with machines that can run Windows, and how much memory you will need to buy for all of the older PCs with only 640K of random access memory. The data collected by a manual inventory might help with such a calculation, but depending on how long it's been since the inventory was taken to the present time, you'll have less confidence in how accurate the information is and whether it reflects the true state of the equipment used by your remote users. You could send a person out to perform another inventory. But that wastes staff time. And how often will this process need to be repeated? Will you need to do an inventory every time there's a new application to be deployed?

There is a way around this problem—one that reduces the cost of collecting the information compared with the cost of using the manual approach. Take advantage of the connection to the network every time a remote user dials in. To that extent, many managers would like a program that automatically probes a remote computer and performs an asset inventory when the dial-up connection is made.

There are several utility programs that perform this type of task on a stand-alone PC, automatically collecting information such as the amount of memory; how much of that is base, expanded, and extended memory; the size of the hard disk drive; how much of that space is free; what type of video graphics card is used; how many floppy disk drives there are and what capacity each has; how many serial and parallel ports there are; what CPU is in the machine; and what BIOS is used.

This information can be used in several ways. First, it can help troubleshoot problems called into the support department. A program that automatically collects hardware information gives the support staffer answering a call instant access to the most current configuration of the caller's equipment. This can help you analyze the caller's problem. For example, it may be that the user has loaded a new application with the incorrect video display driver or printer driver. Or, in some cases, the caller's PC may not have enough memory for the program to run.

But troubleshooting is only one time-saving benefit of using such hardware inventory programs. Another important use of such programs is to exploit the program's database by adding additional information about devices used by remote users. For instance, as was mentioned earlier, many network administrators now add warranty and service contract information to the database. In that way, they can instantly see if a defective component is under warranty or if it has been serviced recently.

You can also store notes about a device's history in the database. This information can then be used by you and your staff to become more proactive in your support and planning. For instance, the information might be used to identify that one vendor's hard disk drive crashes more frequently than others. If such a trend can be spotted, the component that is more likely to fail can be replaced with a more reliable piece of equipment.

Another way that the information can be used in a proactive sense is to spot trends in usage. For instance, by looking at how much data is being stored on hard disks companywide over several months, you can estimate when server disk space will run out for your small remote offices. Then, rather than waiting for the lack of disk space to become a problem, you can plan disk and storage upgrades in the appropriate time frame to ensure that users will have enough storage capacity to accommodate their files. This will head off problems.

Additionally, the trend-analysis that can be performed by use of the data will help convince management that there is a problem in the making that needs to be addressed. This hard data that you've collected should make it easier to justify an expense, such as hard disk upgrades, to management.

There are two industry initiatives that should make the process of collecting information from remote sites and single user locations easier. As was the case with software inventory, the Desktop Management Task Force's (DMTF) DMI initiative will gather much hardware information from remote systems and make it available to a centrally administered asset management system. The other initiative, called the remote monitoring (RMON) management standard, will make it easier to track and manage network devices such as hubs, bridges, and routers in small remote offices.

The thrust of the DMTF is the Desktop Management Interface (DMI) that specifies a common way of accessing the hardware and software components in a desktop PC. The main function of the DMI is to provide a way for management systems to access the information about a PC's internal components. The way the DMTF accomplishes this is through the use of a common application programming interface (API) that will make it easier for third-party network management software vendors to write applications to access information about a desktop PC's components.

One obstacle to full acceptance of the DMTF is that many network systems are already managed by the Simple Network Management Protocol (SNMP). In fact, SNMP is the de facto standard for managing most network equipment—virtually all higher-level management systems use SNMP as the common ground to gather information about problems on networks. Because of the universal acceptance of SNMP, the DMTF felt there should be a level of interoperability between the two management approaches so that products that complied with the DMTF specifications could also be managed through an SNMP management system.

In that way, a network manager could essentially choose one higher-level management system, such as an enterprise management system, and use it to manage everything on the network from the PC's internal components to the internetworking equipment linking all of the devices.

The way to link the two systems (DMTF and SNMP) is to let both access the management information each system stores about devices. With the DMTF, descriptive information about PC components is stored in Management Information Files (MIFs). With SNMP systems, the information is contained in a management information base (MIB), which is a database of network objects controlled by a management console. MIFs and MIBs, having been developed for different purposes by different organizations, have different structures. That means MIFs must somehow be converted or mapped to MIB format in order to be of any use with an SNMP management system.

The second of the two initiatives, RMON, will also make automatic network inventory and assessment easier. RMON was developed by the Remote Network Monitoring Working Group of the Internet Engineering Task Force.

The idea behind RMON is to distribute, throughout a network, probes (called *RMON agents*) that will collect information about the operation of the piece of hardware they are installed in. RMON technology has already been incorporated into devices such as hubs, routers, and servers. In a typical application using RMON, one probe would be located on each LAN segment. The probe would monitor data transmission on that segment and organize the information it collects into a format that is easy for the management system to use.

The type of information an RMON probe might collect is how many packets and what size packets are transmitted on the LAN segment. It will also look at the number of packets broadcast and collisions. Among other things, this information could be used to spot a defective adapter card on the segment that is bombarding the LAN with bad packets, causing poor performance. Such information would be quite useful when users in a small remote site call complaining about slow network response times. You could dial into the LAN in the remote office and retrieve the pertinent RMON data to help you diagnose a performance problem.

As was discussed in Chapter 10, RMON probes can also collect a trace of the traffic on the LAN segment over time. This can be used to study traffic patterns and perform trend-analysis of the bandwidth demands of the users on that segment. One of the most important features of RMON is that it can also be used to send alerts and alarms to network management systems when a preset threshold of some network parameter has been exceeded—for instance, if collisions exceed a normal level.

The benefit of RMON is that it automatically collects information about the traffic on a LAN segment that is in a remote location.

Without RMON, if you're responsible for LANs in several remote sites, you might have to purchase diagnostic tools for each location or have LAN staffers inefficiently use their time driving from site to site with one piece of equipment. RMON makes the process more efficient in several ways. First, it acts as the analyzer on each segment. That immediately reduces the amount of diagnostic equipment you need and cuts down on the time your staff spends moving equipment around. Second, unlike using a traditional diagnostic tool, you don't have to physically go to the LAN segment having trouble to diagnose the problem. You can access the information from a centrally located management console. And third, RMON, by virtue of letting you preset performance threshold levels, can spot a problem in the making, alert you to the problem, and let you take corrective action before the users on your network notice anything has happened.

More Intelligent Upgrades

Having good asset information is essential to cutting support costs. But the same information can also be used to more intelligently plan major upgrades and full-blown migrations.

To give you an idea of how a good inventory of remote equipment can help you plan major software changes, ask yourself the following questions. Do you know how many PCs are in all of your remote sites and telecommuters' homes? You could probably make a ballpark guess at the number. But could you quickly estimate how much memory you'd need to buy to bring every machine in the corporation up to, say, a minimum of 16MB each? Probably not.

Unfortunately, this type of information is essential for budgeting. And it's not just a matter of knowing how many XTs, 286s, 386s, 486s, or Pentiums are installed in remote sites and telecommuters' homes. You need to know the detailed configuration of each machine.

After all, if your company decides to standardize on an application that only supports SVGA (super VGA) or higher resolution displays, you will need to know how many video adapter cards and monitors to buy to upgrade PCs with lower-resolution graphics. Or if you are upgrading everyone to Windows 95, you need to know how many remote PCs have the processing power, memory, and hard disk space required to run the operating system.

When it comes to purchasing software, there are several ways a good inventory helps in the planning process. Mostly, you can leverage the information in an asset database to, in many cases, pay less for software by taking advantage of volume purchasing deals and by buying based on usage trends and not by head count.

For many corporations, the cost of using software is out of control. Support costs and upgrade fees can dwarf the initial licensing fees over the lifetime of an application. And in most companies, software purchasing is decentralized, which leads to higher per-license fees for commonly used applications.

Savvy administrators cut the costs of software ownership by studying software usage patterns within their organizations. They use this information to help guide their software purchasing and support strategies. The key to such cost-reduction efforts is having information available to make a more intelligent choice of a product.

What information is important? It can be something as simple as knowing that only half of the people in one division use a particular application. Or, it could be something more complicated, such as determining that one department is responsible for a disproportionate number of calls to a helpdesk with questions about using an application. To gather information about software usage patterns, companies typically turn to software metering and inventory programs.

The basic function of a metering or inventory program is to ensure that the terms of software licensing agreements are abided by. Metering programs do this by allowing you to limit the number of users who simultaneously access a particular application. For instance, if a company has licensed Microsoft Word for 300 users, a metering program would let 300 people run Word and refuse all other users until one of the 300 quits the application, freeing up a license. Metering can easily be applied to remote sites that connect to the central network. And, if your telecommuters are entering the network in remote node mode, their use of some centrally maintained applications can also be metered.

Software inventory programs offer a more passive form of license compliance by allowing managers to know what is running on their network and in their remote sites. Inventory programs produce lists of the applications residing on network and local drives, and these lists can be matched to software purchasing invoices to demonstrate that the company has indeed obeyed the terms of the licensing agreements.

Usually, corporations buy metering and inventory programs with the intent of using them for these compliance tasks. They can often justify the cost of the metering or inventory program based on the reduced liability risk of fines that would result if, for example, unlicensed software was discovered in an audit by the Software Publishers Association (SPA, Washington, D.C.).

However, you can exploit the more advanced features of metering programs, such as logging usage by application and the ability to manage licenses so that they can be shared, to drive down software costs.

One way companies save money using the advanced features of metering and inventory tools is to reduce the amount of money they spend on licenses. Many companies license software by the node—buying one license per desktop—instead of opting for some form of concurrent licensing agreement.

Often companies that license *one-for-one license-per-user,* say there are good reasons to do so. For example, many believe this method of purchasing software guarantees compliance with licensing agreements and avoids trouble with SPA audits. Secondly, many companies say that they are decentralized (at least when it comes to software purchasing), and they leave the software-buying decisions to each department.

While both reasons are valid, metering and inventory tools can be used to make sure there are no licensing agreement violations and that departments still have some control over their purchases. At the same time, a company can still save money.

For example, you could let individual departments choose their own desktop applications, but still maintain some centralized control over purchases. This would let your organization leverage volume-purchasing strategies that could lead to discounts of as much as 60 percent, based on typical volume discounts and site-licensing agreements offered by application vendors.

This is the simplest way to save money on software. To reap these savings requires better management of the software purchasing process. After all, most remote sites will settle on products from one or two vendors for each desktop application (for example, WordPerfect or Word for word processing, and Lotus 1-2-3 or Excel for a spreadsheet). Yet they purchase the applications separately in small quantities.

A software inventory program can help manage the process by letting you determine which applications are in use and in what quantities. By knowing the real number of licenses that you need, you can negotiate price with vendors.

Another way to save money on licensing fees is to move from one-for-one license-per-user, to *concurrent licensing.* And metering programs allow this change. So instead of licensing software by the copy and putting it on each remote user's workstation, you would put the software on a server and license by use, allowing you to maximize your software investment.

With concurrent licensing, a corporation pays for a certain number of licenses that is less than the total number of users on their network who will run the application. For example, a company may pay for 800 licenses even though 1,000 users may use the program. However, only 800 can use the program at one time. Most metering programs let you extend the metering service to remote sites and to telecommuters dialing into a network using remote node connections.

Metering programs, as noted, ensure a company is complying with concurrent licensing agreements by letting an administrator set a threshold that blocks access once the licensed number of users is running the application.

The savings from moving from a one-for-one basis to concurrent licensing are about 30 percent, according to the Personal Computer Assets Management Institute (PCAMI, Rochester, New York), a group of vendors and users that studies the cost of managing hardware and software assets in organizations. Some say that 30 percent figure is a little low, estimating that the savings can be closer to 40 percent.

Such savings can be substantial for organizations. For example, if concurrent licensing saves 30 percent compared with the cost of buying individual licenses, that translates into a one-time $90,000 savings if you have 1,000 users and you're buying a $300 program, such as Microsoft Access v2.0 for Windows or Lotus 1-2-3. The savings can be even greater for programs that perform a special function, such as an organizational flowchart package or a mapping program that prints directions between two locations. Such packages are often used by many people within an organization, but only a few times a year. Seldom are there more than a handful of people running the program at the same time. So instead of buying 1,000 copies of such a package, a company might be able to get away with a concurrent license for only six users.

Determining how many licenses are needed in a concurrent agreement is the tricky part. But that's where a metering program comes in. Using a metering program, you can study usage patterns and determine the proper number of licenses for each application.

One way to do this is to let users run all the applications they need without restricting access. Most metering programs let you run in this mode to gather data and then visually display the information so it is easy to spot the patterns. Examining the information from an unrestricted metering test, you can determine how many licenses are needed.

One note of caution. There's some debate in the industry about the liability risks when collecting information in this manner. Hard-liners in the licensing agreement legal area say that allowing more users to access an application than you have valid licenses for is a violation of the licensing agreement, and your company will be subject to fines. But others in the industry say that if you only do such exploratory runs to determine the proper number of licenses, you should be okay.

However, to strictly comply with the terms of licensing agreements, this method of letting users freely access applications is not okay. Acknowledging this, some companies choose to forego this method and take a best guess as to the number of licenses they need. Once the application is on the network, they use a metering program's data-collection ability to study usage trends and to adjust the number of licenses in future purchases.

Still, the ability to examine trends in usage and to license accordingly will save money. How much can be saved varies by application, company, and even by department.

For example, Household Credit Services (HCS), a consumer finance firm responsible for several private-label "affinity" credit cards, such as the GM MasterCard and the Ameritech Complete MasterCard, said it would save $800,000 over a two-year period just on the licensing fees for one software package, Microsoft Office.

Microsoft had recommended that Household, which has 4,300 nodes connected to 53 file servers in three sites, choose a per-seat license for Office. However, by using a metering program (SiteMeter from McAfee), the company measured concurrent software usage for each server and found that concurrent usage of Microsoft Office rarely exceeded 10 percent. As a result of the findings, HCS decided to purchase a concurrent usage license instead of the per-seat license. The company estimated the initial savings of approximately $312 per user for customer service personnel, who rarely use Office, and $31.25 per user for administrative personnel, who use Office more frequently.

With concurrent licensing, cost savings can vary depending on whether a company licenses for the *maximum* number of users or the *average* number of users. Licensing based on average use for an application saves more money because fewer licenses are needed. The choice between licensing for average demand or maximum demand often has a lot to do with corporate culture. When licensing for average demand, there will always be peak periods when some users are blocked from an application. Some companies find this unacceptable and license for maximum usage.

However, if your company does choose to license for average usage, many metering programs make life a little easier than you might imagine. For instance, most display a message (with the relevant information such as how many other users are waiting) on the blocked user's screen telling them they've been placed in a queue. When a license is freed up, the user is notified, and he or she has the option of taking the license or passing. This is acceptable to many users.

Many metering programs have an option that allows certain classes of users to always have access to licenses. For example, a network administrator may designate that ten licenses out of 500 are only to be used by the company's ten executives. Or, you can ensure that marketing has more licenses for a presentation manager application available to it than, say, the engineering department does, even though users in both departments may frequently use the application.

One sociological aspect that you might find when metering is used is license hoarding. It's the nature of people to hoard when quantities are limited, whether it's food or software licenses. License hoarding can be intentional, but often it is unintentional. Many users simply load every application they ever need into their StartUp Group within Windows. This may seem logical to them. And they may even think they are saving the company money by being more efficient—having the application a mouse click away when they need it, instead of having to wait for it to load each time they use it.

However, these users may not realize they might be blocking access to an application for a user who really needs it. To help in matters such as this, some metering programs have *inactivity trackers* that can determine when a user simply loads a program and never uses it. Such programs use agent software, which intercepts common calls, that detects when a window is open. This helps the metering program to determine, for example, whether a program is being used or is simply sitting on a user's desktop as an icon or is minimized within a Windows desktop.

Knowing how long programs sit idle on users' desktops can help you negotiate with department heads when it comes to purchasing additional licenses. For example, one department may lobby upper management to buy additional licenses of Excel because they simply cannot tolerate having any of their personnel locked out of the application. A preliminary check of the software usage pattern may indicate that everyone in the department runs Excel (when licenses are available), so the purchase of additional licenses may indeed be warranted. However, with the use of an inactivity tracker, a network administrator may also find that people are loading the application and not using it.

Information such as this allows you to make a sound decision. If the software is sitting idle, loaded but not being used, you might simply send out a memo explaining to users that they are costing the company money. On the other hand, if it turns out that all of the loaded applications are being used and many people are locked out of accessing the program, more licenses should be purchased. It doesn't matter what the decision is, as long as it is based on actual usage and not guesses.

Concurrent licensing is not the only way to save money with metering. Another way is to reallocate or share underutilized licenses. This results in buying fewer licenses and can reduce overall software expenditures by as much as 30 percent, according to the PCAMI.

It happens all the time. Many companies have software licenses that simply go unused. For example, an accounting department may have 100 licenses for Lotus 1-2-3, but the most licenses they ever use is 75. At the same time, an expanding marketing department brings in 25 new employees and buys an additional 25 licenses of the same package. The company could have saved the cost of those additional licenses by reassigning the 25 unused licenses from accounting to marketing.

In 1995, the PCAMI estimated that U.S. companies, government, and military organizations would spend as much as $2 billion on software they already owned. Situations such as this can be avoided using a software inventory program that would let you know what software is sitting on the network and the local drives, as well as on the drives of remote users. With this information, you could easily size up the situation and, in the preceding example, save the cost of 25 licenses, or about $7,500 (that's based on an average retail price of Lotus 1-2-3 Release 5.0 for Windows of about $300).

Besides saving money by identifying unused programs and shifting them to departments that need them, many metering programs allow for the dynamic reallocation of licenses between servers. This is different than simply finding unused licenses within a company and making a one-time transfer of those licenses to another department. With license sharing, the licenses are transferred between groups on an as-needed basis.

For example, suppose the same accounting department only uses the 75 licenses at the end of the month to balance the company's books, but on a typical day uses a maximum of 60 licenses. By dynamically sharing the 15 licenses that sit idle for most of the month with another department, a company could save the cost of an additional 15 licenses.

Such dynamic reallocation can be conducted between sites. So, for example, if one small office needs three licenses of Word today, they may simply have them allocated from a server in the main office. Some companies took license sharing to the extreme by dynamically reallocating licenses across time zones—for instance, allocating them to users in Europe during their working hours, and then, after the close of business in Europe, reallocating them to users arriving for work on the West Coast. Thus, they got double duty out of each license and essentially cut the cost per license in half. This cross-time zone sharing was a short-lived phenomenon, since most application vendors reexamined their licensing agreements to plug this loophole. Several application vendors have said they never anticipated users would be able to do cross-time zone license sharing. Even if the licensing agreements were left the same, wide-area reallocation is an extreme for many companies. Most companies can save money by dynamically reallocating licenses within a smaller geographical area.

And the cost savings are not limited to 1,000-plus node networks. For example, consider the metering of 25 remote users in five remote offices. You may purchase a metering program for license compliance, but, like many managers, also find that you can save money on license purchases using information gather by the metering programs in conjunction with the blocking feature once the licenses are purchased. For instance, you might be able to cut the number of concurrent licenses for a word processing application from 16 to ten (a 37.5 percent savings) and purchase three instead of the current six licenses for a $150 project management application (for a $450 savings on that one application).

Cutting Support Costs with Metering

Metering programs can also be used to help cut support costs. A metering program will link application usage with a particular user. You can use this information about software usage and become more proactive in managing your remote users. For example, you might link software usage patterns with frequency of calls to a helpdesk to plan training programs that will reduce recurring calls.

Or, the program could use information to develop a hardware upgrade plan. For example, if you want to replace older computers with newer models, you may do so in a prudent manner. Instead of upgrading everyone in a day or week, the migration can be done gradually, leaving your staff time to handle normal duties.

The upgrade can be done in a way so that the people who need the replacement the most, get it first. For example, an engineering department that runs CAD/CAM programs would need the replacement sooner than a marketing group that is using a desktop publishing program.

Yet another way to reduce support costs is to use the information about software usage to charge-back the costs of support. With a decentrally managed network with many remote users, it is often hard to quantify support costs. And it has generally been impossible to properly bill-back the charges.

By use of the logging functions of metering programs, which track how often a person uses a program, you can charge-back support costs based on usage. Most often, these costs have been included in your department's operating budget because there is no way to fairly bill-back support charges to the departments. Metering programs, which track usage, allow equitable charge-backs for support.

The charge-back concept is not new. It's similar to a mainframe environment, where costs were charged-back based on usage of processing resources. It's not coincidental that software management strategies are in a sense reverting to the methods used in mainframe days. For many years,

LANs and equipment in remote sites have been allowed to proliferate without any centralized management. Now corporations are finding that the huge hidden costs of managing their resources such as software on these systems needs a centralized approach. Companies that have adopted such strategies are finding there are tremendous cost savings to be gained. The following list summarizes the major benefits from using software-metering applications:

- Ensures compliance with licensing agreements to avoid fines
- Centralizes software purchases to reap volume discounts
- Bases license purchases on usage, not one for each user
- Employs usage information to charge-back support costs to end users
- Links usage patterns with helpdesk calls to plan user training

Cutting Installation Costs

Metering can help you plan software purchases and helps control usage once an application is on the network. Getting the applications there is another task that can be automated for great cost savings.

In mainframe and minicomputer environments, software distribution was straightforward—a magnetic tape containing a new program or new version of an existing program was shipped to each site for installation. In contrast, the process of installing and updating software in today's distributed LAN-based environment is usually a time-consuming task where software is manually installed on every client workstation.

As networks get larger and users are more dispersed, there is a growing need to automate the software installation process. Enter *electronic software distribution* (ESD) software. ESD goes beyond the cloning methods of mainframe and minicomputer software distribution, where a program was simply copied from one machine to another. Such replication/cloning distribution programs are okay only if every client is the same. But that's hardly ever the case with PCs. Even machines with similar hardware can have vastly different software configurations.

When software is loaded onto a client, most often other files (such as autoexec.bat, config.sys, and .ini files) on the client need to be modified for that application to work. Additionally, there are a number of parameters (such as what type of monitor and printer the client uses) that must be set before the application can be installed.

ESD software automatically handles these tasks. Without ESD, you or one of your staffers would normally have to run from machine to machine in a remote site, editing files and entering answers to questions in an installation program. ESD packages eliminate the human element by including a centralized database of information about each client (including such items as amount of memory and type of network interface card drivers used). Such information is needed to properly install a new application.

When you start to use ESD software, the first step is to build this database of information. This can be done automatically by use of software and hardware inventory programs. Once the information is compiled, the ESD program is ready to run. From that point on, software can be installed automatically. For example, you might cascade an installation process so that a server in a small remote site is updated first. Then every user in that remote site will get the new software the next time they log onto that server. Similarly, when a telecommuter dials into a network in remote node mode and logs onto a server, the installation can start. For mobile workers, it might make more sense for their software installations to be done when they are in the office. For instance, if the mobile user has a docking station and connects his or her laptop to the network in the office, use that opportunity to install new software.

In a typical installation procedure, the ESD software would check the database before installing the software. It might find that one user's workstation has a VGA monitor, is attached to a LaserJet II Printer from Hewlett-Packard, and has a config.sys file set up for a large number of files (for example, FILES=60). Another workstation on an adjacent desk may have a super-VGA monitor, a medium-performance laser printer from Hewlett-Packard, and a different config.sys file (for example, FILES=20). The software would then take these factors into account when installing the application. It might, for instance, add a line in the config.sys file.

ESD saves you from performing monotonous, repetitive routines when loading new software. And this time savings translates into cost savings. Without ESD, software distribution and installation cost a company 21 percent more over a five-year life cycle of an application than the licensing fees for the software itself, according to the Gartner Group. Virtually all of the expense of installing and distributing software is the cost of labor by you and your staff. There are no hard figures that can tell you exactly how much time an ESD package will save if one is used on your network. However, some users claim ESD cuts the time to install and distribute software to somewhere between a fifth to a tenth of what it used to take without ESD.

While time savings is the primary advantage to using ESD, there are other reasons to use it. ESD also reduces the cost to support end users, because it performs a number of tasks that head off some typical problems that can occur when new software is installed. For instance, when a new version of a program is installed, its default settings may have a different printer driver than an existing program. When a user prints a document with the new package, an incorrect printer driver would produce either an unintelligible mess, or there would be nothing printed.

In either case, you or your staff will get calls from disgruntled users complaining that there's something wrong with their printers. That's if you're lucky. More often than not the caller will not pinpoint the problem that accurately.

Typically, you get a call saying there's something wrong with the network. And then you will have to start from ground zero with the process of troubleshooting the complaint. This could require a visit to a remote site and/or several hours of troubleshooting before the source of the printer problem is isolated.

The extent to which you automate software distribution may depend on corporate philosophy. Some companies give the LAN staff complete authority to make software changes. For example, you might notify everyone that in two weeks, on a particular night, all users will be automatically upgraded to the new version of a particular application. In this way, users do not have to get involved in the installation process at all.

That may be fine for some organizations. However, there may be cases when a department or a single user would rather wait a day. For example, if the accounting department needs to get quarterly statements out and is fearful that any small glitch that might arise with a new release of an application will derail their task and make them miss an important deadline, you can let that department postpone installation.

To accommodate different users, some ESD packages allow the user to decide when to make the upgrade. The deliver options are generically classified as *ESD-push* and *ESD-pull*. With push, you set a time and the delivery occurs. With pull, the user is notified upon logging onto the network that they are due for an upgrade and asked if they would like to start the process now.

Users like this option because it lets them start the upgrade or installation process at a time when it does not affect their work. For instance, one user might be a fast starter and want to get several tasks done right as the day begins. If he or she has to wait for a program installation to be performed, it might interfere with a deadline.

The downside to giving users the option of when to install is that you quickly have a network running different versions of the same application. This can add to the burden of supporting users. The faster you can synchronize all copies of an application, the better.

Some managers provide users the option of installing on logon or not. But many will give the users a time frame in which they must allow the installation process to occur. This approach satisfies most users and limits the time that you will have to support multiple versions of an application.

The Role of the Internet

Electronic software distribution (ESD) offers some interesting cost savings for remote users. But generally ESD has the most benefit when you're upgrading LAN-attached users in remote offices. That is because most of the ESD software is LAN-based and relies on a user connecting to a server for the installation process to take place.

Such software leaves out remote users who are not LAN attached. To help your telecommuters, you might get around this problem by performing software distribution when the user connects to your corporate network in remote node mode. But then you are dealing with the issue of paying for bandwidth to send the software over the dial-up connection. Such charges can be substantial if you have many long-distance users and you are installing, for example, something like Microsoft Office that requires in the tens of megabytes of data to be installed.

One way to avoid telecommunications fees is to perform software distribution over the Internet. Commonly, your remote users will pay a set amount per month for their Internet connection. Also typically, the remote user will only require a local telephone call to connect to the Internet instead of a long-distance call to your company.

ESD programs aimed at the Internet are just starting to emerge. One of the first that offered the high-end feature that would be needed in a corporate ESD application was introduced in summer 1996. At that time, a software and document distribution package called the Web Transporter was introduced by Megasoft Online (Freehold, New Jersey). Web Transporter addressed many of the problems that had limited the usefulness of web-based distribution programs.

Web Transporter offered a secure way to install software and transfer documents while also providing tools to monitor, track, automate, and customize the distribution process over a corporate intranet or the Internet.

This can be quite useful in a number of ways. For example, this process can be used to distribute new applications, updates, and patches to existing applications.

The web-based distribution program made use of three components—a server module, a client module, and a module called a Packager—to provide the mechanism not only to transfer files and documents, but also to track the entire process.

One component of the package is the Web Transporter Server module, an add-on that plugs into a standard web server and requires the use of Netscape Navigator 2.x and Netscape Commerce Server.

The server module provides activity tracking and reporting features. For example, when a new version of a software package is made available, a manager can see which users have (or, perhaps more importantly, have not) downloaded this newest version. The client part of the Web Transporter runs on each user's desktop system and operates as a plug-in to the Netscape Navigator browser.

To download software, a user simply points his or her browser at the server running the Web Transporter Server module. In a typical operation, the manager will have set up a web page on that server that shows a user all of the software packages or documents that are available for download. A user simply clicks on the package he or she wants to install. At this point, the client module runs a series of operations that enables the installation and configuration of the software.

The way this works is that the client software executes instructions contained in a file, called a *wrapper file*, that is created by the Web Transporter Packager. The Packager is a server-based tool that lets a manager automate the installation process. A manager can specify what level of authorization a user must provide before software is downloaded. Additionally, a manager can program the system to perform some common checks that will aid in software installation. For example, the instructions in the wrapper file might pass along the file sizes and ask the client software to check to see if there is enough disk space on the desktop computer. You can even include an online license registration form for the user to fill out and instructions to launch an installation program on the client once the files are transferred to the client.

The program is equally useful in delivering documents. For example, the client can be instructed to acknowledge receipt of an electronic document, logging this transaction in a database (something that is increasingly being required in some industries such as insurance and finance). Additionally, you can easily make current information (a price list for a salesperson, for example) available to remote and mobile users.

Distributing documents over the Internet offers lots of advantages over straight dial-up methods, according to analysts at Forrester Research. Mobile users have the most frequent customer contact, and document delivery on demand is essential for these people, according to Forrester.

Web Transporter is just the first product in the ESD market to make use of the Internet while also addressing many of the issues you would need to cover for a widespread Internet-based ESD plan. Megasoft's Web Transporter offers a number of features that improve on the commonly used simple file transfer approach to distributing software over intranets and the Internet. Table 17-1 summarizes the issues that you will need to address before using an Internet-based software distribution program. A tool that meets these conditions would let you get new software and upgrades to your remote users over the Internet while making the installation process an automatic one for them.

Feature	Its Use and Importance
Security	Manager-selectable levels of security range from the use of a simple password to user authentication linked to preassigned access rights.
Built-in acknowledgments of file delivery	Client software sends acknowledgments to server verifying that files were received.
Tracking system	Server software tracks operations so managers know, for example, which users have the most recent version of a software package.
Compression	Supports standard compression programs so files can be more efficiently transported over the network.

Table 17-1.   *Features Required with an Internet-Based Software Distribution Package*

Chapter Eighteen

Coping with User Isolation and Frustration

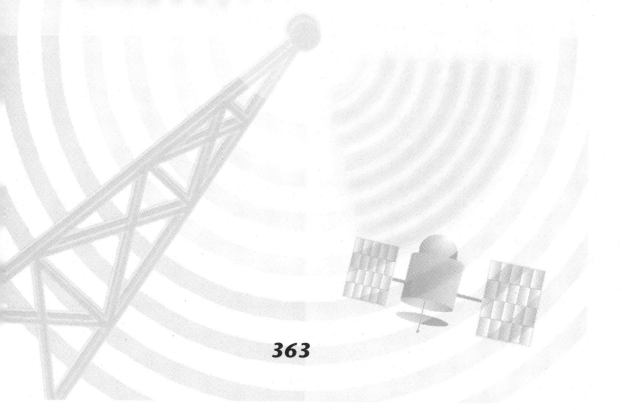

I t isn't easy being a road warrior. Not only are they dealing with time crunches, lost luggage, and the vagaries of life outside the office, they are also suffering from isolation from the rest of the corporation, and the incomplete communication that such isolation brings.

Your Role as the Communications Gatekeeper

As a network manager responsible for remote communications, you're maintaining the umbilical cord that keeps your remote users not only productive, but also connected—professionally and socially—with the happenings at the home office. No matter how well you do your job, you're going to find that your remote users occasionally feel neglected and uninformed. Luckily, however, there are many things you can do to improve communication with your remote users and lessen their feelings of isolation and frustration when they do occur.

Here are a few things that have worked for me.

Don't Rely on E-mail Alone

E-mail is quick, easy, reliable, and nearly universal. Therefore, it's very tempting to use it as your only means of communication with remote users. After all, e-mail is the foundation of remote communication, and was probably the first and foremost reason your remote users started demanding remote access to the corporate network.

Tempting as it is, however, e-mail is a slippery tool for communicating effectively with remote users. As anyone who has used electronic mail knows, it's hard to convey the appropriate tone via this medium, and thus it's very easy to misunderstand and/or misinterpret the intent of an electronic missal. This can quickly reinforce the remote users' pre-existing feelings of isolation, and lead to a breakdown in communication rather than a bolstering of it. In fact (as nearly every network manager has experienced), misconstrued e-mails have bred hostility and even instigated corporate wars.

Furthermore, electronic mail often has the feeling of being a form of mass media, with the same message being directed to the entire world. Remember that your remote users are probably already feeling some separation anxiety and its accompanying anonymity, much of it brought on by the very electronic innovations that enable them to do their jobs. Therefore, it's important to base

your communications on a more personal relationship with your users. Here
are some ways to do that.

Administrative Considerations

The first set of suggestions all have to do with how you administer your
remote users as a group. Because their use of and needs for accessing the
corporate network are far different from that of your local users, you'll need to
consider special ways to manage them.

Directory Services

Have your remote users in their own group (see Figure 18-1) so that they
receive special messages and services when they log in. Remote users have

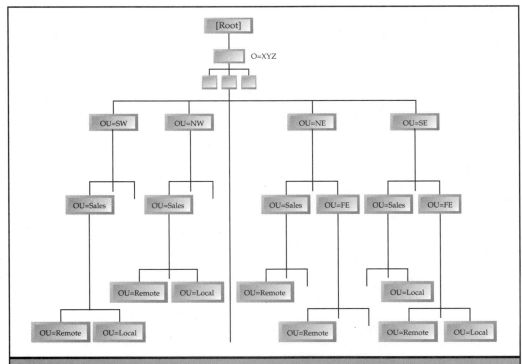

Figure 18-1.   *Setting up remote users as a separate group (shown here
in Novell Directory Services) can make for more effective
communications*

special needs, and creating a special group for them makes it easier and more efficient for you to meet those needs. Sending broadcast messages, special e-mail instructions, and remote access client software updates, are all facilitated by using a separate group for remote access users.

Training, Training, Training

All remote users should receive thorough training before being set free to roam the streets and access the corporate network at will (see Figure 18-2). As the network manager, you should take the initiative to ensure that all remote users are adequately trained.

This initial requirement for training is going to be met with a lot of resistance. Remote users by their very nature are scattered far and wide, and come to the main office very infrequently. Nonetheless, in all but the most extreme circumstances, remote users should be required to come into the main office for a training session before their remote access login is activated. This gives them a chance to

- Become thoroughly familiar with the procedure for remote logins
- Understand software upgrade requirements and schedules
- Learn corporate remote access policy
- Learn how to avoid problems with remote access
- Acquire basic troubleshooting skills
- Meet the support staff that will be helping them with problems

Figure 18-2. *Scheduling training for remote users is a challenge, but it's well worth the effort*

Not only does this help prepare remote users for the situations they will encounter using remote access in the field, it also prevents potential remote access problems. Most important of all, it helps build a personal relationship between the network management staff and the remote users, facilitating effective communication among them.

Documentation

You're probably thinking, "I have time to either manage remote access or document it—but not both." I understand the dilemma, but good user documentation is critical to a successful remote access system. Second only to training, documentation is your most important aid in getting remote access users self-sufficient and productive.

Make preparing effective remote user documentation a top priority. If you truly don't have the staff to accomplish it in-house, you may want to hire a contract documentation expert to develop your remote access user documentation. Having excellent documentation is vital to the success of your remote access system, so it's definitely worth the extra expense.

Whatever means you choose to develop your documentation, it should be in the form of comprehensive, step-by-step instructions on how to dial up, log into, and use your corporate network via your remote communications system. It should also include a section on troubleshooting, as well as how to get help—before, during, and after regular work hours—from the network management staff. When you're traveling, the term "business hours" loses meaning. Often a remote user desperately needs help that can't wait until the office opens in the morning.

Communications Hints

The second group of management tips falls under the heading of effective communication. Although communication is supposed to be what remote access is all about, simply implementing a remote access system doesn't automatically mean that you as a network manager will communicate frequently and effectively with your remote users.

Broadcast Messages

In conjunction with establishing a separate group for remote users via directory services, broadcast messages can be a great help in conveying vital information to remote users the moment they log in. A broadcast message addressed only to remote users will splash across their screens right after they enter their passwords, informing them of impending software updates, virus alerts, changes in corporate remote access policy, and other critical information that must be disseminated immediately. See Figure 18-3.

I have used broadcast messages successfully for years for managing both local and remote users. I began using something as simple as the broadcast feature in Saber's menuing tools. These days, there are even more sophisticated tools for composing and delivering broadcast tools. One in particular, PointCast's I-Server, shown in Figure 18-3, ties into corporate intranets, delivering critical data concisely and pointing to the appropriate page on the corporate intranet for amplification.

Intranet

Speaking of intranets, it's a good idea to have a special page for remote users. This provides a familiar place for them to go to find all the necessary information quickly. This page can include pointers to online training sessions, documentation, online troubleshooting help, and a place to leave e-mail messages for help desk staff members.

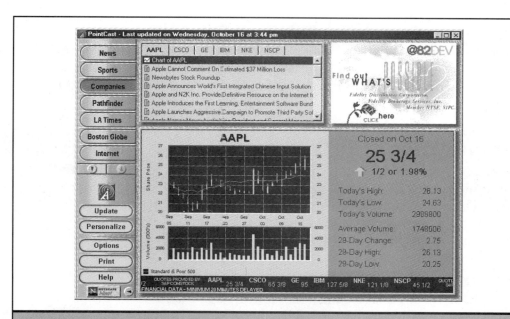

Figure 18-3. *Broadcast messages can improve communication with remote users. This one is from PointCast I-Server.*

Electronic Conferencing

Electronic conferencing is another effective means of communicating with remote users. By its very nature, it lends itself nicely to bringing together a group of widely dispersed users to share information that all of them need. It also enables remote users to get to know one another and share any tips they've discovered for better using remote access and solving any problems they've encountered with it.

Hold Periodic Road Warrior Meetings

Depending upon the nature of your organization, this may not be feasible after the first training sessions. However, if your remote users have occasion to visit the main office (such as quarterly sales meetings), it might be a good idea to organize a Remote User Meeting to discuss any problems they may have had and any plans you may have for the future of the remote access system. From my experience, I do have a couple of hints for holding a successful Road Warrior Convention:

- Be sure it's at a convenient time. You can't please everyone, but try to avoid major scheduling conflicts.

- Make it brief. Remote users are by definition people on the go. Make the meeting thorough, but concise.

- Feed them. Nothing attracts people like food. Road warriors are no exception.

Don't Do Anything Without Several Weeks of Pre-announcement, If Possible

Road warriors don't always check in as frequently as you'd like—and they *never* check in as often as local users. This means that several hours or even days may pass before they check their electronic mail. Therefore, it's very easy for them to miss an e-mail sent at, say, 4:00 P.M., announcing that the electronic mail gateway will be down from 6:00 P.M. until midnight that same night. Such short notice can easily leave your remote users high and dry without access to the corporate network.

It's especially vital for remote users to have access to the corporate network *when* they need it. Cutting them off because they missed an upgrade or a password change is dooming them to failure and potential embarrassment in front of clients (imagine trying to dial in to pull up the latest price list, and having your-login fail because your password is invalid).

Newsletters Are Always Nice

It may be an electronic world, but you can't discount the continuing affinity for paper. After all, you can't fold up an e-mail, stuff it into your pocket, and peruse it over lunch or a quick cup of coffee at an airport counter.

The newsletter doesn't have to be elaborate. It can be little more than an informative flyer, as shown in Figure 18-4. Just remember that it's a supplement to your communication with your remote access users, not the foundation of it.

Consider Establishing a Remote User Hot Line

This can be a pager number, a special 800 number (this is especially important for remote users, since they need quick and easy access to this information, and long-distance credit card calls aren't always that easy to make).

The Road Warrior Chronicles
The Source of News for
XYZ Corporation's Remote Access Users

August 1996

Software Upgrade!

Be prepared for some delays when you log in next Tuesday. As part of our ongoing effort to ensure that we have the best client software to meet your needs, we will begin a system-wide client software upgrade that day. The latest version of Symantec's PCAnywhere will be automatically downloaded when you log in. The upgrade schedule is:

Sales Department   Aug. 1 - Aug. 5
Field Engineering   Aug. 6 - Aug. 20
Field Operations   Aug. 21 - Aug. 31

If you have any questions about the schedule, or encounter any difficulty during the download/upgrade, please contact **Jeri Johanssen at 972-555-8824.**

Southwest Regional Remote Access Server Unavailable

The remote access server for the Southwest Region Sales staff will be down for routine maintenance on Saturday, August 16, from 12 noon until 6 p.m. You will be unable to dial in to the corporate network during this time.

Password Change Coming!

This is just an advance reminder that mandatory quarterly password changes will go into effect on Monday, September 30. When you log in via remote access on or after that date, you will be required to select a new password. Start thinking up a new password now!

Figure 18-4.   *Sample newsletter page*

Now You Can Use E-mail

Of course, there's always good old e-mail. Use it liberally, but:

- Consider it a supplement to the other types of communication
- Be considerate

Using e-mail can add the personal touch to communications with remote users—something that a broadcast message can't always do. However, don't clutter their mailboxes with unnecessary and/or disorganized information. You don't want them to set up a rule excluding all your e-mails!

Keeping all your remote users informed and productive isn't easy. However, you're wise to consider it a vital part of your job. As I described in this chapter, you have several means at your disposal to bring your road warriors into the loop. The more ways you use, the less confusion and frustration both you and they will experience.

Chapter Nineteen

Loyalty and Enforcing Corporate Policy

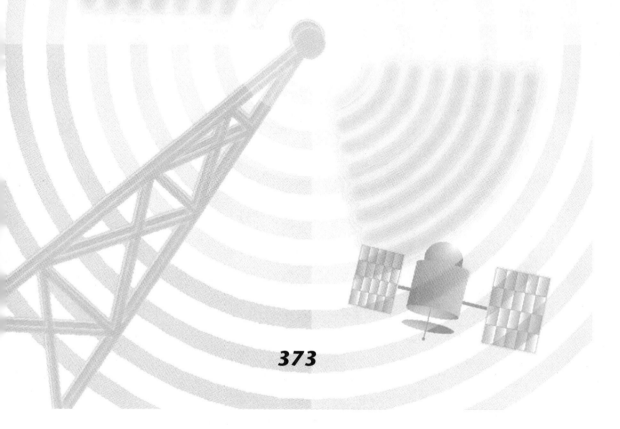

Implementing a remote access system is a mixed blessing. It gives your mobile and remote users a level of access to corporate network resources that they could never have otherwise. The resulting increase in communication and productivity benefits both remote access users individually and your company as a whole.

However, remote access also presents its share of problems. There are the common, everyday problems of designing, installing, and managing the remote access system. There are also issues surrounding users and staff alike in the proper use and maintenance of the system. Further, you also have another, potentially more serious issue: with all those remote users running around loose out there, how do you enforce corporate equipment standards and security policies?

Developing Corporate Remote Access Policies

Although I don't have a magic formula for developing and enforcing corporate policies, I do have a few ideas that have certainly helped me implement and maintain sound guidelines for remote access use. Following them can make your policies more sound, as well as make it easier for your users to abide by them.

Have a Written Policy

This may sound obvious, but you'd be surprised by the number of network managers that have never put their company's remote access policies into writing. Writing down and distributing the guidelines for using remote access services will eliminate many questions and many inadvertent misuses of the remote access system and the corporate network resource.

Your written policy should include:

- Who may use remote access services
- How users may request and acquire remote access services
- Training requirements
- Supported equipment and software lists
- Communication procedures
- Security policies

■ Procedure for submitting special requests for remote access

■ Technical support procedures and contacts

Take Time to Explain the Policy

Your users may wonder how so many policies and procedures can surround something that they view as a simple process. In fact, if you've done a thorough job of implementing the system and training your users and staff, remote access users will probably think policies are unnecessary and even dictatorial. It's hard to make the effort to adhere to what seems like a pointless and intrusive policy. Therefore, you need to make a special effort to explain why you are implementing remote access policies.

Explaining the corporate remote access policies is an opportunity for you to educate users on the corporate network, its complexity, the amount of time it takes to keep it up and running, and the consequences of improper maintenance, using unsupported equipment and software, and/or a security violation. The more the remote access users understand the hassles you face in keeping the corporate nerve center running smoothly, the more likely they are to support you in upholding the corporate policy.

Make Policy Training a Part of Remote User Training

If you present corporate remote access policies as part of user training, you accomplish two things: you ensure that each and every remote access user receives and understands the corporate policy, and you have the opportunity to explain the reasons behind the policies.

Consider a Signed Agreement

At first blush this may sound a little like a loyalty oath, but it really isn't. Asking employees to sign a statement saying that they have read and understand the corporate human resources manual has been a standard operating procedure for years in many companies. In that light, extending the practice to include corporate remote access and data security policies doesn't seem an extreme measure.

Ensuring that your remote access users have read and understand the corporate policies surrounding the system accomplishes three things:

- Ensures that users are aware of corporate remote access policies
- Eliminates confusion and support calls due to ignorance of remote access policies
- Gives you some indication (in the event of a security breach) that the problem is one of malice and not misunderstanding, thus preparing you to take appropriate measures.

Withhold Helpdesk Support to Those Not Adhering to Policy

This may sound a bit draconian, but it really is best for everyone in the long run. Users who refuse to follow security measures, adhere to supported equipment and software lists, and/or follow other remote access policies, can't be allowed to monopolize the support staff with problems that would have been avoided had the users followed the corporate remote access policy. If they are, you will lose the support of the users who *are* following the procedures, and soon. Your remote access policies will be nothing but worthless scrap paper. You may even find that employees stop using the remote access system because adhering to the policies surrounding it is just too difficult.

Have a Review and Amendment Procedure

As Tennyson said, "the whole world changeth, the old order giveth way to the new, lest one good custom should corrupt the earth." (I believe that's from *Morte d'Arthur*, but apologies to you Tennyson buffs if I'm wrong. Actually, apologies anyway.) Change is inevitable to everything, and your remote access policies are no exception.

Make sure that your corporate remote access policies aren't too rigid to survive. Have a procedure for users to submit additions and amendments to the policy, and be sure that the suggested changes are reviewed by a panel of network technical staff, administrators, and other users.

The Loyalty Issues

Everyone knows you can't dictate loyalty, especially among employees. Fortunately, however, most employees really do want to uphold corporate policies and procedures—provided, of course, that they can support corporate policy and still get their jobs done. Your mission is to make sure that your remote access policy doesn't unduly inconvenience the people that your remote access system is supposed to help.

To receive the loyal support of your users, the corporate remote access policy should be fair, flexible, reasonably easy to follow, and thoroughly explained. Having the policy reviewed and ratified by a representative group of users, administrators, and network technical staff will lend it credibility and authority. Employees will put far more energy into upholding policies they voluntarily accepted than policies that were dictated to them from on high.

Education: An Ongoing Task

As you've probably guessed by now, the key to successful enforcement of corporate policy is education: both yours and your users'. Never stop trying to learn more about how your company's employees are using the remote access system and what they need from it. And never stop explaining the remote access system to your users: its features, limitations, and requirements. Most important, spend as much time as you can instructing users on how to get the most from it. You'll find that not only will your users be happier and more cooperative, but also that your job will be a lot easier.

Index

LAN TIMES Free Subscription Form

○ Yes, I want to receive (continue to receive) LAN TIMES free of charge.　　　○ No.

I am　○ a new subscriber　○ renewing my subscription　○ changing my address

Signature required _____ Date _____

Name_____

Title _____ Telephone _____

Company _____

Address _____

City _____

State/County _____ Zip/Postal Code _____

Free in the United States to qualified subscribers only

International Prices (Airmail Delivery)

Canada: $65　Elsewhere: $150

○ Payment enclosed　○ Bill me later

Charge my: ○ Visa　○ Mastercard　○ Amer. Exp

Card number _____

Exp. Date _____

All questions must be completed to qualify for a subscription to LAN TIMES. Publisher reserves the right to serve only those individuals who meet publication criteria.

Which of the following best describe your organization?

(Check only one)
- ○ A. Agriculture/Mining/Construction/Oil/Petrochemical/Environmental
- ○ B. Manufacturer (non-computer)
- ○ C. Government/Military/Public Adm.
- ○ D. Education
- ○ E. Research/Development
- ○ F. Engineering/Architecture
- ○ G. Finance/Banking/Accounting/Insurance/Real Estate
- ○ H. Health/Medical/Legal
- ○ I. VAR/VAD Systems House
- ○ J. Manufacturer Computer Hardware/Software
- ○ K. Aerospace
- ○ L. Retailer/Distributor/Wholesaler (non-computer)
- ○ M. Computer Retailer/Distributor/Sales
- ○ N. Transportation
- ○ O. Media/Marketing/Advertising/Publishing/Broadcasting
- ○ P. Utilities/Telecommunications/VAN
- ○ Q. Entertainment/Recreation/Hospitality/Non-profit/Trade Association
- ○ R. Consultant
- ○ S. Systems Integrator
- ○ T. Computer/LAN Leasing/Training
- ○ U. Information/Data Services
- ○ V. Computer/Communications Services: Outsourcing/3rd Party
- ○ W. All Other Business Services
- ○ X. Other _____

Which best describes your title? (Check only one)
- ○ A. Network/LAN Manager
- ○ B. MIS/DP/IS Manager
- ○ C. Owner/President/CEO/Partner
- ○ D. Data Communications Manager
- ○ E. Engineer/CNE/Technician
- ○ F. Consultant/Analyst
- ○ G. Micro Manager/Specialist/Coordinator
- ○ H. Vice President
- ○ I. All other Dept. Heads, Directors and Managers
- ○ J. Educator
- ○ K. Programmer/Systems Analyst
- ○ L. Professional
- ○ M. Other_____

Which of the following best describes your job function?

(Check only one)
- ○ A. Network/LAN Management
- ○ B. MIS/DP/IS Management
- ○ C. Systems Engineering/Integration
- ○ D. Administration/Management
- ○ E. Technical Services
- ○ F. Consulting
- ○ G. Research/Development
- ○ H. Sales/Marketing
- ○ I. Accounting/Finance
- ○ J. Education/Training

- ○ K. Office Automation
- ○ L. Manufacturing/Operations/Production
- ○ M. Personnel
- ○ N. Technology Assessment
- ○ O. Other _____

4. How many employees work in your entire ORGANIZATION?

(Check only one)
- ○ A. Under 25
- ○ B. 25-100
- ○ C. 101-500
- ○ D. 501-1,000
- ○ E. 1,001-5,000
- ○ F. 5,001-9,999
- ○ G. 10,000 and over

5. Which of the following are you or your clients currently using, or planning to purchase in the next 12 months? (1–Own; 2–Plan to purchase in next 12 months) (Check all that apply)

Topologies	1	2
A. Ethernet	○	○
B. Token Ring	○	○
C. Arcnet	○	○
D. LocalTalk	○	○
E. FDDI	○	○
F. Starlan	○	○
G. Other	○	○

Network Operating System	1	2
A. Novell Netware	○	○
B. Novell Netware Lite	○	○
C. Banyan VINES	○	○
D. Digital Pathworks	○	○
E. IBM LAN Server	○	○
F. Microsoft LAN Manager	○	○
G. Microsoft Windows for Workgroups	○	○
H. Artisoft LANtastic	○	○
I. Sitka TOPS	○	○
J. 10NET	○	○
K. AppleTalk	○	○

Client/Workstation Operating Sys.	1	2
A. DOS	○	○
B. DR-DOS	○	○
C. Windows	○	○
D. Windows NT	○	○
E. UNIX	○	○
F. UnixWare	○	○
G. OS/2	○	○
H. Mac System 6	○	○
I. Mac System 7	○	○

Protocols/Standards	1	2
A. IPX	○	○
B. TCP/IP	○	○
C. X.25	○	○
D. XNS	○	○
E. OSI	○	○
F. SAA/SNA	○	○
G. NFS	○	○
H. MHS	○	○

6. Is your Organization/Clients network...(Check all that apply)
- ○ A. International
- ○ B. National
- ○ C. Regional
- ○ D. Metropolitan
- ○ E. Local
- ○ F. Other _____

7. What hardware does your department/client base own/plan to purchase. (Check all that apply)

	Owns	Plan to purchase in next 12 months
A. Bridges	○	○
B. Diskless Workstations	○	○
C. Cabling System	○	○
D. Printers	○	○
E. Disk Drive	○	○
F. Optical Storage	○	○
G. Tape Backup System	○	○
H. Optical Storage	○	○
I. Application Servers	○	○
J. Communication Servers	○	○
K. Fax Servers	○	○
L. Mainframe	○	○
M. Network Adapter Cards	○	○
N. Wireless Adapters/Bridges	○	○
O. Power Conditioners/UPSs	○	○
P. Hubs/Concentrators	○	○
Q. Minicomputers	○	○
R. Modems	○	○
S. 386-based computers	○	○
T. 486-based computers	○	○
U. Pentium-based computers	○	○
V. Macintosh computers	○	○
W. RISC-based workstations	○	○
X. Routers	○	○
Y. Multimedia Cards	○	○
Z. Network Test/Diagnostic Equipment	○	○
1. Notebooks/Laptops	○	○
2. DSU/CSU	○	○
99. None of the Above	○	○

8. What network software/applications do you/your clients own/plan to purchase in the next 12 months? (Check all that apply)
- ○ A. Network Management
- ○ B. Software Metering
- ○ C. Network Inventory
- ○ D. Virus Protection
- ○ E. Menuing
- ○ F. E-mail
- ○ G. Word Processing
- ○ H. Spreadsheet
- ○ I. Database
- ○ J. Accounting
- ○ K. Document Management
- ○ L. Graphics
- ○ M. Communications
- ○ N. Application Development Tools
- ○ O. Desktop Publishing
- ○ P. Integrated Business Applications
- ○ Q. Multimedia
- ○ R. Document Imaging
- ○ S. Groupware
- ○ Z. None of the above

9. What is the annual revenue of your entire organization or budget if non-profit (Check only one)
- ○ A. Under $10 million
- ○ B. $10-$50 million
- ○ C. $50-$100 million
- ○ D. $100-$500 million
- ○ E. $500 million-$1 billion
- ○ F. Over $1 billion

10. How much does your organization (if reseller, your largest client's company) plan to spend on computer products in the next 12 months? (Check only one)
- ○ A. Under $25,000
- ○ B. $25,000-$99,999
- ○ C. $100,000-$499,999
- ○ D. $500,000-$999,999
- ○ E. $1 billion

11. Where do you purchase computer products? (Check all that apply)
- ○ A. Manufacturer
- ○ B. Distributor
- ○ C. Reseller
- ○ D. VAR
- ○ E. System Integrator
- ○ F. Consultant
- ○ G. Other _____

12. In which ways are you involved in acquiring computer products and services? (Check all that apply)
- ○ A. Determine the need
- ○ B. Define product specifications/features
- ○ C. Select brand
- ○ D. Evaluate the supplier
- ○ E. Select vendor/source
- ○ F. Approve the acquisition
- ○ G. None of the above

ICS1639

fold here

Place Stamp Here

LAN TIMES

McGraw–Hill, INC.

P.O. Box 652

Hightstown NJ 08520-0652